A Broadening Conversation

Classic Readings in Theological Librarianship

Edited by
Melody Layton McMahon
David R. Stewart

The Scarecrow Press, Inc.
Lanham, Maryland • Toronto • Oxford
2006

SCARECROW PRESS, INC.

Published in the United States of America
by Scarecrow Press, Inc.
A wholly owned subsidary of
The Rowman & Littlefield Publishing Group, Inc.
4501 Forbes Boulevard, Suite 200, Lanham, Maryland 20706
www.scarecrowpress.com

PO Box 317
Oxford
OX2 9RU, UK

British Library Cataloguing in Publication Information Available

Library of Congress Cataloging-in-Publication Data

A broadening conversation : classic readings in theological librarianship / edited by
Melody Layton McMahon, David R. Stewart.
    p. cm.
  Includes bibliographical references.
  ISBN-13: 978-0-8108-5853-4 (pbk. : alk. paper)
  ISBN-10: 0-8108-5853-3 (pbk. : alk. paper)
  1. Theological libraries. I. McMahon, Melody Layton, 1957– . II. Stewart,
David R.
Z675.T4B76   2006
027.6′—dc22
                                               2006010139

This anthology is dedicated to the legacy of Julia E. Pettee, Raymond P. Morris, and all others who by their lives and work have left the sense of what is possible in theological librarianship much deeper and broader than they found it.

Contents

Foreword

Simeon Daly

Being retired, I am now out of touch with the day-to-day concerns of the library operation, but I am constantly aware of how my 51 years in the library, and almost 15 years in roles of leadership in the American Theological Library Association, have shaped my character. The appearance of this volume speaks well of the generous efforts of ATLA librarians to be of service to one another and to the profession. I could not say that ATLA is completely unique in its ideals of cooperative service, but still would suggest that it is exemplary in its efforts to be an organization of and for its members.

From its very beginnings, exceptionally gifted and competent people have put their stamp on the organization, and it was always the idea of working for the common good that lay beneath its actions and activities. For almost 40 years the Association could not afford salaried staff and relied almost entirely on the generous expertise of librarians already heavily engaged in the activities of their own institutions. I myself was in the throes of building a new library facility during the two years I served as President, and it was always a marvel to me how hard-working and dedicated were the men and women who kept the Association going for so many years.

The early years of the ATLA lacked participation from Catholic libraries and librarians. Whatever the reasons for ATLA's own decision in that regard, the fact is that Catholics would not have been interested in participating at that time, in part because there was a somewhat parallel movement afoot among their own educational institutions—the National Catholic Education Association was established in 1904, and it had a seminary section from the beginning. In 1921, the Catholic Library Association was established under the aegis of the NCEA and met regularly, conducting its own programs within the association's schedule. By the mid-sixties, a compelling need was felt in Catholic circles for the accreditation of theological schools. It no doubt took considerable fortitude on the part of the leadership of both groups even to consider a move toward closer collaboration, and discussion went on for several years until an agreement was reached in 1967. Three or four Catholic seminaries applied immediately, my institution among them. My first meeting with ATLA was 1969 at Pittsburgh on the campus of Pittsburgh Theological Seminary.

While some of the major Protestant seminaries that had long histories were on a solid footing by the 1930s, the situation of many others was somewhat more tenuous: under-staffed, under-funded and under-appreciated. Surprisingly, a "ripple effect" of the accreditation program in AATS was to highlight, rather than offset, these weaknesses. Very few Catholic seminaries had professional librarians in the forties. Most libraries were watched over by a faculty member, who may have done what he could, but he lacked the staff and the resources to accomplish much. In my own institution, the staff was comprised of volunteers. The collection was small and uncataloged. We gradually began to address this problem, and by the time I left the library we had over 170,000 volumes fully cataloged.

The classification of theological collections was a problem from the beginning. The Library of Congress classification system simply did not meet the needs of Christian theological collections. The Dewey Classification system had generic subdivisions, but the published editions did not reflect adequately the complexities of a theological collection. Several attempts were made in Catholic library circles to supplement Dewey, but none of them really caught on.

The Catholic Library Association published Jeanette Lynn's *Alternative Classification for Catholic Books* in 1937, and we used this from 1950 to 1976. As time went on, and as the LC Classification system began to be the system of choice of all the larger libraries, reclassification to LC became a major industry. Although most would find that the LC system is still a problem for Catholic theological works, it was politically and financially feasible to accept the classification given or adapt the schedules as best one could. The move to increased automation made this process harder to resist, and most theological libraries went ahead and reclassified their religion collections from Pettee, Lynn, or Dewey into LC.

ATLA has been a catalyst for establishing collaborative projects of other kinds as well. The years of meeting together, of being supportive of one another, have been most fruitful. Librarians who saw specific needs created projects or programs to address the issues: Religion Indexes One and Two, the microfilming project of key journals, and the duplicate materials exchange program, for example.

Service is a keyword in leadership and management. It was my willingness to say "yes" when asked that set me on the path of my career in ATLA. It was not a matter of my being the best-qualified person, but of my willingness to serve and to learn. Learn and serve I did. Although some of it was natural to my personality, I think I was able also to be compassionate toward minorities and loners. As one of few Catholics in a Protestant-dominated organization I knew what it was like to be an outsider. I tried to cultivate an ethos where there were no permanent outsiders, first and foremost by striving to communicate well. I knew most of the members by name and almost as many by their faces; I used personal correspondence almost to a fault; I made a point of keeping the members informed on all the major issues we were dealing with during all the years I was in a position to do so, through our various publications.

Although now it is but a distant memory, I was convinced of the importance of the Summary of Proceedings of our annual conferences. When I took office we were three years behind in having them published, and even before that they only appeared a year after the event.

I am grateful for this opportunity to express my thanks to so many significant people in ATLA who enriched my life in those latter years. I received wise counsel and established deep friendships with the folks who mentored me and walked with me in serving the Association. I believe that what I learned in ATLA made me a better manager at home and provided me with tools that made me comfortable and confident in setting goals and creating strategies to accomplish them. ATLA has stretched me, and I discovered qualities that would otherwise never have been tapped in the course of my daily life in the monastery and school. I daresay that most of my confrères had little idea of the "double life" I was leading, and, perhaps, would be more surprised that it was in a role of leadership.

It is my hope that these reminiscences of mine, and the contributions included in this volume from ATLA colleagues of the past and presents, will serve as a tribute to the people and the work of ATLA over the years.

Introduction
Voices from the Attic

Melody Layton McMahon and David R. Stewart

> Our memories grow bright and dim and bright again, and we never
> know exactly what it is we learn and forget, and what it is we remember.
> What is certain is that the act of reading, which rescues so many voices
> from the past, preserves them sometimes well into the future, where we
> may be able to make use of them in brave and unexpected ways.
>
> —Alberto Manguel, *A History of Reading*

This uncommonly curious book can be read as the findings of an exploration
of the "attic" of the American Theological Library Association. An attic
ought not to be mistaken for an archive, even though in family settings it
often serves a similar function; it is where things are put when they are not
likely to be needed or thought of so much anymore. Yet not quite lost forever: neglected, in some disarray, and frequently a little on the dusty side,
but still there for the rediscovering when the impulse arises.

The impulse in this case was our recognition that much of what was richest
and most memorable in the annals of theological librarianship from the last
few generations was still there, just beyond the reach of most of us. True,
there were approximations of an *inventory* of the attic's contents (print
indexes, limited access to contents through the ATLAS serials project), but
that is not at all the same thing as climbing right in and looking at what's
there.

Like most attics, ATLA's contains a combination of what is kept but not
especially memorable, *and* (buried within that) its share of genuine treasures,

which on being rediscovered almost make one shudder at the possibility of their ever having been lost to memory. In our work as editors, we could not have known how vast the contents were, what a challenge it would be to separate the treasures from the other material, or how rewarding the entire process would prove to be.

This anthology has been shaped in several stages, and by a number of influences. Chief among these is the notion of a *conversation*, and this requires some explanation. No matter how terrific the program has been, it's often the case that what ATLA members value most about time spent at annual conferences is the *discussions* they have had while there: with friends old and new, regarding (though by no means limited to) the work of theological librarianship. As theological librarians, it is often evident that we are imbued with a sense of good fortune, at having found (or perhaps been found by) such an enriching vocation: that we enjoy talking about it wherever and whenever we can makes perfect sense. Before it is anything else, this collection is a means of extending and broadening, not only topically but over time, that conversation in which we are all of us partners already. Here is a very good way of listening in on what the shape and nature of the ATLA conversation, which energizes our vocation perhaps more than anything else, has been at any given moment since its founding at Louisville in 1946.

To decide which installments of the conversation most warranted a fresh hearing required of us some interesting choices. For one thing, there were well over one thousand possible entries to choose from, but it didn't take long to realize that (for perfectly good reasons) some pieces may have been timely, but lacked at least that trace of timelessness we were looking for. In other cases (e.g., chapter 2 by Ray Morris and chapter 42 by Julia Pettee) selections were *so* unique, lucid, or field-defining that their inclusion was all but automatic. For the rest of the selection process, however, choices were often more difficult. It was essential to us that this conversation do justice to the elements of continuity and of change that make our work so intriguing. The inclusion here of many voices from outside of ATLA—theologians, administrators, publishers, etc.—serves to remind us that ATLA's dialog has constantly been enriched by interested participants from a much wider spectrum: a *broadening conversation* instead of an echo chamber. With the celebration of sixty years of ATLA in mind, we wanted to honor the past without being nostalgic about it, and at the same time to shed light once again on the intrepid character theological librarians have exhibited in approaching the ever present changes and challenges of their day.

Readers of this book will have no difficulty in recognizing the variety of voices engaged in this enduring conversation. Some have been more entertaining, and some more workmanlike; some have been rich with anecdote and humor, and some have assumed a more cautionary or even prophetic role. Certainly they don't agree about everything, and we made no effort to make it appear that they do. There was an impressive sub-list of candidates for inclusion in this book who were given careful consideration but were set aside in the end: interesting, but not germane, or perhaps already covered better elsewhere; learned, but not of enduring interest, and so on. Conversely, there are some topics which we felt absolutely *had* to be retained in this extended conversation, even while wishing that we had had more (or better) entries to choose from.

What we have brought together here is, we believe, a fair and vivid representation of what has always been at the heart of the ATLA experience: good work and good people, engaged in rich conversation around topics that are both timely and timeless. It has been at the same time an honor and an education for us to listen in, and we hope that the effect of this project will be to enrich the understanding, practice, experience, and enjoyment of theological librarianship for our ATLA friends and colleagues.

1

THE DISTINCTIVE CHARACTER OF THEOLOGICAL LIBRARIANSHIP

1

Introduction

Anne Richardson Womack

"The distinctive character of theological librarianship": what is it that makes our chosen profession unique, distinguishes it from other areas of librarianship? The following seven essays written over a span of 50 years by former presidents of ATLA offer an opportunity to glean answers to this question and to assist us toward a richer understanding of the distinctive nature of our vocation.

At first blush, it might seem counter-intuitive to learn that these seven essay contributions are remarkably similar in focus. Indeed, we would have difficulty identifying the decades in which most of these essays were written were it not for the introduction of terminologies such as "video" or "electronic media." Although the approaches differ, with each essay written in individualistic style and theme, clear similarities underscore the special elements of theological librarianship. This essential unity leads us to an understanding of what constitutes the core identity of a good theological librarian.

A motif that is shared and consistent through all of these essays is a recognition that very few institutional colleagues are aware of the complexity of our work. All of us have experienced the sense that there are few persons in our seminary, or our school, who see the contradictory demands, the range of responsibilities and the sudden shifts (e.g., in technology) that characterize our vocation. We may contribute to this obfuscation simply by a reluctance to articulate the ingredients of the stew of tasks that occupy our days.

In one week's effort, we can find ourselves facing water leaks, computer system dysfunctionality, complaints about temperature variations, foreign language purchase invoices, and class assignments on the topic of eschatology in various religious traditions. Additionally, for many of us, our pastoral training leads us to the personal expectation that we minister, in some way, to our community. Theological librarians are at once all these things: academic professionals with sophisticated language skills, information technology experts, building managers, budget jugglers, pastoral counselors, and stewards of our institutions' learning resources.

This variety can bring a stimulus for creative energy to our task, certainly. But often that task is complicated by limited resources; theological librarians must do much with little, "building bricks without straw." Because our seminaries and divinity schools often struggle with the limited funding of faith-based, service-oriented education as well as modest financial resources of alumni, theological library budgets can be quite thin. The very complexity of our services and programs can force theological libraries to request more financial resources than our boards, our presidents, can readily sustain. As a result, we become adept at doing a lot with little. This dynamic results in one of the remarkable benefits of theological librarianship, the necessity and desire to share with other theological librarians. We need each other's skills, talents, and resources in order to make the mortar that strengthens the building that we construct with those often strawless bricks.

Theological librarians possess a strong work ethic. Those of us who have spent time in other areas of librarianship may recognize this quality, accompanied by a feeling of relief, when finally finding a library that allowed us to work 80 hours a week and not feel out of place. Our essayists address this in different ways, but a safe summary would go something like this: we should work 40 hours each week and then read theological texts an additional 40, flexing both our intellectual and spiritual muscles. Needless to say, theological librarianship is "a total lifetime commitment." It is the giving of ourselves through our work. We may disagree whether or not this quality of our profession is a positive or negative one, both for our individual health and for the health of our institutions. But the characteristic is evident; theological librarians work hard and long hours in service to our constituents.

A deeper understanding of this strong work ethic emerges from these essays, in the form of theological librarianship as an outlet for priestly zeal. We are drawn to this discipline because we care deeply about faith, either as strong supporters of an established faith tradition, or as participants in the ongoing discussion about the role of religion in history and the current world. As theological librarians, we develop a "pattern of a lifetime," a way of being that incorporates the sensibilities of our unique calling into our quotidian purpose. We do not leave our work when we walk out the door; rather, our work encourages in us habits and awareness that strengthen and enrich our lives outside that door. At our best, our community of sharing, respect, dependency, and truthfulness girds us for the challenges of reality outside that community.

Being faithful stewards is another identifier of theological librarians, stewards of the faith lives of our students as well as stewards of our collections. We are involved in the lives of our students and committed to protecting and enhancing access to the materials necessary for their education. We are stewards of their training as future leaders of the faith, working to instill in them "a sense of the true and a sense for the good." Development of our students' faith understandings in relation to the world around them is an essential component of the stewardship practiced by the theological librarian, according to the contributors. In a profession that generally eschews power in the worldly sense, we actively participate in the responsibility of formation of our students' faith lives. We participate in fortifying the will of our students, in shaping their character, in determining their life choices. This commitment to caring for our most precious resource, the members of our community, helps mark the special nature of our professional activity.

The other area for our practice of stewardship—that of our collections— holds particular meaning for theological librarians. We are persons of "The Book," a religious phenomenon, regardless of faith tradition. Caring for texts whose lives cover thousands of years creates a particular depth of tending, protecting, sustaining. The texts placed in our care are the very ones whose meaning has nurtured and sustained our historical forbears on their faith journey. At its best, our profession is involved in the core of human activity, at the heart of civilization and culture.

At our best, we bring to our profession a particular aptitude for understanding human nature. Indeed, the metaphor of "family" appears in more than one of the essayists' contributions. Theological librarians often view relationships with their colleagues, staff, and students in familial terms, proffering an avuncular or maternal side as needed. The argument for the place of *meditatio* in our professional and personal lives provides the vehicle by which wisdom enters our hearts, minds, and souls. Perhaps it is the very discipline of deep reading and deep thought that nurtures theological librarians' energies for committed grappling with the challenges of human interactions. We respond to the gift of God's love for all humanity by devoting our energies to the respect and care of our staff and students, and we are energized by the reflective component of the theological enterprise.

Theological librarianship encourages another talent among its practitioners, a capability for "a catholic and universal grasp; . . . a flare for omniscience." This sense of universality can be thought of as our participation in a "pattern of service to unity." A book invoice from Kurdistan, a mission trip to China, a church records workshop in Madagascar . . . these examples underscore the international reach of theological librarianship, in both its practical and its ministerial aspects. We cannot but embrace the world, knowing something about every faith tradition, or at least knowing how to learn about each one. Over our years of work and service, a rich awareness of cultural, philosophical, and theological perspectives emerges. We respect the differences of others because we must know and understand much about others' beliefs in order to perform well in our professional service. This respect engenders remarkable collegiality in an organization composed of individuals whose religious, cultural, and social perspectives vary widely. Indeed, it is that very variety among us that allows theological librarianship to reflect the identity of the wider religious world. Our joy in developing professional and personal relationships with those whose faith perspectives differ markedly from our own is a pleasure that we wish upon our colleagues in other disciplines.

The strongest strain running through these decades of reflection by the leaders of our profession is the sense that theological librarianship at its best is a ministry. Indeed, Raymond Morris, a founding member of ATLA and its president in 1953, entitled his inaugural contribution "Theological Librarianship as a Ministry." What is particularly significant about Dr. Morris's piece is that, although a scholarly, widely read person, he attached that discipline of intellect to the primary goal of his ministry in the Yale Divinity School Library and broader community. His sense of the theological within his professional calling is underlined by this insight: "You and I in our work have as the beginning and the end of our daily task the perennial mystery of talented young people eager to serve the Kingdom." We extend this concept of ministry to the realm of scholarship, speaking of institutional cooperation in order to serve not only individuals, but to also enrich theological scholarship and ministry more broadly. Even though worlds away, we can relate to the Chinese student who was selected by her church leadership to train as a theological librarian. In trust, she "committed herself to a vocation, a calling, a profession in the truest send of that word." As theological librarians we express our own sense of call or vocation as we support those training to serve their faith tradition, either through direct church work or through scholarship. Those of us who serve in secular institutions also participate actively in the life of the spirit and in the process of education about humanity's relationship to God.

The essays in this section can yield the benefits of insight and inspiration for our profession, its daily practice and its long-term mission. What will serve us best will be to read each of these essays with the application of *meditatio*. If we read energetically, deeply, and patiently, our harvest will be rich and rewarding. The formative gifts that our forbears offer to us can best be received with the same caring and thought that went into their creation.

2

Theological Librarianship as a Ministry
8th Annual Conference, New York, 1953

Raymond P. Morris

It is difficult, if not impossible, for anyone to talk about "Librarianship as a Ministry" in any other terms than a confession. With your forbearance this is what I propose to do.

I feel honored on this occasion to address you. I am reminded of the account of a worthy citizen of China who was being honored by his fellows for conspicuous contribution to his community. To do the matter up right they arranged a procession with the honorable gentleman sitting in a sedan chair—a vehicle for traveling used by dignitaries, consisting of a chair placed on two long poles and carried on the shoulders of attendants. Unfortunately in this case the seat of the chair became loose and fell out, leaving the poor fellow in an extremely uncomfortable and awkward position. Following the celebration one of his friends asked him how he enjoyed the affair, to which he gave the reply, "Apart from the honor I'd just as soon have walked."

In our comments about "Librarianship as a Ministry" I should like to stress what I would call the human side of librarianship, our involvements with persons and people. The very nature of this assignment requires me, it seems, to talk about our jobs from my own point of view, largely from the way I see things. You will understand, I am sure, that I know that there are viewpoints other than my own which are equally valid or even better.

I have always felt that in some fundamental way my work as a librarian has been in a true sense a work in the ministry of the Church of Our Lord and Savior, Jesus Christ. I find that I am, in matters of profession, a somewhat amphibious creature and that in my vocation I have striven to combine the profession of librarian with the profession of minister. I feel this even though I have remained a layman and have never sought ordination. I think that there have been times when as a librarian within the library profession there have been distinct advantages for the Church that I have been a layman and not an ordained minister. I have been able to work within the American Library Association and to exert influences for the cause of religion which otherwise probably would have been denied to me had I been a "Reverend." I do not suggest that for others this pattern would be wise or even desirable. I would, however, at this time emphasize that in speaking of the librarian as a minister we should go beyond the stereotype of the minister which is held in popular conception. Librarianship can be, and for our type of institution, it ought to be, thought of as a ministry. This is so for all levels of our work. I feel that anyone working in the library of a theological institution, other things being equal, will do better work and will be happier and more content if he feels a sense of commitment to the institution he serves. Theological librarianship is at its best a ministry.

What are the basic ingredients of the practical workings of our job? It might be helpful if we would see our jobs as others see them, and then compare this with what they actually are, which is quite another thing. By others I mean the administration, the faculty, the students, and so on. For librarianship, like the ministry, suffers from a stereotype in the minds of the public. You are familiar with this picture of the librarian. It is a rather contradictory picture. There is the austere busybody behind the circulation desk, with the needless clutter of details and red-tape, a sort of glorified administrative secretary. We are the "hander-outers and checker-in-ers." There is, on the part of those who use the library, very little knowledge of a concrete kind of what goes on behind the scenes; there is very little knowledge of the complexities of our jobs, very little appreciation of such things as the need and reason for details, regulations and procedures. There is almost no knowledge that all librarians must try to do too much with too little, that we must be adept in "building bricks without straw." How many times have you had students ask you if you read all of the books you add to the library? How many times have you had faculty members or others act as if you never read any books? We are supposed to understand the school when altogether too frequently we are not permitted to share in the responsibility of the school, and people learn through assuming responsibility. We are expected to talk the language of the specialists, to have a considerable flare for omniscience. The sheer impossibility of our tasks in terms of an intimate knowledge of the literature we must handle is unknown even to the most widely read scholar on our faculty. Faculty members, by and large, simply fail to grasp the ramifications and extent of the literature of the Christian traditions. Theirs is a specialized and a parochial while ours must be a catholic and universal grasp. It is hard for them to understand the magnitude of our task, if it is to be properly done, or even the difficulties of book selection from the range and mass of the literature of religion, much of which is old and much of which is uneven in importance. I doubt if there is another literature as difficult to assess as theology. It is no small task to do this, that is, to do this intelligently, and to bring it into organization and to offer effective service upon it is a job of great magnitude. It is small wonder that at times we fail to see the forest because of the trees.

Yet ours is a much appreciated profession. We are the good angels who can, with almost the stroke of magic, uncover the needed book, or identify the garbled quotation, or dig out the relevant material with dispatch and promptness. We earn in good faith the honorable mention found in prefaces of stout volumes for our contribution to these works of scholarship. We make good midwives.

The facts are, my friends, the profession of librarianship by its requirements for success insists upon contradictory factors of human aptitudes. A librarian is an unusual creature when he is properly put together. Librarianship requires the aptitudes of the administrator, the aptitudes of the scholar, and those aptitudes which lead one to understand human nature—which makes one attractive to people, which leads us to be helpful in human relationships. To the degree that one fails to combine these factors with some measure of balance, he risks failure as a librarian.

Let us trace these factors through a day's work. If I may be pardoned by a personal reference to my calendar for one day this past month, I had planned that this day would be relatively free for what I call routine library work—book selection, classification and cataloguing, reference, the care of correspondence, and general administrative duties. This is really my job as the outsider sees it; this is what I am expected to do. On this day I tried to assist in the task of classification and the assignment of subject headings. As I recall we were dealing with some books of a rather specialized nature, those miserable things which librarians put aside because they are square pegs which do not fit the round holes of our neatly designed classification schedules—you know, books that don't fit anywhere. I gave some dictation, some of which was much overdue. "I am sorry to be so late in answering your letter," is one of my favorite clichés. But then my projected day broke down in mid-passage. I changed my schedule to see three students who were in arrear in their work and with the approaching end of the school year were now becoming panicky. I discovered, in talking to one, that his trouble seemed to lie in the fact that he was a slow reader, so that I arranged for him to have the diagnostic and remedial reading tests. I discussed a possible dissertation topic with another and ended our session by making a few bibliographical suggestions to get him on his way. I tried to reflect on plans of how to stretch the budget to get through the year. I had, that day, a long session with another student contemplating psychiatric care. This person was insecure, he was afraid, and he needed the assurance and counsel of friendship and human interest. And so on.

Now one does not go through that kind of a day without spending himself. You don't do these things without giving of yourself. I went home tired and nervously exhausted. I spent an hour or so with my family. One should not have a family if he does not intend to honor their claims and if he does not value their claims. Then I settled down for a couple or three hours of solid reading, constructive study—something which I have found I must do if I am to pursue successfully the job which is mine. To fail in this is to court disaster. As Mark Twain once quipped, "The man who does not read good books has no advantage over the man who can't read them." This is the Achilles' heel in what is sometimes otherwise a commendable library career.

I won't say that this was a typical day. One of the characteristics of our jobs is that no day is typical. Our days are unpredictable. But I would say that this day was in no sense unusual. I am sure that there are few persons at the Divinity School who appreciate the complexities of my work, the contradictory demands, the range of the responsibilities, and the quick shifts in the nature of the demands which are placed upon one, all the way from the demands of scholarship and research to administration and personnel counseling.

Your day will not be my day. What we do varies from institution to institution, from job to job, and from person to person. You will do your job in an equally important way, and perhaps in a more effective way. Though the details of our tasks will vary, our days have this in common—they are crowded, they are unpredictable, they are varied, and they are demanding. It takes flexibility, knowledge, insight, and physical and nervous stamina to be a librarian. We don't sit around in our offices, in the atmosphere of quiet and order, unmolested, pursuing the contemplative life. If we are doing our jobs, we are engaged deeply and in a truly fundamental way in the life and process of the school, in the complexities, the tensions, the drive of a community which is at work and which is throbbing with vitality. Always we work under a sense of pressure. Each of us, if he is truly effective, will participate in this in his own way and in his own time.

The important aspect of all of this which we are stressing is the human side of our task, the problem of human relations. As this is largely a confession, so let it be an honest one and let me say that the greatest mistakes which I have made as librarian have been mistakes in human relations. I have never been a better librarian because I didn't understand people. I should like to press upon you that the thing which gives importance to our jobs is that it involves people and human destiny.

It may be said that much of this which we have been describing is really personnel work and secondary administration and not the work of a librarian. After all, the librarian may better restrict his activities to that which is more central to his task, such as book selection, book purchase, classification and cataloging, reference, and circulation. But is this the whole truth? It is true in that we must do these things and that we must do them well. These duties are our peculiar responsibility. But to say that a librarian's influence and responsibility is to stop at this point is to ignore the very process of education itself.

It is important for us to remember that in the process of education the whole person goes to school. May I make reference at this point to a statement found in Moberley's *Crisis in the University* where he says:

> To live in college and so to be thrown together with those who have come from different regions and different types of home, with different temperaments and interests and subject of study, is a continuous exercise in mutual understanding and adjustment. Meeting one another in Hall, in Chapel, in Common or Combination Room, on the river or playing fields, and most of all in their own rooms, they acquire insensibly some appreciation of the point of view other than their own and some power of living and dealing with people. The outside world has dimly sensed this.[1]

Perhaps this concept of education as a social dynamic process involving the whole individual has nowhere been put more eloquently than by John Henry Newman in his *Idea of a University*, where he insists that the fundamental principle of the university as a community of teachers and learners should be conceived of in terms of a family. "A university is," says Newman, "an Alma Mater knowing her children one by one, not a foundry, or a mint, or a treadmill."[2] If one were driven to a choice, as happily he is not, between the formal instruction in the classroom and this wider and informal aspect of education as it is carried on outside of the classroom, Newman would take the latter as the more important. Education is carried forward in the context of community life. No teacher can teach with his greatest effectiveness until he knows his student and no students will learn as readily as when he knows his Master. Our work in the library is no different. An effective library is not an institution within an institution. An effective library is a very central, a very vital, and a very important part of a community in which it participates in a major and intimate way.

Most of us, I am sure, are aware that Adolf von Harnack was a fellow librarian, at least by vocation. It was Harnack who transformed the Royal Library from what Mommsen once called "one of the worst libraries of Europe" to the status of one of the great libraries of the Continent and the World. There can be no doubt about Harnack's competence as a scholar. I should like to remind you that it was Harnack the scholar who, as librarian, introduced novelty and innovation into the then accepted German library procedures. For one thing, Harnack insisted upon the circulation of books outside of the library when that procedure was questioned by German libraries. Repeatedly, we find him stressing his conviction that libraries are "neither museums nor cabinets of curiosities; that their function was not so much to conserve books as to put them to use, and that the best adornment of a library was a book worn in service." This is the way he put it on one occasion: "When the German scholar is praised for his particular diligence it seems to me not unlikely that the possibility of taking library books home and studying them by lamp light has a large share in it." This is the same Harnack who at another place insisted: "Our task must be to save for our Fatherland as many precious old books and particularly old German manuscripts as possible." The man who insisted that "manuscripts are the heart of the scholarly library" was also the scholar who understood the reader as a person. Likewise, the stature of Harnack as librarian is enhanced in our eyes when we know that he insisted that the professional librarian be freed from purely routine duties, that in Harnack's busy life of research and scholarship he found time to interest sub-professional assistants in the larger aspects of their work by personally conducting a course in the principles of scholarship in the hope of widening their appreciation. "He even found the way to the hearts of the workingmen," says an admirer, at the time when the book collection was moved from the old to the new library building.[3]

My friends, it can be done. We cannot be excused from a primary interest in personality under the false assumption that our interest and responsibility is primarily in the world of books and scholarship, in the eternities of erudition and not in the temporalities of human behavior.

J. Donald Adams, writing in his column "Speaking of Books" in the *New York Times* Book Review section, quotes Mark Van Doren as saying: "The important thing about a poem is the reader." Adams is speaking of the needs of contemporary American literature. He goes on to say: "the great sin of the New Critics . . . has been that they have forgotten or ignored the nature of the relationship between writer and reader. . . . Too many . . . write for one another or for the critics who misled them."[4] The great sin of our profession can be that we forget the relationship between the book and the reader. We can forget the process of education, the process of growth, the process of creative endeavor. We can forget the living and vital stuff which makes library work important. We can too easily judge ourselves in terms of external standards, procedures, techniques, equipment, budgets, size and wealth of holdings, our reputation with bookmen, or by criteria which are secondary and not primary to our tasks as educators. In doing so we may miss the very thing which tells us the most about the success of our work, the reader, his growth and creative activity. And for me, this is where work becomes fun.

All of this is to say, as I see it, that our jobs are carried on in the context of life, in the context of living things, primarily with persons, not inanimate objects. We are dealing with people in a very vital way. We are dealing with growth in understanding, with the shaping of points of view, with developing and living philosophies, with the stuff which shall shape the promptings of conscience and ethical and moral perception. We are dealing with situations which will fortify the will, which will shape character, and which will ultimately participate in the destiny of men. It does not take a gifted imagination to gauge the scope and importance of our work. You remember George Santayana's formula which he gave in the third volume of his autobiography, *Persons and Places*, the volume entitled *My Host the World*. It is here that he speaks of the two ingredients essential to rational living. One is that we must know ourselves, which is really the Socratic key to Wisdom. The other, we must have "sufficient knowledge of the world to perceive what alternatives are open" to us and which of them are favorable to our true interests. "The fear of the Lord is the beginning of wisdom," is a more normal expression in Christian tradition. This is our task and it is here that we find our ministry.

You and I are dealing with people and if we are to serve effectively we must learn to deal with them in such a manner as to gain their confidence in us. I am in some way responsible for every student who does not achieve his fullest abilities or measure up to his greatest stature in the Divinity School. I am responsible in some way for every student who fails in the Divinity School, and I am responsible in some way for every member of my staff who fails to make good on his job. The place to begin is with our own interest in people, with persons as primary in our sense of values. To do this there must be integrity. You remember the dialogue in T.S. Eliot's *The Cocktail Party* where Edward says to his wife Lavinia:

> One of the most infuriating things about you
> Has always been your perfect assurance
> That you understood me better than I understood myself.

And Lavinia replies:

> And the most infuriating thing about you
> Has always been your placid assumption
> That I wasn't worth the trouble of understanding.[5]

Let us be sure that our inner spirits will find us out. We cannot indefinitely appear to be bigger or other than we are. We cannot conceal our failures to influence people by being busybodies hiding behind a facade of books.

We must not underestimate those factors which reveal our very spirits and our true natures to other people. I say we must not do this. Let me add, we cannot conceal what we are from others. The work we do will be no bigger than the persons we are.

If one were called upon to assess the effectiveness of a library program, if one were called in to survey and appraise a situation involving a library on a campus, he could learn much, and a decisive much, perhaps, if he never went into the library concerned or if he never once talked to the librarian and his staff. He could do this simply by coming to an institution and talking to those for whom the library is intended, to gather the gossip and "scuttlebutt" of the community, to sense the impact that the library is making on the institution, and to learn the general reputation enjoyed by the library. This would be enough to provide a fairly accurate clue to the success and efficiency of the library program. Even silence can be damning. One would not, of course, be so stupid and unfair as to stop with this. He would want to examine the book stock, its organization, the financial structure of the library, the traditions and expectations of the institution, and he would want to talk long and at length with the librarian and his staff. Even then, perhaps, he would not know enough. But we should not minimize our reputations in a community in terms of public relations and our impact upon persons and institutions.

When I suggest that librarianship is largely a matter of dealing with persons, I do not mean to imply that one can be a good librarian by just being a good person. Success of librarianship involves more than diligence, or being a good friend, or being an interesting person. People come to us as librarians expecting to find a set of skills. They come for help of a very special kind. They expect us to know our business. It is true that they are less likely to come, or to come back again, if we have a forbidding personality, or a deadpan countenance, or if we are all aflutter, or if we are simply stuffed shirts. As librarians we need to be endowed with charismatic grace. The personal encounter of librarian and reader should be pleasant, inviting, and helpful. This involves more than sentimentality and a pleasant disposition. There is no substitute for the command of information and the mastery of skills which enables one to turn to the job to be done and to do it with precision and dispatch. Scholarship and a knowledge of scholarly ways, a sound knowledge of books, special knowledge of special tools, bibliography, methodology, imagination, and judgment are the tools of our trade. We need to know what we are doing, what our institution is doing, what is the end of it all. There is no one present whose job does not demand more of him than his abilities command. We must take these requirements seriously. We must learn and we must grow. To be thought of as nice persons is not enough. We must be helpful persons in very demanding situations. There are too many who feel that by simply holding a job they grow in grace and wisdom. The only thing that is surely happening to them is that they are growing older. One grows only through the process of growth which always entails hard work.

A librarian who drops the cares of his job at five o'clock in the afternoon is not going to get far as a librarian. We cannot expect to work in an institution where faculty members burn the midnight oil and we have our social evenings free and expect in the long run to command the respect of our community. Students are sensitive to these differences on the campus. We do not rid ourselves of devils of ignorance through "prayer and fasting" or just sitting. We rid ourselves of the shackles of ignorance through sweat and tears. May I add that I as librarian have never found that I was too well informed about books or that I knew too much to do my job as it should be done. We are never wise in our own conceits. We must remember that limitations in such matters place serious limitations on the effectiveness of our work. For it is inevitable that we, as librarians, project our personalities and abilities into the library itself. We set the atmosphere in which others must do their work.

As this is a confession, I can now ask myself if I have ever been sorry that I am a librarian. I am sure of the answer: "No, not for one moment." I am in the job that I want to be in. I cast no envious eyes at greener pastures. I do not want to teach, I do not want to preach, I do not want to crack rock in a quarry. I just want to be left where I am and I hope that I have the gumption to make the most of what can be done. It is all very challenging and worthwhile. Only there is too much to do. In good Yale tradition, I can say: "I regret that I have but one life to give to my country."

Now not to let you down too much, I invite you to look at the task we have to do. Where else could you go to have a better opportunity to work with, and perchance to influence, young life than the place where you are now? Consider then the kind of people you and I are asked to deal with. Not only is it young life with its enthusiasm and vigor, but, being young, it is interesting life in that it is always unconventional and always new. Youth has all of the promise of life set before it. Furthermore, the young people whom we have in our institutions have found what they want to do and are focused on a commanding purpose. Sometimes they may irritate us by becoming professionalized and "set" too soon. But, by and large, they know what they want to do. They feel a relevance in the work they have to do. You and I in our work have as the beginning and end of our daily task the perennial mystery of talented young people eager to serve the Kingdom.

What profession touches life at a more impressionable time? What profession more richly combines as its resources the gifts of personal encounter and personal achievement with the treasures of the ages? Where can you go to find such a combination that will include aesthetics, the process of learning, the restless search for truth, the adventure of discovery, the joy of new insight, and the anticipation of creative achievement? Not only do we work with the intangible things of the spirit, but there is the tangible tool itself—the book and the collection which frames our efforts with a monument rich because it has been built by many hands from many countries over many ages. I never walk up and down the stacks of our collection at Yale without in some measure receiving an almost mystical experience. For these are not just dirty old tomes which have outlived their times. Here are Plato, Aristotle, Augustine, Aquinas, Luther, Calvin, Wesley, Kierkegaard, Barth, and others, a veritable apostolic succession of Western culture. Here indeed is there a visible communion of saints. Here speak Amos, Isaiah, and Jeremiah. Here is Job. If we listen we can hear the intonation of the Psalmists and the noble preaching of Paul. Here is the tenderness of Francis of Assisi; the "dark night" of John of the Cross; Bunyan with his Pilgrim, and Brother Lawrence serving God by wiping the pots and pans in the kitchen. Here is the horror of the Inquisition, the courage of the crusader, Damien and his lepers. What vitality and what power! Here in the Holy Scripture are found the words of the Master preserved with pristine eloquence by the unfailing page of the printed book. And there they stand, these books, with patience and modesty, waiting for the curious mind and the pilgrim soul—an unmeasured potential of human experience and wisdom, waiting to be introduced by us, their guardians and custodians, to these our times. What an opportunity for one if he is able! What nobler monument could we desire? Truly, as Elihu Root once remarked:

> The statesman, the scientist, the man of affairs, all pass away and are forgotten. But to have builded oneself into the structure of an undying institution, to have aided in the development of a priceless possession of civilization, is to have lived not in vain, but in perpetuity.

Nor is this an idle flight of fancy and rhetoric concocted for this occasion. We are not drunken by the wine of our profession. We have no reason to discount the importance of our task. Rather, you and I run the danger of underestimating the importance of our tasks. We are not called forth to do something which is on the periphery of human interest or human need. We are dealing with the very heart of human experience, with the stuff that lies at the center of Western civilization and Western culture. You remember Lord Acton's dictum: "Religion is the key to history." Again and more recently Professor Tillich has reminded us that "religion is the substance of culture and culture the form of religion."[6] This then, is our task, our work, our opportunity, and our ministry. This is why our work is so everlastingly important. In the noise and confusion of a troubled time, we work with the wisdom of the ages and we are moved by the conviction that "what is highest in spirit is always deepest in nature, that the ideal and the real are at least to some extent identified, not merely evanescently in our own lives, but enduringly in the universe itself."[7] That this most high glory is within the reach of the most lowly is the substance of our ministry as librarians in the Kingdom of Jesus Christ.

NOTES

1. Walter Hamilton Moberley, *The Crisis in the University* (London: SCM Press, 1949), 34.

2. John Henry Newman, *The Idea of a University* (London: Longmans, Green, 1910), 144–45.

3. Cf. Felix E. Hirsch, "The Scholar as Librarian; to the memory of Adolf von Harnack," *Library Quarterly* 9, no. 3 (July, 1939).

4. J. Donald Adams, "Speaking of Books," *New York Times*, 19 April 1953, 2.

5. T. S. Eliot, *The Cocktail Party* (New York: Harcourt, Brace & World, 1950), 96.

6. Paul Tillich, *The Protestant Era* (Chicago: University of Chicago Press, 1948), 57.

7. William Pepperell Montague, *Belief Unbound; a Promethean Religion for the Modern World* (New Haven: Yale University Press, 1930), 6.

3

The Theological Librarian:
His Commitment and Strategy
19th Annual Conference, New York, 1965

James J. Kortendick

Over the entrance to the Theological School at the Catholic University of America is the inscription: *Bonitatem et Disciplinam et Scientiam doce me.* It is from verse 66 in Psalm 118 in the Vulgate. "Teach me goodness and discipline and knowledge, for I have believed in your commandments." In the newer versions it is Psalm 119 and is translated "teach me good judgment and knowledge." In either case it is a good and appropriate prayer for the well-disposed young man as he enters the seminary to take up his studies for the ministry. Goodness, discipline, and knowledge are the bases for good judgment, and they outline rather succinctly the objectives of the seminary: to provide the means and the opportunities for the students to develop the Christian virtues, to develop self-knowledge and self-discipline, and to develop in wisdom and understanding. The seminary which effectively provides this kind of moral, intellectual, spiritual, and pastoral formation is the best assurance that the future minister will be a zealous and effective pastor of soul.

Two general areas of formation are discernible, the moral and spiritual and the other the intellectual and pastoral. The two aims are complementary and the one must include the other. The literature on theological education stresses the relationship and emphasizes that this formation or development must be related to the apostolate, that is, that scholarship, knowledge, and virtue must be so solid and established that it will follow the young man into

It seems appropriate to pass on to you a story which Secretary Wirtz of the U.S. Department of Labor told us recently in Washington at the annual meeting of the President's Committee on Employment of the Handicapped. A newspaper editor dispatched his star reporter to Hell and to Heaven to develop a feature story on relative conditions there. The reporter's first stop was in Hell and he was struck by the apparent opulence and attractiveness of the grain fields and orchards. There seemed to be plenty of everything. Tables were laden with food, but the people all looked hungry, emaciated, and unhappy. He soon saw the reason. Their arms were stiff and they could not bend them at the elbows. Hence they could not bring food to their mouths. This was the Hell of it. In Heaven he discovered the same plenty of everything; tables here, too, were laden with all kinds of delicacies. But he noted to his surprise people in Heaven also had stiff arms. Nevertheless they all seemed happy and obviously hearty and well-fed. And then he noticed they were feeding one another.

The most rewarding and satisfying part of our strategy is our communication with students. If we are neglecting personal, individual contact with our students in the library we are robbing ourselves of the greatest joy in our profession. I'm not thinking here only of the practical ways we can help them collectively or individually by instruction in the use of the library, significant and necessary as this is for them now and later in their ministry. Our awareness of them as individuals with their own unique personalities, hopes, their special talents and potentials for development, their own gaps of knowledge, their difficulties, fears and needs, their good will, their prejudices, their desire to succeed for Christ, our awareness and interest and a sensitivity to each one provides so many bridges of communication and opportunities for us to share our library treasures with them. "The right book to the right person, at the right time" can make a great difference in his life. But we need to know the individual as well as the book in order to be an effective and tactful middle man. Here we can contribute our unique share in the seminary's work of helping that student to gain "a sense of the true and a taste for the good."

We need in our strategy to plan the workday to allow time to be accessible to students, to be "in attention" to their needs. The bonds of service and friendships established will follow through the years, and the alumnus pastor remembering pleasantly this association and your resourcefulness will be inclined as new needs arise to return to his Alma Mater for renewal and updating. If the library reflects the activities of the ministry for which the student is being prepared, the student sees and will recall the source of answers to his needs. In turn our knowledge of the demands made upon clergy in their work-a-day world will sharpen our focus in the development of a more meaningful collection. We will think twice about purchasing an expensive *incunabulum* and weigh its value against the more practical needs.

Most of you are too young to remember the popular song of the '20s, "Don't buy me posies when it's shosies I need."

Seminaries need good libraries for the reasons I've selected to discuss, and for many other reasons of which you will increasingly become aware. But a library is just about as good as its librarian. Its growth in the right materials and services will be in proportion to your growth and renewal in professional competence, to your growth in experience, and skill in strategic planning and cooperation, to your growth in imagination and ingenuity, and to your further development of commitment and identification with seminary goals. I presume that what we are all talking about and hoping for is that we will have theological librarians.

4

Developing Professionally on the Job
27th Annual Conference, Bethlehem, PA, 1973

David W. Faupel

John Henry Newman in his *The Idea of the University* entitled his seventh discourse "Knowledge Viewed in Relation to Professional Skill," reminding us that we are continually faced with the problem of theory versus practice, the "why" and "what" held in dynamic tension to the "how."[1]

The primary purpose of our formal library education was to lay a broad theoretical base for skill in our professional work, not to develop that skill.[2] It is the presupposition of this paper that all too often the handling of our task quickly degenerates into clerical routine. Such tendencies must be forcefully resisted, and the dynamic tension of "theory" versus "practice" must be maintained through professional development on the job.

I find myself in agreement with W. J. McGlothlin when he states that "though we once may have thought that competence once won would live on unnurtured throughout the length of a career, we can no longer. If one does not find ways to increase his competence as knowledge expands and situations change, his knowledge and skill can rapidly become obsolete, declining from competence to relative incompetence—from there it is not far to the extremes of incompetence which are quackery and fraud. Continued professional development is no longer a luxury, nor a privilege but it is an obligation inherent in executing your function as a professional in the contemporary world."[3]

THE AREAS FOR
PROFESSIONAL DEVELOPMENT

The beginning librarian must start filling the gaps of his formal library education, i.e., gaining a grasp of the reference collection, mastering the particular classification scheme of his particular library, comprehending the range of book selection tools, etc. In a smaller library, management, administration and public relations must be quickly developed.

Secondly, he must grasp the contextual setting of his library with regard to the fundamental task of the institution, the needs of his clientele, and the relationship to the larger community. Only by such a grasp can librarianship achieve the professional criterion of service orientation. If the librarian works only within the established boundaries of his own profession, he will find it impossible to formulate solutions for problems which cut across other professions. It is essential to expand his knowledge in the behavioral sciences, educational and management theory, communications theory, logic, etc.

Many seminaries require their professional librarians to have a basic theological degree, but growing theologically is necessary as we maintain our ultimate "service" goals. The professional needs to grow as a person as well as a professional—every procedure, relationship, and act must be assessed to be truly effective.

Finally, we obviously need to keep abreast with exploding developments in our field and enter into dialogue with the new roles proposed for our profession. Like other disciplines, ours is in a state of constant flux.

The resources for professional development are in our own backyard—our libraries. Professional reading, seminary courses, lecture series, and forums are available at our doorstep. Maintain membership in at least two professional associations. Do not overlook formal continuing education courses. And how about cultivating friendships which stimulate professional growth?

IMPLEMENTING PROFESSIONAL
DEVELOPMENT

Development doesn't just happen, it requires planning. Set forth a long-range goal. What do I wish to accomplish in my lifetime? Then project specific objectives for one to five years as stepping stones. As situations change, objectives and goals will need reassessment but should still serve as "guiding lights." Now let me suggest small steps for the implementation of this general plan of action:

- Become a 3-by-5 pack rat. Jot down and file bibliographical material, references to articles and books for off-duty reading, and ideas for possible articles as they occur.
- Learn foreign languages. For many, a dozen vocabulary words and/or rules of grammar can be learned easily during the day without distracting from your work. Add 15–20 minutes of concentrated effort off duty and great dividends will be produced.
- Keep a journal. You need not make daily entries, but this exercise in continual reflective thinking will aid immensely in professional development.
- Develop the power of observation.
- Write a systematic analysis and evaluation of at least some of your reading. This will force you to crystallize your thinking.
- Practice speed reading so that you can sift through chaff quickly to get at the heart of the matter.
- Take advantage of institutional opportunities: audit courses; attend forums.
- Create teaching opportunities—at the reference desk, in orientation programs, in short-term non-credit courses and in term courses for credit. This forces one to think of the user's approach to the library. It may demand some evening work, but such sacrifices will be well rewarded by new insights and professional satisfaction.
- Subscribe to and read professional journals regularly. Only by systematic reading can one keep abreast of the exploding knowledge of librarianship and your school's curriculum areas.
- Seek to publish. But view publication not as something necessary to get ahead but as personal and professional development. Undertake at least one major research project each year. Consider working vacations at a pleasant retreat where half days can be spent bringing together the results of research in written form while enjoying the rest of the day with the family. And vacation travel can be planned to become an educational experience for the family.
- Participate in continuing education. If the above suggestions are implemented in your professional life, it should soon become obvious to your administration that librarianship is a very vital part of the educational process. Therefore such benefits as sabbaticals, leaves of absence, travel expense for professional meetings, etc. which are normally granted to classroom faculty will also apply to professional librarians. In each case the ultimate benefit will come to the institution.

Obviously, what is spelled out is more than an eight-to-five, five-day work week; it is a total lifetime commitment to your job. You may often burn the midnight oil, but the rewards are enormous. A well-planned, organized life will have ample time for the family, church work, and community affairs, and these in turn will dovetail into making you a better professional.

NOTES

1. Marjorie I. Kelley, "Knowledge and Professional Skill, or Is There a Place for Field Work in Library Education for Tomorrow?" *Atlantic Provinces Library Association Bulletin* 33 (June 1969): 13.

2. Kelley, "Knowledge and Professional Skill," 13.

3. W. J. McGlothlin, "Continuing Education in the Professions," *Journal for Educational Librarianship* 13 (Summer 1972): 3–16.

7

On Spiritual Reading and Religious Reading in Peril: President's Address

53rd Annual Conference, Chicago, IL, 1999, and 54th Annual Conference, Berkeley, CA, 2000

Milton J. (Joe) Coalter

ON SPIRITUAL READING

The membership and staff of ATLA have created an association that not only nurtures the profession that we share but has also initiated and perfected a set of research tools that uniquely benefit both discipleship and scholarly religious research.

In like manner, each of us is part of library staffs who work hard to gather competent collections for our home communities, to develop new avenues of access beyond our holdings, and to teach students, faculty, and patrons how to locate the particular items most appropriate for their research or soul searching.

I continue to be amazed by the industry of this community of librarians both as an association and individually. But there are days, my friends, when I find myself feeling more like an information pusher offering dime bags of data ready-made for injection into the papers of degree-hungry students rather than a faithful midwife to an age-old dialogue between the voices of past theological sages and contemporary seekers, disciples, or researchers.

Recently, this disagreeable feeling hit me with renewed vigor during a conversation with a faculty member who teaches early and medieval church history. Our talk centered on that perennial topic within educational institutions—curriculum revision. My colleague noted that she felt that our seminary did a pretty good job at conveying information about the various disciplines of theological studies. But she longed for a curriculum that would facilitate students becoming not just learned in the data but wise in the spirit. Wisdom connoted for her range of spiritual vision and a depth of religious understanding that the learned may or may not have. But such insight is, nevertheless, highly prized and regularly expected in spiritual leaders and scholars of religion.

This conversation brought to mind a fascinating study by another medievalist whose research has periodically tormented my sense of vocation in recent years. The medievalist is Mary Carruthers of New York University. In her work, *The Book of Memory*, Carruthers recovers an understanding of the act of reading that captures for me one, if not the primary, motive behind our vocation as theological librarians. I say Carruthers recovers this insight because Carruthers unearths it from the writings of a number of medieval theologians who long before the advent of formal seminaries or divinity schools recognized that reading meant more than efficiently skimming a text for the surface cream of information. They knew that the nutrients of truth to be found in any worthwhile religious text could only be harvested by ruminating over its content, much "like a cow chewing its cud, or a bee making honey from the nectar of a flower."

Medieval thinkers imagined reading as a two-step process. It began with *lectio*, or an exegesis of a piece of literature using the tools of grammar, rhetoric, and history. This notion of *lectio* was not unlike the "critical thinking" that modern educators so prize and seek to instill in students.

This carving up of the text was but the alpha to an all-important omega in medieval reading practice, however, since *lectio* prepared the reader for the more penetrating work of *meditatio*. *Meditatio* represented the distinctly nourishing act of imbibing and absorbing a text's truths into the memory and revisiting that depth meaning repeatedly through the medium of the memory until its nectar was fully absorbed by the reader.

Meditatio was not so much a function of the eyes as of the memory, and the intended imprint upon the memory was much more than rote learning a text's surface appearance so that it could be regurgitated on command in the exact form that the reader found it. No, memorization by this almost devotional practice of *meditatio* stamped the lesson of a text into the very viscera of a reader's body so that the truths that had been extracted from the text through repeated reflection on it found embodiment in the person of the reader.

Of course, this high ideal for the reading act exceeded the reach of many in the Middle Ages as it does today. Yet ideals such as this had their place then and do today because they press us to raise the bar of our expectations of ourselves beyond the easy or the comfortable.

Meditatio as the omega point of theological reading, it seems to me, does lie at the heart of the reasons libraries and librarians remain part of the formation of religious leaders and scholars. *Meditatio* is, however, an exceedingly lofty goal for the work we do as librarians. It certainly is easily overlooked in the hustle and bustle of selecting, purchasing, circulating, and indexing materials for our patrons' use. It is further complicated by the way theological education has developed.

I know of no seminary, divinity school, or university worth its salt whose curriculum has not expanded exponentially in the number of disciplines taught or the opportunities that it offers in practical applications. But with this wealth of perspectives and field work has come a concomitant decline in the time available for or attention to teaching the students the ancient practice of *meditatio* on the texts they are reading out of class, discussing in class, and using to write papers for class.

There are no evil spirits here conspiring to obstruct this essential step in the path to spiritual wisdom. We need only look at our own house, ATLA, to see that our attempts to facilitate access to an ever-growing mound of literature that increases each day is intended for good and, indeed, does good.

But I wonder as we go about in this good work whether we collectively as an association and individually in our home shops should not be raising our voices to remark that precious little place or space remains for *meditatio* in the theological education of which we are an integral part and contributor.

At ATLA's 1998 annual conference in Washington, D.C. and during sessions at this past conference in Chicago, members from our number have discussed and debated the relative value of electronic versus print media. These discussions are helpful and informative. But they miss one point that theological librarians are uniquely poised within their communities of theological study and formation to make. That is that the practice of *meditatio* is a key to moving learned students beyond to that ultimate goal of becoming wise. Yet *meditatio* requires just as much time today as it did in previous ages before the number and availability of literature, first in print and later electronically, expanded beyond the grasp of any one scholar or disciple. *Meditatio* requires just as much time today as it did in previous ages before the number of disciplines claiming time in the curriculum stretched the capacity of a three-year education to the breaking point. And *meditatio* requires just as much time today as it did in previous ages before the presence of second-career students with families and all the outside demands that go along with such commitments proliferated.

Advocacy for place and space for *meditatio* in the theological curriculum may seem at first blush an odd goal for us to take on. But the depth encoun-

ter of the reader with that being read lies at the core of why we collect, catalog, access, and index in the first place.

Librarians of every sort have long been advocates of literacy and the ready
availability of literature to people of every condition. The theological literature for which we serve as stewards, however, should lead us to demand
more than literacy or availability. An acquaintance with theological materials
after a cursory read of its contents, we all know, is not enough to make religious leaders or scholars either learned or wise. Instead, theological reflection must be digested.

This, of course, takes time and a measure of training. Yet time is what the
current theological curriculum is often least able to give and, unfortunately,
training in the ancient art of meditating upon the word must vie with the
need felt equally urgently by professors to put their students in contact with
as much of the ever-expanding literature in their disciplines as they can.

What does all this mean for our practice as theological librarians, both in
association and individually? I can think of several actions that seem pressing. But at a minimum two would certainly be called for. First, we should be
as vigorous in advocating for time in theological curricula for students to
meditate upon their readings as we are already in aggressively soliciting
funds and staff to collect, process, and index materials for them to read. ATS
in its current standards requires that each degree program of a school have a
community of scholars with which they can consider, discuss, and debate
the content of their studies. But what good is a community of scholars or a
library of rich resources, for that matter, if the scholars assembled have only
enough time to skim the surface of their studies because of the press of their
curricular and extracurricular responsibilities?

Second, we should perhaps expand our notion of library instruction to
include training in the discipline of "reading in depth" once a student has
learned how to locate appropriate quality texts for study. This would, no
doubt, require us theological librarians to flex some intellectual and spiritual
"muscles" that neither our training nor our current job descriptions may
have pressed us to develop. Yet *meditatio* does lie at the heart of why we do
what we do.

Indeed, the vocation and profession that this organization seeks to support and promote originated in the recognition that revelation and the accumulated recorded wisdom about that revelation must be collected and
transmitted to present and future generations because it is vital to spiritual
well-being. If this is so, then our calling remains only partly fulfilled if we
collect, catalog, and index that literature, but we ignore the fact that the
intended recipients of these words have neither the time nor the training to
listen to the "Deep" calling to the depths of their souls in the collections
that we steward.

I hope that in the next year as we go about our work, we will survey our home curriculum and library program to see if we see the discipline of *meditatio* too little in evidence. If we do, I trust that we will begin discussions with our colleagues at home and other librarians in this association about how we might restore this discipline to the formation of religious scholars and leaders.

We theological librarians are more than information pushers. We are also more than caretakers of collections. We are, instead, stewards of a form of literature that demands we speak out whenever the activities of theological education or religious studies threaten to squeeze out reflection on the very source wisdom that we try so hard to make accessible and our institutions seek to transmit.

RELIGIOUS READING IN PERIL: A CHALLENGE TO THE VOCATIONAL SOUL OF THE THEOLOGICAL LIBRARIAN

The theme of this conference, "Embrace the Diversity: International Theological Librarianship," recalls a tension in the life of this association that has occupied my mind as I have served as ATLA's president over the past two years. On one side of that tension have been the efforts of our association to expand the diversity of our membership and collaboration with our colleagues elsewhere in the world. Certainly, some measure of increased diversity in our number and in our cooperative activities is needed and imperative.

But simply bringing together people with varied gifts and backgrounds from different races, nationalities, and religious traditions does not automatically an embrace make. As Andre Geuns from the Bibliothèque Européennes de Théologie observed in a session on international theological librarianship, an embrace requires two, and I would add, it involves two individuals, each distinctive and aware of their distinctiveness.

This brings me to the second half of the tension that I have experienced, for I have also had several occasions to communicate with other library associations this past year. This correspondence, plus discussions in the Board, and among the membership during this conference about ATLA's core values, has led me to ask: Why an ATLA? Why are we a separate organization? Why do we not place ourselves under the umbrella of some larger library association much like the Public Library Association operates within the structure of the American Library Association?

Put another way, what is it that we hold in common and distinctively that leads you, leads me, leads all of us to associate in a self-standing association known as the American Theological Library Association? After all, in one fundamental way, we are like every other library and librarian under the sun in that all our collecting, cataloging, indexing, storing, preserving, and instruction are for naught if that which we hold in our libraries is never read. Although we associate to make ourselves better librarians, to improve our libraries' individual and collective holdings, and to aid our patrons in becoming adept retrievers of information, we remain little more than conscientious caretakers of textual mausoleums if the revelation, commentary, and studies that we treasure and preserve are not picked up and read.

In this we are like all other librarians in North America and beyond. Whatever its special field of expertise be, every library collection requires that all-important reader in order to bear its intended fruit.

However, theological collections are called to gather a distinctive type of text—religious texts—and in this simple fact may lie the source of a special responsibility incumbent upon theological librarians if we are not just to preserve the pool of revelation in our holdings but also to release its life-giving properties.

Last fall I encountered a very interesting book by Paul Griffiths titled *Religious Reading*. Griffiths is a philosopher of religion, and he suggests that religious reading is a spiritual discipline striving against bad odds to survive in an environment that is currently hazardous to its health. If Griffiths is right, religious reading is different from the type of reading practiced, if not actually taught, in many universities and theological schools today. Griffiths contrasts religious reading with what he characterizes as "consumerist" reading. Such reading is found throughout the culture as "consumers treat what they read only as objects of consumption, to be discarded when the end for which they are read has been achieved."[1] At their worst, consumerist readers skim works, preferably with the speed of Evelyn Wood, in order to cull the rudimentary outline of a publication's argument.

In this milieu, texts are not so much read as gutted. In the momentary fire of fleeting current interest or in service to the impending threat of exams or just because Oprah recommended it, texts are eviscerated and then cast off and forgotten, assuming they were ever committed to memory in the first place.

This consumerist mentality reverses the equation for what is valuable in a text by honoring the "quick read" over the "studied response," by preferring the executive summary or the synoptic abstract over the full text, by fancying the dictionary entry over a bibliography of authoritative sources to be examined, and by favoring the course reserve reading list laid out like the smorgasbord of the semester rather than the research project where sources must be uncovered, pondered, and then shaped into a thesis.

When I was in graduate school, I remember sitting with a group of students in the home of a professor of colonial American history following a seminar he led. Our professor was entertaining us students with stories of former academic conferences, and in order to calm fears that we harbored about our inability to absorb the texts listed in his syllabus, much less the voluminous literature available in the field, he told us a tale of one memorable confessional during a gathering of his colleagues after an American Historical Association conference. Following a large dinner well-lubricated with alcoholic beverages, the group began to confess to one another the classics in their field that they had never read. Through the good services of review literature, these scholars had acquired sufficient command of the central notions put forth in these seminal works to carry off later "intelligent discourse" with fellow academics and graduate underlings without ever having themselves cracked the pages of the books in question.

Such a confessional, I imagine, could be replicated by a goodly number of our patrons—both students and faculty. Indeed, if the truth be known, these sins of omission have been aided, abetted, and even taught by a few librarians—librarians who, in our zeal to help and our enthusiasm for the reference sources that are our stock and trade, forget that the goal of the texts we offer up for consumption is not only or simply the speedy extraction and transmission of the information that they hold but rather an unhurried contemplation of the wisdom harbored therein.

Griffiths suggests that religious reading draws it strength from the peculiar nature of the texts being read. For the religious reader, a work of revelation and its attendant legion of documents discussing that revelation and its implications for human life are understood as "a treasure-house, an ocean, a mine: the deeper religious readers dig [Griffiths insists] the more ardently they fish, the more single-mindedly they seek gold, the greater will be their reward. The basic metaphors here are those of discovery, uncovering, retrieval, opening up: religious readers read what is there to be read, and what is there to be read always precedes, exceeds, and in the end supersedes its readers. . . . For the religious reader, the work read is an object of overpowering delight and great beauty. It can never be discarded because it can never be exhausted. It can only be reread, with reverence and ecstasy."[2]

Indeed, such texts must be reread and read yet again, for the ultimate goal of this ancient practice of piety is digestion and absorption into the memory so that the source revelation can so infuse the person of the religious reader that the revelation itself is embodied yet again in that individual.

Religious reading is certainly different from consumerist reading and perhaps even all other types of reading. It, among all forms of reading, requires an unhurried feeding on the text—a thorough immersion in its word—again and again so that its insight soaks the soul, permeating the persona of the religious reader with the aroma of the revealed.

But if religious reading is so distinctive, then so too should be the task of the librarians who individually, and in association, harbor in our collections the textual catalyst for this metamorphosis, wherever in this great and grand creation we are called to serve. How we foster such religious reading in an age that finds this essential spiritual practice rather outmoded, if not outright tedious and alien, is a question easily overlooked in our eagerness to find better ways to collect more widely, to catalog more precisely, to store more compactly, to preserve more efficiently, to digitize more broadly, to instruct more effectively, and to retrieve more quickly.

But I think that we ignore this question at the peril of our own profession for what does it profit us to associate for collecting, cataloging, indexing, preserving, and digitizing the whole corpus of theological literature and yet lose our vocational soul—or, perhaps better put, lose our vocation's sole reason for being? It is my hope that even as we celebrate the diverse situations, skills, and offerings of theological librarians and their libraries throughout the globe, we remember this distinctive calling that we share across time and space, namely to be agents for the recovery and sustenance of a central practice of piety in communities of theological education and religious studies—communities that, ironically, have become almost too busy for "religious reading."

One might say that our colleagues on the faculty in our home institutions have far more impact on this matter than do we. After all, they either designate what is to be read or assign projects that require further reading.

But I would suggest to you that no one on a seminary or university campus is better situated than the theological librarian to recognize the ever-diminishing time and attention given to "religious reading" in contemporary curricula. Consequently, you and I, both individually and as an association, have a singular responsibility to advocate for the recovery of this neglected exercise in spiritual enlightenment, to insist that space be recovered for its practice in our students' curricula, and to mentor its practice on our campuses and throughout theological education. In this, I believe, lies at least one source of a common sense of who we are as librarians and as an association—a mark of distinctiveness and individuality that we bring to any embrace of diversity.

NOTES

1. Paul J. Griffiths, *Religious Reading: The Place of Reading in the Practice of Religion* (New York: Oxford University Press, 1999), 42.

2. Griffiths, *Religious Reading,* 41–42.

8

Power and Responsibility: Reflections on Theological Librarianship
56th Annual Conference, St. Paul, MN, 2002

Sharon Taylor

I have been told that a Presidential address should be a somber reflection on some topic of interest to the whole group, a learned exposition, a meaty, scholarly, well-documented oration—illuminating, scintillating, and thought-provoking. I have heard some great ones over the years. Someday I hope to give one myself. P.G. Wodehouse is supposed to have said that his books were better than Tolstoy's because they were shorter and had more jokes. Today I aspire to a type of speechmaking that would make Wodehouse proud.

WHERE HAVE WE BEEN?

Permit me some personal reminiscences here. In September 1972 (yes, almost 30 years ago) after getting my MLS, I took up my first position in a small seminary library in Jackson, Mississippi. This was the "uttermost ends of the earth" to me at that time. I was the first professionally trained librarian in that library, and over the years I did a little bit of everything—cataloging, processing, reference, administration. I had the Pettee Classification system memorized to the second decimal. I set up the first OCLC computer and learned to use it. I took apart the Xerox machine and put it together again. I could walk to the shelf and pick out almost every title without bothering with the card catalog. I was in my ideal world—and I loved it. Even when I lost my job I knew that I had found a great vocation. This has been confirmed to me over the years as I met colleagues in the field and discovered that they, too, had invested themselves in doing something that they love doing.

I believe that John Trotti, of Union Seminary in Richmond, was the first theological librarian I met outside my own library. I stumbled into him, quite literally, getting off the train for that first—now famous—Princeton Institute in 1980. A group of us had gathered to learn what it meant to be better theological librarians. I was a newbie. I had been director of the library for only a year or two and I was desperate for someone to tell me what I ought to be doing. I found a whole group of people who were willing to share their knowledge, their enthusiasm, and their trials and tribulations. I found many informal mentors (also known as friends) and a more formal one in Charles Willard when he was librarian at Princeton Seminary and I was his assistant. Talk about trials and tribulations! I am not sure which of us was the trial and which was the tribulation. But I learned a lot from him.

As I thought about my own career and the twists and turns it has taken over the past three decades, I hearken back to what our noble forebears had to put up with in working out their calling. I love the picturesque description of the medieval Benedictine librarian that Henry Petroski gives in his *The Book on the Book Shelf:*

> On the Monday after the first Sunday in Lent, before brethren come into the Chapter House, the librarian shall have had a carpet laid down, and all the books got together upon it, except those which a year previously had been assigned for reading. [Each brother was assigned one volume.] These the brethren are to bring with them, when they come into the Chapter House, each his book in his hand . . .
>
> Then the librarian shall read a statement as to the manner in which brethren have had books during the past year. As each brother hears his name pronounced he is to give back the book which had been entrusted to him for reading; and he whose conscience accuses him of not having read the book through which he had received, is to fall on his face, confess his fault, and entreat forgiveness.
>
> The librarian shall then make a fresh distribution of books, namely, a different volume to each brother for his reading.[1]

Ah, what power and responsibility! Can you picture the first faculty meeting of the year handing out to faculty members their one book for the year? Can you imagine a student facedown on the floor in front of the circulation desk begging forgiveness for not having read the book she checked out? Neither can I. By the way, Petroski reports that the present custom of academic libraries of recalling faculty books at the end of each academic year traces back to the Benedictine practice.[2] So you can thank that ancient brother librarian the next time you try to wrest back that long-overdue book from a faculty member who is convinced that it is his or her inalienable right to keep it until retirement or death—whichever comes first.

Ah, what power and responsibility! What power it was to be the one who would know each title in the collection through and through. What a responsibility it was to be able to discern exactly which book would be most helpful, the most remedial, the most life-changing for the individual who stood before you. This brought to my mind Joe Coalter's presidential address at the ATLA conference in Berkeley two years ago on the place of devotional reading in our theological education.[3] What would a seminary education look like if we lived with just one book for a year? Or even two or three books?

Ah, what power and responsibility! To have such total control over a collection. To know where every book is every minute. But we shouldn't imagine that this hyper-protection of the book was just a Catholic obsession. The Anglicans in merry old England kept up that ultimate of security practices and chained the books to the shelves. Of course we are enlightened people these days and we don't do that now—we save the chains to lock down our computer equipment.

I have been reading quite a bit in our seminary's institutional history for my dissertation. Andover Theological Seminary, a precursor to Andover Newton, was founded in 1807, the first graduate Protestant theological school in the United States. Establishing a library was one of the first orders of business. A professor was promptly sent on a book-buying trip to Europe, and this precipitated one of the earliest of countless squabbles within the faculty. The question was: should every book first be evaluated for its theological orthodoxy before being placed in the library since it might become a corrupting influence upon those who read it? One historian commented that this faculty contingent didn't go so far as to suggest an *index expurgatorius*—but no doubt some thought this might be a safer route.[4] However, an open policy prevailed and all manner of foreign and domestic biblical criticism and theology came to find a home in the library. It was a model other seminary libraries emulated.

In the early days, each student paid a library tax of three dollars per year. Access, however, was haphazard and for the first few years the library was open to students one hour a week. By 1830 the library was open one hour on weekdays (from 1 to 2 p.m. in the afternoon—that prime study hour) and two hours on Saturday "so as to save wear and tear."[5] Saturday was the only day that books could be checked out. To maintain a proper decorum in the hallowed inner sanctum only four students were allowed into the library at a time. Faculty members were allowed to check out a maximum of 12 books and students only 3, except for those used in class. And, in one of the earliest attempts at material preservation, all library books were to have paper covers placed on them, and policy dictated that the shabbiest copy was circulated first.

While the rules were different, the Andover librarian had some of that same power and authority that the early Benedictine caretakers possessed. He (and until I became director in 1988 all the head librarians were male) was entrusted with the oversight and the protection of the collection. He even had to post bond for its security. One of the foremost professors of the seminary was criticized for permitting someone to carry books out of town without the express consent of the librarian. The matter went to the Board of Trustees, who asked for a written explanation from the professor. I can't even imagine a scenario like that today.

Ah, what power and responsibility! To be totally in charge of the library. To be the one to make the rules. To even be able to keep those troublesome faculty members in line. To be the terrestrial gatekeeper. To determine who could come in the door and who could touch the books.

Ah, what power and responsibility! To be the overseer of a collection of theological works whose breadth could take readers outside of their own denominational leanings or theological convictions or national or social affiliations. To select books whose content one finds off-putting or offensive or even heretical, but whose ideas are worthy to be read and analyzed and critiqued. What a responsibility to be able to judge what ideas are worthy and what ideas are merely trivial or inconsequential. What a responsibility to guide generations of students though a vast literature, offering both praise and cautionary warnings about the books around them. To actually shape someone's thinking about God, about the world, about one's behavior and belief. An awesome responsibility!

WHERE ARE WE GOING?

Does anybody know? The world has changed before our eyes. The profession has changed. Our jobs have changed. The good news is that most of us still have jobs. It was not that long ago that we were hearing from ATS and denominational leaders that up to one-third of the seminaries in the United States and Canada would close before the year 2000. Decreasing enrollments and escalating costs were going to drive many of our schools out of business. And yet they hung on. And in fact—thanks in part to the propensity of Baptists to pick up their marbles and go play somewhere else when they disagree—the number of accredited schools or those seeking accreditation from ATS has actually increased.

And now the not-so-good news. Will we be able to fill jobs in the future? Malcolm Hamilton, who for several years directed personnel matters for the

Harvard University Libraries and for the past three years or so has been interim librarian at the Harvard Divinity School, told me recently that there were 501 librarians in the Harvard system; 35% will retire in the next ten years. There are 85 librarians who are ranked in upper management. Of these, 57% will retire in the next ten years. The Harvard administration is very concerned about this employment trend. And they are already strategizing about how to develop persons to fill these positions.

How will we fare in theological libraries? Probably not much different. Granted most of us work with much smaller numbers in our institutions. And we do have a crop of younger colleagues coming up in the field. But there are many of us getting a little long in the tooth (and probably a little more gray-haired as we watched our retirement accounts shrinking this last year). How are we as a profession going to meet these needs for future theological librarians? With the vastly increased numbers of second-career folk in many of our schools we don't often have the privilege of watching some young, energetic scholar—someone who started out shelving our books as a student assistant and learned to love the environment—move into the field. Many of those who would have come into field have gone the route of information or computer science designing web pages or programming databases. Where we used to get 20 or 30 applicants for a position we now get 3 or 4. I have frequently talked to presidents and deans who tell me they just can't get a pool of qualified people, particularly for director's positions. Why the disparity?

My first response is: Why would anybody in their right mind want to be underpaid, overworked, harassed by irate patrons and faculty wanting special privileges, beleaguered by water leaking in the archives and a totally dysfunctional computer system, a broken door lock, a building that is too cold or too hot, two invoices in German and one in what I think is Urdu that don't match with anything ordered—and that was all just in the last week. But lest I discourage any of you aspiring to this high calling, I will move on to less subjective reasons.

For one thing the library field has changed dramatically in the last 20 years. And the expectations have likewise changed. The March 2002 supplement to the *Library Journal* was entitled "Movers and Shakers: the people who are shaping the future of Libraries." Just listen to the list of attributes that these folks were to have embodied (and note these people were not just directors of libraries): community builders, visionaries, mentors, activists, innovators, collection developers, scholars, team players, service providers. Makes me feel tired! Those aren't the things I learned in library school. There was no course in Vision or Innovation 101. Not once did the list mention: "loves books and reading." Yet this was far and away the number one reason that librarians chose the profession according to a survey in 1999.[6]

Even more revealing is the compendium of qualities that was compiled in an article on university library directors which appeared in *College & Research Libraries* this past January.[7] There was a long list headed General Areas of Knowledge—things like scholarly communication, knowledge of financial management, information technology, public relations, and facilities planning. (Note: there was nothing about being able to fix the computer when someone manages to stick a CD-ROM into the old 5.5- inch floppy drive.)

There was a much longer list of managerial skills, things like: is willing to make tough decisions, facilitates a productive work environment, builds a shared vision for the library, is able to function in a political environment, sets priorities, communicates effectively with staff. (There is something excruciatingly painful and humbling about saying these things when members of my own library staff are sitting in the audience. I can hear them now: "Wish we had a director like that!")

But the longest list of attributes that one would wish for in a director, 46 traits to be exact, are what they called Personal Characteristics. And I would offer these as characteristics that all of us as theological librarians—not just directors—should nurture and develop. These include being trustworthy, keeping commitments, being evenhanded, treating people with dignity and respect, being self-confident, having a sense of perspective, having a sense of humor, committed to a set of values—that is, having integrity, able to handle stress, being comfortable with ambiguity, being honest, intelligent, resilient, intuitive, being change-focused and having organizational agility, being enthusiastic, and understanding that one does not have all the answers.

Walking on water wasn't listed—but it might have been. These are characteristics to which we can all aspire, and a journey that may take a lifetime.

So how do we find potential librarians to fill our vacancies? Well, we can actively recruit. I received in the mail some days ago an (other) invitation to join AARP—the American Association of Retired Persons. Notice in particular that they don't wait for you to retire before they try to sign you up. They presented me with a list of benefits and services—and a temporary membership card with my name on it. In the same mail, because I am a *bona fide* tuition-paying graduate student at Boston College, I also received a nice poster and an invitation from the United States Army. They explained that as a college graduate I could apply for Officer Candidate School. Check it out—up to $65,000 to pay back college loans; an enlistment bonus of up to $20,000 to spend as I like; guaranteed training and immediate responsibility; strategic thinking and management skill training; a chance to become an officer and a leader. Surely we ought to be able to compete with that!

When I visited seminaries in China a couple of years ago I met a young woman, a recent graduate of a brand-new theological school, who had just been appointed as librarian. She was being sent off to get library training and then she would return and manage the seminary's collection. She was handpicked by the school—one of the best and the brightest—called to make a vocation of theological librarianship. The seminary didn't wait for someone to filter up through the system. They didn't wait for someone to "feel the call" or to volunteer themselves—the self-selection process that we in North America tend to favor. They called and she responded. The school committed itself to providing education and opportunity; she committed herself to a vocation, a calling, a profession in the truest sense of that word. It may be a model we will have to try out more conscientiously.

Ah, what power and responsibility! Is there a future role for ATLA in helping schools identify and select librarians—particularly directors of libraries? How about an ATLA job consultant who can meet with search committees and presidents to help write job descriptions, help formulate the list of personal qualities and professional qualifications one needs to be an effective theological librarian? One who could meet with individuals and help them shape their career goals in the field? Maybe even touring our theological schools and library schools introducing students to the field. Or at least putting it all on a video? Maybe we could even have an ATLA manual for presidents and deans outlining the nature and purpose of the library, how to evaluate library programs, how to evaluate the librarians, how to find a director when openings occur. Something not tied to an accreditation process. If we don't act for change we risk becoming even more a sideline to the educational process of our institutions.

Ah, what power and responsibility! We—yes, each one of us—can help shape a whole profession. We have had to reinvent ourselves when new technology changed how we did things. Now we can push each other along to learn a little more, to trample some of those old stereotypes. We can work on those traits that will make us more effective in our work and in our lives. We can learn the literature deeply and broadly. We after all are the models that future theological librarians will look to and pattern themselves after. Isn't that a scary thought!

HOW WILL WE KNOW WHEN WE GET THERE?

Beats me. Well, this ended up being a lot longer and a little more serious than I intended. So let me close with a few words from one Edmund Pearson. Pearson perpetrated a tongue-in-cheek hoax when he published *The Old Librarian's Almanack* purported to have been written in 1773 by one Philobiblios, a fictitious 18th-century librarian. Hear what he has to say:

> There is none so Felicitous as the Librarian, and none with so small a cause of Ill-content, Jealousy or Rancour. No other Profession is like his; no other so Happy. Of the Clergy, I speak not, their Calling is sacred and not of this World.

The Physician & Lawyer administer to the ills and evils of Mankind. The Merchant's happiness is conditioned upon his pecuniary Success.

But the Librarian, so far removed from any of these, ministers to the wisdom and delight of Mankind, increases his own Knowledge, lives surrounded by the Noble thoughts of great Minds, and can take no Concern of pecuniary Success, forasmuch as such a thing is not within the boundaries of Possibility . . .

The Librarian, as he cannot hope for Wealth (nor fret his Mind about it), so he cannot expect to achieve Fame. Where is the Monument erected to a Librarian? Great Monarchs and Warriors have theirs; in ancient times it was even the custom to honour the Poet. But the Librarian lives and dies unknown to Fame; the durable results of his Labours are not visible to the Eye, and if at all he receiveth Honour it is for his private Character as a Man. His Brother Librarians may know and Esteem him as an Ornament to their Profession, and that is his sufficient Reward.

He lives protected, avaricious neither of Money nor of Worldly Fame, and happy in the goodliest of all Occupations—the pursuit of Wisdom.[8]

No doubt Pearson meant his words to be sardonic, but I found them to be oddly touching. There is more than a grain of truth to be found there. We cannot mark our ultimate success as professionals or as individuals by our salaries, though my addictions to eating regularly and having a roof over my head make me think a lot about that. We have made a lot of progress. I figured out the other day that my salary is nine times higher than that of my first job as a theological librarian—and, yes, I am still underpaid.

Nor can we mark our ultimate success by worldly fame. Not many of us will have "She was a Really Good Cataloger" etched on our tombstones. Or have libraries named after us. I, for one, will be really happy if anyone remembers my name.

Perhaps our prize at the end will come from having known some great colleagues, from having done our best work, from having been an effective and positive influence on the students, faculty, and other colleagues around us. To be that bright shining ornament to the profession. Retiring and thinking not "Thank God that's over with!" but "Thank God I was able to be a part of something really significant, something purposeful, something life-changing, something to get excited about, something ultimately fulfilling." May we all be so fortunate.

NOTES

1. An 11th-century description of the "general monastic practice" of English Benedictines cited in Henry Petroski, *The Book on the Bookshelf* (New York: Alfred A. Knopf, 1999), 41.

2. Petroski, *The Book on the Bookshelf*, 41.

3. Milton J. (Joe) Coalter, "Religious Reading in Peril: A Challenge to the Voca-

tional Soul of the Theological Librarian," in *Summary of Proceedings. 54th Annual Conference of the American Theological Library Association* (Chicago: ATLA, 2000), 69–72.

4. Henry K. Rowe. *The History of Andover Theological Seminary* (Newton, Mass: Andover Theological Seminary, 1933), 143.

5. Rowe, *The History of Andover Theological Seminary*, 145.

6. Rachel Singer Gordon and Sarah Nesbeitt, "Who We Are, Where Are We Going: A Report from the Front," *Library Journal* 124, no. 9 (May 15, 1999): 38.

7. Peter Hernon, Ronald R. Powell, and Arthur P. Young, "University Library Directors in the Association of Research Libraries: The Next Generation, Part Two," *College and Research Libraries* 63, no. 1 (January 2002): 73–90.

8. Edmund L. Pearson, *The Old Librarian's Almanack* (Woodstock, Vermont: Elm Tree Press, 1909), n.p.

2

THEOLOGICAL LIBRARIANS AT WORK

9

Introduction

Monica Corcoran

While reading these essays I was repeatedly impressed by the thought that although we have come a very long way since the 1940s in the ways in which we approach our work, the fundamentals of what we do and why we do it have changed very little. Our methodologies may have changed, but the basics remain: the seemingly endless quest for adequate funding, the periodic regrouping, the process of asking ourselves what can be cut from the collections budget, and wondering how best to improve access to current holdings and to enhance the collection for future needs.

LIBRARY STAFFING

Gilbert provides some useful ideas that still remain helpful to librarians of today. For example, patrons are still prone to assume that whoever is working at the circulation clerk is a fully-trained librarian. While we may never change that perception, we are still wise to work with it in mind. Two minutes' time to review an hour-long orientation held last semester may be all the clerk has at her disposal for reference work. We can reduce the failure rate of our patrons in finding needed materials by being proactive in supporting our circulation staff. This can be accomplished by having ready finding aids clearly arranged and organized at the circulation desk and at the public OPAC terminals. Keeping a log of unanswered questions and of recommendations by the frontline staff for streamlining procedures is another helpful tool.

It is still valuable and important that we reshelve books in a timely manner because to our patrons there is no practical difference between a lost and an unshelved book, and most of them will not ask for help. But "rough re-shelving" can be less helpful than no reshelving at all, resulting in more "lost" books, which will only be retrieved during the next inventory. Such a technique may work well in smaller collections, but most of ours have grown considerably since the early days of ATLA.

CATALOGING

It amazes me that even within library circles catalogers are sometimes viewed as being expendable, or interchangeable, as if "one size fits all." In my library our cataloger has been on staff for thirty-one years, and she is the first person I approach for help in finding materials and in deciphering what may or may not be suitable for our collection.

With the prevalence of copy cataloging, and with the advent of electronic catalogs, correct and accurate cataloging is more vital than ever. In addition to having a scholarly grasp of the scope and mission of the institution, today's cataloger needs to know what kind of help to ask of the IT department when poor search results reflect some kind of the technology malfunction rather than poor cataloging.

ARCHIVES VS. SPECIAL COLLECTIONS

In many cases, a library receiving archival documents must scramble to find volunteers to accession and arrange the materials. We are very wisely exhorted in this part (Macleod) to appoint to the work a supervisor who understands the principles of future retrieval and how best to accommodate that work. However, the plea for a simple system of cataloging special collec-tions made more sense in the '50s when Cappon was writing than it does now. With electronic cataloging systems, we need to use standard fields for identifying these papers, letters, and photos. In an era when scholars expect to be able to search its holdings online before deciding whether to visit a given library, we need to be as savvy as possible in determining what kind of metadata will be most helpful A label of "Dulles letters, box 1" is insufficient for users who will be searching for archival material in the web-based cata-logs of many libraries.

A number of institutions have digitized or are planning to digitize their manuscript collections. This approach deserves serious consideration. The initial work required is considerable and costly, but the finished product can help overcome many of the limits presented by our archival collections. Even digitizing a portion of the collection will give scholars some idea about the depth and quality of materials in the collection. Since our libraries are usually the repositories for the records of major religious bodies, it is still a good practice to facilitate the safekeeping of these records in years to come. Our experiences help us to anticipate many of the records which will find their way into the archives of the institution, and there is much we can do to foster their use.

FROM A COLLECTION TO A LIBRARY

The steps taken in building a library are faced periodically by all of us: stretching frugal budgets, mustering volunteer help, converting cataloging records. Of special concern is the need to make the case for adequate staffing, of making thoughtful and systematic changes such as the choice of a classification system, or decisions about classification standards when merging two or more collections, and of providing the best kind of library advocacy to administrators on a regular basis.

There are good reasons for discouraging too great a reliance on the help of part-time staff instead of full-time workers. In some cases, part-timers work very well, but communications can become strained when their work hours do not regularly overlap with those of full-time staff. Where the option exists, enlisting the help of interns from graduate level library science programs seems to be a better solution than relying on volunteers.

COLLECTION DEVELOPMENT

Written policies can be used to justify budget increases, to document needs, and to maintain the library's "institutional memory" from era to era. In my experience, this last point is one of the more cogent justifications for maintaining written policies. How often does a new staffer arrive only to be met with very different explanations of mission and policies by various people within and outside the library staff? It is true that the writing and updating of such documents can seem like a drain on valuable staff time, but having them in place can prevent months or even years of floundering. Anyone who has been hired during a period of high staff turnover knows how difficult an orientation can be, with or without written policies.

The mechanics of collection development have changed only slightly since the presentation by Whipple. We still rely on the reputations of individual publishers, book reviews, automatic (approval) ordering plans, and bibliographies. Quantitative analysis, although still utilized, seems a less reliable measure. Citation analysis can still be misused by careless scholars. Materials selection by librarians rather than faculty is still normally the better approach. And, of course, sacrificing collection depth for faculty leanings remains a poor strategy. However, areas of past strength should be maintained if the value of the collection is to remain high. When a library has been collecting materials in a particular subject area and has established itself as an authoritative or even a strong collection in the subject, maintaining that area of strength will help to keep the collection strong and coherent, and will also help to maintain the institution's academic reputation. There can be, under specific circumstances, very sound reasons for shifting the emphasis of a collection, but if the curriculum is supported by the subject area and if the scholarly community relies on the institution, it can only enhance the reputation of the library to continue collecting in that area.

WRITING ABOUT OUR PROFESSION

Unless a profession writes about its work it cannot measure its own progress; it cannot look to early members in the field for direction and comparison. We are aided now by the availability of a wealth of electronic resources. We also can find inspirational sources, among them *A Benedictine Library in a Disordered World* and *How the Irish Saved Civilization*, when we need a reminder and a renewal of purpose. The first describes a collection which was lost forever, but the fact that it even existed, and at such a high standard of excellence, served to inspire future generations. The second tells the story of how a network of traveling priests and monks managed to quietly rescue and save valuable writings during a period of political upheaval and rampant plundering in Europe. Without the quiet work of these few people, much of our written history would have been lost to us. We, as a profession, can find guidance and wisdom in these kinds of writings, and should continue to write about our profession both for the advancement of the profession and as a legacy to those who will follow us.

CONCLUSION

There is a wealth of excellent advice to be found in these essays. Much of it can still be commended as a source of wisdom for handling various aspects of our work in theological libraries. The means by which we do our work may have changed, but much of the resourcefulness, the thought and planning needed to do the job well remains unchanged. For this reason, the recording and preservation of our collective knowledge is of utmost importance. It is in the sharing of our experiences and discoveries of a better path that we help our colleagues perform to a higher standard, and light a beacon for those who will follow us.

10

The Cataloger and Instruction
6th Annual Conference, Louisville, KY, 1952

Helen B. Uhrich

A paper on the cataloger and instruction could easily become so general that it would be useful to no one. In this case, however, the group to be addressed, the American Theological Library Association, clearly determines the direction such a presentation should follow, and the paper, therefore, will be slanted toward the theological seminary library as found in this country and the participation by the cataloger in its educational program. We realize, of course, that the possibility for generalities still exists, but it is hoped that its usefulness will not be limited to the academic exercise of a cataloger who, now that the writing of this paper has been done, has been politely reminded of the following jingle:

> Cataloging, we admit,
> Is work that is extolled by none,
> Because you never notice it,
> Unless it isn't being done.

In order to suggest how the cataloger may share in a creative, educational process we shall examine the distinctive nature of theological literature and the library in which the theological cataloger works; the task of the theological library and its relation to the program of the school and the cataloger's share in the development of this program; the qualifications she will need for performance of these tasks; the functions and aims of cataloging and classification; and the effective use and value of the catalog in an instructional program.

First of all it is essential to understand something about the literature with which the cataloger in the field of theology is concerned. No other discipline has produced so old or so extensive a documentation. Man's efforts to understand himself and to relate himself effectively to the world about him have resulted in a literature that is characterized by its variety of expression, its diversity of viewpoint, and its unevenness. It is the nature of the theological process to draw upon the past, to relate itself to tradition, to precedent, to that which has gone before. That is to say that the new book is not always the best book, theologically speaking. There is a process, a movement, a constant renewal which possesses a creative and dynamic quality. The cataloger is thus constantly confronted with "something old and something new," neither to be preferred to the exclusion of the other.

The task of assembling and organizing the literature in the field of theology falls largely and naturally to the theological or seminary library. While all departments of knowledge are represented in the theological library, there is a unifying core or point of view that ties this material together. Thus the collection, by relating all topics within it to theology and religion, becomes a homogeneous unit. But books organized around a point of view will not in themselves make a library. A library is more than books and material and buildings. As President Sproul of the University of California has said, "Books are not a library any more than blood is a man, although they are just as indispensable to it. A library," he said, "is a collection of books, housed adequately, and if possible nobly, but most important of all, organized for use and directed by highly trained personnel toward the ends which it has been established to serve, whether these be recreation or research."

By definition, then, a theological library is not just a collection of books in a subject area but a collection organized for use with a very specific purpose in mind. It is developed and organized through intelligent selection and well-defined aims, consistently and persistently adhered to over a span of years, and constantly related to its purpose, which is the school and its program.

The function of the theological library is twofold. Not only does it serve as a repository for the literature that will document man's religious history and development, but, perhaps more important, it exists to implement the educational program of the school. Actually, these two aims are interdependent in that by conserving the past and organizing and preserving human knowledge and ideas in all of their media, the library makes it possible for this knowledge and these ideas to be revitalized and put to use in the education of others. This dual function to serve the school's present needs and at the same time anticipate the needs of a generation hence, to approach the work on both a vertical and a horizontal line, to be both timely and timeless, presents a challenge that can only be met by great wisdom and inspired work. To perform a task which must be so obviously of the present and still transcend it may be what T. S. Eliot meant in his Quartet:

> To apprehend
> The point of intersection of the timeless
> With time is an occupation for the saint.

This may, indeed, be our distinctive claim to sainthood.

Recalling ourselves abruptly from this heavenly vision, we realize that along with the emergence of the library from its role as a repository of books to that of an educational agency comes the accompanying demand that librarians be more than custodians. This concept of librarianship takes us far beyond what Archibald MacLeish has described as "the hat check boy in the parcel room of culture." The library must not cease to function as accumulator and organizer of books, periodicals, and other materials, but it must also be an active force in the teaching, research, publication, and extension programs of the school.

The library is not an end in itself. While there are many duties and routines it has to perform in schedules and technical processes, these must be kept as the background to the efficient performance and promotion of the educational objectives, policies, and practices of the institution. It follows then that there are definite implications for the entire library staff. If the library is to perform these functions properly, the staff must understand the institution's administrative and educational policies and maintain close contact with its activities. Staff members must know a great deal about the particular institution of which the library is a part, and they must be familiar with the school's history and traditions, program, philosophy, and aims. This should be more than just a passing acquaintance. It must be intimate enough so that all actions are determined and modified by the purpose and program they are intended to advance.

While this is true for the library staff as a whole, it is especially true for the cataloger. Once the resources for carrying out the objectives of the institution in the fields of instruction and research have been provided, probably no other person on the staff is in the same strategic position for implementing this program as the cataloger. Organization of the resources of the library for efficient use constitutes one of the fundamental essentials to the successful operation of the library and its integration with the teaching and research program of the school. The cataloger very quickly takes a prominent part in the educational program of the institution.

The factors that will guide the cataloger in organizing and interpreting the collection are essentially the same as those that should determine its scope and development. A knowledge and understanding of the situation in which the library will function, the service it will have to provide, the immediate and ultimate use of materials are necessary if the cataloger is to relate her work to it effectively. A cataloger who is not concerned with the relationship of her work to the school or how it could serve it more adequately is not performing her task to the utmost of her possibilities or potentialities. There is a job to be done and the cataloger must share in it. The aim is a library shaped by a very specific purpose. Integrated and coordinated with all parts of the school in its educational program, the library takes its place along with the classroom and the professor's study, and all members of the library staff become contributors and sharers in something larger than their physical boundaries of book stacks and catalog cases.

We assume that the cataloger has the required qualifications for her job. She must have native ability, aptitude, and those qualities which give a person the potentiality of scope, depth, and growth. You cannot take a little person and give her a big job. To these qualifications must be added a sound technical training, a genuine skill based on an acquired technique, a professional interest, mental curiosity, imagination, flexibility, drive, the "book-sense" which William Warner Bishop describes as an ability to move quickly and easily among printed things with an instinctive appreciation of values. Lest she be a technician only, useful in a limited way, she must bring vision to her task to know which aspects of the technical program are necessary for the particular tasks of her library and which may be omitted without educational loss. The cataloger will need all the language equipment she can muster if she is going to advance beyond the elementary stages of cataloging in this discipline. She will need bibliographical competence of the highest order if she is going to move freely and easily in this literature and deal intelligently with it in all of its varying degrees of complexity and diversity. The cataloger who would serve scholars must be something of a scholar, or as Miss Pettee has said, she must be a "near-scholar."

Specifically, then, how can the cataloger help to implement the educational program of the school and contribute to it? How can she, by performing the tasks of her profession, participate as a teaching instrument? The answer, broadly stated, must obviously be found in the areas normally designated as her responsibility—the classification, cataloging, and assignment of subject headings—in other words, in the organization and interpretation of the library collection. Why do we classify books? To make them more easily accessible. Why do we catalog books? To enable the readers and staff to use them more easily. These simple rudiments are so fundamental to the educational process, so easily assumed and taken for granted as the natural, normal situation in our libraries that we easily fail to understand how important they are for the process of instruction itself.

The cataloger, then, stands between the acquisition of books and the final servicing of these books, and it is here that she makes her unique contribution to the instructional program of the school. Between these two actions all the implications of the curriculum, new courses, additions to the teaching staff, size of student body, will have to be understood and interpreted by the cataloger. Changes, additions, and new plans in the school's program will affect the use of the library and library materials, and the cataloger must anticipate what these will mean in her work. The significance for the cataloger is clear. She must emphasize and support the educational objectives of the school and become identified with them.

Since most of our libraries combine the cataloging and classification processes either in one person or in one department, reference in this paper to cataloging will, unless qualified, imply inclusion of classification and subject cataloging. By the cataloger will be meant that person who performs the three determinations, classification, subject heading, and descriptive cataloging, which govern the placement of the book on the shelves and its recording in the catalogs.

The primary aim for the cataloger as stated in the Editor's Introduction to the second edition of the A.L.A. *Cataloging Rules for Author and Title Entries* "is to make the collection of books and other materials accessible to all who have a legitimate claim on its resources. These persons include not only readers and research workers, but members of the administrative, order, reference, and cataloging staffs of the library itself."

In the organization and interpretation of the library collection the action specifically designed to make books accessible and available is classification. We could make little headway in meeting the demands placed on our book collections without some system of arrangement for the volumes on the shelves. The problems involved in the circulation of books, in the answering of reference questions, in locating specific titles of books, in meeting requests for definite (or indefinite) subjects, all make it imperative that the library have a scheme for allocating its books which will make possible prompt and effective service. Without some means of getting at these books and of finding them quickly and easily, they are of little value to the staff, the student, or the professor, and the most magnificent educational resources are literally useless. As Dr. E. C. Richardson has said: "Libraries are not gotten together as a museum to exhibit what we have called the fossils of knowledge. . . . The books are collected for use. They are administered for use. They are arranged for use; and it is use which is the motive of classification."

It is largely this principle of making books accessible and available for use that has made the library-instructional program at Stephens College so effective. By emphasizing the essential unity of library work and instruction, they have made the library an integral part of the teaching program. They have made books easy to get at. They have placed books where they will be used. They have made books available at the time needed or wanted. While they have accomplished this by dispersing their collection over the campus in classrooms, offices, dormitories, laboratories, etc., it is not this physical arrangement in which we are particularly interested. In fact, it might be an entirely unsatisfactory disposition for most libraries. The two principles here that are of primary importance to us and that can be appropriated to any institution are first, the library understands the institution and what it is doing, and second, the accessibility of books.

These two factors, then, have definite implications for the classifier if the collection of books is to become an instructional tool. The use of books is not an incidental or accidental aspect of instruction, but central and primary. Complacency at the point of classification and organization will not produce the maximum availability of the library's resources that is needed for educational effectiveness.

This brings us back to our original definition of a theological library as a collection of books in a special subject area organized for *use* with a specific purpose in mind. What does this mean for the classifier of theological literature? It means, very briefly, that she must know something about the books she is classifying if she is to relate them to a program whose aims and objectives are theological training. She must have a sound knowledge of the subject matter and be able to class books so that they will aid and not hinder the educational process. The literature must be arranged in an order that lends itself to the subject divisions in theology and it must be logical to those who know and are familiar with the subject. It must "make sense" to the specialist in the field. The demands of the intelligent reader follow pretty closely the literature itself, and the finished job must be well-defined to meet his expectations. Classification must follow the "joints," the natural breakdowns in the field, and not the proclivities or the personal whims of the classifier. The usefulness of the classification will be determined to a large extent by the degree of accord between the user and the arrangement of the books.

Classification must not be forced or artificial, and fuzziness and false distinctions must be avoided. If it is necessary to toss a coin to see which of two numbers to use, the lines of distinction between them have been drawn too closely. The classifier must avoid the inclination to overclassify on the one hand or to underclassify on the other. The first extreme will result in a collection difficult to use because too much detail has been introduced. Minute distinctions may be apparent to the classifier, but their significance is lost to the user. If classification is too broad the book collection will be unwieldy because too few subdivisions have been introduced and the natural lines of cleavage are not apparent.

Much in theological literature is both new and also very old. The classifier must be able to recognize new trends and developments and be able to identify them correctly and relate them to the past. She must be alert to the constant stream of old doctrines in new dress, to new orientations, and must be able, so far as possible, to understand their meaning and importance. It is her task to detect these recurring motifs and to relate them to older or similar ones.

The classifier will do well to remember that books are not written with classification schedules in mind, and for many square pegs there will be only round holes. Life is not static and therefore books are not. Classification schedules are artificial arrangers of knowledge and do not "stay put." Unless the classifier is unusually astute, she will create a tool that quickly becomes dated and outmoded. She must be cautious lest she be carried away by all that seems new. She needs a certain abandon to know when to let herself go. She must have enough perspective so that she will not be looked upon as a child of today, loved today and despised tomorrow. ("Will you love me in December as you do in May?")

Classification alone is not sufficient to reveal the complete resources of the library. It must be supplemented and augmented if the library's holdings in a given field or on a special topic are to be uncovered. This complementary function is performed by subject analysis and its related devices. Without subject headings in the catalog the library records provide only a one-dimensional picture of the library's resources.

Many of the same principles employed in giving significance to the classification are also applied in the assignment of subject headings. Subject cataloging, like classification, will be good or bad according as there is a common context, great or small, between the terms of the cataloger and those of the user. A common experience must furnish this context. The cataloger must not only assume but must know that the term has the same meaning for the user as for herself. As an educator she should be aware of how the mind of the reader works and must learn the lingo and vocabulary of the theologian. If the cataloger is going to make subject cataloging fully effective, the choice of terms, structure, and arrangement must correspond as closely as possible with the reader's approach.

The cataloger's work with subject headings finds an echo of similarity in the experiences of Ronald Knox in his work as a Bible translator. His task in translating the Bible, he said, was to reduce words and phrases to the equivalent idiom of his own language and to find the word that had the correct meaning and association for the user. To get a real translation, he said, the channel must be connected with its surroundings, instead of being sealed off at both ends. This is not too different from what the cataloger aims to do through her work.

In order to make available the work of classification and subject headings, it is necessary to have records describing the contents of the library collection. In the American academic library this is usually a dictionary catalog containing the author, subject, title, reference and other cards intended to enable the reader to find a definite work or a class of works and to choose different books or different editions of a work on the basis of information given on the catalog entry.

The public catalog is usually, and no doubt rightly so, regarded as the principal tool resulting from the work of the catalog department, so far as the users of the library and the staff are concerned. Miss Margaret Mann, in her *Introduction to Cataloging and the Classification of Books,* says that the preparation of any library catalog constitutes one of the most important and painstaking tasks in the field of library science, not alone because it is a piece of work requiring the greatest care and intelligence, but because effective use of the book collection by the staff and readers depends on the perfection of its execution. All activities of the library will depend upon this tool and be influenced by its guidance.

The catalog is the point where the student, the teacher, and the library staff, not only today but tomorrow as well, approach the library collection. The catalog will be a good tool or a poor tool in the degree that the resources of the library have been adequately and thoroughly identified, recorded, and made accessible, and in the degree that it meets the needs of the school it serves. The cataloger must be alert to whatever will contribute to the effective fashioning of this tool as a repository of useful and accurate information. The effectiveness of the library in the program of the school will depend in no small part on the excellence of the catalog and the skill with which it has been constructed.

Miss McCrum, in her book *An Estimate of Standards for a College Library,* refers to the catalog as a loose-leaf reference book whose general characteristics should be those of any reliable, serviceable reference work. It should be planned to give a guidance to books as encyclopedias do to knowledge in general. It should act as an index to subject matter with sufficient notes and cross references to make the contents available to the type of person using it. The card catalog must remain the essential index by which related subjects in separated books are brought together. The physical burden of making scattered books available in one place, at need, at a given time, is the obligation of the library staff.

There are certain demands which may reasonably be made of the catalog and there are certain specifications it must meet. It must be accurate, consistent, predictable. Inaccuracies in transcription of call numbers, wrong dates, incomplete citations will discount not only the work of the cataloger but of the entire staff. The information must be as correct as the cataloger is able to determine it. Names must be spelled accurately and dates of authors given correctly so that persons whose names appear in the catalog can be identified. Information must be full enough so that one edition of a book is not confused with another; so that a citation can be given that will be respectable as the place, publisher, and date; or that a bibliographical reference can be verified. There must be enough physical description as to pages, bibliographies, and notes so that books may be selected for a particular purpose.

The catalog must also meet the requirements of consistency and predictability. By this we do not mean that all cards in it are alike as to final detail in form and content, but that sound policies have been established and executed, and that a reasonable degree of standardization and uniformity is maintained. While the information may be simplified, it must be reliable and necessitate no further verification on the part of the user. According to Miss Mann, simplification does not consist in the elimination of essentials; it means a recognition of essentials and their most effective use. The cataloger's aim, then, is to ascertain those lasting principles which have been found most useful in library cataloging and which are not subject to change, even though the rules which attempt to apply those principles to specific books are reworded from time to time. The most accurate, consistent, and predictable catalog, obviously, will be the most useful.

What will this kind of catalog mean to the research man? It means that he can depend upon it for accurate information and that he can rely upon it for his bibliographical research without further checking. One of the cataloger's main services to the scholar will be in the provision of reliable author entries. If he can be confident that he will not be let loose on a wild goose chase for phantom or ghost titles, the cataloger will have contributed much to the teaching and research program of the school.

While it might appear that these specifications for the catalog are necessary for the research library only, it should be pointed out that the catalog in the small library also needs to be developed with accuracy and attention to bibliographical details. For one thing, the small library becomes the large library, and careless or inadequate cataloging will have to be done over as the library grows or as it fails to expand with the book collection. It is perhaps more important for the small library to develop subject headings, added entries, and references in greater detail and more extensively than the large library, simply to use its collection to the fullest. The basic shape and outline of a large library is determined in no small measure by the type and depth of the foundation under it. As for careless, inaccurate, and ignorant work, it has no place in an academic setting where scholarly work is going on.

It soon becomes apparent to the cataloger that the academic level of those who use the catalog varies from the beginner whose questions will be general and broad and who may not even know the elementary sources in the field to the highly trained and experienced person whose questions will be detailed and specific and well beyond the general aspects of the problem. The catalog will need to provide service from the most simple requests of those who use it as a finding list to the most advanced who are considering a topic exhaustively and who, with a minimum of time and effort, want to gather their material.

The functions of the catalog, then, will range from providing casual information to aiding the scholar in extensive research in his field of study. Of this the cataloger is aware and she intends that much of the information provided by the catalog will not be needed by all of its users. She includes this information so it will not interfere with the use of the catalog on its various levels. The catalog very quickly becomes a complex affair beyond the ability of the untrained person to use. It is made for the staff quite as much as for the public. In short, and this is a point too often overlooked or not even understood, much of the information in the catalog exists only for the skilled bibliographer and the librarian who has been trained how to use and interpret it. Unless we are given the right kind of a catalog tool and the skills to use it, it will be impossible for libraries to perform some of the most important tasks given them to do.

We can illustrate the use of the library on the advanced level of research by citing an article by Edward G. Lewis that appeared in *College and Research Libraries* for April 1952 entitled "A Political Scientist in the Reference Library." The author says that the questions the more experienced political scientist will bring to the library will likely be about small factual details. He knows where to find the major pieces of information and has probably worked out the general aspect of his problem and has done an exhaustive amount of digging for facts before turning to the reference librarian for aid. What he is looking for is the elusive detail, the sort of detail that can almost never be found in the obvious places. This is in contrast to the beginning political scientist who will lean heavily on the bibliographical help which the reference librarian can provide. "Judging from my own experience," he writes, "I feel that the political scientist of some experience does not expect from the reference librarian help on the body of the material, but on the all important and often incredibly elusive peripheral details."

If Mr. Lewis's approach to the library is typical of the use made by advanced scholars in other subject areas, what does this tell the cataloger? If he is correct in analyzing his use of the library, what can the cataloger learn from it that will be significant for her work? Briefly, it tells her that what is valued most on the simple level of library use is valued the least by the specialist. What John Smith wants to know on the beginning level is already known to the researcher of some experience. What the specialist wants is the information over and beyond what he has been able to uncover in his rummaging about. Catalogers would be most remiss in their service to this level of use if the tool they created answered only the question, "Do you have a certain book and where can I find it?" Much of the value in the library could never be tapped or uncovered with this kind of catalog.

Miss Mudge, writing against the background of her experience as the head of the reference department of the Columbia University Library, has gone so far as to say, "I have yet to find any item of information called for in the rules for adequate description of the average book which some reader, of his own accord, will not make good use of." Confronted with statements like this, the cataloger is placed in a dilemma, and it is against these opposing pulls that she must constantly work. She is besieged for more and more cards and detail in the catalog and at the same time she is asked to keep costs down. The cataloger is faced with a paradox—on the one hand the inclination to include detail on and beyond the law of diminishing returns and on the other, the inclination to simplify because of immediate pressures and not because of real and lasting economy. The faculty, if given their way, would have everything analyzed. "It will be used if we know we have it," they say. The reference and order departments add similar pleas and requests. Obviously, the cataloger will be hopelessly bogged down if she attempts to carry all these requests to the extreme. If she catalogs in the detail the faculty, the reference, and order departments would like, costs go up and cataloging output is reduced. Actually, she must have the good judgment to determine when she can simplify and effect real economy or when, by cutting corners, costs go up and service deteriorates. "True economy," according to Mr. Charles Martel, "is to make an entry which answers the purposes for which persons to whom books are necessary consult catalogs . . . an entry not ornate and elaborate, but correct, complete, and withal as concise as possible."

Very few of us would argue for a blind or senseless elaboration of detail or for indiscriminate cataloging as though all books were of equal worth. Not every book needs to be cataloged as though it were a rare book. Just as there are different levels of service to users, so there are different levels of cataloging for various categories of materials. Too much cataloging has been in the "rare book tradition" influenced by the scholarly research collections and by following standards that have made our cataloging far too elaborate at many points. Conversely, since the catalog is a permanent reference work and not a temporary one or one that will be done over every generation, it is wasteful and extravagant to put into it inadequate and slipshod work. At Yale we are still recataloging books that were hastily put on shelves twenty years ago on "temporary cataloging and classification." Frugality practiced on bibliographical detail may mean saving in the catalog department and books more quickly cataloged, but may be more than outweighed by increased costs in other departments of the library.

As a matter of fact, a catalog can be kept simple only to a certain point, and the theological library catalog is no exception. It very quickly becomes involved and complex. This is due to the very nature of the material described in it. Bible entries, for instance, do not lend themselves to easy arrangement or use. There are also the difficulties presented by corporate entries for church bodies, societies and institutions, and their publications. These headings are further complicated by the divisive nature and the movements for ecumenicity within the denominational scene. We have not even touched on the problems involved in voluminous authors, such as Thomas Aquinas, Saint Augustine, and others; or the difficulties encountered in names that are entered in the vernacular or classical form, as Hieronymus for St. Jerome, and Clemens Romanus for Clement of Rome, or in entries for sacred literature other than the Bible.

Because of the complexity of the catalog, the cataloger will employ all possible devices to increase its value and assist the reader in his search for material. She will not set up an expensive tool with no further signals or instructions for use. The catalog will very quickly get beyond the point where it can be used profitably without guide cards and references of various kinds and description.

Some of the more obvious of these devices to enhance the reliability of the catalog are subject guide cards for major terms and their subdivisions; guides displaying the various sub-schemes of card arrangements; name guides; information guide cards explaining the use of the catalog; explanatory cards defining or delimiting a term; reference guides to other material, such as the vertical file, special collections, and the like. In addition, there are the "see" and "see also" cards to correlate subjects or entries and to bridge the lack of context between the terms of the catalog and those of the user.

It is impossible to tell a cataloger what form these cards and references should take for her catalog. While she is guided in their construction by her cataloging codes and the requests from users and the reference department, their choice will ultimately depend upon her imagination and ingenuity, her knowledge of the subject matter, the extent of the research that has gone into establishing a particular heading, and other peculiarities that become obvious as she handles the material. Her aim is to organize material for efficient use, and if by providing guides and reference cards she can save the user's time, or enable him to proceed more directly to his subject, or investigate a topic more exhaustively, she has accomplished that end. The value of all of this for the reference and the order librarian and for users on all levels, including research, is plain.

True, many of our efforts to be helpful turn out to be obscure or amusing. We are all familiar with the story of the literal-minded person who reacted to the reference, "For complete information see main entry," by looking for the front door. Directing the reader to statement of contents or more complete information may result in a card similar to the one we found in our catalog recently. The title read, "What is hell?" The note read, "For contents see main entry." Sometimes the detailed description of a rare book produces rather startling effects as, for example, the note on the card for Archbishop Laud's funeral sermon preached by himself from the scaffold on Tower-hill, 1644: "Bled at top and outside edge." These examples, I am sure, could be matched by all of us.

Another point at which the cataloger can be of service to the library and to the school is in the development of the collection. Through the years she acquires a tremendous knowledge of the book stock and the library's resources. This intimate knowledge of the library can be of invaluable help in building and developing the collection, making recommendations for purchase, pointing out lacks, indicating weak areas, and so on. Her critical searches through bibliographies and reference tools will often uncover valuable suggestions for purchase. In fact, the cataloger may do a better job of helping to build up the collection than those who are teachers of the subject because she has a more objective point of view toward the complete library resources.

Since no other person in the library is in quite the same strategic position as the cataloger for acquiring a familiarity with the material, its organization, and how to uncover it, she is often unexcelled in reference work, and the question is how to tap this knowledge. How to provide the reference librarian with the skills and knowledge that result from the discipline of cataloging and classification is another problem. Realizing that the best training for reference work is in cataloging, many libraries start their new people in the catalog department. Some libraries withhold advancement for reference librarians until they have had experience in cataloging because they believe their value to the library is limited without it.

It has been suggested that this objective may be effected in part by an interchange of personnel within the library. True, nothing is more helpful for the cataloger than to observe at first hand how the catalog is being used, whether it is effective, and how it might be improved. Much can be learned in a short while from contacts with the public. On the other hand, it is doubtful whether a casual exchange can provide the requisite training for the reference librarian. It is a worthy objective, but the solution is complicated and quickly creates problems, largely administrative, in the matter of adequate personnel to support such a program, the disruption of planned work, loss of time, and similar difficulties.

We often say that the reference librarian is the liaison between the school and the library, at the direct point of contact between the student and the book. Here the final interpretation of the library collection takes place and the process in bringing books and people together becomes complete. The success with which this is accomplished will depend in large measure on the reference librarian and the skill she brings to bear upon her work, not only in educational methods, but in the use of her tools. To do this effectively she must have her reference material, of which the catalog is the major tool, under perfect control. Thus the acquisition of the book, its organization, and final servicing may be integrated with the educational objectives and procedures of the institution.

And now, what have we said about the cataloger and instruction? What is her share in making the library effective in the educational process and integrating it with the institution as a whole? By the very nature of her profession the cataloger works at the center of materials that preserve human knowledge and ideas. She is an active participant in a creative process wherein men are in search of the thought and experience of the past and seek in turn to contribute their interpretation to the extension of this knowledge. By performing the tasks of her profession she can make the resources of the whole library accessible and available to all. By organizing and interpreting the library collection she can constantly relate the library to the school and share in the promotion of its educational program. Her labors here and now are meant for tomorrow as well, and how effectively she performs her task will be evident as time goes on. As Kierkegaard has said, "Life must be understood backwards. But . . . it must be lived forwards." Future generations may not rise up to call her blessed, but perhaps somewhere along the way the cataloger can snatch a tiny bit of sainthood for herself.

11

Problems in Manuscript Cataloging
10th Annual Conference, Berkeley, CA, 1956

Julia H. Macleod

Youth is often criticized for brashness and conceit, but there is an even greater daring and complacency that comes with age and grey hair. Perhaps it is from these, as well as my quarter century of experience at the Huntington Library and the Bancroft Library, that I am emboldened to formulate some ideas about dealing with manuscripts.

"But women's work is never done!" is part of an old saying which holds true for cataloguers—especially manuscript cataloguers—of both sexes! Just as we have some hope of finishing the task at hand, to say nothing of the arrears, along comes a new—and usually large and heterogeneous—collection of material demanding immediate attention! But despite our grumblings over insufficient help, insufficient space and time, pressures to make material available for use, and the ever-increasing demands for reports and guides to holdings, few manuscript cataloguers would trade their work for any other.

Most manuscript cataloguers have been "on the job" trainees. Some have had library school training before they have had to cope with manuscripts. Their professional training, however, has usually been book centered and not always too helpful in respect to many of the problems encountered in arranging and cataloguing manuscripts. The basic philosophy in book cataloguing and classification is to bring together on the shelves works on the same and related subjects. Few collections of books acquired by a library are kept intact but are scattered throughout the library, perhaps with identifying bookplates to record their source. On the other hand, the keynote of archival practice is to keep together material from a single source and make appropriate references in the catalogue to the various parts. Where this basic principle has been violated in respect to an archive, and the various parts scattered, trouble in the future is usually the result.

Whatever our backgrounds, I think we will all agree that our work with manuscripts is largely "a playing by ear" technique, acquired from experience, rather than the result of formalized training. The summer training courses or "Institutes" given in the last few years by the American University under the direction of Ernst Posner, and by Radcliffe College and the History Department of Harvard, under the direction of Earle W. Newton, represent the most important training programs for manuscript and archive workers yet offered. There has been nothing of the sort given in the West. The A.L.A. preliminary report on manuscript cataloguing represents the first attempt at standardization of procedure. Most repositories have developed their own methods to meet their own needs and convenience. And regardless of the future availability of workers with some specific training in handling manuscripts, and the adoption of procedures for manuscript cataloguing by the A.L.A., many of these repositories will continue to go their own way due to their own varied problems of budget, staff, space, and holdings.

I would like to differentiate between the terms "archive" and "collection." I believe the term "archive" is generally understood in cataloguing parlance to mean the natural accumulation of papers by an individual, an organization, or a family in the course of their activities over the years. On the other hand, a "collection" usually designates the papers collected by an individual or organization for some specific purpose. The term "collection" has often been used, however, to refer to an archive; the terms "papers" or "records" are more correct. When a repository refers to its collections it usually refers to both "collections" and "archives," as well as all its related material.

In dealing with the "collection" the cataloguer is more justified in taking liberties with the arrangement than when dealing with an "archive." While it is important to retain the identity of a "collection," the purpose of the collector in accumulating the material can be taken into account. "Collections" have often been achieved by destroying "archives." Dealers, autograph and rarity collectors frequently do this. The interests and needs of the repository can more correctly enter into its treatment of a "collection" than of an "archive." However, great care must always be exercised in breaking up a collection, even when its parts seem to have little relation, one to the other, that something of value in the fact that the collection was assembled is not lost in the process.

An "archive," on the other hand, must be more carefully treated. When books and printed matter are acquired along with personal papers, it is pretty standard practice to separate the two. Most repositories have separate catalogues for their manuscript and book holdings. Ideally, a list of the material so separated should always be retained as part of the "archive." Sometimes this is done, but more often, due to the pressures of time and shortness of staff, it is not. Thus, valuable association information is apt to be lost. However, if the printed material were retained with the manuscripts, it would either become buried or create terrific problems of cataloguing and shelving. Each repository has to solve such problems in its own fashion.

For pictures, perhaps, the problem is a little easier. Here at the Bancroft, since we have established a Picture and a Portrait File, it is easier to keep track, with consecutive numberings and cross references, of the photographs, tintypes, and the like acquired with an "archive" or a "collection." But I am sure there are many pictures and portraits and, possibly, some printed material, in some of our unprocessed groups of papers. Also, it is very possible that the identity of some of our pictures and portraits could be definitely established if better acquisition records had been kept in the past.

This leads me to the importance of "provenance" records. The source of an "archive," "collection," or single item should always be carefully recorded. The name of the dealer (but not necessarily what was paid for it) should always be available to the user, as should the name of the donor, unless specifically wishing to remain anonymous. This information sometimes provides valuable clues to the location of additional papers, or to the authenticity of material which has been copied. And, as time elapses, this information becomes increasingly valuable.

The first step in making a group of papers available for use is their arrangement. Very few archives or collections come into a repository in such shape that there is nothing to do but give the containers appropriate finding symbols, put them on the shelves, and make a few cards for the catalogue. The mere transportation of the papers often destroys any previous arrangement. Literature and training both emphasize the fact that the guiding principle in respect to the arrangement of an "archive" should be the *"respect du fond"* or retention, where possible, of the original arrangement of the papers. With most groups of family papers or the papers of an individual long dead, there is no pattern to be followed. Usually what comes into the repository is merely what has survived the hazards of "women, water and mice" as someone has described the perils which can destroy manuscripts. When a group of papers is in a hopeless mess, the cataloguer has a free hand and can create some sort of order from the chaos with no qualms whatsoever. When a group of papers has some sort of recognizable arrangement, that should be carefully scrutinized to see whether it can be retained and still have the papers readily serviceable. Many systems of arrangement suited the needs of the individual whose papers they were, but are not so easily administered by the repository.

It seems to me that in the interests of security and ease of servicing manuscript material, the repository is justified in making some modifications on arrangement of large groups of papers. These changes must be done carefully, and it must always be borne in mind that the material itself determines the arrangement. No one should undertake to destroy an existing system of arrangement without carefully going over the papers to find out just what is the significance of that arrangement. No one should undertake to arrange an archive arbitrarily. A system which can be used on one group of papers may not be the best one for another group of papers, even if, at first glance, they seem somewhat similar. However, the vagaries and "vaguaries" of some file clerk need not be perpetuated. We have one archive of a former public official in which we found that crank letters were all filed under "N" for "Nuts." I would also like to point out that the sorting and arrangement of a group of papers should be undertaken by the most highly trained and experienced staff members and not the casual help. It seems very hard to convince "the powers that be" that this is so. Casual help can often be used under direction, but should not be turned loose on any group of manuscripts. Valuable information concerning enclosures in letters, related items, identification of unsigned items, etc., can all be lost, and very difficult if not impossible to reconstruct, by careless handling of material in sorting. Hasty searches at the behest of a client are also dangerous. When the sorting is being done, however, the material can be identified with a rubber stamp so that when any item is removed from its container it can be recognized. Casual help can be trusted with this task, and, perhaps, some phases of the sorting.

I have often wondered if the principle laid down by John C. Fitzpatrick in his little brochure on the arrangement and cataloguing of manuscripts in the Library of Congress, that a chronological arrangement was the best arrangement for any group of papers, was not slightly influenced by the fact that it is possible to put untrained personnel to work on papers in that fashion. A date is much easier to read than a name, and a much more definite guide to arrangement. However, in a large group of correspondence, unless you have recorded the date of every letter by every correspondent, you have no means of producing the letters of any individual. Even if you can do this, the work involved to produce them in an extensive correspondence is terrific. It is seldom that the reader is interested in the whole archive. For one reader who wishes to go through the entire mass of papers, you will have a hundred readers who are interested in some one or more correspondents. You may also be asked to have parts of an archive filmed or photostated, which means locating single items and then replacing them. Here at the Bancroft Library, we have effected a compromise. In several of our large groups of modern papers, where we have letters received and the carbon copies of replies, we have separated these, making penciled note of the date of reply on the letter received, and date of the letter received on the reply. The carbons of replies or "out letters" we have arranged chronologically; the "in letters" we have grouped alphabetically, arranging each group chronologically. In this fashion the chronological picture of the archive is maintained, yet it is possible to produce the letters of any one individual without going through all the papers. This method of arrangement seems to have satisfied the users of these "archives."

In arranging a large group of papers, I believe, it is always permissible to separate correspondence from accounts, diaries, legal papers, and the like, making the necessary cross references for related items. It is likewise permissible to remove some personal correspondence from general correspondence. A man's letters to his wife and to his children can well be made into separate units apart from his general correspondence. A willy-nilly chronological arrangement of a large group of papers can produce an awful mess— useless to most readers and impractical to administer. A subject approach to arrangement is, also, almost impossible to achieve. Particularly in papers of an earlier age, very few letters dealt only with one subject! Subject entries in the catalogue, where appropriate, seem a better solution to this problem. But I cannot emphasize too strongly my belief that the nature of the papers must determine their arrangement. It is impossible to set down hard and fast rules except that it is impossible to deal with every large group of papers in the same fashion. The judgment of the arranger always enters into the picture, and for this reason the arranger must have some knowledge and experience on which to base the judgments. The increasing demand for microfilm makes the problem of arrangement a very pressing one. It is possible though arduous for a reader to go through a mass of unsorted papers, but a mess of papers on microfilm is practically useless, and almost a complete waste of money.

After papers have been arranged comes the problem of containers. Should they be bound or put in folders? It seems to me that binding is the least satisfactory method of housing manuscripts. Once a group of papers is bound its arrangement is fixed. What about the undated or unidentified items which later, with additional information, you are able to put in their proper places? Also, if one item is called for, the whole group is handled. The difficulties for photo-duplication are greatly increased. The metal-edged boxes, like those used at the National Archives and elsewhere, are very satisfactory.[1] They can be laid flat to house very fragile material which should not be stood on edge, or used vertically as file boxes. We also use large carton-like containers, which can hold either the regular-sized or legal-sized filing folders. These cartons are also useful for housing groups of small or fragile volumes, and the miscellaneous material which sometimes makes up an archive. Portfolios of various sizes, with flaps and ties, are very useful for holding small groups of papers and fragile single items. We use an acid-free blue folder for our early manuscripts and letters, placing groups of folders in boxes or portfolios, depending upon the number to be kept together. We use manila folders in both regular and legal sizes, sometimes with blue folders to subdivide the material, in filing our large groups of modern papers. These we have placed in both the metal-edged boxes and cartons, as file drawers. Boxes and cartons on the shelves take up much less room and are more easily serviced than material in steel or temporary file drawers.

In cataloguing manuscripts as well as books, the important first step is to develop an entry. Sometimes this is very simple. The diary, letter, account, or even the "archive" is readily identifiable. The writing is clear, the signatures are decipherable, the dates are known—all is smooth sailing. But many times this is not the case. Much manuscript cataloguing demands considerable research, and there are no Library of Congress cards, British Museum catalogues, and the like to help. One of the most important attributes of a good manuscript worker, in my opinion, is an "eye" for handwriting. Often the ability to recognize handwriting similarities and differences is the key to identification of material. While some people seem to have more aptitude than others, I believe that by study and practice one can develop this skill. And it is important to know whether a letter, a manuscript, or a document is an original or a copy. One cannot always trust the dealer or the donor. Forgeries are not unknown. Also, if a manuscript has been copied, to know who copied it is sometimes an indication of the reliability of the copy. Very specialized knowledge of a period or locale is frequently needed to identify an author or addressee. To know something about paper, inks, postmarks, and writing customs aids in fixing dates. Many more people wrote letters, diaries, and the like than published books. The sleuthing which is sometimes necessary for identification is one of the cataloguer's compensations for the more boring routine tasks. But along with research must go a little imagination. The cataloguer cannot be too literal. A letter addressed to "Miss Overland" was not recognized as having been sent to Millicent Washburn Shinn, long-time editor of the *Overland Monthly* in San Francisco. Another earnest worker identified the writer of a letter as one "Belle Slippet," when the poor lady was just apologizing for the smears, with a note under her signed given name, that her blotter had slipped! And, of course, to the unwary, the signature of a bishop, with his Christian name and See, often results in an error of identification.

The cataloguing of a single item is relatively simple. One can usually establish an author, an addressee, or a title as well as the date or approximate date, and whether the item is an original or a copy. It is the large group of papers which presents the greatest problems. By using multiduplication processes it is possible to make cards for subjects and added entries, as well as main and shelf list cards, at not too great cost. We have also availed ourselves of multiduplication to get the names of correspondents or authors in an archive or collection into the catalogue. By treating these as analytics and having skeleton cards multilithed, to which only a minimum of typing must be added, we have made cards for much of the material which, in a large group of papers, usually is listed only in a report or guide. When a group of papers is arranged, the catalogable unit determines its position. Corporate entries, with necessary cross references, are established according to standard procedure. Cards are made direct from the folders. The shelf list, containing a copy of the main card followed by the analytics, serves as an index to the archive or collection. The main cards for both the group and the analytics are filed, along with the subject and added entry cards, in the Manuscripts catalogue. What may seem to be a heavy investment in mimeographing or multilithing facilities can save many times the cost in man (or woman) hours.

I noted with considerable interest and appreciation the article by Dorothy V. Martin, "Use of Cataloguing Techniques in Work with Records and Manuscripts," in *The American Archivist*, October 1955. Her excellent bibliography gives the more important works on manuscript cataloguing up to 1945. Various numbers of the *Archivist* have had many helpful articles, but Miss Martin's emphasizes the importance of cards. It seems to me that the emphasis should always be upon the catalogue. That should be the chief repository of information concerning the manuscript holdings. The names of the correspondents or authors in an "archive" or "collection" should be entered in the catalogue along with those of single items which are acquired. Sometimes the standard of what and whom to enter is hard to determine, but here again, the needs and holdings of the repository can be the guide. For a reference department to have to go through descriptive lists, in order to answer inquiries as to holdings, is very time consuming and wasteful. Also, there is always the possibility that some important group of papers will be overlooked. Cards for the catalogue, particularly when some of the shortcuts to card making are employed to reduce the work, could better have been made in the first place. With the contemplated "Union Catalog of Manuscripts" for which the A.L.A. preliminary report on manuscript catalogue procedures is undoubtedly a harbinger, we may all be forced to make more cards.

I would like, also, to make a plea for *careful* arrangement and cataloging or none at all. When a large group of papers has been properly identified and carefully arranged, it should never need rearrangement. When an item or a group of papers has been fully catalogued it does not need to be recataloged. It is the successive working over of material which is wasteful of time and effort. Also, the preparation of guides and reports of holdings can be greatly simplified if adequate cards are to be found in the catalog. These could even be reproduced from the shelf list by one of the photoduplication processes.

I have not gone into the matter of classification or finding symbols. Each repository has to work out these for its own needs and holdings. Some simple combination of letters and numbers is the most flexible. The call number or symbol plus a colon and sub-number can always identify the analytics of

an "archive" or "collection." Here at the Bancroft Library we have based
our classification system on that devised by Hubert Howe Bancroft for the
primary material he accumulated, which forms the nucleus of our manuscript holdings. Secondary material in manuscript is catalogued and classified by our book cataloguers under the Library of Congress system. By
leaving number gaps in all of the divisions and subdivisions Bancroft established for the manuscripts, we can always differentiate his original collection
from the other acquisitions. Since the public does not have access to these
shelves, it is very convenient to place material merely in numerical sequences.
The simpler the system, the easier it is to find and replace material, particularly if you have a frequent turnover of pages or stack attendants.

I believe I have touched on the most important phases of work with manuscripts. I can only add that I have certainly enjoyed my work. What all these
years of being paid to read other people's letters have done to my moral scru-
ples I will leave to *your imagination.*

NOTE

1. In regard to containers, an article by Victor Gondos Jr., "A Note on Record
Containers," in the July 1954 (v. 17, no. 3) issue of *The American Archivist*, gives a
description with dimensions, and notes on sources of supply for both the nationally
advertised Fibredex, metal-edged documents container, and a carton similar to the
one we use. The portfolios we have had made up by our own University Press. We
get the document containers or Fibredex metal-edged boxes and the cartons from the
Zellerbach Paper Co., San Francisco, from whom we also get our blue folders.

12

Archival Good Works for Theologians
12th Annual Conference, Boston, MA, 1958

Lester J. Cappon

In addressing a group of librarians, an archivist may feel that his remarks should be guarded and discreet. In the history of the world I am not sure which occupation is the more venerable, that of librarian or archivist; but in the United States the latter is the younger professionally by a half-century. Some librarians had served in the capacity of archivists and helped them establish their new profession. Where no archivist is employed, the librarian still feels his responsibility for the records. Proof of this feeling is his concern today about the records of theological schools, where archivists are still seldom to be found.

In addressing a group of theological librarians, the professional archivist must regard himself very much as the layman in terms of subject matter of the records. Yet the archivist as historian deals with the records of a divinity school not with a narrow concern for their service to administrative and internal operations, but rather to reveal evidence of the school's impact on other institutions in the past and on the issues of the present. A dynamic society never lacks controversy. A dynamic theological seminary is perennially involved in religious and educational controversy. In one generation it may be between Old Lights and New Lights, in the next between slave owner and abolitionist, at another period over the relationship between church and state. Yet how many seminaries have archives worthy of the name to shed light on the past, thus making it possible to illuminate the present? How many are engaged in selecting and preserving current records for future use? The specific answers to these questions ought to be determined, for they would undoubtedly be provocative of what needs to be done.

I shall direct my remarks, therefore, to an analysis of the problems inherent in the field of theological and religious records. I shall try to explain how the records of the seminaries ought to be correlated with the larger bodies of religious material. In asking why we have not been more dutiful and steadfast in acknowledging an archival obligation and translating duty into good works, I find some justification for trespassing in the open spaces of homiletics, fortified by a text from the Old Testament and another from the New.

In the thirty-first chapter of Deuteronomy the following verses reiterate a previous statement in the same chapter:

> And it came to pass, when Moses had made an end of writing the words of this law in a book, until they were finished, That Moses commanded the Levites, which bare the ark of the covenant of the Lord, saying,
>   Take this book of the law, and put it in the side of the ark of the covenant of the Lord your God, that it may be there for a witness against thee.[1]

And in the third chapter of the Epistle of Paul to Titus:

> This is a faithful saying, and these things I will that thou affirm constantly, that they which have believed in God might be careful to maintain good works. These things are good and profitable unto men. But avoid foolish questions, and genealogies, and contentions, and strivings about the law; for they are unprofitable and vain.[2]

As you know, much of the Book of Deuteronomy is devoted to the Hebraic law: the fundamentals of morality in the Ten Commandments and a kind of codification of the laws of religious observance, crime, and punishment—"the statutes and judgments, which ye shall observe to do in the land, which the Lord God of thy fathers giveth thee to possess it. . . ."[3] When these laws were actually written down is uncertain, but in the story of Moses their preservation was the responsibility of a particular tribe, the Levites, who were to keep them within the Holy of Holies. We may regard this ancient recording of the law as symbolic of the foundation of our own civilization, with its government of laws, not of men, shaped by law and modifying the law. Indeed, the laws, duly recorded, may be taken as symbolic of other basic records which stem from or contribute to them. In this sermon of mine, how shall we apply the text and the principle to theological schools?

"What is to be considered as material for American *religious* history?"[4] asked Professor Allison when he began his *Inventory of Unpublished Material for American Religious History*, compiled fifty years ago. Source materials pertaining to religious history are difficult to delimit except by definition so circumscribed as to fall short of its very objective. The religious manifestations in the lives of most persons are not so separate and distinct that they can be isolated for examination, nor would such detached data yield reliable conclusions. Certainly the manuscript records of individuals are seldom accumulated in well-labeled bundles, for men do not live by classification schemes concocted by librarians or archivists. Certain religious records, however, do lend themselves to separate treatment by denomination and thus by related institution, whether Catholic or Protestant. In fact, we are so accustomed to thinking of Christianity in terms of various sects that most depositories of religious materials have been established under their auspices, each concentrating on its particular brand of Christian doctrine and organized activity.

However much some scholars may complain about the wide dispersal of these sources for their research, we should not be surprised to find this condition prevailing in a country predominantly Protestant; for fragmentation, not unification, is inherent in Protestantism. The spirit of religious liberty and individual freedom not only appears repeatedly within the records but is reflected in their widespread existence in the custody of countless autonomous organizations.

One segment of these diverse religious sources consists of the records of theological schools. I am referring to those materials which archivists clearly define as the official records, printed as well as manuscript. They are created during the daily administration—policy-making, financial, pedagogical, social, even extracurricular—and operation of the school and, by benefit of an enlightened policy, they are refined as archives for permanent preservation and use. The basic archival problems of the theological seminary are no different from those of any other institution of higher learning. The archives, if they were established, would serve both administrative and research purposes. But this "would be" condition, contrary to fact, has long prevailed in the area of college and university records. Only a limited number of such archival establishments worthy of the name have appeared during the past twenty years of nurture by the Society of American Archivists.[5] Yet many of these institutions have collected and preserved historical materials of great research value, and some theological schools have contributed notably to this cultural achievement. What is the explanation for this oversight or neglect?

The pioneer American historians and collectors envisioned the past in the heroic individual. The man was sufficient measure of the institution. The records most sought after, therefore, were personal papers, while selected individual documents were valued chiefly for the signatures they bore. The records of institutions, political or theological or educational, were preserved piecemeal for their personal associations rather than for their integrity and organic unity embodying institutional life and growth. The official records were not converted into archives; survival *in toto* or in fragments was usually accidental; preservation was seldom planned. Among such discarded volumes, old account books were seldom recognized for their historical value. The treasurer's accounts of Harvard College, 1669–1693, for example, were found in the stables of the Hancock House, Boston, when the property was destroyed.[6] Minister-historian Lucius R. Paige of Cambridge discovered in the library of a deceased neighbor the quarter-bill books of eighteenth-century Steward Thomas Chesholm of Harvard, "a priceless record of college life and economy."[7] In the early 1930s, after inquiries by the librarian of the University of Virginia into its early records, letters of Thomas Jefferson concerning the University came to light in the bursar's office. This discovery, and the indifference toward the records it implied, strengthened the movement for organizing the University's archives.[8] But college records are not easily assembled and converted into archives. Normally scattered throughout the campus, they reflect in their very decentralization the local autonomy that is customarily defended against administrative directives. Sometimes archival programs can be initiated only in crisis!

The old question, "What's wrong with American education?" which is rampant currently with a new setting of satellites, has precipitated an abundance of prolix and inconclusive answers. Insofar as they result from ignorance of the past, one may presume that the source materials of educational institutions, of trustees, faculty, and students, have not been effectively utilized. In the field of higher education, as we have suggested above, only a few colleges and seminaries have organized archives and made their records serviceable. It is a paradoxical situation that in a number of instances the preparation of a university history has *preceded* the assembling of the records for inception of an archival program. This cart-before-the-horse sequence has proved at least that the records were useful, while the historian carried on his research under most disadvantageous conditions and brought to light valuable evidence to witness the need for the archives.

Thus, instead of the old saying, "No archives, no history," the new aphorism runs: "No historian, no archives." Professor Cheyney's *History of the University of Pennsylvania* (1940), for example, revealed records widely scattered and indifferently cared for. His labors suggested the desirability of a university archives, established forthwith at the close of World War II.[9] Professors Curti and Carstensen strengthened the case for an archival department at the University of Wisconsin which could have eased the labor on their two-volume *History* (1949);[10] the archives were eventually organized in the new University Library building. But among the numerous histories of colleges and universities published during the past quarter-century, often occasioned by centennial celebrations, few bibliographical references to the official records are to be found and fewer to anything in the nature of archives. It is still a strange, ill-defined, if not unknown, term on most campuses.[11]

Although historians have contributed to the development of college and university archives, the history of education is a special field which, by and large, the professional historian has neglected. And where he has failed to tread, the educationist has rushed in, usually without adequate historical background, perspective, or the discipline of historical study for his sociological approach. If the crisis in education is assessed historically, we shall have to understand what education meant to past generations, as ideal and actuality, in theory and practice. Only when it is seen in its proper context can the past be of valid use to the present. To fill this gap the Fund for the Advancement of Education has recently called upon historians to provide the essential information on the history of American education.[12]

The case for the records of institutions of higher learning in general leaves much to be desired. Among them, theological schools are also found wanting in the care and evaluation of their records. A brief survey of the evolution of these institutions and the historical function of their libraries will help to explain why this is so. The theological seminary did not come into existence in America until the end of the eighteenth century. The primary purpose of the colonial college was to train men for the Christian ministry, whether Anglicans at King's College or Congregationalists at Yale or Presbyterians at the College of New Jersey. The professional school was still in the future. Besides, many a young man got his instruction in tutorial fashion from a theologian of repute who chanced to be minister of the local church,[13] just as the young apprentice in the legal profession read law with a well-established lawyer in the local community.

The theological seminary came into its own during the first half of the nineteenth century as a vigorous expression of evangelical Protestantism. It flourished in an atmosphere of denominational independence; it engaged in many a controversy on the right wing and on the left concerning doctrinal beliefs as well as freedom of thought. The eighteenth century had its Great Awakening and its deism; the nineteenth century had its gospel message and its transcendentalism. As the Rev. Dr. John Holt Rice, distinguished Presbyterian of Virginia put it in 1829: "The evangelical men are disputing, some for *old* orthodoxy, and some for *new* metaphysics."[14] During the first quarter of the century, the leading denominations founded institutions for theological training and scholarship that have continued down to our own day. Among them Andover led the way in 1808. Union in Richmond, Virginia, dates from 1812 and Princeton Theological likewise; both Presbyterian General (Episcopal) in New York and the Episcopal Seminary in Alexandria, Virginia, appeared in 1817 and 1823, respectively; Colgate (Baptist), at Rochester, New York, in 1817; and the Lutheran Seminary at Gettysburg, Pennsylvania, in 1826.

Some of the colonial colleges had received public support as affiliates of the Established Church, but the new seminaries, dependent upon private funds, bespoke the spirit of the Revolution in the separation of church and state. In harmony with the prevailing temper of independence and evangelical piety the seminaries were influential in advancing the American demo-

cratic faith and the "Mission of America" in an age of progress.[15] They
multiplied steadily in numbers until by the mid-1880s there were some 140,
including those of the Roman Catholic faith. As one writer pointed out at
this time, "Not only ministers of the Gospel in the strictest sense . . . but
editors of the religious press, college presidents and professors, secretaries of
ecclesiastical boards and other associations for advancing the kingdom of
God on earth, are mostly graduates of these institutions."[16]

As the increase of seminaries developed hand-in-hand with the expansion
of the churches that supported them, some churchmen began to inquire into
the past of their denominations in order to trace their origins and to measure
the contemporary progress of the Gospel. During the second quarter of the
nineteenth century the nationalism of the American people gave vent to
spontaneous expression as they witnessed the phenomenal growth of the
Republic and material betterment for the common man. Their feeling was
confirmed by the first generation of historians who wrote the early history
of the colonies and the Revolution with undisguised pride and patriotic bias.
Theologians were also spurred by this spirit of historical inquiry and documentation; indeed this generation of churchmen made some notable contributions toward assembling the sources of religious history and began to
utilize seminary libraries as depositories for collections of church records.

This historical movement is well personified by the Rev. Francis Lister
Hawks, who projected a great documentary collection on the Anglican
Church of colonial America to pave the way for later historical writers.
Hawks pointed out that the ecclesiastical history of the United States was
"as yet an almost untrodden field." He helped to rectify this condition by
writing a history of the Episcopal church in Virginia and a second volume
on Maryland.[17] In 1836 he was in England making transcripts of SPG and
other records pertaining to the church in America; seventeen folio volumes
were ultimately placed in the custody of the Church Missions House in New
York City.[18] As historiographer of the Church, Hawks was one of the founders of the Protestant Episcopal Historical Society in New York City in
1850.[19]

The Presbyterians, to cite another example, were moved by a similar spirit
of historical inquiry. Ebenezer Hazard, pioneer archival collector and editor,
began, with the blessing of the church authorities, to assemble materials for
a history, but it was not completed.[20] In 1839–40, the Rev. Charles Hodge,
alumnus and professor of Princeton Theological Seminary, published a heavily documented, two-volume *Constitutional History of the Presbyterian
Church in the United States* down to 1788, based upon available official
records. He called for a comprehensive history of the Presbyterian Church
throughout the United States, to be prepared perhaps as a cooperative work
organized by states or regions, and without delay. "Much has already been
lost," he lamented, "which the men of the last generation might have pre-

served."[21] Hodge's labors and pleas doubtless help to explain the publication in 1841 of the Minutes of the synods of Philadelphia and New York for the period 1706–88, authorized by the General Assembly of the Presbyterian Church.[22] These were also the early years of ministry of another Princeton theologian, the Rev. William B. Sprague, who served the Second Presbyterian Church of Albany for forty years. An avid collector of manuscripts and imprints, he gave the Princeton Seminary a valuable set of nearly a thousand pamphlets to enrich the library.[23]

During the nineteenth century, in every denomination certain seminary libraries became centers for its historical collections, varying from official minute books of the highest administrative bodies in the ecclesiastical organization to records of local churches. These national, regional, and local archives, though seldom designated as such, received, usually from relatives and descendants, the correspondence of clergy and laymen who had played influential roles in the life of the church. Thus almost imperceptibly at first, seminaries acquired research materials; by steady accretion their holdings became notable, attracting scholars and stimulating further research. Before the twentieth century, however, since these repositories did little or nothing to publicize their holdings, many a scholar overlooked them. Nevertheless, the seminary was a vehicle for religious history in providing facilities, convenient and to some degree quite accidental, for preserving source materials of its particular denomination.

The Allison *Inventory,* published in 1910, which provided the first guide to manuscript materials for American religious history, had some serious limitations. It was confined to Protestant Christianity; the data from areas south of Maryland and Kentucky and west of the Mississippi River were derived only by a questionnaire circulated by mail; and, among the institutions represented, the amount of detailed information available varied widely.[24] Nevertheless, this *Inventory* has been of lasting value. Nothing comparable has appeared since, except a limited number of Inventories of church archives, by denomination, state by state, compiled by the Historical Records Survey under the Work Projects Administration twenty years ago.[25] Among the institutions included in Allison are seventeen theological seminaries, listed either directly with their manuscript holdings or subordinate to other denominational records. In no instance, however, are the official records of the seminary itself listed in any detail. Instead, one finds, for example, according to the librarian of Auburn Theological Seminary, that it has the minute books of a few presbyteries of the neighboring New York State area and a few "biographical sketches of a local nature"; or that the record books of the Board of Trustees and of two local societies of Lane Theological Seminary were in the custody of its library; but most of the seventeen seminaries made no mention of their own records or archives. Only Andover supplied more than the most meager information of this kind; here the records were "kept in the office of the treasurer of the seminary." Fortunately the Harvard University Archives were already well established and included "various records of the Divinity School."[26]

If theologians have neglected the records of their own seminaries, the foregoing survey may serve to explain how and why they have been absorbed in the wealth of other historical religious materials close at hand. But it is high time that they took stock of the records within their own bailiwicks before the forces of man and nature further dissipate and destroy them. It is high time that theologians in centers of learning give thought to archival good works in their midst which are good and profitable unto men. Here is an almost unexploited field for historical research: not merely on the histories of theological schools, but on innumerable other subjects in American civilization to which seminary life and thought have contributed and left some evidence in the records. But first these records must be organized before they can be effectively used.

Such an archival project must take into consideration three basic principles. First, the current records of today become, by proper evaluation and reduction in bulk, the archives of tomorrow. This is accomplished through the techniques of records management, i.e., the setting of standards for paper, ink, etc., used in creating the records; the coordination of record-keeping among the various offices which create and file them; the designation of record groups in accordance with administrative organization and functions; the establishment of uniform practices in classification, filing, and servicing; the operation of a unified system of retention and disposal of records of temporary value; and the maintenance of an orderly procedure for transfer of non-current records to the archives. The second principle to be noted has already been implied in one of the foregoing points: viz. that the records should be maintained as they were originally filed, to serve the administrative functions for which they were created and to assure their optimum use for historical research. This is the *respect pour les fonds* which every knowledgeable archivist insists upon when he takes over from the records manager. It emphasizes the role of administrative history throughout the life-history of records.

The third principle concerns the dual service of the archives. The records of the seminary, like those of any other institution, are created primarily for administrative purposes. Even after the non-current records of enduring value have been segregated for maintenance as archives, they will still have administrative use—the basic *raison d'être* for establishing the archives. (Note that records do not qualify as archives primarily because they are old, but because they have continuing value.) The second use of the archives is for research, chiefly historical research in its broad connotation. The older the records the less they will be consulted for administrative matters and the more for historical investigation. Yet the cultural functions of colleges and universities and theological seminaries are so diverse that first-hand information concerning the distant past, preserved (not buried!) in the archives, may have a significant bearing on current problems; and those problems may involve institutional policy—theological or political or ethical. Thus the administrator as well as the scholar has sound reasons for advocating the establishment and maintenance of the seminary's archives.

A recent *Appeal for Archives in Institutions of Higher Learning*, by the Rev. Henry E. Browne, then archivist of Catholic University of America, is a forthright statement of the case. "It should become increasingly evident," he wrote, "to the administrators of American Catholic colleges and universities that a well-ordered and functioning archives is not a luxury but an obligation they owe to the past, the present, and the future."[27] This statement may serve as the Catholic counterpart to my own references to Protestant institutions, and I suspect that conditions are no different in Jewish colleges and seminaries.[28] Many churches have established historical collections in conjunction with their national or regional headquarters, where the national archives of the denomination are preserved. Many of these are well known to scholars and are often cited in historical works. But theological seminaries, with a few exceptions, have yet to find their archivists and put them to work.

The crisis in education ought to stimulate archival activity at the nerve-centers of education, the institutions of higher learning. When the author, whoever he may have been, of the pastoral letter to Titus, admonished against "foolish questions, and genealogies, and contentions, and strivings about the law," he held to the vain hope that such issues could be avoided among Christians. Since they are an inevitable part of man's religious striving, they are interwoven in the records and add zest to the archivist's labors as he helps to make the past more meaningful to the present and as he contributes to the solution of our contemporary problems. Let archival good works be performed *by* theologians as well as *for* them.

NOTES

1. Deuteronomy 31:24–26; compare verses 9–11.
2. Titus 3:8–9.
3. Deuteronomy 12:1.
4. William H. Allison, *Inventory of Unpublished Material for American Religious History in Protestant Church Archives and Other Repositories* . . . (Washington: Carnegie Institution of Washington, 1910), iv–v.
5. The Society's Committee on Institutional Archives reported in 1944: "Rarely is there evidence of a systematic policy with reference to the transfer of records (if an educational institution) from administrative offices to the archives." *American Archivist* 8 (1945), 81.

6. Justin Winsor, "The Present Condition of the Archives of Harvard College," *American Antiquarian Society, Proceedings*, new ser., 9 (1893–94), 111.

7. S. E. Morison, "Chesholm's Steward's Book," *Colonial Society of Mass., Publications* 31 (1935), 9.

8. Cf. W. Edwin Hemphill, "A Bibliography of the Unprinted Official Records of the University of Virginia," *Sixth Annual Report of the Archivist, University of Virginia Library for the Year 1935–36* (University, Va., 1936), 9–10.

9. Edward P. Cheyney, *History of the University of Pennsylvania, 1740–1940* (Philadelphia: University of Pennsylvania Press, 1940), vii–ix.

10. Merle Curti and Vernon Carstensen, *The University of Wisconsin; a History, 1848– 1925* (Madison: University of Wisconsin Press, 1949), II, 597–601. "The University's records . . . are abundant, though as yet uncentralized. Many are still uncared for. . . ." Compare the conditions described in Samuel Gring Hefelbower, *The History of Gettysburg College, 1832–1932* (Gettysburg, Pa.: Gettysburg College, 1932), v–vi.

11. There are important exceptions among the older colleges and universities, but very little has been published about the content of the archives. Note the Inventory of the Harvard University Archives, to 1800, in Samuel Eliot Morison, *Harvard College in the Seventeenth Century* (Cambridge: Harvard University Press, 1936), II, 662–681; Cornell University, Collection of Regional History and the University Archives, *Report of the Curator and Archivist, 1950–1954* ([Ithaca, 1955?]), 17–32.

12. Paul H. Buck and others, *The Role of Education in American History* ([New York] The Fund for the Advancement of Education, [1957]), 16 pages.

13. George Lewis Prentiss, *The Union Theological Seminary in the City of New York: Historical and Biographical Sketches of Its First Fifty Years* (New York: A.D.F. Randolph, 1889), 4.

14. Prentiss, *The Union Theological Seminary in the City of New York*, 7.

15. Ralph Henry Gabriel, *The Course of American Democratic Thought, an Intellectual History since 1815* (New York: Ronald Press, 1940), ch. 2.

16. Prentiss, *The Union Theological Seminary in the City of New York*, 3–4.

17. Francis L. Hawks, *A Narrative of Events Connected with the Rise and Progress of the Protestant Episcopal Church in Virginia . . .* (New York: Harper, 1836), viii; the volume on Maryland was published in 1839.

18. Allison, *Inventory*, 98–99; Edgar L. Pennington, "Manuscript Sources of Our Church History," *The Historical Magazine of the Protestant Episcopal Church* 1 (1932), 19–21. Hawks' contemporary, Professor William R. Whittingham at General Theological Seminary in the late 1830s, became a great collector of church materials. Bishop of Maryland for almost forty years, he willed his collection to the Diocese and thereby gave scholarly prestige to its Library. Cf. William F. Brand, *Life of William Rollinson Whittingham, Fourth Bishop of Maryland*, 2d ed. (New York, 1886), I, ch. 8; Whittingham's will, in II, 369–370.

19. *The Historical Magazine of the Protestant Episcopal Church* 1 (1932), 3–4.

20. Hawks, *Narrative of Events . . . Virginia*, xi, note.

21. Charles Hodge, *The Constitutional History of the Presbyterian Church in the United States of America . . .* (Philadelphia: W.S. Martien, 1839–40), I, iv–v.

22. *Records of the Presbyterian Church in the United States of America . . .* (Phila-

delphia, [1841?]). The first leaf of the earliest records were missing. The Methodists also thought enough of their early *Minutes of the Annual Conferences, 1773–1828,* originally issued as pamphlets, to assemble them in one volume (New York, 1840).

23. Hodge, *Constitutional History of Presbyterian Church,* II, vi; H. E. S[tarr], "Sprague, William Buell," *Dictionary of American Biography,* XVII, 476–477.

24. Allison, *Inventory,* iii–v.

25. Work Projects Administration, *Check List of Historical Records Survey Publications,* rev. ed. (Washington: Federal Works Agency, 1943), 49–56.

26. Allison, *Inventory,* 22–25, 65, 94, 143.

27. *American Archivist* 16 (1953), 226.

28. The American Jewish Archives was established at Hebrew Union College, Cincinnati, in 1947, but during the ten years' publication of the quarterly magazine of the Archives there has been no indication that the records of the College are embraced within the program of the AJA. *American Jewish Archives* 1, no. 1 (June 1948), 2–5, 23–26, *et seq.*

13

Changing a Pile of Books into a Library
24th Annual Conference, New Orleans, LA, 1970

John J. Shellem

When Dr. Scherer suggested the title for this paper, he could not realize the train of memories and emotions the title would evoke. The pile of books to which he referred numbered some 150,000 volumes, give or take—much confusion. The pile constitutes the library of my venerable alma mater, St. Charles Borromeo Seminary, Overbrook, Pennsylvania and the large but very undernourished stepdaughter of our library, the Collections of the American Catholic Historical Society of Philadelphia.

St. Charles Seminary was founded in 1832. The first trunks of books for the library arrived in the port of Philadelphia the next year. They were the gift of the Rector of the Irish College in Rome. The gifts continued at a rapid rate until the number mentioned above was achieved. The Historical Collections began with that Society in 1885 and were trucked out to Overbrook in great confusion in 1933. The books begat books, and the papers begat papers, until the confusion seemed insurmountable.

The administration of the library from that year 1833 into 1967 was given over from generation to generation to a duly assigned seminary professor. The interest of these professors varied over the century and more, from Sacred Scripture to Canon Law, and indeed included for a time in the 1880s one whose prime interests were Sanskrit and the Indian Wars. Library Science, unhappily, escaped the scope of their hobbies.

The Professor-Librarian was assisted from time immemorial by an army of student volunteers. These young men skilled themselves in such arts as devising classification schedules, binding, adapting all sorts of Cutter tables, goldleafing call numbers, mimeographing catalog cards, microfilming, and many other marvelous activities. Alas, every bit of it was done without professional supervision.

The budget for this long history was remarkably frugal. How all that was accomplished on such little annual sums is a source of wonderment. The contributed elements of both work and materials were for so very long taken for granted.

Finally, aided by serious student reaction, a swift reappraisal of the library circumstances was made. A professional librarian was assigned and after a minor struggle the first year's budget of $75,000 was approved.

Librarian consultants were invited in to examine and recommend. Some went away shaking their heads. The consultant for the Middle States Association, a distinguished College President, and sometime librarian, said after a thorough tour of all our problems and storerooms full of books, "Father, I have seen many problems in my time but I think this is it!" I found the statement consoling. It somehow excused my uncharitableness when I was assigned to the library. I am accused of having remarked, "Lord, such a job. It is like being assigned as master of the engine room on the Titanic—after it hit." The remaining storage rooms of books still constitute our iceberg below the surface.

THE RECLASSIFICATION PROJECT

Since the student librarians of old had done amazing feats of misclassification after the fashion of Dewey numbers, such as providing nothing but several zeros beyond the decimal point in a few instances or putting hundreds of books on the shelves marked simply: "200.", it was earnestly recommended that we move directly to the Library of Congress classification. This continuing reclassification process is a step we have never regretted.

Reclassification means that for several years, of course, we will have two libraries in operation, two public catalogs, and two shelf lists. I have seen reclassified projects where the new L.C. entry was filed into the older Dewey catalog, new cards constantly eliminating the old. Our old catalog was so derelict with erroneous entries and misfiling that we would not dare put the new cards with it. We just quietly watch the old catalog lose its usefulness, and covet the drawer space.

First preferences for materials to be reclassified in L.C. were haphazard. Some faculty members agreed to select essential titles from the Dewey collection, then these were recataloged. (I am inclined to use the term recataloged, rather than merely reclassified, because in the overwhelming majority of cases the old cataloging was useless save for the presence of an occasional L.C. card.) Another motivation to transfer classification has been the borrowing of a book from the Dewey section. When a Dewey numbered book is returned to the library it travels through reclassification. As a result circulation of books from the Dewey collection obviously declines at a rapid rate. At present it represents only 6% of the total circulation, while Dewey books still represent two-thirds of the book collection.

Sometimes reclassification can be delightfully easy, as in the case of the 400-volume set of Migne's *Patrology*. Two call numbers for the two separate units of the work, and that was that. The month that was done, our classification statistics jumped enormously. The effort to gather statistics to demonstrate to management our activity does not often come so readily.

In comparing our reclassification needs with those of another college just completing the project, we discovered one most important element. If what you have to start with is a well-cataloged collection with predominantly L.C. cards present, then the transfer is orderly, if not automatic. If the starting material, classification and cataloging, is the product of a patchwork quilt of lengthy and faulty design, then consider you are beginning fairly close to start and argue your needs for staff from that point of view.

BUDGET PLANNING

We ran aground in budget planning dealing with this factor of reclassification. Funds are needed almost exclusively for work hours and relatively little for materials, the materials aspect of the reclassification being that mighty latter-day Moloch of the library, the Xerox machine. In the subsequent debate with the committee, established by our Board of Trustees, to consider funds for the reclassification project, I began to develop a new sympathy for Luther's confrontation with the Cardinal at Augsburg.

With the aid of Dr. George Bricker of Lancaster Theological Seminary and Sister Dennis Lynch of Rosemont College Library, who were my defenders before this committee, we arrived at the compromise of a separate allotment for reclassification. This figure would gradually decrease over five years. The amount of the decrease would be absorbed into the budget through the demand of increasing costs. We are still left, however, without a clear definition of reclassification costs. The activity of reclassification flows through the regular pattern of acquisitions, cataloging, classification, and processing. When there's any lull in the processing of new books, quantities of the old collection are dumped into the machinery.

GATHERING STAFF

When the initial budget was approved, the first step was to find help. When word got around that the seminary library was to experience a rebirth, local college librarians were most helpful in recommending people to us. Even the local parish clergy lent a hand in directing office help toward us. After the first few were employed, the ancient principle seemed quickly to apply itself: "Excellent staff members recommend excellent new staff members, etc."

In the hurry to gather staff, we too quickly added persons with experience, but with only opportunity for part-time work. I remember a very capable library administrator scolding me for adding so many part-time people to staff. I recall I could not see the immediacy of the argument. Now I do. Work patterns in processing seem never to move smoothly if part-time staff numerically dominate any function. Our staff is now 10.9 full time equivalent persons, exclusive of student help.

PUBLIC RELATIONS

As was hinted at earlier, student reaction motivated the library renewal. The library perforce was obliged to develop no little public relations in order to sell itself, in the face of great prejudice, to both the faculty and student. The library was long disparaged as the burial ground for libraries of deceased priests. Therefore, no current literature was ever expected to be found there. Anything good quickly disappeared, and might be returned via a bequest a generation or two later. One of the first things I did, after digging into the office, was to lock the library when I was not available to tend store. During one of these times, before we had staff, a sign designed by a clever student appeared on the locked door. The sign read: "Library closed—will reopen January 1, 2000 A.D. Books are fermenting." Another student said frankly, "You ought to use those books for something practical, mulch!" Plainly, the book collection had no eye appeal. So, against the advice of a couple of librarians, we introduced the use of plastic jackets over dust covers for all new books. The contrast now between the L.C. collection and the old Dewey collection is startling. I have always, as a librarian, been for the plastic jacket, beyond its pragmatic purpose. People do judge a book by its cover.

Repeatedly, in the beginning, the matter of the image of the library in the academic community became a concern. To alter this view, the place of public relations was of prime importance. The minor seminary, now the seminary college, lost its very sickly junior-college-type library. The students were now expected to cross campus to the much larger theology school library. In the traditional separation of the two schools this was interpreted by students as an abandonment of their needs. To reverse this, the small minor seminary library was stripped of its large collection of old high school books. The room was greatly remodeled and a college reference collection added, duplicating material in the main library. And the room has become a pleasant study center with audiovisual facilities for college needs.

The faculty had a library of many ancient manuals and large, aging, unused sets of theology and a small periodical reading room to go with it. These facilities were quietly abolished. The explanation that the faculty should always involve itself with the main collection of the campus was not the best public relations ever invented. Persons of habit took the transition poorly.

The value of publications, bibliographies, a library manual, an annual report, etc. has been motivating in countless ways. The monthly publication of the new book list with a cover letter of library news, exhortations, and veiled threats has motivated some faculty members to develop book lists and even one department to publish its own bibliography. The solemn, yet I hope attractive, annual reports evoked the delightful back-handed compliment: "It seems the world was created to use the seminary library!"

The "Ryan Memorial Library Guide," the guide to the use of the library, has impressed on students the facilities and services we have available. It becomes a most useful text in library instruction in classes where staff members have been invited to present the cause of the library in individual subject areas. As an outgrowth of these lectures, the library staff has developed and offered as an elective a course entitled "Theological Materials in Research."

PUBLIC SERVICE

Library service beyond the needs of the regular seminary program, as in any large library, takes on a variety of dimensions. The presence of the collections of the American Catholic Historical Society of Philadelphia presses upon us a service to scholarship which we have yet to master. This other library on our campus includes such varied items as almost 4,000 bound volumes of 19th century Catholic newspapers, 20,000 volumes in American Catholic Church History, many of them rare Americana, a pamphlet collection of perhaps 40,000, and a manuscript collection estimated at 150,000 items. The manuscripts contain everything from a letter by Thomas Jefferson to letters recently discovered in an accumulation there, in the hand of Jefferson Davis. The Society has no budget to maintain this library. So it falls upon the Seminary to preserve and offer it to scholarship. Since the arrival of this material at Overbrook in 1933, the element of much donated student labor and goodwill has brought a modicum of order. This important library, however, still lacks a professional plan and budget. Since local scholars do have an inkling of the materials located there, it is the obligation of the Seminary library to make them available.

Another facet of the Seminary's holding under the supervision of the library is the art collection. It is an accumulation, through gift, over the century and more, of some 350 oil paintings plus many sketches and prints. Through the interest of volunteer help our collection of paintings by Thomas Eakins, the most renowned painter in the history of Philadelphia, was given much worthwhile publicity recently. This group of volunteers, happily, named the "Friendly Daughters of St. Charles," achieved a quality of public relations for our school that no amount of professional planning could have achieved. They want to involve themselves in other cultural projects for the Seminary. I prayerfully hope that our 15,000 rare books may catch their attention and become both cultural and research assets to our Seminary.

Since our Seminary in the past had sponsored two renowned scholarly publications in Catholic academic circles, the *American Ecclesiastical Review* and the *American Catholic Quarterly*, it was thought that the library might motivate, what with all its staff, a latter-day publication. Hence, out of the variety of activities in the library building a periodical, *Dimension: Journal of Pastoral Concern*, is now in its second volume.

PROFESSIONAL INVOLVEMENT

An ingredient in developing library service as well as staff competence is involvement in professional organizations. The guidance and assistance garnered from these important associations should not be underestimated. In our area, we are fortunate in having access to the experience of library service groups such as: The Southeastern Pennsylvania Seminary Library Cooperative, The Library Public Relations Association of Greater Philadelphia, The Tri-State College Library Cooperative, The Union Library Catalogue of Pennsylvania, The Pennsylvania and Local Catholic Library Association Unit, etc. Each of these groups opens up to us information and experience that does not necessarily repeat itself. The meetings, minutes, and publications provide stimulus for a variety of phases of our service. While no one will deny that serious involvement in such groups takes much needed time, I insist that it is time well utilized.

CONTINUING EDUCATION

Since a sizable budget and costly development of library facilities have been undertaken at St. Charles, the idea that all of this material and effort should serve just a college and theological school seemed too confining for the possibility of service to the church in our community. Books and services are made available readily to scholars and students from theology schools and religion departments in the colleges and universities of the area. Religious personnel, priests, brothers, and sisters from our archdiocese are invited to use the facilities.

Because of the potential of our campus for religious education, a School of Religious Studies, a master's program primarily for teaching Sisters, and the School of Pastoral Studies, a master's program for the parish clergy, have been inaugurated in the past year. These new part-time students, numbering under 400, obviously utilize library services. They create new aspects of service potential which heretofore were not even thought of.

THE EVALUATION

This past spring after frantic, speedy, and finally frenzied preparation our Seminary stood for the Middle States Association and American Association of Theological Schools evaluation. It was a double-barreled performance that had us frantic to say the least. The visitor for the library evaluation very many of you, I am sure, know quite well, Dr. Robert F. Beach, Librarian of Union Theological Seminary, New York.

Having been much cloistered in Catholic library circles until these latter days, I had not met Dr. Beach. So I asked members of our Southeastern Pennsylvania Library Cooperative what should I expect for the visitation. To a man they spoke of the visitor in high praise, how competent he would be. One member of the group observed: "He's a no nonsense man." I replied: "Lord, I'm ruined!" If there's anything I've had to do these past three years to gain attention for our library, it was to throw a great deal of nonsense in the air!

Dr. Beach was a wonderfully thorough, helpful member of the evaluation team. His observations were both generous and constructive. They provided no end of motivation and fuel with which to confront the now harried Board of Trustees.

In the story of this development of the library, the ingredient of professional consultation from the beginning to the evaluation cannot be underestimated. The wisdom, advice, and experience of other librarians is the teaching we need for a given chore. When I failed to apply instruction given, I quickly learned the hard way!

As every librarian well knows, projects strongly begun easily breed new programs for services and development. Our Board of Trustees recently received in our budget proposal recommendations for plant development and expansion. Whether they shall tolerate this latest outrage for the good of religion or whether the fate of the librarian will match that of Savonarola will make another chapter of the continuing saga of one man's library!

14

Collection Development in a Theological Research Library
38th Annual Conference, Holland, MI, 1984

Caroline Whipple

For the purpose of this paper I will use the term "theological research library" to mean those libraries and theological collections which must supply the needs of research degree programs and the research needs of faculty and visiting scholars within certain defined subject areas.

POLICIES FOR COLLECTION DEVELOPMENT

The best way to achieve an institutional understanding of library needs is to have written policies worked out with faculty and administrators that set forth the mission of the library and spell out the scope of the collection. These policies can be used to document library needs and justify budget proposals. Because an understanding worked out one year can easily be forgotten or overlooked when head librarians, deans, or presidents change, it is imperative that the library rely on written policy statements to assure the continuity of a library's mission and purpose.

Chief among these policies should be a *written statement detailing the subject areas and the languages* in which the library is expected to develop its collection. This document must be understood by all as official policy necessary for meeting the purposes of the curriculum, the degree programs, and faculty research. Defense of the materials budget, then, becomes a defense of school policy and not simply a defense of library preferences.

Frequently libraries will have *agreements with other libraries* to develop special subject areas in order to avoid duplication and to promote the best use of limited resources. It is one of the ironies of our profession that after years of arguing that cooperation is the key to cutting materials costs we find that cooperation can cost money from the standpoint of those responsible for approving the library budget. This is true because cooperation involves a pledge on the library's part to develop portions of its collection regardless of immediate curriculum needs. Hence, it is crucial that these agreements be formalized in writing and accepted as institutional policy.

Librarians need to be alert to the ways these agreements can be changed unknowingly or inadvertently modified by faculty action. I am referring to the long-standing penchant on the part of faculties to inaugurate *new programs and new areas of study* without addressing the question of library funding.[1] Even if the faculty grapples with the problem of increased library funding before inaugurating a new program, its members may not understand the expense of, or even the need for, retrospective collection development until after the programs are launched. It is crucial, therefore, that collection development officers maintain open channels of communication with all faculty members and try to insure that costs will be realistically addressed prior to beginning new areas of study.

PRACTICES IN COLLECTION DEVELOPMENT

After establishing policies, librarians must turn their attention to developing the collection. *Adequate, yearly funding* is the key to collection development. Books go out of print too rapidly, inflation drives up costs too fast, and budgets are too limited to assume that the library can maintain its excellence when funding is severely restricted, even for a limited time.

The next most important aspect of collection development is *selection by librarians*. While every good acquisitions program will involve faculty, the final decisions should be made by librarians. This may not be possible in those institutions that give departmental allocations to faculty. Faculty members as a whole rarely make good selectors.[2] The result is likely to be an uneven collection with faculty members selecting materials for areas of their greatest interest, some making no selections and some selecting solely on the basis of publishers' announcements. Faculty selection can result in injudicious decisions at the end of the fiscal year to expend their library allocation. Unfortunately it will be the library, not the faculty, that will bear the brunt of criticism for the inadequacy of the collection.[3]

Selection by librarians who are subject specialists, confer regularly with faculty, and know the curriculum and the degree programs is the primary way to assure that the areas covered by the collection development policies are treated fairly. It is important that these librarians build as much confidence as possible among the faculty in their ability to develop the collection and that they report regularly to faculty on their purchases.

One of the problems that most theological librarians have is the need to acquire material *at the time it is published* rather than wait until book reviews disclose the importance of the material. This means that librarians must develop skill in separating the worthwhile from the less important in order to make the most of restrictive budgets and do so prior to reading reviews of the material and prior to knowing how much relevant material will be published in a given year.

Experienced librarians have developed different ways of coping with this problem. Probably the most frequent way is to rely on the reputation of the publisher or the author for books to be ordered when announced, and then to rely on book reviews for the more specialized or less obvious material. Another coping strategy is to use the various forms of automatic ordering, such as approval plans and standing orders, to acquire those titles whose selection can be made routine. The staff time saved can subsequently be used for checking of bibliographies and for extensive reading of book reviews.

Approval plans, if properly designed and carefully monitored, can play a valuable role in relieving librarians of the time-consuming task of examining publishers' catalogs, trade announcements, book reviews, national bibliographies, and the like.[4] However, the choice of a vendor is critical, and profiling must be done carefully.[5] At its best, an approval plan can overcome some of the hazards of ordering from publishers' announcements by permitting the library to examine the book prior to adding it to the collection.[6]

For larger libraries the blanket order plans offered by some vendors and presses may prove worthwhile. Smaller libraries, like most theological libraries, will find that they are not cost effective.

With the approval and the standing order plans supplying the self-selecting books, the librarians should find time to engage in the truly difficult job of collection development, namely the checking of library holdings with standard bibliographies and with book review sections of scholarly journals. Their work will continue with the monitoring of such bibliographic tools as *Religious Studies Review, Theologische Literaturzeitung, Revue d'Histoire Ecclésiastique,* and the listings in *ADRIS* and *Scholar's Choice.* The checking will further include bibliographies found in dissertations and catalogs of reprint publishers and used book dealers. This work is the heart of professional collection development and, in my judgment, is the primary means of assuring quality and depth in the collection.

TOOLS FOR COLLECTION EVALUATION

Skillful management requires the use of *tools for collection evaluation which will help those to whom librarians report* determine the quality of the collection and the quality of development policies. The most familiar of these tools is the volume count. Governmental and private agencies to whom we report annually request this information. Librarians in charge of collection development should compare the figures reported by other libraries with their own in order to gain a perspective on their collections and report these to their superiors.

More appropriate *quantitative measures* can be developed than comparisons based on volume count. Collection development officers should familiarize themselves with the various means of quantitative comparisons, such as those recommended in the "Standards for University Libraries."[7]

In addition to quantitative data showing comparisons with other libraries, collection development officers should perform studies which attempt to *measure quality and performance* as well as quantity. These studies could take the form of reports on varying bibliographical checks made during the year. What is known as "citation analysis" can also be useful.[8] Citation analysis can be carried out by librarians on their own collections using, for example, the bibliographies of dissertations submitted to their schools for determining how well their library is meeting the needs of the research degrees.

Citation analysis has recently come under criticism regarding its assumptions, not the least of which is the suspicion that students engaged in research may cite only available material.[9] Whether citation analysis, interlibrary loan analysis, or bibliographic checking are used, an effort should be made to keep a record of the results for reporting purposes.

In 1979, Allen Kent and his colleagues startled some members of the library profession by performing a *use study* of the University of Pittsburgh Library which showed that 40% of the books acquired by the library were not used within a seven-year period. The conclusion they drew was that in an age when library materials budgets were escalating out of control, scientific acquisitions management would concentrate on providing the material that has a high probability of circulating. Interlibrary loan, it was argued, could be relied on for the material requested infrequently.[10]

Use studies are not new. As early as 1976, Richard W. Trueswell[11] had shown that between 30% and 60% of the titles in the collections he studied would satisfy 98% of the circulation needs.[12] The growth of automated circulation systems with their ability to provide unprecedented statistics on circulation has encouraged a growing body of literature on the use of the collections. Frequently the premise of these studies is that collection development ought to concentrate on materials with a high probability of frequent use. It must be kept in mind that many of these studies are done with university libraries in mind. Their value to theological libraries has yet to be demonstrated.

The popularity of use studies has caused the premise on which they are based to function as a kind of self-evident truth within some academic circles. A related premise is the assumption that library development for present curricula is a sufficient goal for the library. For this reason I want to address the drawbacks of a theological collection policy based mainly on these premises.[13]

To concentrate purchases on materials of probable high use would require the library to adjust its purchasing strategies year by year depending on curriculum changes. In practice this would mean adjusting collection development to the courses that are taught, to faculty interest, to current student interest, to factors such as whether the school has a vacancy on its faculty, or whether its faculty tends to be liberal or conservative. At this point the words of Leon Pacala on seminary libraries are straight to the point:

> Our schools can tolerate ideology when it touches faculty; it (i.e. our schools) can tolerate ideology when it bears upon administrators, but it (our schools) can hardly tolerate ideology or limited perspectives where the library is concerned. There you must serve not only the advocates of a single resolution of an issue but you must cover the bases for either change or addition in whatever resolution an institution will adopt.[14]

A one-sided emphasis on high use as the primary determinant of quality can mean sacrificing the collection depth needed to attract new faculty members. It can also mean sacrificing depth in those areas where the faculty is in transition, and may ultimately reduce the national or international reputation of the library. To quote from Ronald Powell:

> Those librarians who rationalize their unwillingness to fight for the research collections by using the argument that a high-circulating collection will do just as well are doing both the scholars and the institutions a major disservice. The end result will be the impossibility of carrying out effective scholarly research on those campuses, particularly if no other extensive collections are easily available in the immediate area.[15]

Far from being more cost effective for a theological research library to restrict its purchases to material with a high prospect of use, it may in fact be more expensive. The reason is that the institution's past investment in its holdings will deteriorate. A subject area that is not maintained quickly loses its value. The "Acquisition Policy Statement" of the University of Illinois says it well:

> If we were to discontinue buying in the field in which we are now strong, there would be a rapid deterioration in the value of our present holdings. If we were to decide to start building up a previously neglected area, we would find that great research strength cannot be established quickly or at small cost.[16]

Theological research libraries should not operate on a policy that would hinder in principle any of the following:

- The purchase of special collections when offered for sale
- The purchase of collections of primary and secondary sources on microfilm
- The acquisition of the more unusual and specialized materials
- The development of an excellent reference collection
- The development of those areas of historical strength
- The building up of areas of past weakness
- The library's ability to make purchases on the basis of the long-term need for preservation, such as participation in the ATLA program for the preservation of religious monographs

Some of this material can be very expensive and may have little immediate use. Yet it is the careful and considered purchases of these kinds of material that can give the library collection its lasting value.

In summary, collection development in a theological research library is an exercise in policy development which has as its goal the acquiring, maintenance, and preservation of the literature of theological studies for today's scholars and for tomorrow's heritage. As such it requires sophisticated practices of collection evaluation which assume the importance of the library's stewardship of the historical record which will be our children's legacy.

NOTES

1. J. Periam Danton, *Book Selection and Collections: A Comparison of German and American University Libraries* (New York and London: Columbia University Press, 1963), 8.

2. Danton, *Book Selection and Collections*, 71.

3. Danton, *Book Selection and Collections*, 74.

4. Robert G. Sewell, "Managing European Automatic Acquisitions," *Library Resources & Technical Services* 27 (1962): 397–405.

5. Robert C. Miller, "Approval Plans: Fifteen Years of Frustration and Fruition," in *Shaping Library Collections for the 1980s*, ed. Peter Spyers-Duran and Thomas Mann (Phoenix: Oryx Press, 1980), 49.

6. Cf. William A. Katz, *Collection Development: The Selection of Material for Libraries* (New York: Holt, Rinehart and Winston, 1980), 164–65.

7. "Standards for University Libraries," *College and Research Libraries News* 40 (1979): 101–10. These standards were prepared by a joint committee established by the Association of Research Libraries and the Association of College and Research Libraries.

8. Cf. Marion L. Buzzard and Doris E. New, "Research Notes: An Investigation

of Collection Support for Doctoral Research," *College and Research Libraries* 44 (1983): 470.

9. Cf. Linda C. Smith, "Citation Analysis," *Library Trends* 30 (1981): 83–101. This article presents an excellent analysis of the presuppositions on which citation analysis is based, including the citation indexes.

10. Allen Kent et al., *Use of Library Materials: The University of Pittsburgh Study* (New York: Marcel Dekker, 1979), 105–41.

11. "Growing Libraries: Who Needs Them? A Statistical Basis for the No Growth Collection," in *Farewell to Alexandria: Solutions to Space, Growth and Performance Problems of Libraries*, ed. Daniel Gore (Westport, CT: Greenwood Press, 1976), 72–104. One of Trueswell's concerns was finding a method of weeding a large university collection and of identifying material that could be moved to remote storage. For such tasks his methodology is highly useful.

12. Stuart A. Stifflear, "Core Analysis in Collection Management," *Collection Management* 5 (1983), 137.

13. It needs to be emphasized that use studies can be very valuable when properly applied and when they are not used to rationalize away a research library's need to acquire the rare and seldom-used, but frequently valuable, material.

14. Leon Pacala, "Theological Libraries Revisited," in *Summary of Proceedings, Thirty-fifth Annual Conference of The American Theological Library Association* (American Theological Library Association, 1982), 5.

15. "An Investigation of the Relationship between Quantifiable Reference Service Variables and Reference Performance in Public Libraries," *The Library Quarterly* (1978), 13.

16. University of Illinois Library, "Acquisition Policy Statement," mimeograph, 1959, 1. Quoted by Danton, 11.

15

Circulation in Theological Libraries: Seeking and Saving the Lost
41st Annual Conference, Berkeley, CA, 1987

Thomas F. Gilbert

"For the Son of man came to seek and to save the lost."

—Luke 19:10

When I first considered theological library work as a profession, my main impetus was to serve the cause of the peculiar brand of evangelical theology at the seminary I attended. I felt that the dissemination of these Gospel truths through the men and women who studied there would have a genuine impact on the Church and the world. However, the other reason I got into librarianship was the sight of so many patrons who were obviously "lost" in the library. People would waste hours using the library inefficiently, and then come up to someone in the library (often a student worker with just minimal knowledge of the organization of the library) who could direct them to appropriate library resources in minutes. It was these "lost" people that I felt called to "seek and to save," and I submit that the library's main purpose is to pursue and help such poor souls. The appropriate place to receive such aid in most of our libraries is the circulation desk. Few of our libraries can afford full-time reference staff, and even those who can afford full-time reference staff realize that the reference staff is not able to staff the library all the hours it is open. I believe that it is well to organize circulation work around the theme "seeking and saving the lost."

THE PUBLIC SERVICE FUNCTION OF
CIRCULATION: SEEKING AND SAVING THE
"LOST" PATRON

The first person a new patron sees when he or she walks in the door of a library is usually a circulation librarian. No matter what training that library staff member has, to that patron he or she is the librarian. If the patron has skipped your wonderful orientation tour for new students (I feel lucky if half of the new students show up for the tour) or is not a student, the circulation staff has two minutes at most to cover the ground you took half an hour to cover on your tour. Needless to say, those are two very important minutes. If they are well spent they will save staff and patron time in that repeated directional questions will not need to be asked. I believe it would be well if the basic two-minute speech could be outlined so that one could always be sure to cover the basic questions about the catalog, location of collections, and loan and fine policies of the library. It would be well for those who will be registered borrowers to have brief but essential information regarding hours and loan and fine policies printed or stamped upon their library cards along with the library's telephone number. We should encourage circulation staff (and indeed all staff who happen to be working in public areas) to take the first step and try to greet the patron unknown to them who seems to be floundering a bit. The patron will be much more likely to ask a question of someone who has "broken the ice" with them.

I have a theory that circulation work makes you crazy. Why is that? I see three basic reasons:

1. The constant interruptions of patrons while doing complex record control tasks that require a high degree of accuracy, such as creating overdue notices, filing book cards, maintaining patron registration lists, and sometimes even processing books, and catalog maintenance tasks such as labeling and card filing.
2. The impossibility of meeting every patron's need for library material.
3. The fact that most patron contact occurs after a patron has tried and failed to find what they need in the way of library materials.

Being interrupted by patrons who can't find what they want and blame the library can be maddening, especially if one is in the middle of a complicated task that requires a high degree of concentration. By greeting patrons as described above we can reduce the patron failure rate and cut down on the third kind of contact. Other ways of reducing failure rate will be discussed below in the document delivery portion of the paper. However, reasons one and two are nearly unavoidable. We must try to make sure that circulation staff get regular breaks and relief from these interruptions by scheduling some work time when another staff member has primary responsibility for meeting the public demands so the circulation person can concentrate on his or her record and document control tasks.

THE DOCUMENT DELIVERY FUNCTION OF CIRCULATION: SEEKING AND SAVING THE "LOST" BOOK

Every library has the task of accounting for and providing fair access to the library materials it owns. These tasks belong to the circulation department. As far as the patron is concerned, every single item he wants is "lost" when he or she walks into a library. Out of tens of thousands of items, the patron wants the relevant library material on say "infralapsarianism" or perhaps wants some known item that someone has recommended. How do we manage to meet these demands? The obvious first answer is collection development. Collection development is usually the province of the library director or subject bibliographer. Acquiring new titles and purchasing old collections to fill in gaps in the collection is one of the fun parts of a director's life, and he or she devotes much time and energy to it. This work can aid the circulation staff considerably if it is done in a timely fashion as the library materials in demand by patrons will with any luck already be in the library and fully processed by the time students and faculty hear about them through reviews or word of mouth. Finding that you have already owned a title for three months that the academic dean thinks is hot off the press is always a terrific feeling. However, once titles are purchased, how much thought does the director give to maintaining access to those titles? That task is often delegated completely to the circulation staff. Just as most directors take an avid interest in how library materials are acquired and cataloged, so should they be interested in how they are shelved and circulated. In particular, the following four areas should be attended to.

Shelving

Returned library materials should be shelved promptly and accurately. If there is a large shelving backlog, no matter how well organized it is, there will be an increase in patron frustration, all the more because of the fact that books that circulate tend to circulate again. Thus, one title that has recently been checked out is more likely to be in demand by the students and faculty than the "ninety-nine" titles that are still on the shelves. The book is "lost" to the patron until it has been reshelved. Rather than be certain that your backlog is in perfect order, just put it in rough shelf order by 100s if in Dewey or by two letter code if in LC (with perhaps some subdivisions in the theology sections of LC), and have the students or staff spend more time actually putting the books back on the shelves. The shelvers will spend a bit more time walking the stacks using this method, but I believe the distances to be short enough in most of our libraries that it will be more efficient this way. Better still, hire enough regular shelving help to reshelve books every day and avoid getting a backlog altogether. It goes without saying that every shelver must be well-trained in whatever classification scheme used to avoid shelving errors. Once a title is misshelved it is "lost" until the next time inventory is taken, unless you just happen upon it.

Circulation and Overdue Record Control

Do everything you can to have as few files of circulation cards as possible, two files at the most; one for current and one for overdue materials. When a patron is at the circulation desk, distraught because he or she cannot find a title on the shelf, they are in no mood to wait until the staff member checks three or more files. One can use color coded book card covers to indicate reserve books, faculty books, overdue notices sent, and any other subgroup of books you like. This eliminates the need for extra files and reduces the chances of misfiling the cards. Overdue notices should be sent regularly. Very few of our libraries have a lot of extra staff time to do this work, but it is essential in maintaining the circulation of library materials. Access to a microcomputer and the appropriate database-type software can simplify and speed up this task considerably. Before we had a PC, we were lucky if overdues were sent twice per semester on those typed three-part forms, and the filing of all those slips was a real pain. Now, we can notify people of overdues every other week without putting undue strain on the circulation and student staff.

Loan and Fine Policy

Most of the library literature on circulation has to do with these two matters. What loan period is best? Should libraries charge fines? One survey of 42 California college and academic libraries indicated that the majority of loan periods were in the three- to four-week range.[1] A survey of medical libraries showed that two weeks was their favored loan period.[2] A study of North Carolina libraries yielded the following results:

- Patrons do pay attention to loan periods. Most books that are lent by libraries return either shortly after they were loaned or very close to the due date.
- Libraries charging stiffer fines get a better return rate. The highest fine charged was ten cents/day.

- Restricting borrowing privileges of patrons with overdue books was effective in securing their return.
- Quick first notices (within 15 days of the book being overdue) get the best results.
- Those libraries that charged fines by the notice rather than by the day got better results (though the libraries with this policy were a very small part of the sample).
- Billing patrons for the cost of materials after three notices (usually six weeks) was effective in getting books back.
- Phoning patrons with overdue books was ineffective.

I quote from the study, "Libraries that take overdues seriously were the ones that would get their books back."[3] I understand our reluctance to charge fines and confront borrowers. It doesn't seem like very "loving" behavior. We need to realize two things. First, it is in our current patron's best interest to make sure we have these materials available to as many people as possible. Caring for our other patrons requires that we be tough in enforcing loan policies. Second, the longer materials are out the more likely that they will stay out and the title could be lost to the library forever. I have just finished reviewing the books in our library that have been checked out and not returned for over six months. Out of 99 titles, only 33 were still in print, and I will be lucky if I get all of those. As you know, some of the older items listed in *Books in Print* are not really in stock and may be in the process of going out-of-print. These titles represent a real loss to our library's patrons and will probably never be available again unless found by accident (or providence if you're Reformed) in some gift collection.

Inventory and Replacement of Missing Books

Inventory is a highly effective way to foresee and forestall a patron's frustration with our libraries. Unfortunately, it is a very time consuming and labor intensive procedure and therefore many of us do not even attempt it. A middle way that has been useful is to identify and inventory certain heavily used sections of the collection. The Biblical Studies section of our LC collection was inventoried last year and many volumes replaced that were in high demand for exegetical work. It took about 50 hours of staff time and was fully accomplished two weeks after the project began. Another effective means of inventory is to follow up systematically every patron report of a missing title, and if it remains missing for a certain period of time to replace it. An added benefit of both these methods is that if a title is indeed lost, it is removed from the catalog and thus is not requested by the patron again. Libraries can't own the universe of bibliographic materials, but by knowing what we have and what we don't we can better provide effective interlibrary loan service for our patrons.

CONCLUSION

Having spent one day per week this year staffing the circulation desk, I have seen how important it is that we provide good orientation of "lost" patrons and good follow up to "lost" library materials, whether they be "lost" in the intricacies of the subject headings or not on the shelf where they belong. Patrons may not see or especially appreciate the effort of circulation staff to account for and demand the return of material, through inventory, overdue notices, and fines, but without such effort patron frustration with our libraries grows and the object of the library to provide and encourage the reading of theology is diminished. Circulation work can make you crazy, but if you don't work hard at saving the "lost" patron and the "lost" book it will make you crazier.

NOTES

1. Henry DuBois, "From Leniency to Lockout," *College and Research Library News* 47 (December 1986): 698–702.

2. Sarah Lyons, "Loan Periods in Health Science Libraries," *Medical Library Association Bulletin* 69 (July 1983): 326–329.

3. Robert Burgin and Patsy Hansel, "More Hard Facts on Overdues," *Library and Archival Security* 6, no. 2/3 (1984): 8–16.

16

Parchment, Paper, PDF: The Literature of Theological Librarianship
57th Annual Conference, Portland, OR, 2003

David R. Stewart

The American humorist Will Rogers once visited Paris, and during his stay he went on a tour of the Louvre. As he followed the group through the galleries his attention was captured by the famous statue known as the Venus de Milo. After looking at it for a few minutes, he hurriedly left the tour and found the nearest gift shop, where he purchased a postcard displaying the Venus, on which he eagerly wrote a note to his 11-year-old niece back in America: "See this statue? This is what will happen to you if you don't stop chewing your fingernails."

I mention this story to illustrate the role of a dilettante: "a dabbler in an art or a field of knowledge." It's fair to say that of all the folks strolling around the Louvre that afternoon, many of whom knew a great deal about art, nobody saw the Venus in quite the same way Will Rogers did. But he made his point, and his is the perspective we remember.

My point is that I am not tackling this topic as an historian, but as something of a self-confessed dilettante, though certainly an enthusiastic one. I can't help but be encouraged by the fact that there are so many of you who have an interest in this subject as well. And I have no doubt that our being here and giving this whole matter some thought will have a direct and positive result in altering the landscape of the literature of theological librarianship.

Let me give you a few reasons why I think this is an important issue for us as ATLA members.

EDUCATION FOR
THEOLOGICAL LIBRARIANSHIP

As most of you are aware, for the past couple of years, at the appointment of Dennis Norlin, two successive task forces have been busy doing the initial planning for an introductory course on theological librarianship. The idea is to begin by designing an introductory workshop, which might eventually be expanded to a full-term, credit course. The obvious target groups for this workshop are: a. people who are considering a career in theological librarianship, but feel the need for an orientation; b. people who are working already in theological libraries, but who came into their positions without the kind of vocational overview they needed.

If ATLA is going to take on this educational responsibility, what could we offer students for a bibliography, or for a textbook? In other words, what is unique about, or germane to, our vocation, and where can one find it described in print? What are its roots and development? Why does this work matter so much, and what is the need for it to be done with excellence? (This last is all the more poignant in times of "restraint," when institutional decision makers who have no idea of what we do are looking for ways to save money.)

VOCATIONAL IDENTITY

Many of the same concerns apply when we look at the issue of vocational self-identity. I don't know of any group of people which is imbued with such a sense of good fortune—at having found (or having been found by) a kind of work which is historically so well grounded, which serves the academic, ecclesiastical, and educational communities' processes so well, and has quite the same eclecticism—as this company of theological librarians.

But even the wisest among us would find it a challenge to articulate all of this to prospective colleagues. Likewise, in our collaborations with the Association of Theological Schools, the Wabash Center, and other groups with which we share some common goals and interests—we have plenty of advocacy at a personal level, and can point to any number of cases where our work has demonstrated its value. But almost none of this is in print, at least not in any cogent and compelling form.

Whether for the sake of justifying our work or commending it to others, it helps to have a corpus of material to point to—"here, read this"—rather than merely testimonies and anecdotes.

PERSONAL GROWTH AND PERSPECTIVE

Whether consciously or not, in this kind of work each of us builds on work done by those who have preceded us, and sometimes we are reaping where others have sown. Isaac Newton said, "If I have seen farther than others, it is because I have stood on the shoulders of giants." And at least on our good days, we know something of what this means. I'm not here to advocate the development of an ATLA-sponsored line of theological librarian action figures, or "bobble heads." Yet it's a good thing to acknowledge that there are people who have done this work with great distinction, and we need to know what they brought to our vocation that is of enduring value. We need, for our own sakes and for those who are looking to join us, to be able to draw on the wisdom and perspective of the "giants" in our vocation.

I'm sure you have your own excellent reasons for being interested in the literature of theological librarianship, but these are mine, and I think we all have something to gain by giving this some collective thought today.

OVERVIEW OF THE LITERATURE OF THEOLOGICAL LIBRARIANSHIP

In describing the general state of the literature of theological librarianship, I would offer the following comments: a. there isn't much out there, and yet there doesn't *need* to be a lot. But there does need to be more literature of theological librarianship than is currently available, and it needs to be of a high caliber; b. what is available is unevenly distributed, and is of uneven quality. But we could begin to change this with just a few well-conceived projects.

The literature is diverse, scattered, and stretches over more than two millennia. I'd like to look at the following dimensions of this literature, and show some examples.

General History

While I was still in Vancouver, I wrote for ATLANTIS a review of William Johnston's *Recent Reference Books in Religion*.[1] I thought it was a very fine book, and sent the author a copy of the review. He was very gracious and appreciative, and a few months later he asked me if I might be interested in writing a few entries for a new *Encyclopedia of Monasticism* he was going to be editing for Fitzroy-Dearborn Publishers. To be honest, my ignorance on the subject of monasticism was close to being comprehensive, but I was about to take a job in a very good theological library, and I can read voraciously when I find something that interests me. So, I was delighted to accept the assignment.

As I began to pull together sources, I found that what was out there was interesting, but on the whole pretty fragmentary and dated. So I gamely started pulling stuff together, and this eventually provided the impetus for what is now on the ATLA server. Here are examples of sources I have found in this line:

1. St. Jerome. A very thorough entry on one of the "patron saints" of librarians, from the 1917 edition of *The Catholic Encyclopedia*.[2] This wonderful resource provides the full text of articles and their bibliographies in HTML format.

2. Lionel Casson, *Libraries in the Ancient World*.[3] This little book is most interested in the pre-Christian era, but it is a concise and engaging introduction to how libraries functioned in the ancient world. Here's an excerpt, describing the sack of a major library in Alexandria, during the 7th century A.D.:

> A Greek savant, who was a friend of the commander of the army that took over the city, asked him for the library as a gift. The commander prudently turned the matter over to his overlord, Caliph Omar, who was told: "If these writings of the Greeks agree with the book of God, they are useless and do not need to be preserved; if they disagree, they are pernicious and ought to be destroyed." And destroyed they were, by being handed over to the city's baths for fuel, and, the story specifies, they sufficed to feed the furnaces of all four thousand of them for six months.

Pretty barbarous, admittedly, but it does provide an intriguing snapshot on early approaches to what we now call "de-accessioning."

3. Cassiodorus, the work of James O' Donnell. We're all too familiar with instances where the best source on a given subject is not available in any electronic format. But with James J. O'Donnell's Ph.D. dissertation on Cassiodorus, we have a rare exception. Again, here is a snippet which sheds some light on the library career of this fascinating figure:

> One of the remarkable things about the [Vivarium] enterprise is the comparative richness of the library. This is the more surprising since, as we have seen, Cassiodorus' earlier collection at Rome, whatever its institutional affiliation, had clearly not been transferred to Squillace. Nevertheless, within a very few years of Cassiodorus' return (the first draft of the *Institutiones* can be confidently dated to about 562[[21]]), there was a bountiful library of scripture and scripture commentaries, histories and grammar books, miscellaneous useful guides (e.g., Columella), and the Greek works set for translation. To our picture of Cassiodorus, therefore, abiding impatiently in Constantinople, taking thought of the monastery to which he would return, attempting to salvage something of his notion of a school of Christian learning, we should add the likelihood of his becoming actively involved in the procurement of manuscripts for the library of that institution.[4]

4. David Stam, ed., *International Dictionary of Library Histories* (Chicago: Fitzroy-Dearborn Publishers, 2001).[5] Earlier summary essays by Gapp and Hadidian[6] are badly out of date. I attempted to provide an updated summary in this newer volume in an article titled "Christian Libraries."[7]

5. Felix E. Hirsch, "The Scholar as Librarian: to the Memory of Adolf von Harnack."[8] To be completely accurate, Harnack was not a theological librarian, but he was a brilliant and distinguished biblical scholar who was so unusually alive to the importance and potential of library work that he accepted an invitation to be the director of the State Library of Prussia. This story is told in a lively and respectful manner in the article from the 1930s.

6. The work of Norman Kansfield: Just in the past few weeks I have gotten permission to post both the graduate thesis ("The Origins of Protestant Theological Seminary Libraries in the United States") and the doctoral dissertation ("Study the Most Approved Authors: The Role of the Theological Library in Nineteenth-Century American Protestant Ministerial Education") from the University of Chicago of Dr. Kansfield. I don't know of any better sources for understanding the development and contribution of theological libraries in North America.[9]

There may be other sources of this kind, and if you know of any by all means pass along the citations to me. I would only add that, as valuable as these individual pieces are, it would be even better if there were bigger, more integrative, and more recent works in the field. That might be a project which interests some of you.

Local History

You may have noticed that I posted a question on this topic to the ATLANTIS listserv a few weeks ago. I'd estimate that no more than a dozen of our member libraries reported that they have a history of their libraries on hand, in any form. Not surprisingly, some libraries have gotten more attention than others. The Burke Library of Union Theological Seminary in New York, for example, was the subject of a full doctoral dissertation,[10] but it's regrettably long on facts and short on readability. Here are some representative examples of local histories:

1. Eastern Baptist Theological Seminary (Philadelphia), "Austen Kennedy de Blois: A Man with a Mission." This pamphlet outlines the career of a distinguished teacher, librarian, and administrator.[11]

2. Yale Divinity Library. Paul Stuehrenberg, Director of the YDS library, wrote an overview history of the library, "A Library Worthy of the School" in 1994, and it not only provides an engaging survey of the library and its development since its inception in 1932, but provides a model of how a concise treatment can do justice to a library's story.[12]

3. Andover-Harvard Theological Library. Here is an example of how a less-is-more approach can offer library patrons a summary of a library's history in a web medium.[13]

This is one aspect of "the literature of theological librarianship" where I would be happy to see some new initiatives. Local histories do not always demand a book-length treatment. But the story of how local resources and staff have been organized in the service of their parent institutions and the church is important, and there is a lot of local character which is unique. What's certain is that if people like us don't preserve those stories, nobody else will.

Technical Services (and Library Operations)

I'm using Technical Services here as an example of how current practices in one core sector of Theological Librarianship can be written about in a useful and engaging manner. Admittedly, it's a bit of a stretch at times to term this sort of technical report format as "literature," yet it would be an oversight not to identify it as germane to the representation of our vocational endeavors.

1. *Theology Cataloging Bulletin*: A quarterly newsletter of ATLA's Technical Services Section. It contains listings of new and changed subject headings and classification numbers in appropriate subject areas as well as other information of interest to religion/theology catalogers. It is available by print subscription, as well as online.[14]

2. The writing initiatives of individual ATLA members: A good example of an ATLA librarian's personal interest and initiative getting published—and there are many of them—is Chad Abel-Kops' study of the tricky issue of bibliographic control of homiletical material in the online journal *First Monday*: "What Has Straw in Common with Wheat? A Selective Review of Bibliographic Control in the Field of Homiletics."[15] The opportunities for more of this kind of activity are very good.

Reflections on "Best Practices" and Distinguished Careers

There have been some good efforts in drawing attention to the work of individual librarians whose efforts have almost single-handedly "altered the landscape." A couple of examples are:

1. Richard Spoor's overview of the life and career of Julia Pettee (mostly at the Burke Library of Union Theological Seminary), "Julia Pettee and Her Contribution to Theological Librarianship."[16]

2. Helen Bordner Uhrich's article from *Special Libraries*, "Classification and Cataloging in Theological Libraries." (1952). Works of this kind provide a fascinating snapshot of what the issues were at a given time, as well as what the practices and priorities were in a given library (in this case the Yale Divinity Library).[17]

It would be naive to think that this sort of literature is of equal interest to all ATLA members, yet it provides by far the best indicator of how we understand and value our own work.

Theological Librarianship in the "Heroic Tradition"

At this point I'm going to be completely idiosyncratic and add a final category because I think it is important that we acknowledge those persons or historical settings in which our work has been done at the highest level. We learn from reading such literature, we may even draw strength and inspiration from it, and I think we owe it to ourselves and our colleagues to provide some examples. Again, you may have your own favorites, but here are some of mine:

1. Richard W. Southern, "A Benedictine Library in a Disordered World."[18] This is the text of an address delivered by this distinguished historian at the opening of one of our ATLA member libraries. As well as giving vivid examples of our work at its best, this work illustrates with great beauty why theological librarianship really matters.

2. Michael Grant, *In Search of England*.[19] I especially recommend the chapter entitled "Heritages and Destructions: the Troublesome Journey and Laborious Search of John Leland." Leland, a brilliant classicist, was commissioned by Henry VIII to travel throughout the land taking inventory of the holdings of the great monastic libraries. This account of his career captures the bittersweet character of that pivotal moment in British history prior to the Dissolution of the Monasteries, 1536–40.

3. Thomas Cahill, *How the Irish Saved Civilization. The Untold Story of Ireland's Heroic Role from the Fall of Rome to the Rise of Medieval Europe*.[20] I re-read this book on my flight here earlier in the week. I'm not sure it would always pass muster from a historian's point of view—it has the quality of a "tale" or "yarn" at times—yet I could not recommend it highly enough as an illustration of how important the work of collecting and preserving books and manuscripts can be. An excerpt:

> In a land where literacy previously had been unknown, in a world where the old literate civilizations were sinking fast beneath successive waves of barbarism, the white Gospel page, shining in all the little oratories of Ireland, acted as a pledge: the lonely darkness had been turned into light, and the lonely virtue of courage, sustained through all the centuries, had been transformed into hope.

4. James Charles Roy, *Islands of Storm*.[21] Covers very similar terrain to Cahill's *How the Irish . . .* , but in greater detail. It is most interested in the land, the culture, and the spirituality of Celtic monasticism.

5. Raymond P. Morris, "Theological Librarianship as a Ministry."[22] This is the best thing I have ever read about our vocation. It captures the intrigue, the romance, the difficulty, the variety, and embodies the perspective of a distinguished theological librarian, hard at work, and profoundly thankful to be doing exactly what he is doing.

Current Projects

In the months leading up to this year's conference, I have been surprised to learn that there are more ideas and even works-in-progress in the literature of theological librarianship than I had been aware of. At least two ATLA members are working on articles for publication, and I have asked both Jack Ammerman (Editor of *ATLA Scarecrow Bibliography Series*) and Ron Crown (Editor-designate for the *Journal of Religious and Theological Information*) to outline some of the opportunities that are open for publication through those venues. Here are some other current ventures I am aware of:

1. Bibliography: my friend and former colleague, Ivan Gaetz (Dean of Libraries, Regis University) and I received an ATLA grant to undertake a complete revision of Coralie Jenkin's *Theological Libraries and Librarianship: A Bibliography*.[23] This project should be close to completion during the summer.

2. A recently published book of essays: Gregory A. Smith (Liberty University) has edited a new book of essays, *Christian Librarianship: Essays on the Integration of Faith and Practice*.[24] I have looked carefully at the book, and I know of a couple of reviews which will be appearing soon. Two comments: a. this volume is much more oriented to the context of the Association of Christian Librarians, which serves a different constituency than ATLA, and b. especially for the strength of its bibliographies, it is well worth taking a look at.

3. An ATLA retrospective anthology: Though we haven't talked about it today, it's a fact that the greatest single source for literature on theological librarianship is the ATLA *Annual Conference Proceedings*. Not many of our member libraries are fortunate enough to have an entire set from 1947 onward, and it requires a lot of diligence to sift through the materials that are not of sustained interest. Yet some of the addresses, the presentations, etc. are absolutely terrific. So I have come up with the idea of resuscitating some of this material by putting a selection together in an anthology. I have an outline, and a proposal, and am currently looking for a publisher. It might be that some of you would be interested in writing an introduction for one of the topical sections, once this idea moves forward.[25]

CONCLUSION

The survey of the literature of theological librarianship I have offered here has been impressionistic and cursory, but it provides a fair representation both of what is out there and of what needs to be filled in. There is every reason to believe that the possibilities we have identified here, and your own interests and initiatives proceeding from your work, can go a long way toward enriching the literature further in the months to come. I will do what I can to make sure that we have ways of keeping in touch on our own projects, and look forward to seeing your contributions come to fruition in the months ahead.

NOTES

1. William J. Johnston, *Recent Reference Books in Religion: A Guide for Students, Scholars, Researchers, Buyers, and Readers* (Downers Grove, Ill: Inter-Varsity Press, 1996).

2. Louis Saltet, "Jerome," in *The Catholic Encyclopedia*, http://newadvent.org/cathen/08341a.htm (November 15, 2005).

3. Lionel Casson, *Libraries in the Ancient World* (New Haven: Yale University Press, 2001), 138.

4. James J. O'Donnell, *Cassiodorus* (Berkeley: University of California Press, 1979), http://ccat.sas.upenn.edu/jod/texts/cassbook/chap6.html (November 15, 2005).

5. David Stam, ed. *International Dictionary of Library Histories* (Chicago: Fitzroy-Dearborn Publishers, 2001).

6. Dikran Hadidian, "Seminary Libraries," in *Encyclopedia of Library and Information Science*, ed. Allen Kent, Harold Lancour, and Jay E. Daily (New York and Basel: Marcel Dekker, Inc., 1979), Vol. 27, 215–241, and Kenneth Gapp, "Theological Libraries," in *The Twentieth Century Encyclopedia of Religious Knowledge*, ed. L. Loettscher (Grand Rapids: Baker, 1955),Vol. 2, 1101–2.

7. David R. Stewart, "Christian Libraries," in *International Dictionary of Library Histories*, ed. David Stam (Chicago: Fitzroy-Dearborn Publishers, 2001), Vol. 1, 48-54.

8. Felix E. Hirsch, "The Scholar as Librarian: to the Memory of Adolf von Harnack," *Library Quarterly* 9, no. 3 (July 1939); Online at: http://www.atla.com/sources/index.htm (November 16, 2005).

9. Norman J. Kansfield, *The Origins of Protestant Theological Seminary Libraries in the United States*, M.A. Dissertation, Faculty of the Graduate Library School, University of Chicago, 1970; Online at http://www.atla.com/sources/PDFs/kansfield1-toc.htm; and *Study the Most Approved Authors: The Role of the Theological Library in Nineteenth-Century American Protestant Ministerial Education*, Ph.D. Dissertation, Faculty of the Graduate Library School, University of Chicago, 1981; Online at http://www.atla.com/sources/PDFs/kansfield2-toc.htm (November 25, 2005).

10. Thomas P. Slavens, *The Library of Union Theological Seminary in the City of New York, 1836 to the Present*, Ph.D. Dissertation, The University of Michigan, 1965.

11. Norman H. Maring, *Austen Kennedy de Blois: A Man With a Mission; Eastern*

Baptist Theological Seminary President, 1926–1936 (Wynnewood, Penn: Friends of the Library, Eastern Baptist Theological Seminary, 2000).

12. Paul F. Stuehrenberg, *A Library Worthy of the School; A History of the Yale Divinity School Library Collections* (New Haven: Yale Divinity School Library, 1994).

13. Harvard Divinity School, *Andover-Harvard Theological Library; Mission and History,* http://www.hds.harvard.edu/library/about/history/ (November 14, 2005).

14. *Theology Cataloging Bulletin,* available through the American Theological Library Association at http://www.atla.com/member/publications/tcb.html (November 16, 2005).

15. Chad Abel-Kops, "What Has Straw in Common with Wheat? A Selective Review of Bibliographic Control in the Field of Homiletics," *First Monday* 6, no. 3 (July 2001); http://www.firstmonday.dk/issues/issue6_7/abel/index.html (November 14, 2005).

16. Published in M. Patrick Graham et al., eds. *The American Theological Library Association: Essays in Celebration of the First Fifty Years* (Lanham, Md.: Scarecrow Press, 1996). Also online at http://www.atla.com/sources/index.htm (November 15, 2005).

17. David R. Stewart, ed., *Theological Libraries: Historical Sources,* http://www.atla.com/sources/index.htm (November 14, 2005).

18. Richard W. Southern, "A Benedictine Library in a Disordered World," *The Downside Review* 94 (July 1976): 163–77. Also online at http://www.atla.com/sources/index.htm (November 16, 2005).

19. Michael Grant, *In Search of England. Journeys into the English Past* (Berkeley: University of California Press, 1999).

20. Thomas Cahill, *How the Irish Saved Civilization. The Untold Story of Ireland's Heroic Role from the Fall of Rome to the Rise of Medieval Europe* (New York: Doubleday, 1996), 163–64.

21. James Charles Roy, *Islands of Storm* (Chester Springs, Penn: Dufour Editions, 1991).

22. Raymond P. Morris, "Theological Librarianship as a Ministry," *Summary of Proceedings. 7th Annual Conference of the American Theological Library Association* (Chicago: ATLA, 1953): 31–39. Also online at http://www.atla.com/sources/index.htm (November 15, 2005).

23. Coralie E. J. Jenkin, *Theological Libraries and Librarianship: A Bibliography* (Adelaide: C. E. J. Jenkin, 1984).

24. Gregory A. Smith, *Christian Librarianship: Essays on the Integration of Faith and Practice* (Jefferson, N.C.: McFarland & Co., 2002).

25. Editor's note: The present volume is the outcome of this idea, first put forward publicly at ATLA's annual conference in Portland, Oregon, June 2003.

3

THE THEOLOGICAL LIBRARIAN AS EDUCATOR

17

Introduction

Roger L. Loyd

How is the theological librarian an educator? Traditionally the response might have been, "through offering reference service," "through biblio-graphic instruction," "through appropriate collection development," and/or "through working with faculty when requested." Librarians holding doc-toral degrees might have gone further than this, by offering credit courses in their fields of study. But is this vision, even in a best case scenario, large enough to guide theological librarians for the future?

Collaboration and *information literacy* are the prevailing themes found throughout library literature relating to this discussion as the twenty-first century begins. They represent two insights into the work of the librarian as educator that extend the vision.[1]

In this part, we bring into our conversation voices from earlier times, regarding theological librarianship today, and focusing on the topics of col-laboration and information literacy as ways theological librarians can be educators.

COLLABORATION

The notion of collaboration between faculty and librarians is not itself new. Raspa and Ward reach toward a definition of the term in these words: "col-laboration is a more pervasive, long-term relationship in which participants recognize common goals and objectives, share more tasks, and participate in extensive planning and implementation. Collaborators share the give-and-take listening that creates the bond of belonging to a learning community."

They suggest that five factors occur in true collaborations: passion, persistence, playfulness, project, and promotion.[2]

What might some specific types of collaboration involve for theological librarians? From the information gathered by Eileen Saner,[3] many librarians collaborate on educational initiatives through offering bibliographic instruction courses. This form of curricular collaboration, while not immediately working with a faculty member, contributes to the overall good of the institution's curriculum as does any other course. Others collaborate in writing grants and then carrying out projects with faculty members (digitizing materials, for example). Conversations with faculty regarding their research interests have motivated some librarians both as they have reflected on their own collection development processes and also as they have designed library services to support that research.

Indeed the authors whose contributions comprise this part all call for collaboration between librarians and faculty members (and administration) on topics as varied as accreditation, ecumenical dialogue, and the use of books itself. James Dunkly affirms the mission of the theological librarian as a partner with the faculty, and calls attention to the wider assignment carried by librarians, "representing the widest possible sweep of the world of learning." Dunkly makes a case for incorporating theological librarians into theological education more profoundly, by realizing their distinctive professional identity. All of the theological librarians in the group offer the insight that librarians who collaborate with faculty bring a significant set of resources into the enterprise.

INFORMATION LITERACY

Gragg defines information literacy as the development of critical thinking in the areas of (1) locating, evaluating, and using information effectively; (2) learning how to learn; and (3) lifelong learning.[4] Librarians have led the way in educating library users for use of the Internet, database searches, and electronic communication. However, the really important challenge is to expand that into a more full-fledged information literacy program, in collaboration with the faculty and administration. Rockman frames this challenge as follows: "Students may have picked up the skills to send electronic mail, chat, and download music, but many have not learned how to effectively locate information; evaluate, synthesize, and integrate ideas; use information in original work or give proper credit for information used."[5]

The program for the 2005 annual conference of the American Theological Library Association included a discussion of three different strategies for development of information literacy: the course-for-credit model (Associated Canadian Theological Schools), the course-embedded model (University of Calgary), and the across-the-curriculum model (Candler School of Theology at Emory University). The program also included a critique of the notions of information literacy by two theological librarians.[6] This level of interest is illustrative of what an active concern ATLA members have in making the most of related opportunities. Though the essays in this part come from an earlier period, in which personal computing was not yet so pervasive in education, they do provide foundational insights into the issues of developing critical thinking in students and encouraging faculty members to teach toward its development in their own courses.

How does the theological librarian promote information literacy? It is crucial to realize that this effort is not exclusively the responsibility of public services librarians and directors; rather, the way the library's website (for example) presents students with worthwhile tools to use in their internet research (websites, purchased databases, electronic journals) will largely be in the hands of the catalogers and website designers. If they do their work well, and if faculty and other librarians collaborate to teach information literacy, researchers will turn to the library's website as well as to generic search tools like Google or Yahoo. To me, the key sentence found in this part for considering information literacy is in Andrew Scrimgeour's contribution: "I have been chagrined to learn that dazzling students with reference works without providing *mental shelves on which to place them* is not of enduring value" (emphasis added). Helping library users construct the mental framework on which to hang the thoughts they are developing would be a good goal to pursue.

A generation or so ago, Pacala saw the need for clear thinking about the future of theological libraries, and (in collaboration with ATLA) the Association of Theological Schools received funding from the Lilly Endowment to underwrite a study known as "Project 2000," led by project director Stephen L. Peterson.[7] Its results were published in 1984. Does the conversation among the authors in this part help to make a case that another such study is due? If so, I would hope its participants would continue Peterson's reflections on roles, material resources, personnel resources, physical resources, and coordinating structures. After reading the essays in this part and reflecting on theological librarianship in the near future, it seems clear to me that that such a subsequent study should focus on collaboration and information literacy as endeavors which can benefit greatly from greater library participation.

NOTES

1. They were also key themes in two recent workshops at the Wabash Center for Teaching and Learning in Theology and Religion: "Colloquium on the Role of the

Theological Librarian in Teaching, Learning and Research" (November 3–8, 2004), and "A Conversation about Strategies for Involving Theological Librarians Effectively in Theological Teaching and Learning" (May 9–10, 2005). I helped lead the first workshop, and have the benefit of Eileen Saner's summary of theological librarians' collaborative activities from the second.

2. Dick Raspa and Dane Ward, "Listening for Collaboration: Faculty and Librarians Working Together," in *The Collaborative Imperative: Librarians and Faculty Working Together in the Information Universe* (Chicago: Association of College and Research, 2000), 1–18.

3. Eileen Saner (esaner@ambs.edu). "Faculty/Librarian Collaboration at ATS-Accredited Institutions." Email to Roger Loyd (roger.loyd@duke.edu). June 8, 2005.

4. David R. Stewart, ed., "New Directions for the Timeless Quest—Theological Libraries in an Era of Change [issue focus]," *Theological Education* 40, no. 1 (2004). Cf. especially Melody Layton McMahon, "Librarians and Teaching Faculty in Collaboration: New Incentives, New Opportunities," 73–87, and Douglas Gragg, "Information Literacy in Theological Education," 99–112.

5. Ilene Rockman & Associates, *Integrating Information Literacy into the Higher Education Curriculum: Practical Models for Transformation.* (San Francisco: Jossey-Bass, 2004).

6. Contents of the panel and program were published in the 2005 edition of the *ATLA Proceedings.*

7. Stephen L. Peterson, "Theological Libraries for the Twenty-First Century: Project 2000 Final Report," *Theological Education* 20, no. 3 (1984), Suppl., 3–114. Also by the same author, see "Project 2000 Revisited," *Theological Education* (1987).

18

Seminary Libraries and Theological Education
2nd Annual Conference, Dayton, OH, 1948

L. R. Elliott

Shortly before the first World War, a student entered a school of theology, a member of this Association from its beginning. The professors were scholars and teachers of renown. The school had a large enrollment and was well established. It possessed an ample library. The student remembers the teachers, the classes, and some of the textbooks. Of the library he recalls only two or three timorous visits, which had no curriculum-related purpose. The teaching method was based on textbooks and professors' lectures. The library had little relation to the students' learning processes.

This experience represents the kind of teaching which was normal in the United States through the first quarter of the present century. In 1926, Charles B. Shaw, discussing the weakness of the library's function in accredited colleges, said, "Among the leading universities and colleges of the country there are no officially established and enforced regulations concerning matters vital to the well being of their libraries. Other factors in academic life have this protective legislation. But the librarian and his staff may be professionally inadequate; the staff may be insufficient in number; all may be overworked and underpaid. The book collection may be pitifully small, unsuited to the legitimate demands made upon it, and growing at only a snail's pace."[1]

During the following years this condition began to change. The periodical articles on library improvement that are a trickle in the twenties became a stream in the thirties and forties. Since 1930, the *Education Index* lists more than a hundred articles on college libraries, most of which stress the new awareness of the library's importance to higher education.

The first World War turned back in large measure the flow to German universities of American graduate students. This gave the American universities a new stimulus to strengthen their graduate schools, which affected their libraries and those of other institutions.

The college surveys conducted during the twenties and thirties focused fresh attention on the libraries, revealing inadequacies and suggesting improvements. In 1937–38 Dr. Harvie Branscomb directed the survey of the Association of American Colleges. It was a cooperative effort, nationwide in scope. The results were published by the director in his now well-known and oft-quoted work, *Teaching with Books.* It contains much that is pertinent to theological library problems.

The accrediting associations during this period revised their library standards in the direction of quality of resources and extent of use by teachers and students. From the Middle States Association in 1937, "It cannot be too strongly urged that the library is the heart of any higher educational institution. The very first consideration is the degree to which the books it possesses support and supplement the instruction it offers and the extent to which both faculty and students actually use such books. The Commission will insist above all else that a college library shall not be a repository. The modern college cannot justify itself without a library which gives evidence of constant and productive use."[2] And from the Southern Association in 1942, "During the past two decades, the major interest in college libraries has been in their growth, in suitable buildings, and in librarians technically trained. At present, the prime concern of college teachers, librarians, and administrators is in the effective integration of the library with the teaching processes. The achievement of such integration calls for a clarification of the functions of the college library and for continuous planning and cooperation on the part of the administration, faculty, and a qualified library staff."[3] This preamble is followed by a well-analyzed discussion of the services to be expected of the modern college library.

DEFINITION

What is the basis for the educational function of the library? In brief it is this: A student whose curriculum requires extensive reading, under faculty guidance, of the important literature of each subject will be better trained than the student who is required only to stand examinations on textbook assignments and professor's lectures. If this thesis is accepted then the library must be regarded as an educational more than an administrative unit;

it must bear an important share with the faculty in the total educational program offered the students; the professional members of the library staff must be regarded as educators, their professional qualifications and the character of their service justifying such recognition.

This thesis is the inspiration for the extensive literature to which reference has been made. The following extracts are representative. R. G. Sproul, "A librarian should be more than a keeper of books; he should be an educator. The library is the heart of the university. No other division of the university articulates with all departments of instruction and research on the educational side, and certainly no department can rank with the library, which conserves and makes available the thought and capitalizes the experience of all mankind. It is indeed far more than a department; it is the common meeting ground and unifying influence for all departments. The intellectual growth and vitality of every school and every division, of every professor and every student depends on the vitality of the library."[4] William W. Bishop, "The proper integration of the college library with college instruction, its work of producing those results at which the college aims, is a matter for most careful study. Precisely those colleges which have developed strong libraries in immediate and carefully planned aid of instruction are those which have spent liberally on their libraries, not money alone but much conscientious thinking."[5] Guy E. Snavely, "This college president looks upon a college librarian as a teaching colleague. In a way the librarian, like the dean, the registrar, the bursar, the purchasing agent and the president himself, is an administrative officer. Unlike these other officers, the librarian is, however, more intimately connected with the teaching phase of the college than with administration . . . it is most desirable that the librarian be of more value as a teacher than as an administrator."[6] Henry M. Wriston, "Aside from the faculty, the most important single instrument of instruction in the college is its library. The character of the library and the temper and methods of its administration have much to do with the liberal quality of the education the students achieve. Amidst all the talk of tests and measurement, few objective indices of the reality of liberal learning are as suggestive or as reliable as the figures kept by the college librarian."[7] J. Periam Danton, "So long as courses were taught with the aid of a single textbook, from which a given number of pages were assigned each day, the function of the library remained negligible; but as soon as it became a recognized educational axiom that a dozen or fifty textbooks were better than one and that it was educationally sounder for students to consult and digest a variety of sources than to be limited to the knowledge and opinions of a single writer, the library began to play a prominent and indispensable role."[8]

"This library trend is developing in the lower grades of education as well as in higher education. Many high schools today have better libraries and make more use of them than did colleges a generation ago. This means that in the future an increasing number of seminary students will have come through secondary and collegiate institutions where the educational program emphasizes the library as an instructional agency. They will have become accustomed to the use of many books in meeting their course requirements. When such students enter the seminary they will expect to find similar methods in use. If, instead, they find course work based on text book assignments and classroom lectures, they will experience a sense of disappointment and frustration and the seminary will suffer loss of prestige and a diminishing ability to render its maximum educational service."[9]

In colleges and universities the new emphasis on the library is especially operative in the humanities and social sciences. The seminary curriculum lies in these areas. The experience of other institutions of higher education will be found equally valid in schools of theology. Some seminary courses may be better managed by the lecture and one or several textbooks, but for most of the work the library method is superior.

"Take, for example, the subject of hermeneutics. Instead of the class passing a memory test on the contents of a textbook, let the teacher outline historically and topically the entire field at the beginning of the course. Let the class spend the remainder of the time in the library getting acquainted with the literature of the various schools of Biblical interpretation—the Jewish literal and allegorical; the Christian typological, allegorical, dogmatic, and the modern historico-critical, with much reading of the literature, such as the Talmud, the Greek and Latin fathers and the leading post-Reformation expositors. Let the teacher hold occasional conference periods with the class in the library to give them guidance as they progress. At the conclusion of the course let the students with free access to all material used prepare a paper which will show their understanding of the subject and its relation to their life work as interpreters of the Scriptures."[10]

"Teaching with books is valid because it makes the student a seeker for knowledge rather than a recipient of knowledge. The old method emphasizes teaching, places the major responsibility on the teacher and leaves the student in a passive attitude. The newer method emphasizes learning, places more responsibility on the student, and creates in his mind an active attitude toward his work. In the classroom students unconsciously hold the teacher largely responsible for their academic progress. In the library the student is on his own responsibility. There he must reach out, take hold, evaluate and assimilate by his own effort. How can a preacher hope to interpret in all its richness the New Testament if he has not become familiar with the large body of new material that records what is now known of the life and thought of the Graeco-Roman world. And how can he know such material unless he has made extensive use of it in the pursuit of his New Testament courses?"[11]

"The test of educational effectiveness is not the degree of knowledge exhibited by the professor's lectures but how much and how well the student learns. Teaching ability consists far more in transferable enthusiasm than in stored erudition. The Greeks understood this when they derived the verb *didaskein*, to teach, from the causative stem of *daw*, I know. Teaching is causing to know. The purpose of the educative process is not primarily to store the mind with factual knowledge, although knowledge is power, but to train the mind to reflective thinking and critical judgment, to condition the mind to functional maturity, to grow in wisdom. In an ample collection of great books the student acquires a consciousness of the essential unity of the race, a sense of historical continuity and of the moral quality and divine centrality of the universe, the awareness that through the ages one increasing purpose runs—the eternal purpose of God in Christ Jesus."[12]

IMPLEMENTATION

If seminary libraries are to make teaching with books a realistic experience in theological education, certain practical measures must be adopted. First of all, the proper authority in each school must agree that such use of the library is educationally valid and must adopt a definite program for implementing their decision. The items on this program will vary from school to school but in general will include budgetary provisions, adequate staff, book resources, service activities, technical operations, building, and equipment. Each of these items is important and needs careful consideration.

The responsibility for this implementation rests on three groups. They are the librarian and his chief assistants, the faculty, and the administration.

The librarian must possess educational skill if he is to make the library a vital part of the seminary's instruction. He must have the point of view and ability of a scholar if he is to cooperate with scholarly teachers. He must comprehend the methods of teaching and the learning problems of the undergraduates. He must know the content of the curriculum and understand its aims. Graduate work in his seminary will be seriously hindered unless he knows the materials and processes of research.

The librarian must also be a good supervisor. How much of the technical detail he personally manages will depend on the size of the institution, the number of his professional assistants, and whether the administration emphasizes the educational or housekeeping side of his office.

The faculty bear a greater responsibility. To a large extent their attitude will determine the value of the library's contribution to the students' education. The best results are achieved when a full and cordial measure of cooperation exists between teachers and librarians.

Such faculty cooperation will issue from the conviction that no student achieves competence in a subject if he does not know the literature of the subject; that the teacher's lectures, however learned, are not the limit of the students' efforts but should stimulate and guide the student to make his own mastery of the literature of the field. In contrast with this attitude is the professor who spends most of the time lecturing and requires the class to read only his own book, or one substantially agreeing with his views. Under such a teacher the student is robbed of his intellectual birthright. A teacher misuses his academic authority if he makes it the end rather than the means of the students' learning efforts.

A certain college professor, eminent as a successful teacher, says, "I furnish the librarian with select reading lists for each of the important topics studied in each of my courses. There are specific references to chapters, and the catalog number is on the margin so that the student can secure the book readily. I constantly keep before the more serious students the necessity of reading oneself into a subject and not depending merely on text or lectures. We have all too little of the type of extensive independent reading for mastery of a subject that is done by the students in the English universities. Our point of view is usually artificial—'Do this collateral so as to pass this course.' To the English student, it is rather a matter of mature reading under guidance for insight and grasp of the subject."[13]

A well-known theological teacher has recently made this luminous contribution, "a theological seminary should be judged by its library and the use made of it by students and faculty . . . the seminary library is an integral part of the students' education . . . the issue is between instruction in a classroom, with its assignment of relative readings, and the inspiration of the student to become a scholar in his own right through the resources which the library supplies, under the careful guidance of a professor-guide. The latter method will certainly imply that the professor will lecture; and it will imply that the classroom will have its place. But the center of gravity will be the truth, and the student will be thrown upon his own responsibility as he is wisely guided to the sources of a subject. A student should not be made responsible to a course or to a professor, but to himself, and to the subject."[14] This means taking the library out of the margin and placing it at the center of the curriculum. It means raising the librarian above the level of a glorified clerk and bringing him into the program of instruction. On this basis the teachers will take the librarian into their confidence, will habitually consult him in developing their courses, and will cooperate with him in plans for improving the library and its service.

Upon the administration rests the greatest responsibility for the character and functioning of the library. "Active cooperation between the faculty and library staff under strong administrative guidance is an absolutely necessary basis for developing the latent possibilities of the library in aid of . . . teaching."[15] The Southern Association expects the presidents of its colleges to provide adequate financial support, lead in defining the kind of library needed, provide a qualified librarian, bring him into vital relation with the educational program, and to insist on the adequacy of the library's resources.[16] Another authority specifically urges "that the library must come first in the thinking of the college administrator for without this basic tool of modern education, the finest buildings, the most competent faculty, and the most rigorously selected student body are rendered to a great measure helpless. The faculty cannot teach, and the students cannot learn without books. And they must be the proper books, in sufficient numbers, adequately housed, efficiently administered, skillfully interpreted. Library costs, therefore, are among the first costs of the college. If they cannot be met, monies spent otherwise may be largely wasted."[17]

The library-minded administrator will bring the librarian into proper institutional relations. The latter should have entire authority over the library, responsible only to the head of the school. A faculty library committee will be advisory and not executive. The librarian and his professional assistants will be accorded faculty status as to salary, rank, vacations, and retirement by the same or similar academic standards that govern the status of the teaching staff. The librarian should be appointed to those faculty committees that consider curricular questions and research programs. Such arrangements are not made to compliment the librarian but they are necessary if the library functions as a vital instructional agency.

CONCLUSION

The foregoing discussion is an effort to digest and interpret the extensive literature now available on the educational function of the library. The authorities quoted and those cited in the appended bibliography are eminent leaders in American education. Although they speak in terms of the college and university library their principles readily apply to seminary libraries.

The members of the American Theological Library Association are grateful for the friendly recognition contained in the invitation of the American Association of Theological Schools to present this discussion on its 1948 program. They appreciate the many generous encouragements that have come from individual presidents and deans supporting their organization for more effective library service to theological education.

Some of our librarians are asking, "What is an adequate library? What is adequate financial support? What is adequate management and equipment?" These questions arise because the librarians earnestly desire to raise the standards of librarianship and library service. They do not expect quantitative rules concerning a subject that is essentially qualitative in character but they could wish that paragraph 5 on the "Library" in the "Standards for Accrediting" might be expanded and made more circumstantial so as to give larger guidance for library development.

You have already agreed to make a study of your libraries during 1948–50. We hope this study will become a thorough survey of the libraries, securing competent survey leadership, investigating all aspects of the libraries and their relation to theological instruction, taking sufficient time to acquire all pertinent data and preparing a report that will receive recognition for its thorough analysis and sound conclusions. We are ready to cooperate with you. We have discussed such a survey and we believe the financial support and survey leadership can be found if the project is cast in large dimensions. We believe its results will strengthen theological education.

A Christian ministry spiritually dynamic and intellectually competent is tremendously needed by this homogenized age. The future success of our theological schools in training such a ministry will increasingly depend on making seminary libraries real teaching instruments. They must be furnished with every element necessary to make them such instruments because without them high standards of instruction cannot be maintained. The teacher of Christian theology and the seminary library are among the first of those means for attaining that sublime objective—"Ye shall know the truth and the truth shall make you free."

NOTES

1. Charles B. Shaw, *Library Journal* 51 (January 15, 1926): 77–79.
2. Quoted by Carl M. White in "Is the Relation of the College Library to the College Program that of Implement or Adjunct?" *The Educational Record* 20 (January 1939): 61.
3. Southern Association of Colleges and Secondary Schools, "The Relation of the Library to Instruction," *Southern Association Quarterly* 6 (November 1942): 468–71.
4. R. G. Sproul, *School and Society* 32 (September 13, 1930): 343–50.
5. William W. Bishop, "The College Library and College Teaching," *Bulletin of the Association of American Colleges* 23 (May 1937): 191–92.
6. Gus E. Snavely, "The College President Looks at the College Librarian," *Bulletin of the Association of American Colleges* 23 (November 1937): 344.
7. Henry M. Wriston, "The College Library," *Bulletin of the Association of American Colleges* 23 (November 1937): 357.
8. J. Periam Danton, "The College Library: A New Factor in Education," *Journal of Higher Education* 8 (October 1937): 379.
9. L. R. Elliott, "The Function of the Library in Theological Education," *Southern Baptist College News and Views* 11 (February 1947): 19–21.
10. Elliott, "The Function of the Library in Theological Education," 20.
11. Elliott, "The Function of the Library in Theological Education," 20.
12. Elliott, "The Function of the Library in Theological Education," 20.

13. Carl M. White, "Is the Relation of the College Library to the College Program that of Implement or Adjunct?" 73.

14. Elmer G. Homrighausen, "The Use of the Library in Preparing Students for the Parish Ministry," *Princeton Seminary Bulletin* 11 (Summer 1947): 13–17.

15. W. W. Bishop, "The College Library and College Teaching," *Bulletin of the Association of American Colleges* 23 (May 1937): 192.

16. Southern Association of Colleges and Secondary Schools, "The Relation of the Library to Instruction."

17. W. M. Randall and F. L. D. Goodrich, *Principles of College Library Administration*, 2d ed. (1941), 10.

19

The Community of Learning: Presidential Address
11th Annual Conference, Fort Worth, TX, 1957

Helen B. Uhrich

In *The Purpose of the Church and its Ministry,* the first volume published by
The Study of Theological Education, librarians are referred to as "those
most catholic of teachers, the competent librarians."[1] In the final volume,
The Advancement of Theological Education, the role of librarians in theological schools and the relationship of librarians to the teaching and learning
process are assessed and described in more detail, with the conclusion that
while this role in the school remains in part a silent one, it is not passive
when rightly conceived. "The librarian," we read, "can be indispensable in
creating the intellectual atmosphere in which minds grow."[2]

While I would not deny that these statements have been taken out of their
context and are quoted without their qualifying footnote, nevertheless these
adjectives are based on personal observations drawn from the data, insights,
and ideas gained as a result of visits to more than ninety theological seminaries; interviews; and consultation of school publications and other information supplied by member schools of AATS and other non-member
institutions.

It is a compliment to our profession that we have been accepted so completely and naturally as teachers and that we share so centrally in the responsibility of theological education. The distinction between the librarian and
those who teach has not been defined too sharply, nor should it be. There
may be a distinction in function but there is such a considerable overlapping

in purpose and procedure that it would not only be unwise but impossible to say the duties of the librarian or the teacher are exclusively this or exclusively that. Nevertheless, it is as librarians that we bring our peculiar skills to the teaching function, and we do it through our knowledge and performance of those tasks that only we can do because we are librarians.

In the second place, it is gratifying to know that the library has not been singled out by the Study Staff as a special problem area. While the library has been considered along with other factors related to the establishment and maintenance of an institution, those who look for a detailed analysis of the library as a problem will look in vain. As a matter of fact, the work of our Association was noted with special appreciation and as an excellent example of what can be accomplished through cooperation.

It is tempting, indeed, to continue in this pleasant and flattering vein and to bask in our future and glory. I propose, however, to be a little less flattering and complimentary with ourselves and conditions than our critics. We are glad that they think well of us and we are duly grateful. But we have fundamental problems before us yet to be answered. Of primary concern to us is the question of creativity, of education, of research, of the learning process and our relationship to it.

The axis on which the school turns, according to the last volume of the Study, is the relationship of teaching and learning. Teacher and student are called "companions in inquiry," and they share in the "companionship in learning." In this relationship, education is not a transmission of knowledge, nor the teacher "a retail distributor of intellectual and spiritual commodities."[3] The school becomes a community of learners, teacher and student, teacher and teacher, student and student, with all the diversity and oneness that characterize this world of learning. As the *Christian Century* stated in its editorial of April 24, 1957: "A seminary is not so much an institution set up once and for all as it is a community always setting itself up."[4]

Continuing the thesis of the Study, in this community of discourse and interest where the theological student is challenged "to enter into conversation with a continuous if not identical group of thinkers," the librarian becomes a teacher and the library a teaching center. Theological studies develop in close relationship to the mediating disciplines in the sciences and humanities. There is a constant dialogue between theology and other disciplines. Thus the setting is provided whereby the library assumes the difficult problem of "mediating a heritage of knowledge and so using a tradition that the powers of the living present be not choked or thwarted but released and directed so that a living generation become not the slave but the heir, conservator, and perfecter of its ancestors."[5]

Consequently it becomes increasingly evident that the library and the librarian share very directly in the fundamental problem of theological education. This problem is set forth by the investigators, in what is perhaps the most important sentence in the book, as "how to help students to become self-educating men who will continue to prepare themselves throughout their lives to meet the changing problems of their ministry, to carry on their theological inquiries and criticisms continuously and progressively in the midst of changing religious and cultural climates of opinion."[6] At this point the librarian becomes the most catholic of teachers and he, together with the teacher in the classroom, fails or succeeds to the degree that he has been able to meet this problem. It is a joint attack, and success or failure will not be credited to either one alone. The bell will toll for all and the warning is for all:

> A theological education which does not lead young men and women to embark on a continuous, ever-incomplete but ever-sustained effort to study and to understand the meanings of their work and of the situations in which they labor is neither theological nor education.[7]

It is this relationship of teaching and learning in which we all share. The elements in the encounter of teacher and/or librarian and student in theological study are for the most part those found in all educational endeavors, though we as librarians are most concerned with the teaching and learning process that goes beyond the classroom. With the theological school defined as "a community of Christian living and worship,"[8] theological teaching is effected in many ways, of which the library is but one area, though an important one, in which "creative mutuality" is achieved.

All this is good, and we see our role in perspective, but concretely and specifically, just how do librarians participate in this teaching and learning process? How do librarians help students become self-educating men who can carry on their own learning process and lengthen study into a life-time pursuit? How does the librarian induce the student into a mental predicament where new abilities are required? How does the librarian recognize the moment of excited curiosity and create thereby a teaching situation unequalled in classroom or seminar?

Perhaps the way to answer these questions is to ask more questions. One of these questions is whether we, as librarians, attempt to set off the research and scholarship that goes on in the library from the rest of the school and its program or whether we set it up in the framework of what the school is attempting to do. Do we understand the educational philosophy of the school wherein we carry on our work? Do we identify ourselves with the activities of the school or do we hold ourselves aloof? Do we attempt to learn what is good and what is poor pedagogy? Do we read books or only book reviews? Last year, for example, out of a total of 12,538 new titles and new editions published, 1,297 were in the fields of religion, philosophy and ethics alone.[9] Do we think we can work intelligently in this subject area if we read less than one book a month, a figure, incidentally, said to be reached by only 25 to 30 per cent of our adult population?

It was more than accident that linked the adjectives "catholic" and "competent" in describing librarians. In our service as theological librarians we cannot be competent unless we are catholic, and the chances are that we shall not be catholic unless there is a high degree of competence and versatility associated with our work. In a community of scholars it is necessary that we speak the same language they do and that we understand them at the level at which they work. We must be able to turn from the biblical scholar to the church historian or the philosopher with the greatest of ease, and be able to answer a few non-relevant questions on the side. In some ways we may know more than they. However, nothing is detected so quickly by the scholar as a lack of understanding and communication or an amateurishness in our conversation with them, and the librarian is often accepted or rejected on this point alone.

This need for familiarity with the idiom of a discipline is described by L. W. Grensted in *Theological Essays in Commemoration of the Jubilee* of Manchester University: Faculty of Theology. Dr. Grensted, in his contribution entitled, "The Changing Background of Theological Studies," states that every field of theoretical study, including philosophy, has necessarily a setting or schema of obligation and reference. The first of these is the obligation of internal reference, which is the demand for fuller coherence and progress within the science or philosophical system itself. He says, "This is in principle an isolating demand, making for an ever greater precision of language and of process which shuts out all except those who are the priests of its mysteries, actively and wholly devoted to their service."[10]

This is just another way of saying that every discipline has its signs and passwords that only the initiated know. Unless the theological librarian learns to speak the language of theology, and until he becomes a member of this community of scholars, he will never be accepted as more than a spectator or bystander, an *ausländer*, unable to understand or to participate in what is going on.

Miss Julia Pettee has called the librarian a "near scholar," a most felicitous phrase. This is to suggest that in our particular subject area the librarian must know the methodology of theology, its structure, its nomenclature; he must go beyond a casual, superficial acquaintance with the field—in short, he must penetrate into the very fibers of the subject.

If, as the Study suggests, our role in the school is not a passive one but an active one, then this participation must be shared in by all the staff, from the catalogers to the reference department and through the various levels of administration. This may range from the minimum requirements that all members of the staff be sympathetic and not antagonistic to the purpose of the school up to those few who have the dedication of a conviction and high calling. This role dare not be nebulous but must be clear-cut, incisive, and trenchant.

Let us elaborate a little more in our specifications of requirements for the various positions in the library. For the cataloger, it means he must know the subject matter with which he is dealing and be intimately acquainted with it so that, in spite of a welter of differences, he can detect recurring motifs and definite patterns, and can recognize dressed-up versions of old doctrines or heresies; he must be able to cope with a quantity of material, a diversity of viewpoint and be equipped to handle a variety of foreign languages; he must have a wide acquaintance with the humanities and general literature. In the processing and organization of material and the preparation of the public catalog, the cataloger must be skillful, consistent, accurate, and trained in the best and most desirable professional methods to do this particular job.

The reference librarian must have a similar set of skills. He must be thoroughly familiar with the catalog, his chief bibliographical tool. He must know how it is put together and how it can be used to uncover the resources of the library. More than this, he must be acquainted at first hand with the library collection. Since this position is at the highly strategic juncture where the school and library meet, the reference librarian will be lost if he must reach for a compass and guide book every time the cry for help is heard. Because of the peculiar requirements for the person who serves in this capacity, and because often the person who is most skilled in the use and interpretation of the catalog is the person who knows how it is put together, many libraries expect their reference librarians to have had previous experience in the catalog department. There is much to be said for this.

Perhaps it would be wise to come back now to the qualifying footnote mentioned at the beginning of this paper and to remind ourselves that not all of us qualify as members of this community of learning, nor is membership bestowed automatically. "It is not implied," we read, "that all theological librarians are competent any more than all the members of other faculty groups are so. But a heartening sign in the present situation is the increase of interest among these librarians in their work as teachers and the increase of concern among faculties for the development of school libraries as teaching centers."[11]

In answering the question how a librarian achieves membership in this community of learning and becomes a "companion in inquiry" with teacher and student, one replies that there is no simple rule of thumb and much depends on the person. Of this we may be sure, that competent librarians of this type will not just happen nor will they appear by chance. We can depend on this—there are some attitudes and habits that will *not* get us into this community of learning.

At the risk of appearing facetious, outspoken, or even injudicious, I am proposing a self-diagnostic test of professional attitudes and habits:

1. Do you drop your work and worries at 5:00 P.M., or even a few minutes before five?
2. Do you think you grow wiser as you grow older? You can fossilize by staying on the job as easily as you can grow.
3. Do you believe that learning is some trick of osmosis, or that enough cultural pollen will rub off in the process of handling books for you to get by in your job?
4. Do you think that being a librarian by profession is nice, but being a professor is nicer? This is known as "the grass is greener on the other side" school of thought. It is a betrayal of respect for your profession. Better be known as a first-class librarian than as a second-class professor.
5. Do you have more interest in keeping a record of things than of ideas, and are you more at home with your day-by-day record file than with the great ideas that have come down through the ages?
6. Do you feud more or less constantly with the users of your library rather than against the powers of ignorance?
7. Do you believe that staff morale and good rapport between the library and the school "just happen"? They don't. You have to work at this constantly, every single member of the staff.
8. Do you work on the basis that because it is new, it must be good or better than what you are now doing, or, equally vicious, that because this is the way you have always done it, that this is the only way?
9. Do you spend your time talking about what the administration is failing to provide for you instead of reading and thinking about what you fail to know or what you can provide for the school?
10. Do you think that a library degree is all it takes to make you a professional librarian? This is a degree that must be won on the job and earned over and over again through good hard work.

This is only a decalogue, but similar questions can provide the kind of self-diagnosis which may explain to a great degree why we are where we are.

When we speak of the librarian entering a community of learning, we mean that there must be participation, active participation, a sharing in inquiry, an unalterable and unswerving concentration on the main purpose, a constant attack on the central problem rather than on the periphery of nonessentials, a holding to the vision that comes on moving out from our narrow confines, the gaining of a true perspective. This is what we mean when we talk about "creating the intellectual atmosphere in which minds grow." This is where the librarian can be indispensable. When this happens, the community has accepted us and we know at last that it cannot exist without us.

To return again to the Study, we are happy indeed that we have made notable progress in our libraries and in our Association and that we have been complimented and commended. We like to read that "There has been steady improvement in the general situation of theological libraries over the past ten years." One can note much progress if one begins low enough on the scale with everything still to be done. Progress is a relative thing. When we look at what we should be rather than what we are, then our progress is not so noteworthy. Actually, we have moved through preliminary and minor problems up to those of a major proportion. There is still more to be done and I would like to lift up some of these major problems that we as a group must face if we are to advance from where we are to where we ought to be. There is little doubt that these problems will be harder to solve than any we have overcome thus far and that the "Ease in Zion" is not yet. I am going to risk the appearance of presumptuousness and outline these problem areas by simple declarative statements grouped under three headings: Personnel, Library Budgets, and Library Standards.

Personnel. We are not going to get stronger libraries and more effective library programs until we recruit stronger personnel and we are not going to recruit stronger personnel until our positions are made more attractive salary-wise and in terms of opportunity.

Library Budgets. Theological education in this country cannot be said to be in a favorable position in terms of training effectiveness as long as so large a proportion of our members must operate on a minimal library budget as they do. Quality libraries, in terms of books, personnel, and plant, cost money.

Library Standards. We have focused so much on the minimum requirements that we have not talked about the necessary or normative requirements. Realistically speaking, what is going to be required from the bulk of our libraries if we are going to play the role which the Study of Theological Education has outlined as commendable for the library? Another corollary of the latter would be whether we have faced our responsibility by failing to call attention to the chaotic and uneven condition of what may be called graduate or post B.D. work in our institutions so far as library implications are concerned. It is common knowledge that theological work on this level is ill-defined and most uneven.

These are some problems that go beyond the ability of this Association to correct. We can lend our support to AATS and encourage them when and if they propose to deal with them. It does lay a heavy responsibility on the Committee which has been appointed by AATS to revise and consider library standards, and on which some of our members are participating. There are more questions which one could raise, but these are enough to tax our ingenuity.

NOTES

1. H. Richard Niebuhr, *The Purpose of the Church and its Ministry* (New York: Harper, 1956), 13.

2. H. Richard Niebuhr, *The Advancement of Theological Education* (New York: Harper, 1957), 133.

3. Niebuhr, *The Advancement of Theological Education*, 209.

4. *Christian Century* 74 (April 24, 1957): 510.

5. Niebuhr, *The Advancement of Theological Education*, 202.

6. Niebuhr, *The Advancement of Theological Education*, 219.

7. Niebuhr, *The Purpose of the Church and its Ministry*, 134.

8. Niebuhr, *The Purpose of the Church and its Ministry*, 112.

9. *Publishers Weekly* (January 21, 1957): 46.

10. Manchester University Faculty of Theology, *Theological Essays in Commemoration of the Jubilee* (Manchester: Manchester University Press, 1954), 23.

11. Niebuhr, *The Purpose of the Church and its Ministry*, 13.

20

Professors and Librarians: Partners in the *Oikoumené*
20th Annual Conference, Louisville, KY, 1966

Paul A. Crow Jr.

This occasion carries more than the customary sense of honor for me. It is prompted by my longtime appreciation for your Association and its dynamic spirit. If such bodies as the American Society of Church History, the American Theological Society, and other learned societies influenced their members and institutions for good as effectively as you, American theological education would reflect far more vitality than it does. But my pleasure is especially heightened because you will install your president-elect and my effervescent colleague at Lexington, Roscoe M. Pierson. In a real sense this address is an outgrowth of a continuous dialogue which began in my seminary days.

The title of this address is in no way designed to call back the antiquated concept which once pitted professors against librarians or vice versa. Rather just the opposite is intended. While those who lecture in the classroom and those who teach from the library have distinct functions, we share a common ministry. Nevertheless this ministry—and this is the thesis of this address— has been radically reshaped by the new ecumenical situation. In theological education we have entered a new era of ecumenical developments and dynamics which call into judgment much within our seminaries, churches, and ministries which smacks of parochialism.

We can appropriately talk about the ecumenical explosion. Librarians surely have suffered from the avalanche of journals, monographs, books, and—I understand even bibliographies—which demand to be ordered, cataloged, and read. This new interest is further expressed through the establishment of numerous ecumenical institutes in different countries, an endless procession of ecumenical meetings, and the prevalence of church union conversations in every major area of the world. Yet beyond the literature and the conferences, the ecumenical movement has developed new relationships among the churches which have pierced the comfortable walls that once separated tradition from tradition. When the churches that constituted the World Council of Churches at Amsterdam in 1948 covenanted "to stay together," they entered a new era of Christian history whose revolutionary implications were only partially realized at the time. Then, along came the new frontiers produced by Vatican II as well as the cautiously let's-talk stance now emerging among some conservative-evangelicals. All these new relations make us more conscious of the reality of the *oikoumené* and the imperatives laid upon our seminaries as we chart our future in order to equip today's ministry for tomorrow's church and world.

In recent years our Roman Catholic brethren have reflected an alertness to the fact that the ecumenical ethos demands radical changes in the education of those who serve the church. The need for ecumenical theological education was clearly stated in the *Decree of Ecumenism* which came from the Second Vatican Council: "Instruction in sacred theology and other branches of knowledge, especially those of an historical nature, must also be presented from an ecumenical point of view, so that at every point they may more accurately correspond with the facts of the case."[1] Subsequently, the American Bishops' Commission for Ecumenical Affairs has established a committee to study problems and make plans related to ecumenism and theological education. Another broader project on the American scene is the recently announced Conference on Theological Education for Ecumenical Dialogue, planned for June 1967 at Chicago, which will bring Protestant, Roman Catholic, and Orthodox teachers together for the first time to discuss strategy and practical ways of seminary education in an ecumenical perspective. The transition is beginning with a new urgency among Protestant seminaries, although a great deal still needs to be thought through and initiated. Surely if his Holiness Paul VI can realistically plan to reform and restructure the Curia, Protestant seminaries can take more decisively their need for ecumenical *aggiornamento*!

But before anyone rushes back to their next faculty meeting with a passel of proposals, we need to remind ourselves of the real meaning of the Christian *oikoumené*, only so can we raise the right issues or avoid reacting against the wrong images. Admitting the root meaning of "the whole inhabited earth," the general usage of this word has been in its Christian context. The most widely accepted definition comes from a document of the World Council of Churches which says the word "ecumenical" is properly used "to describe everything that relates to the whole task of the whole Church to bring the Gospel to the whole world."[2] Another statement by the Central Committee declares: "Ecumenical work means work which helps the existing Churches in process of renewal to become the one missionary Church."[3] Obviously neither of these definitions is perfect, but they do communicate an expansive concept—one which presses the church and the seminaries to their outer limits beyond the stability of our past performances or privately forged schemes.

To really understand what is meant when we say that the seminaries must rendezvous with the fact of ecumenism, we need to extricate two sinister interpretations. First, to be ecumenical is not merely to cast another vote for that sacred word "relevance." I am for relevancy as much as anyone, but ofttimes this seems to mean little more than an adjustment to the latest fad, which in the final analysis may not always be really relevant. This was brought home to me in a story about the publication of the book, *The Vinland Map and the Tartar Relation,* which discloses two recently discovered medieval manuscripts copied about 1440 A.D. from much earlier originals. Among other things the Vinland map gives evidence that the Vikings did travel to, possibly settle for a while on, the North American mainland. The director of Yale University Press, Chester Kerr, who published the book, was justifiably proud that the book attracted so much attention and sold beyond all expectations. As you might guess, a Harvard critic, writing in *Scholarly Books in America*, put this enthusiasm in perspective with a humorous report: Not all Americans were excited about the map and the controversy over whether Leif Ericson or Christopher Columbus should be regarded as the discoverer of America. Chester Kerr happened to meet Richard Halfmoon, a chief of the Nez Percé Indian Tribe, soon after the map was published. Whereupon the chief said to the publisher, "You will forgive me for saying so, sir, but this controversy does not really interest me or my people."[4] What makes any movement truly relevant to the church and theological education is not its novelty or how enthusiastically it is shouted, but whether it arises from the church's charter and makes us more faithful stewards of the Christian message.

Another precaution should be made in the stride for ecumenical theological education. Many would warn against trying to create another specialized discipline in the curriculum. Dr. John A. Mackay has made an able case for the need of technical study of ecumenics in his book, *Ecumenics: The Science of the Church Universal*.[5] Since the ecumenical movement is an event which has changed the course of modern Christianity, all students should be introduced to the history of the movement and, equally important, have experience in the methodology of genuine dialogue. However, while the introduction of a few courses in ecumenics may begin the process, it does not bring the catholic perspective, in the sense of a wholeness of the church in space and in time, to a seminary's curriculum or community life. This only happens, says Professor Nikos A. Nissiotis, the Director of the Ecumenical Institute at Bossey, Switzerland, when ecumenics is "regarded as the basic vision in theology cutting across and thus renewing the origin and the scope of all theological disciplines and enriching Church life."[6] Through such a conception the vision of the ecumenical task should begin to recast *all* disciplines in the seminary, including the criteria which a librarian uses in his craft. Whereas in the past our departments or such fields are often molded by a subtle sectarianism, a not-so-subtle polemics, or at least a confessional orientation, they would be recast in light of the reality of world Christianity. This ecumenical perspective must lead to the reappraisal of all disciplines and fields.

I can testify that the task of church history and its writing has been deeply influenced here. Long used as the tool of polemics, church history can no longer be used in gamesmanship among divided churches. It is the rhythm of the entire drama of God's activity which must be considered. Our separate histories, our denominational histories, find their own validity in their relation to our common Christian history. In like manner the study of biblical hermeneutics would find it necessary to have ecumenically agreed-upon principles in exegesis. Systematic theology would reevaluate its treatment of the sacraments, ecclesiology, and other theological battlegrounds. Homiletics would guarantee that preaching is not merely nurture for the comfortable, but penetrating proclamation to the church's mission. That these perspectives are not universally practiced in our seminaries should be a cause of concern to all of us.

But what are some of the deeper implications of our partnership in the Christian *oikoumené*? Without pretending to have a magic formula which can be added to the standards of the American Association of Theological Schools and implemented next fall in our seminaries, let me propose several frontiers. These are not new to you, but I submit we need to look at them again vis-à-vis our ecumenical ministry.

One of the important frontiers we face, or have not faced, is the contrast between scholarship and specialization. You know that in education as well as at General Electric we live in an age of specialists. Our technocratic culture has the upper hand, and this is not all the work of evil forces. But we may be tempted by an age-old serpent in contemporary dress which would lure us to confuse scholarship with the accumulation of theological ideas and academic competence.

Before you misunderstand and react prematurely, let me affirm my conviction that theological education is an academic experience given to the most rigorous disciplines of the intellectual community—assuming the variety of human limitations. Heaven knows, our American churches have suffered from those who would make ministerial education an a-intellectual or anti-intellectual episode, suspicious of thinking or technical research which does not feed into next Sunday's sermon or resemble a seminar in propaganda. The most controversial corrective to this mood was given in an article by Paul Ramsey entitled "The Status and Advancement of Theological Scholarship in America."[7] Dr. Ramsey ably defends the would-be scholar-teacher who is precluded from real competence in his chosen field because of the numerous calls to preach, counsel with congregations, write popular books, serve on denominational and ecumenical commissions, and other "trivia." (He failed to mention the legion administrative duties carried within the academic community itself!) I agree with certain aspects of Dr. Ramsey's analysis, e.g., the overburden of the calendar. Most of us in the seminaries are chief among the sinners in this respect. But behind such a critique—and this is the heart of our problem—is the desire on the part of some to divorce, or at least keep at arm's length, the minister and the scholar, the church and the academy. When this happens, we run the risk of becoming scholar-teachers who do not truly share the ministry which is the primary function of the institutions we serve.

The seminary is an academy, with all the commitments such a statement applies, but it is an academy of the church. With the freedom essential to serve the church and with the mandate to take the whole Gospel to the whole world, the seminary nevertheless can only fulfill its task as it stands within the life and witness of the church. This means each teacher or theologian is called to be a church-theologian in both word and deed. Likewise each student must discover the exhilarating moment when his scientific studies of the Bible, theology, church history, ethics, and other fields are intimately related to his presence in the church. The church cannot afford specialists who are devoid of a sense of ministry.

The primary clue at this point is whether our seminaries and divinity schools—indeed we, their professors—understand our fundamental task as the proclamation of the Gospel. If we are not called to lead persons to a vital comprehension of the Christian message, then what is our unique business— other than to engage in competitive recruitment (which in our own way compares favorably with the professional football leagues), degrade each other's faculties, and engage in other non-theological niceties which seem to add spice to the theological enterprise. Early in this century Adolf von Harnack, who made his fame as a theologian and historian, and his money as a librarian, published an essay on "The Relevance of Theological Faculties at the University" which was a defense against those who wanted to close down the divinity schools. Harnack's main point is instructive to what is being said here:

> Theology is concerned with religion, and above all, with the greatest historical event which mankind has witnessed, with Jesus Christ and the results which

have followed . . . theological faculties have as their purpose to protect this inheritance. This is their final and loftiest purpose. And they ought not only to preserve, but also present it forcefully.[8]

Parenthetically, we should note Harnack also suggests that not all the faculty members need be Protestants, saying, "How valuable it would be for students of theology at a university to be able to hear church history and symbolics from a Catholic theologian too. Why should we not welcome one to our faculty?"[9] Both suggestions take us back to the heart of our seminary task in light of our ecumenical imperative, namely, to prompt the church—the whole church—to take the Gospel—the whole Gospel—to the world—the whole world.

There is a final dimension to this ministry for our seminaries and those of us who serve them in different capacities. As we plan curriculum, give scholarships, supervise field assignments, administer library procedures, and work with student councils, the process of studying *about* the Christian message is not enough. It must lead to the existential perception of the *truth* of that message and the *experience* of its validity in worship, witness, and fellowship. True scholarship, in the lives of teachers and students alike, will find expression in both learning and devotion. Although these two virtues sometimes seem to stand at odds with others, Roland Bainton's observation is penetrating, "Without warmth of commitment scholarship is barren."[10] Only through the giving of self in loving service does one know the unsearchable riches of the quest for Christian truth. When those we teach move, almost with a sense of awe, from an understanding of doctrines, events, and ministerial functions to personal, real-life participation in the Christian life, then we have more nearly accomplished our task.

This accomplishment will be accelerated or held back, however, to the degree that theological education sees its products primarily as persons, not statistics, lectures, and the like. It always makes special demands to deal with persons, and even more important to use these dealings as part of a redemptive process. Yet here is the glorious but frustrating stance the seminary takes. Our life together focuses upon persons—who are in varying stages of growth and entrenchment, who are threatened by their peers, new ideas, and a changing world, who are reaching out at new creativity. Our shared ministry among the seminaries will bring few joys until we can watch and guide this encounter of persons with persons, and each person with the Person. When this is our rule, however, those who go from our classrooms and ping pong tables will not be connoisseurs about the Christian message, but whole persons who understand the Christian message, who believe it, and who can interpret it to modern man because they have experienced it.

Insofar as we professors and librarians can share in these goals—to lead persons to hear God's calling and the good news it brings, to inquire after knowledge in the discipline of committed scholarship, and to see the ful-fillment of education in the involvement of themselves in God's issues—surely then we understand what John Baillie meant when he said, "Theological study also is a means of grace."

NOTES

1. "Decree of Ecumenism" in *The Documents of Vatican II*, ed. Walter M. Abbott, S.J. (New York: The American Press and Association Press, 1966), 353.

2. Minutes and Reports of the Fourth Meeting of the Central Committee. Rolle, Switzerland, August, 1951 (Geneva: World Council of Churches, 1951), 65.

3. Minutes and Reports of the Tenth Meeting of the Central Committee. New Haven, Connecticut, July–August, 1957 (Geneva: World Council of Churches, 1957), 106.

4. David Dempsey, "What A Way to Grow," *Saturday Review* (June 11, 1966): 46.

5. John A. Mackay, *Ecumenics: The Science of the Church Universal* (Englewood Cliffs, N.J.: Prentice-Hall, 1964).

6. Nikos A. Nissiotis, "Principles of an Ecumenically Oriented Theology," *Criterion* [University of Chicago Divinity School] 2 (Spring 1963): 3.

7. Paul Ramsey, "The Status and Advancement of Theological Scholarship in America," *The Christian Scholar* 47 (Fall 1964): 219.

8. Adolf von Harnack, "The Relevance of Theological Faculties at the University," trans. Mary Jane Mosher in *The Christian Scholar* 47 (Fall 1964): 219.

9. Harnack, "The Relevance of Theological Faculties at the University," 218.

10. Quoted in E. Harris Harbison, *The Christian Scholar in the Age of the Reformation* (New York: Charles Scribners, 1956), 166.

21

Theological Libraries Revisited
35th Annual Conference, St. Louis, MO, 1981

Leon Pacala

I recently received an invitation to address a group of CEOs of minority schools sponsored by the United Presbyterian Church, and I was somewhat taken back by the wording on the invitation. It read literally "We would like the group to bear your presentation." Now, I kind of convinced myself that that was a typographical error but only with limited success. Father Daly was much more careful and much more gracious in his invitation for me to take part in this gathering. He went on to try to convince me that I had something significant to say to this group and also to feel wanted. So I'm very delighted to be here—which proves that the biblical injunction that man does not live by bread alone is true—he must be buttered up occasionally. Now that I'm here in the presence of this somewhat forbidding group, I feel somewhat like the little girl who was very much concerned about her father who was in the habit of bringing home a briefcase full of work every evening and, after dinner, repairing immediately to the study to remain there all night. She asked her mother why Daddy had to work at night and at home. Her mother explained that her father was a very busy and important person who couldn't possibly complete his work during the daytime. "Well," said the worried girl, "why don't they put him in a slower section?" Well, now, in the presence of this professionally oriented and experienced group who preside over an area of our theological communities which remains for many of us a mystery and yet still highly valued, I recognize what a fast track I'm in—or I'm on—at this time and I'm very grateful to be here.

When I was thinking about the assignment and the topic, I was tempted to entitle my remarks "Theological Libraries: A Vanishing Species," and then I did some research on the experience of our theological schools with their libraries over the last three or four decades. I learned, for example, that four decades ago, there were only twelve libraries on the North American continent housing seventy-five thousand volumes or more in their theological collections. Today, there are a hundred and six which exceed that number. I studied ten libraries and their development during that period—ten chosen at random—and learned that, over that same period, those libraries had increased in size from 2.9 to 5.8 times, with an average growth of 3.4 times increase. So, over that long period, we have just lived through, as you know, an unprecedented period of growth and expansion. I then tried to discern something of the trends over the more recent past and tried to analyze some of the indices that have taken place over the last five years. I found that over these five years, contrary to, I'm sure, the full satisfaction of libraries—librarians—that our schools continue to invest an increasing portion of their resources in theological libraries. For example, over these five years, I learned that university-related libraries had increased their appropriation for library support 37% in five years; Roman Catholic schools, 31%; denominational schools, 64%; Canadian schools, 66%; non-denominational and non-university-related schools, 84%. Now, this took place during a period of time when the consumer price index increased 51.5%. Now, what this points out, then, is that, over a five-year period, that at least three of the five categories of schools had at least kept pace with the rate of inflation in the support of their libraries. I know that that doesn't tell the whole story, that the increase in costs of library appropriations and acquisitions has far outpaced the average rate of inflation. So I went back to try to understand what is happening in terms of the acquisitions picture and again this bears out the fact that library costs have exceeded significantly the average increase in inflation. Again, university-related schools over this five-year period have decreased the number of volumes added to their collection by 60%, a figure so startling, in fact, that I'm very suspicious of our data. The same has occurred with Canadian schools, where the number of volumes added has decreased some 50% over a five-year period; for Roman Catholic schools, a decrease of 16%. Denominational schools have increased their number of acquisitions or additions to the library by a modest 28% and non-university-related, non-denominational schools by 4%.

The conclusion one can draw from this brief presentation of statistics, however, stands, namely, that it is the experience of our theological schools that, perhaps more than any other part of the institutional budget, appropriations for libraries have at least kept pace in most instances with the rate of inflation. I suspect there's a closer parallel there, related to libraries, than on any other aspect of institutional budgeting. From this, one can draw, then, at least some implications of the role, the status, that libraries may have in our institutions. But I want to concentrate not upon the financial picture or the constraints within which libraries proceed but to single out another topic for conversation and in the few minutes that we have together I would like to offer an invitation to begin anew a dialogue and perhaps even a debate about the nature and role of theological libraries in theological education, and, furthermore, I would like to include in that invitation the suggestion that persons gathered in this room assume the responsibility of becoming a more constituent part of that discussion and debate.

First, let me try to make clear my own personal perspective. At the biennial meeting of the Association of Theological Schools in 1948, L. R. Elliot, who was then the librarian of Southwestern Baptist Theological Seminary, in one of the major addresses to that gathering, completed his presentation entitled "The Role of Theological Libraries in Theological Education" with this comment—he said, "I believe that seminaries should increasingly be known by their libraries and by the use made of those libraries by students and faculty." Now, I happen to believe that injunction. I also believe that that statement is true of a great many of our schools; partially true of a great many more; and, in principle at least, true of the hopes and aspirations of still a larger number of schools. But I also believe that unless the kind of discussion and debate that I'm about to suggest take place, I suspect that that index of the effectiveness of our theological schools will diminish in the years ahead.

Now, it's been an interesting and illuminating exercise to go back through official documents of the Association of Theological Schools and the official actions taken related to our theological libraries. It seems that at least once every decade it has become a topic of official action by the Association. Interestingly enough, in the 1940s, the major issue, it seemed, was that of trying to transform theological education in such a way as to make learning by books a more significant instructional mode. It's rather startling to realize that, as late as the middle 1940s, the status of theological libraries hung in the balance of the debate and the thesis that a student whose theological education included substantial learning through volumes, important volumes of every subject matter, would be much better prepared for ministry than a student whose theological education turned around standing for examinations on the basis of textbooks and lectures. How far we have traveled since the middle 1940s, at least in principle, in our schools, for learning by books, I would assume, is indeed a proven point beyond debate and discussion in our day.

In the 1950s, there was an official study again made of the role of theological schools—theological libraries—which led to the establishment of accrediting standards for the library to be used in the accreditational processes of the Association. It's interesting to study those standards because they continue to constitute the core of the standards as they exist today. Standards were rooted in the principle that the theological library should be integrated to the purposes of the institution itself and by all means should support the instructional and the research programs of the institution. It also insisted that theological libraries should be indeed the study center of the entire institution.

During the 1960s, the major study of theological education was carried on by a commission on the planning of resources for theological education, and, in the report that was submitted late in that decade, theological libraries were mentioned only in passing, and, in the mentioning, the one point that was singled out was the potential advantage of cooperative mechanisms. A few years later in the curriculum for the 1970s that was published, no mention of theological libraries was made at all.

In the 1970s, there was a joint ATS/ATLA task force on the strategy for libraries, and that report is quite interesting because there again it singles out the need and the advantages for cooperative mechanisms and structures and calls attention to the fact that theological libraries must include resources which go beyond the printed page or the bound volume. And then it ended with something of a pep talk that in times of diminishing resources we must avoid the mood that nothing could be done in terms of regional cooperation or research because of diminishing resources.

Now, as one looks at that history so briefly outlined, one has two very vivid impressions: one, how substantive and decisive was the discussion about theological libraries in the 1940s and the 1950s and, conversely, how much that kind of discussion and debate seemed to be lacking in the 1960s and 1970s, decades when procedures and techniques tended to dominate our attention. I want to suggest that it is time to return to the level of seriousness and substance that engaged the theological communities in the 50s—in the 40s and 50s—so far as theological libraries were concerned. I want to suggest also that this kind of a constituency is an important part of the total context in which that kind of discussion and debate might prove productive. The need for such a debate, I think, is in part less obvious than the need for all the constituents of theological communities to participate in that debate. I don't know a great deal about libraries, but I know enough to understand the problems that you confront as professionals responsible for a segment, an important segment, of your institutions. But I want to suggest that your concerns must go beyond those technical and professional concerns, and, that as members of the full community of theological educators, the concerns and issues which confront theological education as a whole will be decisive not only for the enterprise but also for our libraries as such. Your participation therefore in that discussion is absolutely imperative.

Now, let me point out in very brief outline something of the nature and perhaps the issues around which that future discussion might take place— issues which affect our entire enterprise but which have far-ranging implications for the day in and day out responsibilities each of you shoulder. Let me suggest first of all that the immediate future of theological education will be shaped by the need to increasingly clarify its basic purposes and objectives. Throughout the twentieth century, the instructional programs and curriculums of our theological schools have been shaped increasingly by the conviction that ministry is indeed a profession. And a professional model has been the source for the motivations of the greatest development, additions, and innovation in theological education. Now, for some, that has been a saving grace and there can be no question but what that model has had not only official but lasting impact upon the enterprise. There are others, however, who look upon that fact as something of a curse rather than a blessing and who are calling attention to the fact increasingly that we must be about the task of discerning ways in which that single model should be augmented, corrected, and perhaps even transcended. I want to suggest that you as librarians have an important stake in that discussion. And I recognize something of the anomaly however into which you are placed as a participant in that discussion. Our schools can tolerate ideology when it touches faculty; it can tolerate ideology when it bears upon administrators; but it can hardly tolerate ideology or limited perspectives where the library is concerned. There you must serve not only the advocates of a single resolution of an issue but you must cover the bases for either change or addition in whatever resolution an institution will adopt.

But perhaps in that anomaly itself stands or is included some of your greatest contribution to this ensuing discussion, for you have a perspective that your responsibility will keep alive in striking a balance, in suggesting dimensions of the issues, and in evaluating whatever resolution is projected in the effort to understand the basic purpose for which our institutions exist. Profession or something else—an emphasis upon the nurturing of competence and functions or something else—are we in the business to nurture persons trained to perform according to certain expectations and need or are we in the business to identify and nurture those who will embody a tradition, the experience of a people, a destiny that is determinative and distinctive? That signifies something of the dimension of the discussion which all of us must undertake and be a part of.

A second issue that confronts theological education is of a different kind. The future of our institutions will be determined by their relationships to the rest of higher education. We are learning to appreciate what the 1970s did for theological education. More than we realized as we lived through those difficult years, the 1970s constituted a very creative period in the history of theological education. It was a period of growth probably second to only the 1950s. It was a period of development and of great creativity. But it was also a time in which our theological schools increasingly isolated themselves from important centers of our culture including the other aspects of the fabric of higher education. Now, the history and the elements in that growing isolation are complex. Some of them can be traced to the unprecedented growth in the post–World War II period of university and college departments of religious studies. What happened with that growth and development was that there was an increasingly sharpened division of labor between departments of religious studies and seminaries, the latter increasingly focusing upon their roles as agents of the church, existing for the purpose increasingly singular in understanding of preparing the leadership of the church, and increasingly narrowing the scope of institutional functions attenuated to that increasingly specialized purpose.

Now, I've overdrawn the distinction, but I think there is great truth in the elements and the implications of that distinction. But what has happened as a result is that there is an increasing gulf that threatens to expand into increasing alienation and isolation. Now, it's not difficult to imagine the implications and the consequences if that gulf is permitted to grow and to develop. And yet I'm convinced that one of the greatest threats to our theological schools is that of greater, increasing isolation from other culture-forming, culture-shaping centers in our society, and it's a trend which must be very carefully discerned, assessed, and evaluated. And its implications for theological education must be made very clear. Again, I want to suggest that librarians have a very important contribution to make to that issue and to the discussion that ought to center around that issue, for there is a very real sense in which our libraries should remain the open door to the rest of the world of learning. The size and the configuration of that door will be determined largely by persons gathered in this room. The implications of that determination will be felt by theological education as a whole.

There's a third type of isolation that will increasingly challenge our theological schools which also requires serious thought and assessment. That is the threat of increased sectarianization of our instructional programs. Ecumenicity came to theological education in a very unique way in the 1960s. It was epitomized in 1968 when the first Roman Catholic seminary was accredited by the Association. Since then, every major Roman Catholic seminary has either been accredited or is well on the road to accreditation. During the period, there also developed what comes to as close a consensus in theological education as I know, often times unspoken, even more frequently never debated, and that is the belief that preparation for religious leadership can be best carried out in some form of an ecumenical context. If there is a principle that we have somehow all accepted and embraced in some sense, it's that. And yet, of late, there are signs that that principle is being seriously called into question, not explicitly, but nevertheless, no less effectively. That calling into question is the result of a number of factors, some of which are loose in society as a whole—forces and motivation stressing the separation of groups within our society, stressing distinctiveness; a political process which proceeds according to caucuses and encounter and confrontation. But there are also forces within the ecclesiastical communities themselves contributing to that increasing sectarianization, namely, as our churches have experienced (as most have) a declining support and a declining size of their enrollments; there has been a tendency to guard the ramparts, a tendency to alter or to change or to transform a concern for ecclesiastical identity to an advocacy of denominational distinctiveness, and in that transformation is contained a great threat to the community of theological schools.

Now, again, where responsible denominational identity ends and sectarianization begins is a very important issue that needs to be on our agenda in the immediate future and again I submit that librarians have a great deal to contribute to the clarification of that issue, its implications, and its resolution. Whether our libraries will become indeed denominational archives or whether they will remain centers of theological study in our institutions is not an exaggerated way to pose some of the consequences and implications of that trend.

Let me suggest a final issue and I'm finished. The theological schools in the immediate future will need to clarify for themselves again their distinctive subject matter. Ned Farley of Vanderbilt University has argued, and I think convincingly, that much of the present predicament of theological education stems from the fact that we have lost a coherent subject matter. In place of a single reality that not only shapes and relates our theological studies but also justifies and defines them, in place of a single subject matter, we have substituted a very loose configuration of highly specialized studies, each with its own method, its own objectives, its own purposes, and somehow we have pulled it all together and called it theological study. Now, the issues and the problems implied in the increasing loss of a singular subject matter are indeed complex and comprehensive in scope. It's an issue that touches the very heart of the enterprise we represent, for it deals with the very nature of knowledge, the knowledge upon which our educational enterprise rests. For to raise a question of the subject matter of theological education is to raise a question of the theological nature of knowledge itself. What is the substance of that knowledge? What is its defining form and principle? What should be its organizational forms? Almost overwhelmingly complex questions, and yet questions which no longer can be ignored without extracting a fearful toll from the enterprise itself. Again, what kind of knowledge must our educational systems presuppose? Or, what kind of knowledge is the responsibility of the church? Or, what kind of knowledge is it our responsibility to nurture and to offer to the total pantheon of scholars in our culture and in our times? I want to suggest that we can no longer assume that these answers can come from history or from the way history has shaped our intellectual or scholarly guilds; that as theological schools have increasingly focused upon their distinctive purposes, there may be far-reaching implications and consequences for the kind of knowledge upon which those purposes rest. These are questions which must be phrased, discussed, and debated, and certainly you who preside over the gathering, the preservation and the servicing of that body of knowledge must be a constituent part.

Well, we've hopped, skipped, and jumped over a lot of issues but I want to suggest that the future of theological education requires the contribution that each can make from the uniqueness of their perspectives and that you who are such important parts of the community of theological educators have a distinctive and a very important role to play in that debate. I firmly hope you'll accept that challenge and that you will make it a part of your agenda, not first and foremost as professional librarians, but first and foremost as members of the community of theological educators and out of that basic commitment and assumption I think that there is much to be gained. Now, one doesn't have to be around an academic institution very long to be rather jaundiced about all of the great claims that will be forthcoming from a new venture or an experiment or an innovation of some kind or another. I remember once Robert Hutchins commenting that he had learned that Harvard had decided to alter the size of the diploma. He went on to say that they were either going to make it larger or smaller, he had forgotten which, but he was sure it was a step in the right direction. I want to suggest that your participation in the right kind of debate or dialogue that I have suggested would be indeed a step in the right direction and can make all the difference in the world.

Throughout this first year in office, I have learned a great deal. Part of what I have learned I owe in no small measure to Simeon Daly and his colleagues, who cornered me in one of the buildings of Princeton Theological Seminary early last October and we discussed matters of mutual interest and concern. Well, saying we discussed it overstates it—they talked and I listened. But I came away from that meeting convinced that one of the priorities before the community of theological schools touches upon our theological libraries. It was an impression which grew throughout the year as I increased my knowledge of our schools and their leadership, so much so that, when the executive committee of the Association gathered and I was asked to submit a very small number of priorities to which I thought the Association of Theological Schools should commit itself, included in that small list was the future of our theological libraries. I remain convinced of that.

I'm happy to announce that again with the help of Father Daly and his colleagues, we have formulated a joint project of both associations which we have rather modestly entitled "Theological Project 2000." It's a project which is designed to do some of the things at least that I have been suggesting, a project that will be studied—a study project basically of nature—devoted to two or three important objectives: one, to try to more clearly discern the role of theological libraries in theological education for the remainder of this century; secondly, to try to discern the resources needed to fulfill those functions and purposes; thirdly, to suggest strategies to insure those resources; and finally, to propose possible updating of the standards affecting libraries upon which accreditation rests. That's a presumptuous study to undertake and yet, we're convinced, a timely and essential one. I'm happy to be able to announce, for the first time publicly, that, yesterday afternoon, I received confirmation from the Lilly Endowment that a grant of $70,000 has been approved to underwrite such a study. It will be a study that will be inaugurated almost immediately and hopefully completed some-time in academic year 1982–83. This is one way in which our associations can be about the very essential business that is the main responsibility that you and I share. I'd also like to say that I look forward to not only working on that project but to pledging whatever resources the Association of Theo-logical Schools may command to ensure the success of what will hopefully be a benchmark study in the development and history of theological librar-ies. In addition to the action taken by the Lilly Endowment, I can think of no other more hopeful sign of insuring the success of that project than to indicate that we have received a commitment from one of your colleagues, one of your distinguished colleagues, Steve Peterson, who's agreed to coor-dinate that study for us. I look forward to the result of that and to continued relationships of our associations as we seek to find ways in which to fulfill the important purposes to which we are committed. Thank you.

22

The Structures of Religious Literature: Conceptual Frameworks for Improving Bibliographic Instruction
37th Annual Conference, Richmond, VA, 1983

Andrew D. Scrimgeour

A year ago I submitted to the program committee a working title for this paper. It was dubbed "The Cognitive Structures of Theological Literature." This obtuse title reflected my recent immersion into the writings of educational theorists and cognitive psychologists. It was certainly an unimaginative and unforgivable caption for a talk in the humanities, let alone for theological bibliographers and reference librarians!

I want to change the title and pilfer one from a slender book that is stashed with similar thin volumes among small vehicles, stuffed animals, and assorted contraband in my two-year-old's room. His favorite book bears the title *I Wish I Had a Computer That Makes Waffles*. Let me doctor that a bit to read *I Wish I Had a Computer That Made Sense of All Religious Literature!*

My concern is for a structural understanding of religious literature. This interest grows out of a long-standing fascination with the communication and publishing patterns within and among the various disciplines that make up the theological corpus. But my inquiry has intensified over the past nine years as I have experimented with various approaches to teaching theological bibliography and the craft skills of research. I have been chagrined to learn that dazzling students with reference works without providing mental shelves on which to place them is not of enduring value.

I always feel that I am on sound ground if I find evidence that H. Richard Niebuhr has been there before me. Edward Farley, in his recent essay, *Theologia: The Fragmentation and Unity of Theological Education*, mines again Niebuhr's classic study of theological education in the United States:

> The greatest defect in theological education today is that it is too much an affair of piecemeal transmission of knowledge and skills, and that, in consequence, it offers too little challenge to (students) to develop (their) own resources and to become independent, lifelong inquirer(s), growing constantly while engaged in the work of ministry.[1]

The indictment of the seminary enterprise also indexes my own efforts in bibliographic instruction. It has been too piecemeal, and it has not sufficiently fostered critical, imaginative independence in the soon-to-be minister or priest.

My efforts have taken this progression. My first years in the classroom were as a *magician*. Armed with bibliographies and piles of impressive tomes, I dazzled my students with my glorious wares. It was high entertainment to produce just the right tools for developing papers and projects. Students always found pertinent tools to then use, but a clear overview of the reference works of the discipline was not fostered. Thus, the librarian was needed to perform new feats of white magic when the next round of courses began, and another subject area was broached.

A cluster of sensitivities next influenced my teaching and nudged me away from my earnest but naïve salesmanship. The pivotal role of bibliographic guides in research and steps to locating them became a valuable step to teach. The value of presenting reference tools by genre was also a new pedagogical insight. The bibliographies of these classroom lectures began to be organized by genre and became elementary guides in themselves, particularly when critical annotations were added. These annotations offered fundamental information about the tools, how they compared to similar tools, their idiosyncrasies, and the like.[2]

As my experience in the classroom grew I became less the magician and more the *guide*. Using the assignment that the students were facing, I organized the lecture around their actual project. Tools were thus introduced in the context of the actual work at hand. Search strategies became more important than any single reference work out of context. Bibliographies complete with annotations and call numbers were still provided, but not all titles on these lists were discussed by any means. A second handout became vital— pages from the reference works that documented the search I was conducting.

The latest influence on my teaching is really at the heart of this talk. The performance as well as the understanding of students became demonstrably more sophisticated as I reworked lectures to build on conceptual understandings of the literature rather than the specific qualities of isolated tools. Before presenting two schemes that I have found particularly valuable, let me make a few remarks about my exploration of learning theories as they relate to teaching the craft of research.

The work of Raymond McInnis convinced me of the utter naïveté of teaching lasting research skills without conceptual structures.[3] His work grew out of instructional psychology which emphasized the importance of cognitive structures, or frameworks, in the learning process. He drew also on the recognition that although teaching is obviously directed to promote learning, the learning process itself must be better understood. The combined effect of his work is to fuse teaching and learning theories.

Although cognitive learning theorists disagree on many points, they do have a common ground. First, the use of concepts simplifies a subject for the tyro and makes it more understandable. Second, people are able to retain information that is tied to structured concepts longer and use it more readily than detailed information that is not so ordered. And third, when a student is solving a new problem or working in a new subject field, he or she draws on an understanding of the basic framework of concepts of related subject areas in that effort. This transfer of concepts allows previous learning to facilitate new learning.

There are two conceptual frameworks that I have found helpful to students in bibliographic lectures. They have several qualities in common. Both are designed for use with either beginning or advanced students. Elaboration of the examples of each scheme quickly pitches the presentation to the desired audience level. Both may be used together in the same presentation or used separately. And each is susceptible to a brief presentation or a more lengthy discussion. If the lecture is a standard fifty-minute one, then experience suggests that one should be sacrificed for the other.

The first illustration, "The Religious Scholar: Research, Communication, and Finding Aids," charts the genesis of a scholarly publication from its informal beginnings in lectures to its various printed incarnations. Review literature is pictured as serving to evaluate such publications and to integrate them into the bibliographic network of the subject. The role of the graduate student in the flow of scholarly communication is also placed. The use of three columns delineates (1) the form of scholarly communication; (2) the status of that communication; and (3) examples of the communication as well as finding aids (reference tools) for locating such resources. (See Exhibit 1 at the end of this chapter.)

The second illustration portrays the types and functions of reference works. The teeter-totter or scale is weighted to subject information tools on one side and to bibliographic information on the other. Reference works placed in the middle of the scale uniquely balance substantive material and bibliographic detail. The middle of the illustration parses the blends of subject information and bibliographic information by genres, whether dictionary, encyclopedia, index, or library catalog. The bottom portion of the chart offers illustrations of reference works for each of the five categories. It is a handy model on which to hang the infinite, and often confusing, array of reference tools. (See Exhibit 2 at the end of this chapter.)

I have found these frameworks fundamental enough to provide a foundation for the beginning divinity student, yet flexible enough for refinement as the sophistication of the student grows. These illustrations hardly exhaust the concepts that serve the craft of research in the field of religion. They are offered as two fundamental models that have worked in my own experience.

Charles Willard, my mentor in many library matters, impressed me nine years ago with a telling observation. The faculty member who presents his or her course with a full bibliography *ex machina* may well be doing a great disservice. The *process* by which books and articles are judged as vital to a course may well be among the most important matters to teach. That perspective has haunted me these years and drives me to pursue more effective ways to foster bibliographic literacy in the ministry of the churches.

NOTES

1. Edward Farley, *Theologia: The Fragmentation and Unity of Theological Education.* (Philadelphia: Fortress, 1983), 23.
2. Some early examples appeared as issues of *Renewals: A Bibliographic Newsletter of the B.T.I. Libraries.* See especially "The Black Church in the United States—a Resource Guide" (February 1979), "Locating Book Reviews" (November 1979), and "Current Indexing and Abstracting Tools for Religious Studies—A Selective Guide" (March–April 1980).
3. Raymond G. McInnis, *New Perspectives for Reference Service in Academic Libraries.* (Westport, CT: Greenwood, 1978).

EXHIBIT 1:
THE RELIGIOUS SCHOLAR: RESEARCH,
COMMUNICATION, AND FINDING AIDS

The Individual Scholar's Communication

Informal Patterns (Pre-publication)

Classroom lectures
Graduate seminars
Faculty colliquia

- Ideas developed and critiqued locally
- Examples and finding aids: Locally catalogued, unpublished works or ephemera (Landes, *Biblical Exegesis*). If information on such an item is known, it may often be secured through a national computer system such as OCLC. 2. Tape catalog (Reigner Recording Library)

Invited lectures
Learned society papers
Lecture series

- Ideas honed in more public settings
- Examples and finding aids: Tape catalogs, learned society programs, abstract books, tapes, and issues of its journal (AAR/SBL annual meeting publications)

Formal Patterns (Publications)

Journal articles
Festschriften articles
Anthology articles
Chapters in books

- Ideas formally judged by peers and published
- Examples and finding aids: Journal article indexes (*Religion Index One*), multi-author work indexes (*Religion Index Two*), and citation indexes (*Arts & Humanities Citation Index*)

Books
Monographic series

- Larger projects formally judged by peers and published
- Note: The use of footnotes and bibliographies places them in the ongoing scholarly conversation.
- Examples and finding aids: Book reviews (*Religion Index One*), bibliographic essays (*Religious Studies Review*), and annual subject bibliographies (Society of Old Testament Study book list)

Bibliography

American Academy of Religion and Society of Biblical Research. *Annual Meeting, 1983*. Chico, CA: Scholars Press, 1983.
———. *Book of Abstracts, 1983*. Chico, CA: Scholars Press, 1983.

Arts and Humanities Citation Index. Philadelphia: Institute for Scientific Information, 1978–. Three times annually.

Comprehensive Dissertation Index. Ann Arbor: University Microfilms. Published for various time periods with individual volumes dedicated to specific subject fields, including religion and philosophy.

Kepple, Robert J. *Reference Works for Theological Research: An Annotated Selective Bibliographical Guide.* 2nd ed. Washington, DC: University Press of America, 1981. Consult also Kepple's *Reference Works for Theological Research: Supplement of Additions and Changes.* 1981/1982 ed. Philadelphia: Westminster Theological Seminary, 1982.

Lands, George M. *The Nature and Method of Biblical Exegesis: Including Some Practical Suggestions for the Outline, Structure, and Content of an Exegetical Paper, Based on Either an Old Testament or a New Testament Text.* 6th revised ed. New York: Union Theological Seminary, 1977.

Reigned Recording Library Catalog 1981. Richmond: Union Theological Seminary, 1981.

Religion Index One: Periodicals. Chicago: American Theological Library Association, 1977–. Formerly *Index to Religious Periodical Literature,* 1949–1976.

Religion Index Two: Multi-Author Works, 1976–. Chicago: American Theological Library Association, 1978–. Annual.

Religious Studies Review. Waterloo, Ontario: Council on the Study of Religion, 1975–.

Sandmen, Ernest R., and Hale, Frederick. *American Religion and Philosophy: A Guide to Information Sources.* Detroit: Gale, 1978.

The Society of Old Testament Study. *Book List.* London: The Society of Old Testament Study, 1946–. Annual.

EXHIBIT 2:
THE TYPES AND FUNCTIONS
OF REFERENCE WORKS

The following five classifications, from purely subject information to purely bibliographic information, are adapted from Raymond G. McInnis's "tripartite matrix" in "The Substantive-Bibliographic Continuum and the Functions of Intermediary Sources," *New Perspectives for Reference Service in Academic Libraries* (Westport, CT: Greenwood Press, 1978), p. 136.

Type 1
Subject Information

Dictionary, glossary, or directory
Examples: Van Harvey, *Handbook of Theological Terms,* and *Directory of Departments and Programs of Religion in North America*

Type 2
Primarily Subject Information, Secondarily Bibliographic
Information

Dictionary or encyclopedia (textbook)
Examples: Brandon, *Dictionary of Comparative Religions*, and Cross, *Oxford Dictionary of the Christian Church*

Type 3
Combination of Subject and Bibliographic Information

Comprehensive encyclopedia
Examples: *New Catholic Encyclopedia* and *Interpreters' Dictionary of the Bible*

Type 4
Primarily Bibliographic Information, Secondarily Subject
Information

Index with abstracts, annotated bibliography, and bibliographic guide
Examples: *Religion Index One* and Adams, *Reader's Guide to the Great Religions*

Type 5
Bibliographic Information

Library catalog (card, fiche, online) and bibliographic index
Examples: Humanities index; Williams & Brown, *Afro-American Religious Studies*; and *Books in Print*

23

Theological Libraries and Theological Librarians in Theological Education
45th Annual Conference, Toronto, ON, 1991

James Dunkly

Wisely or not, this Association has for some years invited its presidents to address it (one president per year, I hasten to add!), an invitation that most of us have found hard to resist. But I was asked to consider doing mine in connection with a chapel service, so that it might be thought of as a kind of presidential homily. That invitation, too, I have found hard to resist, not because I think of the ATLA presidency as a liturgical office, and not because I seek to lend these remarks of mine a spurious authority by calling them a homily, but rather because I seek to underscore the connection between what we do *in here*, in the chapel, in our worship, and what we do *out there*, in the meeting rooms of our annual conference and in our own libraries and institutions back home. The fundamental unity between how we pray and how we live our lives is as much to be sought by librarians as it is by anyone else.

The traditional order of worship we are using for this service of matins, or morning prayer, is the order of the daily office, the *officium* ("duty," literally) developed for daily prayer in Christian religious communities centuries ago and built in part upon Jewish synagogue liturgies that are even older. The presupposition of this form of prayer is that it be done regularly—*periodically*, to use a term that librarians will appreciate—and the period is twenty-four hours. This is one way of interpreting those biblical passages that refer to the obligation of the people of God to pray daily—giving thanks, confessing their faith and their faults, and praying for themselves and one another.

But the period for this kind of worship is also one year, the annual liturgical cycle. Thus, while it is indeed odd in a way for us to drop into this daily round of prayer once a year at our annual conference, it is appropriate for us to do so if we think of ourselves as celebrating and seeking strength for the daily round of our work. We give thanks for our common work, we confess our shared vision and our shortcomings (albeit selectively!), and we seek ways to help ourselves and support each other. Our common prayer here thus also represents the *devotion* that is our work as theological librarians.

Theological librarianship is done in the twofold setting of school and church. The library is one of four primary centers of theological education: classroom, chapel, field site, and library. The library is necessary to illuminate, sustain, and advance the relations between the church and the seminary, between the church and the field of theology (and, as well, the field of religious studies, which isn't the same as theology but can't be ignored by the pursuer of theology), and between the church and the world of learning more generally.

The function of the theological library is much like that of any other kind of library: to multiply experience. The theological library's primary function is that of widening experience beyond oneself, beyond one's own institution, beyond one's own church, beyond one's own religion. How? Through multiplying experience. The library invites and impels us beyond this our own world/time/age/order/*kosmos*, and the theological library invites and impels us beyond theology, or at least beyond theology as it is conventionally defined.

Within theological libraries and among theological librarians, there are varieties of sizes and scope, varieties of personality, and varieties of task. Small theological libraries, like small theological schools or small congregations, have most of the responsibilities and problems of larger ones, but the smaller ones have fewer resources. But scarcity of resources in no way diminishes responsibility. Students and teachers of theology in little places need to know the same things that students and teachers of theology in big places need to know, a kind of parity that librarians and administrators must keep constantly in mind if they are to support those students and teachers properly. New means of access to materials owned by other libraries have made it easier to provide this kind of support than it used to be, but it still isn't free, and it isn't automatic.

Theological libraries must all cope with four areas of work: services wanted, materials required to provide those services, a physical environment in which those services and materials are handled, and whatever systems and structures and staff we need in order to cope with the first three. These four areas of work, which correspond roughly to public services, collection development, administration, and technical services, are like puppies in a box: hard to confine, impossible to put back once they've escaped, and offering unlimited scope for diligence. The theological librarian, like the pastor, is a *broker*, a broker of a wide and not entirely predictable range of information and service, offered both programmatically and ad hoc. For this reason, the library's responsibility for the development of its collections is more than the sum of the interests of the people who happen to be on the faculty at any one time. Our collections have to reflect the shape of theological and related learning, not simply the curriculum our institution is using now.

Library administration enables services to be performed and materials to be handled. Administration is not an end in itself, though it does have the crucial role of linking the library to the rest of the school, to the church and to the world. Similarly, technical services aren't ends, either; they are means. But they are means necessary to the successful performance of other functions. Systems, structures, and especially staff are essential to providing service and maintaining collections. A library is not simply a warehouse for books, a point that must be made again and again to administrators and governing boards and even faculty members.

The theological librarian is a partner with classroom teachers, field education supervisors, faculty advisors, church office-bearers, and the whole people of God in theological education and formation for ministry. The library serves the classroom, the field site, and even the chapel; librarians interact (or should interact) with their colleagues in all three locations. The theological librarian serves the theological school in some ways as the professor of theological encyclopedia did in a nineteenth-century faculty: helping to shape questions, not just supply information to answer them; providing special expertise not otherwise available in the faculty; representing the widest possible sweep of the world of learning. And, we must remember, the theological librarian also serves as part of the school's administration. Consequently, it is impossible any longer for one person to serve as *the* theological librarian.

Every school must now depend, and in fact does so depend whether or not that dependence is recognized, upon a collegial body of librarians, not upon a single librarian, to do its work in this dimension of theological education. No one person can do everything that is involved in theological librarianship. In schools with more than one person carrying professional responsibility in the library, *all* those persons—not just the one designated as library director—are active partners in the educational enterprise and should be treated as colleagues. Even if an institution can afford only one staff person in its own library, that person's dependence upon other libraries and professional colleagues is regular and essential, even though the casual observer may be readily deceived into thinking it a one-person show. There *aren't* any one-person shows any more. *Every* school's dependence upon other schools' libraries is such now that its own library program must be shaped in maximum collaboration with other institutions. *Nobody* can go it alone any more.

Librarians are library-based colleagues of classroom-based and field-based theological teachers. We are all in this together, and as a result we ought to work together. Mutual responsibility and interdependence is the name of the game in theological librarianship just as it is in the church at large, and in the world of learning, and indeed in the world, period— however unrecognized that principle may be.

No template exists for the job of theological librarian, and none should. Different types of people, with differing skills and backgrounds and interests, are needed in theological librarianship. There isn't a single right model to which we all have to conform; we are as varied in our personalities and in our strengths and weaknesses as our patrons are. This Association exists in part to help us realize that diversity and learn from it, multiplying our experience in people as well as in bibliography.

There are different kinds of theological librarians, but there is one comprehensive set of tasks and relations for theological librarianship wherever it is practiced. No single model will do, and there is no template. But there *is* a consistently articulated consensus of responsibility; that's what professional identity is all about.

Librarians must be incorporated regularly into academic, organizational, and financial planning, as the guidelines of the Association of Theological Schools insist. Librarians, like libraries and theological faculties, are not simply sources of expense; they are assets to be developed. Continuing education, adequate compensation, and appropriate recognition are essential to that development. This is a word that our schools need to hear, but we must first hear it ourselves.

Librarianship is indeed a profession, and librarians like other professionals see their significance in terms of the services they provide to others. Effective theological librarians can't be technicians only, nor can we be classed as either inferior faculty or superior staff. We are something in ourselves, with a distinctive professional identity.

Effective theological librarians must have a sense of theology as a whole, though we can't be expected to be omnicompetent (nor should we expect omnicompetence of ourselves and then writhe in consequent guilt when we fail to achieve it). Effective theological librarians must have a sense of the church, whether or not we are ourselves communicant members of it. Effective theological librarians must have a sense of the community of scholarship, whether or not we are ourselves scholars. Effective theological librarians must have a care for people, though how that care is expressed may vary considerably in mode and degree of directness from one person to another, for we are not all alike.

Further, theological education can well be seen as ministry, and many theological librarians see their work in specific terms of vocation, in the theological sense. Theological librarianship is a worthy primary vocational option, and students should have it presented to them in that light, not just by a formal presentation at some point in their educational programs but by the way in which we who are theological librarians get incorporated *and incorporate ourselves* into the educational enterprise and experience. The recruitment and training of theological librarians should be set alongside the recruitment and training of theological teachers, or pastors, and of other ministries in the church and in the seminary. To these ends, then, at our annual conference we give thanks for our common calling and for each of the places in which we pursue it. We swap stories to commiserate and to learn. We share in the work of this Association to support each other in our common task. We widen our own experience with that of others here, just as at home we offer our patrons that opportunity in our libraries. We widen the circle of our work and our vision as librarians, and hence widen our prayer, in which we include those whom we serve: our patrons, our schools, our colleagues, our churches.

There is a word to be spread about libraries and librarians in theological education, and it is largely up to us to do the spreading, not by pleading and not by boasting, but straightforwardly and confidently, for the sake of the whole body of theological education. This is a word that our schools and our churches need to hear, but we must first hear it ourselves.

4

THEOLOGICAL LIBRARIANSHIP: CONTEXTS AND CONSTITUENCIES

24

Introduction

Michael Bramah

The five chapters in this part form a pair of "bookends." The first two come from the middle years of the 20th century. The next three, after a hiatus of over 25 years, come from the last 15 years of the century. In some ways the two appear to be worlds apart. But, in other, and equally significant, ways, there is a strong sense of continuity.

This part shifts our focus from the individual theological librarian to the environment in which that individual works. We are invited to think about the *contexts* in which the theological library is situated, and the constituencies that the theological library serves. The conundrum which faces the staffs of theological collections is that while much has remained constant in the past 50 years, much has also changed dramatically.

In simple terms, our traditional contexts have not changed. The environments in which we work continue to be the seminary library, the college or university theological library, or the academic library with significant theological holdings. What has changed almost beyond recognition, however, is the variety of ways in which our collections and our expertise is accessed. With the advent of the electronic age, one of our most significant environments is what has been referred to as the virtual library. Distance education, the electronic classroom, online serials, digitized full-text monographs, and digitized collections of images all contribute to the importance of our online accessibility. The ways in which we interact with both our users and our collections are hugely changed from 50 years ago. One expects that they will continue changing ever more rapidly in future. What does not change is our professional commitment to providing the best informed access to our collections for all our users.

The five chapters also invite us to examine our *constituencies*. The earlier chapters clearly identify our primary constituencies. These were, and remain, our students, administrators, and faculty. The more recent chapters make mention of other legitimate constituencies such as the local community, lay leaders, and other librarians. In the past decade there has been a resurgent interest in spirituality in North America; both traditional Jewish and Christian forms of spirituality, and many others, from aboriginal to New Age. We should consider encouraging these seekers to discover the riches we hold in our collections, and the wide-ranging knowledge of them that we can provide. We might also encourage our fellow professionals in the public library world and the broader secular academic world to avail themselves of our holdings and expertise for those seeking religious and theological information and resources from them. For many of us, the denomination that supports the academic institution is also an important constituency. With increasing emphasis on lay leadership and lay education our collections, knowledge, and facilities can all be put to beneficial use by those involved in these endeavours.

Although our primary constituencies remain our students, faculty, and administrators, what needs to be emphasized is that, for many of us, these primary constituencies have themselves changed radically in the last 50 years. Half a century ago the enterprise of theological education in mainstream North America was engaged in by those whom we now pejoratively call WASPs (the P standing as easily for Papists as for Protestants). Theological education was designed for the young, the single, the male, the campus resident, the candidate for ordination. Our constituencies now comprise a wide diversity of individuals: women; mature students; lesbians and gays; single parents; the divorced; seekers of a second, or even third, career; lay leaders; educators; activists; those who are academically interested, but agnostic, or even non-believers; those who would rock the boat, as soon as bail it (and it is not only students to whom I refer). Our goal as theological librarians remains constant: to provide all our users with the best collections and the most knowledgeable assistance possible.

What the most recent chapters propose are new and potentially fruitful partnerships with librarians not traditionally seen as having an interest, or expertise, in theology and religion, those public, corporate, and secular academic librarians referred to above. While this may prove useful, I believe we will derive more mutual benefit in forging links and strengthening ties with librarians in two other areas. One is the librarians, educators, and collections serving Jewish and Christian institutions outside North America. I am encouraged by our links with BETH, by the international guests attending the annual ATLA conference, and by the presence of Caribbean and Central American individual members in ATLA. What I hope will develop are bonds with those Jewish and Christian librarians and institutions in Africa, Asia, and South America, a kind of theological equivalent of IFLA. Christianity in the developing world is flourishing and vibrant, and thus has a great deal to offer us, both theologically and pastorally.

The other possibility I envisage is reaching out to those librarians and educators and their institutions that are certainly theological, but not Jewish or Christian. Modern North America and Europe are no longer the monolithic, and largely observant, Judeo-Christian societies of 50 years ago. They additionally embrace, and ought to welcome, a multicultural society including Muslim, Buddhist, Hindu, and other theological scholarship and beliefs. In the west we co-exist in a secular world that has little or no interest in any form of religion or theology. These non-Judeo-Christian professionals and their facilities throughout the world surely share our interest in theology, and in serving the people of God. Partnership with them ought to be explored and encouraged.

Christian and Jewish theological librarians will always be relevant in their traditional contexts and to their traditional constituencies. There is no question of this. Our real challenge now is to prove our relevance beyond our traditions; to a 21st century, both in North America and throughout the world that is full of paradoxes, within both Judaism and Christianity, and in their relations with other faiths and in their continued relevance to secular society.

25

Joint Panel Discussion: The Library in the Life of the Seminary
8th Annual Conference, Chicago, IL, 1954

Robert F. Beach, Moderator

INTRODUCTION TO PANEL
Robert F. Beach

It is proper that a joint conference on "Frontiers in Theological Education" devote serious attention to one of the most rapidly changing frontiers of all, i.e., *the library in the life of the seminary.* Do any of us doubt that this particular frontier is changing swiftly? If so, let him compare the situation described by Raymond Morris in the 1934 survey of theological education, familiar to most of us (*The Education of American Ministers*) with the summary as gathered in the figures of the AATS Standards Committee and presented at the joint conference at Louisville in June 1952. The record of development during two decades is striking, judged by almost any standard. As one of our very able seminary administrators has put it: "Ten years ago the weakest part of the seminary program was the library. In the last ten years more progress has been made in the library aspect of seminary work than in any other aspect. We have more books, we have better buildings, we have better facilities, we have more workers and better trained workers. We have better ideals, we have more adequate standards, we have better tools of helpfulness...."

Yet we are not here this afternoon to gloat over our progress, genuine and heartening as it is. We are here to seek mutual answers to basic questions relating to continuing inadequacies. Here are some of the primary questions upon which wisdom is needed:

1. How are we going to make the library a more effective, functioning, educational unit?
2. What philosophy must underlie our efforts?
3. What are the proper respective roles of the administration, the faculty, the library committee, the library staff, in creating and executing such a program?
4. What are our most serious problems? How and why do we so often "miss the boat"?

There would probably not be much theoretical argument in this company as to the importance of having the library command a central place in the seminary program. And I use the word central in more than a narrowly academic sense, for we are concerned with the training of the *whole man*. And yet, I suspect that with all the evidence of library progress, which may be easily cited, we stir uneasily when we realize how inadequately most of us do our jobs. . . . This afternoon, then, we want to be practical and specific in sharing our opinions.

May I proceed to introduce our panel participants and indicate our procedures. The theme we already have before us: "The library in the life of the seminary." Plans for this panel have been developed by Dr. Baker and myself and we have cleared at each step of the way with members of the AATS and ATLA. So this experience is fully a mutual one. Dr. Baker has asked me to serve as moderator, and we have drafted four other participants, each a lively and informed individual, each primed to make a specific contribution in a particular area. We have included a balance between administrators and librarians, between large and small schools, between (if the Far West will forgive me) different sections of the country, and finally, between (if Dr. Newhall will forgive me) men and women! Here, then, are the participants in the panel with their respective emphases:

President Walter N. Roberts: "The library program from the point of view of the Seminary Administration."
Dean Merrimon Cuninggim: "The library as the Faculty would like to see and have it."
Dr. Jannette Newhall: "The library program seen from the point of view of the library staff."
Professor Raymond Morris: "Orientation—an indispensable element in making the library useful."

Our plan is this: each panel participant will have 8–10 minutes for his prepared presentation. In order to save time and keep on the track, we shall save challenges and questions until the fourth participant has concluded. Following the final presentation, each topic will be fair bait for all of us, beginning with the panel members and moving rapidly to the floor. If you care to write down questions, there are cards "in the pews." This is your program. We are merely agents in getting it under way constructively.

THE LIBRARY FROM THE POINT OF VIEW OF THE SEMINARY ADMINISTRATION
Walter N. Roberts

We are trying to think together this afternoon. I would like to think with you for awhile having our thoughts to center around four basic principles of administration which, I am sure, you will recognize as being a condensed form of those seven principles given to us by the late Albert W. Beaven.

The first principle is outlining a task to be accomplished. The second, selecting the people to do this job. Third, placing the responsibility squarely on the shoulders of those selected to do the job and inspire them to achieve; and fourth, showing appreciation when the job is done.

Now, let us think for a moment about this first basic principle. What is the task to be done, to be accomplished? It would seem to me it is a four-fold task. In the first place we want adequate building or buildings. We want a collection of theological books and periodicals and all that goes with a good library. We want this library managed by an alert, competent, capable, and able librarian and library staff, and finally and exceedingly important we want a library program.

It is this last point that I want to amplify this afternoon. How to put across the program. There must be someone or several who have the vision of it. Get others to see the vision and keep enlarging the circle of the concerned, until the whole school, the whole seminary family is in on this program to make the library an effective, functioning unit in the school.

I think we need to remember the fact that the library is not a side issue in the school. It is something of major concern, of central importance and an integral part of the whole school. As we repeatedly say, it is the teammate of the classroom. It should be the study center of the school, a place where books and scholars are brought together in the happy relationship of learning.

This program also needs to be a long-range program because a great library isn't built in a single day or a single year, or even in a few years. Great libraries are built over a long period of time by people who are concerned about them.

In the second place we must select the people to do the job, and these people must enlist others in this program. I want to emphasize here this afternoon that this is a task of the whole school. While the leadership comes from the librarian, and with the librarian, the president, the dean, the library committee, the faculty, and the whole student body, it is an undertaking for the entire seminary family, the whole seminary community. It is my conviction that there are certain people that have here a primary responsibility. The president and the dean of the school, the librarian, the chairman of the library committee, the whole library committee itself, and then emanating from these persons primarily concerned should be an enlarging circle of the concerned. So that this program becomes a program of the whole school.

Another point along this line which it would seem is a fundamental educational principle in this matter is this basic principle that those who *initiate* a program are the ones to *execute* and *judge* the program. Therefore, the more people who come into this program of initiation are the very people who should also come into the program of execution and judging. So that there is created an attitude not of asking why do *they* do it this way, but rather, why do *we* do it this way? This is *our* program as a school and when I say the librarian, the library staff, the president, the dean, the chairman of the library committee, and the faculty, I say, too, the students are involved in this. It is a task for the entire seminary family.

The next point I would like to emphasize is that this responsibility must be placed squarely upon the shoulders of a group and this group inspired to achieve. It seems to me, we must remember that the librarian is the head of the library. The library committee should be an advisory committee and should not take over the administrative functions of the library.

Finally, I would like to emphasize this fourth point of administration, and that is recognition and appreciation for work well done. There is real personal satisfaction that any person has who does a job well. There is an inner compensation, an inner satisfaction and peace; but the need for more than that exists. A kindly word of appreciation is a tremendous force as a morale builder in the life of the school. This isn't a one-way street. This kindly word of appreciation needs to penetrate the entire school. A kindly word of appreciation to the librarian, to the assistant librarian, to the library staff, is tremendously helpful, a kindly word of appreciation on the part of the librarian to other members of the staff.

I often think of the morale that was engendered in the Royal Air Force in Britain during the war, and how those men gave themselves, and many of them gave their lives for the cause; but how much more ready they must have been when a kindly word of public appreciation was given to them by Winston Churchill when he said, "Never in the field of human conflict was so much owed by so many to so few." That is a real morale builder.

Let me summarize all that I have tried to say this afternoon by emphasizing this fact, that while there are those in the school primarily responsible for the library, yet the whole school is responsible for the library. This is the task of all of us and I know of nothing that will help more to improve the situation in all of our schools than this philosophy of feeling that this is our task of making the library an effective, functioning unit in the life of the school.

THE SEMINARY LIBRARY FROM THE
FACULTY POINT OF VIEW
Merrimon Cuninggim

It is pleasant that the topic does not call for embarrassing introspection. The subject does not necessitate treatment of the theme, "The Faculty from (what one imagines to be) the Librarian's Point of View." One is free to pretend that the faculty are not on trial for their use or misuse of the library, and that it is only the library itself under examination. This makes for irresponsible free-wheeling such as my administrative and bibliophilic colleagues on this panel would hardly condone, but which they can do nothing about.

What then do we of the faculty expect of the library? Let's get the obvious things out of the way first. We expect the library to perform at least two functions for us, and then a third of lesser importance if and when the staff have the time. The first of the necessary duties is, of course, the fulfillment of the role of instrument to the classroom. The library must be the *partner of the curriculum*, ready to meet the specific needs of all the courses we teach and all the seminars we learn from. We want our reserve shelves fully stocked ten minutes after we turn in the reading lists, and we want the library staff to set such inflexible regulations, with proper exceptions, as to prevent commuting students from taking out too many books too long, and from complaining that they can't take enough of them long enough. We want plenty of copies of those books to which we make repeated reference, and we want no squandering of library funds on multiple copies of some one title at the expense of broadening the collection. Most of all, we want the library staff so to manage the matter as to spare us completely from the queries of students as to the rules of the game. We are the doctors; the librarians are the pharmacists. It is the doctor who prescribes, but it is the pharmacist who prints the dosage on the bottle.

Here our interest, it is plain, is the *student.* The library's role of partnership to the classroom is that function which underlies the primacy of the student in the seminary's life. Thus the library must be prepared not only to meet the general needs of any one course but the specific needs of each of the students in that course, and of all the students in all the courses. The reserve shelf is only the beginning; the staff must also be prepared to give aid for outside reading, term papers, reports, special projects, theses, and dissertations. This is a large order; it calls for imagination and initiative as well as, of course, for encyclopedic information. Almost any library can handle the reserve shelf problem with adequacy, but those tasks which call for the staff to work closely with individual students are more difficult. For here the staff, willy-nilly, assumes at least part of the role of the teacher. This is the soundest argument of all for giving the professional librarian faculty status, faculty rank, and faculty salary—namely, that he is in truth, if he is doing his proper job, a member of the teaching corps. The librarian is not merely the teaching assistant but is the co-teacher of every course, for it is his duty to counsel, to guide, to instruct the students not merely in the uses of the book collection, but in the learning process itself.

The second necessary function puts us of the *faculty*, rather than the students, in the place of prime consideration. We expect the library to serve as *adequate resource for our independent research* and as measurable help in our scholarly endeavor. We should have no cause for omitting the names of the library staff from the appreciative prefaces of any books we write. Which means, we ought to be able to count on the staff for at least as much personal attention as the individual students receive. As much? More! Our articles and books ought to be more significant than our students' term papers and theses; thus the help we receive from the library staff should be more extensive, more intensive, and more indispensable. Considerations of size and competence of the staff will suggest practical limitations, but as to theoretical limitations of aid to the faculty members as scholars, there are none. If I really mean that, I suppose I'm suggesting that the librarian ought not to stop with collecting material or checking footnotes, but ought actually to write some of our books for us—which probably wouldn't be a bad idea! We wouldn't produce as many bad books.

The third expectation is subsidiary to these first two only in the same sense that, if something has to give, it is this one. Even the librarian can't work all the time, and if time and energy don't allow for all three, then the two functions already mentioned come first. But this third is still important, for it is the task of serving as the seminary's intellectual errand boy for the *community*. Here it is that my administrator's slip is showing for I have in mind the excellent *public relations function* which the library can perform by meeting as many as possible of the requests, both serious and frivolous, which come from friends and neighbors. Such service is not divorced from the academic program of the seminary, for it, like the students' searching, springs directly from the vitality and provocativeness of the faculty's intellectual life. Thus the faculty have a legitimate interest in seeing the library meet the community's needs as far as possible, for the scope and quality of the off-campus requests for aid are measures of our own effectiveness as leaders of thought, of our own success in building the intellectual reputation of the school.

Yet these, as I said, are the obvious things, the tangible things. And I think we of the faculty want something more than the smooth performance of such describable duties as aiding the students and ourselves, and, if possible, the community. We expect some intangibles, some things not so easy to recognize by actual patterns of behavior which the staff may establish, but which, perhaps, are even more real, in the sense of being even more determinative of the place which the library holds in the institution's life. These intangibles are qualities or moods or tempers which we expect the library to foster; I shall name three of them which seem to me to be essential.

First, we want the library to take the lead in the creation of an atmosphere of *earnestness*. Not urgency, for growth in understanding seldom comes through haste, and a library shouldn't be even a mental race track. Not solemnity, for pursuit of learning need not be humorless, and a library shouldn't be even an ideological morgue. Neither urgency nor solemnity but earnestness is the mood to be sought—that study is serious business, that there is no substitute for it, that devotion to its pursuit must be the manifest spirit of the seminary. This we look to the library to provide, in unhurried, good-tempered measure. When classroom gets shoddy, seminar gets picayune, or chapel gets saccharine, the library must call us all to a high earnestness of intellectual endeavor.

Secondly, we expect the library to assume an air of subservience. Like any well-ordered service station, it must do more than furnish gas and oil. It must perform chores of self-abasement—wipe our windshields clear, remove the grime of the dusty road, and map out journeys that lie ahead—and these it must do with an attitude of gladness and an invitation to come again. The faculty must believe that the library is their servant, not their arbiter, and equally the servant of their students, and of literally all who call upon it, as time and energy allow. This is more a matter of mood than it is of mere behavior, and when a library succeeds in creating it, that mood can grow to be part of the whole seminary spirit.

The third desirable temper may seem, initially, the contradiction of the second, for it is the possession of a degree of confidence, a sense of excellence, so great as to inspire in the faculty a recognition of the incompleteness of their own knowledge and the insufficiency of their own studies. Put simply, it is the library that must keep us humble; it is the spirit of *humility* in faculty and students that the library must create. Needless to say, this attitude is not brought about by pretensions to grandeur on the part of the librarian and his staff. On the contrary, the librarian himself must first possess this sincere humility, the realization of the inadequacy of his own intellectual endeavors, before he can communicate it to his faculty colleagues. But when he does, then he may find that a sense of awe before the limitless resources of the institution under his keeping grows and spreads throughout all the members of the academic community, and that the community is immeasurably richer because of its presence.

These things, then, are what the faculty expect of the library: that it develop a program of lively aid for the students, the faculty themselves, and when possible, even the community at large; and that it foster a spirit to undergird that program, a mood of earnestness, an attitude of subservience, and a sense of humility in all who enter its doors. Thus will the library play its rightful and highly significant part in the total life of the community.

THE LIBRARY STAFF VIEWS
THE LIBRARY PROGRAM
Jannette E. Newhall

Much of humor, usually on the gentle side, surrounds the librarian. There is the story of the Harvard librarian of an earlier generation, who was seen hurrying across the Yard. A colleague inquired about his hurry and was told: "All the books are on the shelves except one, and I am going to fetch that." This story is countered by the remark of the long-time director of the Harvard Divinity Library that the only books preserved, when the old University library burned, were those that were out on loan! Somewhere between these extremes we find the goal of contemporary library service.

The Purpose of the Library Program. The type of library program offered in the seminary should depend on the purpose of theological education itself. If the purpose of the seminary were to inculcate the views of its professors, only a few texts and dictionaries would be used. Certainly no library would be needed. But Mark Hopkins and his log are no longer regarded as fully ideal. Seminary students need rich contact with inspiring teachers, but they need far more. Since the aim of the seminary is to develop new generations of creative leaders for the church, the classroom and the library share in opportunities for confronting students with the great personalities and ideas of all ages and teaching them scholarly habits which will last a lifetime. Some required readings are essential, but "the library should not be allowed to become a reservoir for plagiarism" as Edward Clark has warned that it sometimes is.[1] Both faculty and library staff face the temptation of giving the student the "right" answers and the "best" books, when his greatest need may be to learn for himself the art of wise discrimination among lively options and stark contradictions. After all, seminary education is *graduate* education, and an important test of its ultimate significance is the degree to which it stimulates independent and critical reading and thinking. While the library exists to serve first the student and secondarily the faculty, its service must be aimed at indicating resources and methods of research rather than conclusions. The student who does not do the actual work of tracing etymologies or building bibliographies will be handicapped in his later scholarly work. Yet he has been cheated of a part of his rightful heritage if no professor or librarian has introduced him to the exhaustive national bibliographies of Germany and France, England and America, which supplement the card catalogs of even the greatest libraries. Although the staff write no term papers or faculty books, they can also be of service in calling attention to material in current journals and in general literature that might otherwise be missed. The best library program is a cooperative undertaking of faculty, librarians, and students.

The Library Collections. A mere count of the number of volumes in the library gives no sure criterion of adequacy. A century ago the average seminary curriculum rested heavily upon textbooks in theology, ecclesiastical history, and the classical languages of Biblical study. Today the sound theological library must be prepared with dictionaries and other resources to handle a score of ancient and modern languages, and to cover fields as diverse as pastoral counseling, ecumenics, and rural church administration. In many areas no texts are available, and whole courses may have to depend on periodical articles and pamphlets for their library support. In this connection, it may be noted that librarians should be consulted when changes in the curriculum are contemplated, for library collections must support the teaching program.

In building the book collection, faculty cooperation is sorely needed. Our professors might be roughly divided into the timid and the omnivorous when it comes to book selection. We all know men and women who never recommend a book for fear no one will read it. And we also know those eager professors who are so convinced of the vital importance of their own departments that they would gladly spend the entire book budget on their fields. Somewhere between these extremes are the conscientious scholars who keep alert to the best in contemporary literature, and who also watch for basic older works which their library lacks. Of them the librarian fervently says, "May their tribe increase." Students may also play a vital part in building the library collection, and incidentally learn new appreciation of its problems and opportunities. Last spring a group of Boston University students initiated a campaign for book gifts to the library. Many library conferences ensued and much searching of publishers' announcements, and regular book circulation increased by one-third because students were spending more time in the library.

A further important function of faculty and administration is as book-finders when estates are being settled or spring housecleaning is under way. There are still extensive collections, including important periodical sets, in private libraries of former faculty members and ministers that might well enrich our seminary libraries. Such gifts can, however, be a distinctly mixed blessing unless they are received with the understanding that only needed items must be kept by the library.

A Library Staff to Support the Program and Build the Collection. If the educational program of the library is the one we have outlined, and if the library covers the wide area indicated, it is clear that the librarian should be a scholar in his own right, broadly educated in theological studies, and possessing at least the basic library education. Too often in practice, if not in theory, our seminaries have regarded the work of the librarian as a glorified secretarial and bookkeeping job. They have not considered the kind of study necessary for the wise building of book collections, for reference guidance to students and to faculty in a dozen or more fields, or for the intelligent cataloging of volumes in many languages and on abstruse topics.

Ideally the librarian should have the same education as the faculty, should be an adequate scholar in one subject field besides library science, and have a better than average acquaintance with general literature. But such education, and the conviction that it can best be used in the vocation of theological librarianship, must be encouraged by the attitude of administration and faculty toward the library staff. In general, administrators have been more aware of the quality of the work done in libraries than have the faculty, and more ready to give it recognition and support—as is evidenced in pronouncements of the American Association of Theological Schools on many occasions. But there is still work to be done in the area which might be called "human relations" before the faculties of many of our schools will accept the librarian—especially if a woman—as an equal professional partner in the educational enterprise. But faculty status, when merited by education and performance, should not be denied, nor should it be in name only. The practice in some of our hoary institutions of naming a professor as "librarian" and employing an "assistant" to do the work should be recognized as subterfuge.

There is controversy over the question of teaching opportunities for the librarian outside the formal orientation to the library. However, the librarian who has training in a subject field should be able to make a contribution to the curriculum, and would grow in understanding of his task as he shared in both sides of the educational process. Furthermore, actual teaching of a content course may help to change the attitude of faculty and students toward the librarians, who sometimes feel like second-class citizens. One of my faculty colleagues suggested that librarians should be subservient—but the more common meaning of the term is "tamely subordinate, servile, obsequious," qualities which no self-respecting person could adopt. The librarian longs to be of *service* to all members of the seminary community, but with dignity and integrity, not servility.

Our libraries do far too little to support the research of our faculties and we look eagerly for resources and suggestions for fuller service to them. But at one point there is danger of real hostility between the library staff and the faculty, and that is on the thoughtless and perhaps selfish use of library books by some of the faculty. On most faculties there are a few professors who feel like one Harvard professor of my acquaintance who said, "No professor should be asked to return a book. His widow will bring it back!" But when a student assignment is due, and the librarian notes that a professor has the only available copy of the needed book, at least two of the trio are very unhappy.

Lest it seem that only the head librarian is of importance, let me add a few words about the supporting staff. Just as a seminary department has professors and instructors and student assistants, so the library has staff members with varied training and experience. If the institution is large enough, the library will have both professional staff members, with library training and at least two academic degrees, and a clerical staff, with secretarial or other equivalent training. Student assistants usually function at the clerical level. Through our Theological Library Association, we are encouraging superior people to prepare for theological librarianship. A number of outstanding candidates are now available. But library salary scales in our seminaries are still far below what public libraries are offering, and often below what young instructors in the same seminaries are receiving. If worthy staff members are to be held in the profession, obviously salaries and status should be commensurate with the tasks assigned them and the importance of their contributions to the seminaries.

ORIENTATION—AN INDISPENSABLE ELEMENT IN MAKING THE LIBRARY USEFUL
Raymond P. Morris

When Woodrow Wilson, then the newly elected President of Princeton, addressed the Western Association of Princeton Clubs at Cleveland he asserted that "When you settle what the chief end of life is, you have settled everything else." Perhaps this is an oversimplification of the way that the problems of life are met. It will serve to emphasize the need for knowing what is of chief importance in what one proposes to do. When we know what we want to do, many questions fall into their proper place of relative importance.

What is it that we are proposing to do in the libraries of the institutions represented here? There are many things we are trying to do. By these collections we become the conservators of culture. Libraries are, as Schopenhauer reminds us, the only sure and living memory of mankind. This memory is an important witness for the Christian faith. Such collections are necessary for research and creative work, apart from which the Christian impulse becomes sterile and falters. Also, there are aesthetic values, the values of the book collector, and so on. All of our libraries to a degree will participate in these ends.

I suggest, however, that for most of the institutions represented here, I should say even for all of us, the word which suggests more accurately the chief end we have in mind for our libraries is not a repository, or research, or aesthetics—it is education. Our primary interest is that the library may be an effective instrument of education. This is also the place we frequently fail. The goal which we want to keep before us to give our discussion its general orientation, and which should control the policies and actions in our libraries, is, to my mind, best suggested by the word education.

Perhaps we can define this word *education* to give it more concreteness in meaning. The disciplines employed in the education for the Christian ministry are largely those which, through association and rootage, have been the liberal arts or the humanities. Theological education, as is dictated both by our curricula and by the needs of our churches, tries to do two things: (1) to continue the general purpose of the liberal arts program, and (2) to give instruction for competence, skills, and needs peculiar to the Christian ministries. As to the former, John Henry Newman pretty much caught the heart of the matter when he spoke of education as "acquired illumination," as "a personal possession and an inward endowment," as something which "implies action upon our mental nature and the formation of character; it is something individual and permanent," says Newman, "and is commonly spoken of in connection with religion and virtue."[2] It seems to me that this is an indisputable assertion of the primary place of the person—the individual, mature and consecrated, disciplined and informed, the man of integrity, possessed of high native talent, who is a significant person. This is primary and essential for the successful vocation of the church. Theological education recognizes that there can be no substitute for the finished product, no substitute for the significant person. For we can depend upon the significant person to get on in the ministry, even though he may be lacking in skills like preaching or teaching, counseling, etc. At least we can depend upon him to recognize his inadequacies and to make compensation for them.

The second thing that professional theological education does, and I think that also this must be secondary in importance, is to give instruction for competence and skills peculiar to the profession; preaching, communication, pastoral work, counseling, educational guidance, administration, etc. The value and need for these skills, I believe, is obvious.

This is, of course, an oversimplification, but it may serve to direct our thinking to the great end we have in mind so that the few things we may say concerning the place of the book in education will fall into their proper perspective.

What is the place of the book or the library in all of this? In the first place, the library is very much a part of all of it and it cannot operate successfully unless it is in reality a part of all of it. A library is not a minor institution within a larger institution. It cannot be relegated to the realm of the clerical and administrative as apart from that which is instructional and educational. Theology and its cognate disciplines are primarily literary disciplines, and their mastery can only go forward with the assistance of the printed book. The fundamental place of Scripture in our Christian tradition is too obvious for there to be need to labor this point.

Being an integral part of it all, that is, of the educational process, it is important that those charged with the responsibility of directing the policies and the development and the day-to-day routines of the library must themselves understand the high end of theological education. They must know what their institution is proposing to do. They must get this picture clearly in their minds and it must become so imbedded in their feelings and convictions that they are prompted to return to it again and again as they complete their daily round. It will cause them to put first things first in the multitude of duties associated with their job. It will bring to the forefront the proper emphasis of their task. For whether we wish it or not, it is the simple fact that the general tone and outlook of the library, the atmosphere it creates, and the ultimate quality of its service is determined by those who are given the daily responsibility of its administration and care. This person must then be of such a stripe that the end result of his work will be a program and a product that is sharply marked by the educational needs of the school. For the library will cast a shadow or a light over the entire educational work of the school.

When we come to the place of the book in theological education, the formula we suggest is deceptively simple and obvious. If we wish to put it into a phrase, we can say that the educational end of the library is *to provide the right book at the right time*. This is not as easy as it may sound.

What do we mean by the right book? Obviously not just any book. The literature of the Christian tradition is enormous, it is ancient, varied and uneven, and in mass it is overwhelming. May I suggest that the crucial problem of our libraries may not be to collect even a significant percentage of this literature, and certainly not theological literature to the exclusion of supporting literature. Theology becomes distorted when studied in a vacuum. Multitudes of titles may serve only to confuse the student or to block his access to the thing desired, namely, the right book. Let us not be confused at this point. We are not debating the problem of literature and culture, the documentation of Christian traditions, or the provision for research facilities, etc. These problems are more or less common to all of us. We would only suggest in passing that a big library may not be the best library for the purpose of theological education. All of this is just another way of saying that our libraries must learn what they have not learned well, namely, that what makes a book collection important in a given situation is that by design and construction its resources are brought to bear upon the need to be met, and the most important need first of all. We should point with pride not to the size, but to the quality and pertinence of our book collections, the care and wisdom by which these have been selected, and the effectiveness by which they have been made accessible to those who wish to consult them.

A problem common to all of us is that we must compete for the time of the student. Three years of a person's life, with the heterogeneous educational background of the men going into the modern Protestant ministry, with all of the extracurricular activities our students feel they must engage in, with the demands for field work, etc., which divides their interest, time, and energies: three years is a short time to prepare a man for the ministry. The element of time is too precious to place before our students library equipment that is mediocre and does not meet the need.

Now, we know too much about education to suggest that the book is all of it. The whole person goes to school and the whole experience is one of growth in which the book plays but a role, an important role, but not the only role. On the other hand, we need to make no apology for the place of the book in education. It is one of the most productive insights of Christian experience that the human soul grows through contemplation of that which is great and good. This is the highest utility of liberal education. This is the greatest argument for the place of the book. If we may refer to Newman once again where he says:

> Good is not only good, but reproductive of good; this is one of its attributes; nothing is excellent, beautiful, perfect, desirable for its own sake, but it overflows, and spreads the likeness of itself all around it. Good is prolific, it is not only good to the eye, but to the taste; it not only attracts us, but it communicates itself; it excites first our admiration and love, then our desire and our gratitude, and that in proportion to its intenseness and fullness in particular instances. A great good will impart great good.[3]

The formula suggested was to provide the right book *at the right time.* By the right time, we mean *the time that the book is needed.* In the context of learning, of study, of contemplation, of creative work, nothing is more exasperating or frustrating or destructive of getting ahead than to know that the book, or the tool, or the information you need is not at hand. It stops the creative process cold. Conversely, no book will ever be quite as useful as that which may be consulted when one is working at the peak of intensity and concentration, when momentum is at hand. In teaching or preaching or creative literary endeavor there are no substitutes for leisure, for the quiet place of study, or for the atmosphere which is created when one is surrounded by his tools and his books. These ingredients are fundamental, they are crucial.

These are the surroundings in which the human spirit works to its best advantage. The problem of the institutional library is to reproduce these surroundings in so far as it is able.

We need the right book at the right time. In application this means that it is important that books and resources must be made accessible. A library is more than a collection of books; it is a collection of books which has been brought into order. Libraries do this in part through the construction of card catalogs and subject classifications. These are of utmost importance and are indispensable if we are to make the resources of the library accessible quickly to the clientele. No one who knows his business belittles this. Anyone who knows his business also knows that a person does not learn best to judge or to use books by looking at titles in a card catalog. Certainly one does not attain maturity in the use of books by relying upon the few titles which have been segregated on some professor's reserve shelf, and that is about all that some of our students learn about the use of a library or about books. One of the most observable and distressing failures in theological education, as I have been able to observe it, and I believe that this is not an unfair judgment, is that we do not teach our students how to judge and evaluate books, how to keep somewhat abreast in a field of endeavor, how to work alone without guidance and promptings and recommendations and the other "props." In this respect the product of our schools is immature. People learn much in their use or judgment of books by using them in their natural habitats, that is, with other books. Our libraries should be designed, in so far as this is possible, for the maximum ease of access to its resources.

There is one further and important observation which should be made about the library as an instrument of education. Library service, that is, good library service, the kind of library service we are after, is a continuous teaching process. It is a teaching process if the personnel responsible for library operations is capable of teaching. The fact that much library service does not appear as an effective teaching process has very little bearing upon the potential of the situation. I call to your attention these simple facts; there is no other personnel in our institutions who is at once more available or more likely to be present when a student needs help and direction in the use of books than is the librarian. There is no time when a student is more teachable than when he wants help. These two factors alone will suggest the educational potential in the situation. This is the critical moment in the educational process. These situations filled with such potential for educational effort are the constant ingredients of library service, they are the daily work of the librarian. It is true that the "blind cannot lead the blind," but it is also true that one may lead "a mule to water but not make him drink." The indispensable ingredients for counseling or for education are a sense of need and a desire to be helped. Here is the most fruitful context of the learning process. The librarian meets the student at this fruitful context, at this crucial moment again and again. Librarians can teach if they are capable of teaching, and if they do not teach they are missing the very thing which makes their jobs exciting and most useful to their institutions. That they must be persons of stature and ability is not to be debated. That much remains to be desired in this matter we freely confess. Our purpose at this time is only to suggest the need and the possibilities which are in the situation.

NOTES

1. Edward M. Clark, "How to Motivate Student Use of the Library," *A.A.U.P. Bulletin* 39 (1953): 412.

2. John Henry Newman, *The Idea of a University* (Chicago: Loyola University Press, 1927), 131.

3. Newman, *The Idea of a University*, 184.

26

Some Thoughts on the Joint Theological School–Liberal Arts College Library
14th Annual Conference, St. Paul, MN, 1960

Arthur E. Jones Jr.

From the rather peculiar vantage point of a library that College and Research Libraries has strangely bracketed with Columbia and Cornell for statistical purposes, I have frequently been struck by the discrepancies between the situation in which I find myself and what would seem to be the general image, if we can borrow the word from the popular jargon of the day, of the theological library. While I have to deal with both undergraduates and professional or graduate students, with both theologians and physicists, with such publications as *Chem Abstracts*, *PMLA*, and the *Economist* as well as *New Testament Abstracts*, *Qumran Review*, and *Theologisçhe Literaturzeitung*, most of our ATLA thinking postulates a different kind of situation. Somehow the theological school library becomes, under these circumstances, an abstraction. It is one of those arbitrary entities like literary style apart from content or a philosophical idea apart from the social and environmental conditions of its propounders or a football team's passing attack apart from its ground game. In other words, "theological school library," as a term, represents a sort of ideal, abstracted from a real situation for the purposes of analysis, discussion, and, amusing as it may seem, ease of problem solving.

All this is merely a rather fanciful explanation of why I have come to be particularly aware of some of the ramifications of the problems which involve the theological library's relationship to its educational institution. But the point is that I am not, in this, unique. A number of our members are in the same position of having a single library to serve both theological seminary and liberal arts college educational programs. Others are in the middle of debates as to whether the separation of libraries or the joining of them is educationally and administratively preferable.

I seek to use this paper merely to sum up some arguments and to share some thoughts and experiences on the subject of the joint liberal arts college–theological school library which it seems to me may be worth airing. No one, I hope, is expecting me to say that either the joint library or the separate theological library is inherently superior under all circumstances. No one would or should make that kind of claim. On the other hand, to go back to that image of the theological school which I mentioned earlier, I would not be averse to redressing some of the balance. The U.S. Department of Education's definition of a theological school as an institution, not affiliated with a university, giving training in theology leading to a B.D. degree may symbolize a kind of bias, or at least prejudicial predetermination, that could stand some correction. Some of the same attitude appears in the AATS and even in its Standards for Theological Libraries. There, and in a good many places, it appears assumed that the theological school library is a separate institution serving a separate institution and that this is the situation as it is and, by rights, ought to be. In actuality, many of us are in a somewhat different country, and I, for one, am not at all convinced that the difference is wholly disadvantageous. At any rate, there needs some exploration of divergences from the usual image and perhaps more awareness of their implications for our ever-present problems.

At first glance, the problem of the desirability of the separateness of the theological library from other libraries would seem to be tied to the desirability of separateness of the theological school itself. Clearly there are both advantages and disadvantages to the theological school's affiliation with a liberal arts college or a university. The advantages include the possibility afforded for direct contact with the so-called secular fields of knowledge represented by other disciplines. If the theologian is to speak intelligently and intelligibly in this modern world, he must be acquainted with the presuppositions, the evidence, and the conclusions of those who think in the areas of physics and psychology, of philosophy and sociology. The intellectual dialogue between the Church and the world may find one of its most direct expressions in the conversations between members of the theological school and representatives of the full range of subjects taught in colleges and universities. In any event, if the Church is to communicate and to provide moral and spiritual leadership, there must be understanding and engagement, and affiliation may be a means to these ends. In addition to what may be called the theoretical advantages of seminary affiliation, there are such practical advantages as the sharing of cultural and educational programs and the financial benefits from larger operations.

On the other hand, the dangers which may attend affiliation are no less real. The theological school may be dwarfed by the growth of other components. An administration may emerge which either does not understand or is not in sympathy with the nature and goal of theological education. And there are sufficient numbers of seminaries which have had to withdraw from universities in order to maintain their own integrity to underscore both the danger itself and the difficulty of establishing satisfactory structural means of avoiding it. Another peril to the theological school, at least one sometimes mentioned, is the possible effect of lower academic standards in the school with which it is associated. Generally speaking, however, the reverse situation is just as likely. The facts seem to indicate fairly clearly, for instance, that educational qualifications for theological schools do not compare very favorably with those for graduate schools of comparable standing. At least this last argument seems one with little real relevance.

So far as the separation of the theological school itself as an institution is concerned, the trend of recent years has been toward its increase. We have the rather curious situation in which weight of accreditation standards, the emphasis on special professional preparation, and some unfortunate past experience with secularized administrations have tended toward the separation of theological schools from colleges and universities and have encouraged separate libraries. One is tempted to remark that theology, which was once regarded as the queen of the sciences and the handmaiden of knowledge, has sometimes been packed off to a nunnery.

At the same time that the general movement has been toward separation, the seminary curriculum has been broadened; subjects previously compartmentalized as non-theological have been found to bear close relationship to theological training, and theological education has increasingly aimed at ministries other than the pastoral pulpit and widened as it has done so. The recently established honors program at Perkins School of Theology might be cited in this latter connection. Teaching, religious education, chaplaincies, even theological librarianship are increasingly recognized as legitimate ends of theological education and as requiring new means or emphases.

On the whole, there seem to be cogent reasons to support the separateness and distinctiveness of theological education, although there may be advantages to affiliation. The presupposition of a vocation, the essential individual commitment to Christ, and the school's peculiar relation to the Church make for an educational institution with unique characteristics, but supposing we grant the peculiar separateness of the theological school or seminary, even where it is a member of a university or affiliated with a liberal arts college, there seems no necessary reason that its library need be separate, *provided* that adequate safeguards can be established and maintained to insure continuing support for the theological collection and services. But of course, this is the main problem. At least, however, we need to recognize that so far as materials needed for theological study and research are concerned, there is far less reason for separation of a theological library from a liberal arts or university library than there is for the separation of libraries of medicine and law, where the subject matter is far more rigidly compartmentalized, and that there is really no more reason to build a separate library and maintain separate facilities for theological studies than for graduate or professional study of literature, history, or political science.

If neither the nature of theological study nor the materials upon which theological study is based demand separate library facilities, the case for the joint library is made much stronger by consideration of finances, the convenience of the theological student and faculty, and efficiency in the library's technical services. Financially it is axiomatic that you get more for your money in larger packages. Up to the point where Parkinson's Law takes effect, joint operation is cheaper and more efficient. At least where the staff is larger, it is possible to make adjustments to enable professional staff to confine themselves more to professional tasks. Where the collection is larger and more varied it is a distinct aid to convenience to have materials readily at hand, rather than across the quadrangle, somewhere in the same city, or available at a regional center.

Jules Moreau, in discussing serials programs for theological libraries in a paper presented to this group last year in Toronto, underlined the problems created by the multiplication of serials and the increasing fragmentation of special fields to the point where almost no theological library can afford to acquire all of the materials which its users would like to have available. His solution is a degree of completeness in indexes and bibliographies, an emphasis upon the abstracting and summarizing publications, and cooperative accessions where this is geographically possible. With this there can be no quarrelling; it is sound and applies eventually in any library's situation, but surely we know also that our service is better, our patrons happier if we can produce material from our own shelves rather than go through the processes of acquiring it from some other place. And the point is that we have a better chance of producing it and thereby helping to spark that extra research, that trip up an alley of investigation, if our collection is larger and more varied than the budgetary limitations and more strictly defined subject limitations of the theological collection permit.

Moreau also said something in the same ATLA paper that was so well said and has such pertinence to connections between the liberal arts library facilities and those of the theological school that it deserves repetition here. As he put it,

A theological school is an academic institution. Theology is, therefore, . . . an academic discipline upon which it is incumbent that it listen to other disciplines and ask them questions. Further it is demanded of theology that it observe the best of academic methods in order to maintain its own integrity among the family of academic disciplines. It follows naturally that theological education is a process of engaging students in that responsible dialogue wherein disciplines admonish, supplement, and even support one another. In such an atmosphere and on such grounds, the total enterprise of theological study is committed to nothing less than the same goal as the liberal educator but for reasons which ought to be infinitely clearer to the theological educator.[1]

And, while the subject is still the theoretical advantages of the joint library, Ruth Eisenhart's report on the potential of cooperative cataloging in the same issue of the *Proceedings*[2] ought to stir us to further thought. She called attention to the number of theological school libraries which do not have what other libraries would regard as essential bibliographic aids to cataloging: the *National Union Catalog*, the British *National Bibliography*, perhaps even the new *Book Publishing Record*, and then there are the *Library of Congress—Books Subjects*, the *Library of Congress Catalog of Printed Cards*, and the *British Museum Catalog,* to stick to English-language tools. How much would the joint library situation make additional bibliographies of this sort available? If it is a question of funds, I estimate that the presence of the college library at Drew is worth at least $4,000 a year to the book budget of the theological school or that about one-fifth of the college budget for books, periodicals, and binding goes for the purchase of materials important to the library of the theological school. And, of course, something like the same figures pertain in the reverse situation. General encyclopedias; daily newspapers; standard editions of historical and literary figures, like Abbott's edition of Cromwell or the recent editions of Donne or Dryden; general periodicals, from the weekly news magazines to the *American Scholar* and *Yale Review*; even, if we follow the lead of Stanley Hopper and Tom Driver, much contemporary fiction, poetry, and drama; all these and much more are needs common to both the theological school library and the liberal arts college library if each is to perform its proper function. To separate the libraries and then to try to bring them back together again by means of involved union catalogs or some of the ventures that run under the rubric of "cooperative" seems a kind of perverse procedure.

But we have been talking in terms of theory, and in theory it would be difficult to argue that the advantages are not with the joint library. Practically, however, there are serious problems all along the line that demand intelligent anticipation and built-in safeguards or else the theoretical advantages are overwhelmed in practical disadvantages.

If the theological library is to serve theological education effectively within the framework of the joint library system, there must be some degree of separateness, even beyond, I would say, the separateness which pertains in those libraries which have embraced the subject division arrangement, although these libraries, admittedly mostly public libraries, may supply a kind of example and rationale. First, there needs to be separate budgeting for books, periodicals, and microfilm materials. Second, there should be, ideally, separate and distinct divisions in some staff areas of responsibility. And last, in this minimal degree of separation, there ought to be some physical facilities within the library building given over primarily to theological studies. Without these, the service of the theological library to the theological school is seriously threatened by developments which we have already glanced at, and it would be impossible to apply very usefully any kind of standards for the evaluation of library functioning.

I should insist upon separate book budgeting as essential, even though it may mean an arbitrary assignment of some periodical subscriptions and reference purchases. Separate budgeting should not, I think, be necessary for binding or such library expenses as cataloging and circulation supplies, mimeographing, postage, telephone, and equipment. In these instances, as with staff salaries generally, it is probably enough if a fair and proportionate share of the expense is assigned to the theological school. No one has yet worked out a formula, however, for this assignment. The main thing is to avoid usurpation of funds and to assure to faculty and students in theological studies a continued financial base for support of the theological curriculum and basic research.

Whether the head librarian in the joint theological school–liberal arts college should have theological training is a moot point. This much is certain; there must be special knowledge and competence in the overall responsibility for the theological collection. And if the administrative head of the joint library is not theologically trained, the collection needs the supervision of a professional member of the library staff who is so trained. General surveillance by a faculty committee of the theological school is not enough, although such a committee must be strongly recommended. A special theological school library committee which also forms a portion of the general library committee offers the greatest potential assistance. It should go without saying also that theological training is important almost equally in reference work with theological students as in supervision of the acquisition program. It is less essential, although at times most helpful, if some members of the cataloging staff have some theological training.

Obviously what must be guarded against is the danger that the theological school's library, services as well as collection, will be so overshadowed, diminished, or absorbed that its support of the theological school and its curriculum is impaired. The danger, particularly now, is that expanding enrollments in the colleges, not matched by seminary enrollment growth, and the greater attractiveness or profit from undergraduate tuitions, will choke the growth of the theological school library's educational service and seriously impede advancement. It remains easier to get competent library trained personnel than competent library trained personnel with theological training. And the doctrine of the greatest good for the greatest number, although utilitarian, may well pose serious problems.

For these reasons, it is well to add a third general requirement for the theological library in the joint library system. There should be adequate provision for a specialized reference collection housed with seating arrangements somewhat higher than the 30 per cent of the student body that is most usually recommended for general undergraduate libraries. Drew solves this problem with a theological school reading room housing both special reference collection and course reserves and by having this reading room adjacent to the 200 stack level. Something of this sort of physical arrangement seems inescapable.

Adding up this collection of observations, theories, and judgments about the joint library, I can only repeat that there are strong reasons why the library of a liberal arts college and an affiliated theological school ought to be housed together. (There are even strong reasons for the affiliation in the first place.) These we need to recognize and take into account. At the same time much more thought needs to be given to the means whereby the ends that we project for theological libraries generally may be safeguarded within the institutions that have joint libraries. Whatever the agency by which they have been joined, I am willing to say let no man put asunder. But we may well need additional exploration of the special demands which this type library makes and some special standards and criteria to help assure its effectiveness and take advantage of its assets. We ought not to leave a vacuum to be filled by mere expediency.

NOTES

1. Jules Moreau, "A Serials Program for Theological Libraries: A Plea for More Cooperation in Cooperative Accession," *Summary of Proceedings, 13th Annual Conference of the American Theological Library Association* (Chicago: ATLA, 1959): 57.

2. Ruth C. Eisenhart, "Cooperative Cataloging: Dream or Reality?" *Summary of Proceedings, 13th Annual Conference of the American Theological Library Association* (Chicago: ATLA, 1959).

27

The Theological Library: Servant or Partner?

41st Annual Conference, Berkeley, CA, 1987

Claude Welch

I suggested as a title for this talk—and I do intend this as a discussion piece more than as a formal address—"The Theological Library: Servant or Partner?" I was initially tempted to pose the contrast as one between a master/ slave or father/stepchild relation and a marriage relation—but the servant/ partner contrast probably better expresses the contrast I want to draw, even through it is not quite the right metaphor.

The point I shall want to suggest is really very simple. You may write it off as an absurd oversimplification or an idle dream. But then it may be a not unreasonable goal. So let us, to borrow a Kierkegaardian phrase, call it an "experiment in thought" relative to the question "do theological libraries have a future?" or, better said, "what sort of future can and should theological libraries have?" To this kind of question specifically I shall come by and by.

First, however, a few disclaimers regarding my own qualifications to speak on this subject. I'm not a librarian, but an old-fashioned scholar who likes to walk up and down the stacks and browse to see what our librarians have acquired in the subject matters that interest me. I've had no training in library science. I have only a superficial and passing acquaintance with all the new technology of library operation, and I have never done a computer bibliographic search in support of my own studies. Maybe I should have, but actually I have some serious questions whether computer searching is the right model for advance in much of theology and historical interpretation. Surely that can be vital for the natural sciences, where one must build on the latest data and discoveries of others and must know where current comparable research is going on. And in certain areas of the theological disciplines, particularly involving detailed textual analysis, computer searching and analysis can be of enormous value and time-saving. But I am not so sure it is essential for me. For example, must I see all the recent articles and books on Horace Bushnell and Ernst Troeltsch in order to understand them and to say something wise, or at least illuminating and useful, especially in view of the flood of publications in theology and religion of recent years? There is far too little good literature, and there is also too much junk that is published.

Yet I have been, and continue to be, profoundly interested in the theological library as an operation. I have expended a great deal of energy in the past sixteen years on the construction of the new Graduate Theological Union library, and as GTU Dean, or Dean and President, I have been more or less in charge of that library's operation and especially its finances over that time. Further, as nominal chair of the ATS/ATLA Joint Committee on Library Resources, I have had the need to study carefully Stephen Peterson's Project 2000 Final Report, "Theological Libraries for the Twenty-first Century."[1] My colleagues on that committee—Tom Gillespie, David Green, Channing Jeschke, Jean-Marc Laporte, Sara Lyons, and Steve Peterson—have planted some seeds and stimulated me to think more reflectively about the nature and future of theological libraries in general. It is mainly out of such experiences as these that I venture to say anything at all, though I would not want my colleagues on the joint committee to be blamed for any conclusions that I have drawn, even if I borrow unashamedly from their suggestions.

A WORD ON THE EXPERIENCE
OF THE JOINT COMMITTEE

I should, however, as a further preliminary, comment briefly on some of our experience in that committee. The first task we undertook was simply (!?) to stimulate discussion of the Peterson report in theological schools generally, particularly by faculty and administrators. Although in reporting to the 1986 biennial meeting of ATS I tried to put the best face on the results, one must finally say that this endeavor did not meet with resounding success. You might even say it was a failure. As best we can determine, by survey and hearsay, the Project 2000 Report was attended to mostly by library staff in a fair number of theological schools. A few seminary presidents and deans seem to have been aware of the report, even before our attempt at consciousness-raising, but their response was largely to refer it to their librarians. And even after our efforts to call attention to what we believe to be a penetrating, often troubling, and by implication prophetic analysis, faculties seem hardly to have been interested at all. We have done better this past year, I think, by offering some bribes in the form of competitive awards to schools that would make serious proposals to take up some of the kinds of questions raised by the report.

Now I don't want to sound simply negative or cynical here. Some of Peterson's major recommendations are in fact being acted on by this association (whether as a direct result of his report is not important). For example, in relation to material resources, he urged the planning and funding of "a major inter-institutional preservation program." And the ATLA Preservation Project has made a noble start on this, to the point indeed of being a possible model for preservation efforts in other fields. Also, Peterson's argument for the necessity of a theological library collection profile is being addressed in a preliminary way by the ATLA Inventory Project—though I do not see that the conceptualization of this problem and project is as clear as it ought to be. We shall have to see what comes out of the first phase of the inventory and then someone can decide how to get the really interesting data. (After all, nobody will be helped much by discovering that we have 175 look-alike theological libraries.)

On the other hand, nothing significant has been done about Peterson's third major recommendation relative to material resources, namely that "a research and planning project is needed to expedite the development of resources for the study and understanding of Third World Christianity." That is perhaps not surprising because this is an exceedingly complex problem which will call for a kind of coordination and cooperation quite beyond any present realization. Third World materials are collected in a very few places, and given the nature of the materials this probably must be the case. Here is a clear illustration of the importance of access rather than possession. Such materials cannot and need not be everywhere. What is necessary is *accessibility*, which can be provided by current technology, even to the point of document delivery on demand, if the structures of cooperation can be created.

The latter point, incidentally, my colleagues on the joint committee have shown me to be valid also with respect to the preservation in microform of the materials that are now self-destructing. Theological and other schools ought to support the preservation project not in order to possess all those microfiche, but so that the material will be permanently accessible to whoever wants and needs it.

But I don't want to fill up my time by going through all of the kinds of recommendations that Peterson has made. Rather, I want to go back in a way to the question why theological schools, and particularly their faculties, have not yet gotten excited about the Peterson report or about the future of their libraries in general. The answer to that question, which I think is implicit in the report and which I want to propose more directly, is something like this: what is called for is a radical reconception of the role of the theological library in the life of the theological school.

CONTEXTS AND PARAMETERS
FOR RECONCEPTION

In order to move toward that kind of reconception, we need to note at least briefly some of the "givens" in the current theological school and theological library scene to which any reorientation must attend. There are both problems and possibilities. I list only a few, not necessarily in order of importance.

Need I mention the problems of financial support? I do so mainly in order to comment that I believe these are becoming more intense. Theological schools are hurting, at least most of those related to ATS and ATLA. They will probably hurt more in the future, and not merely because of continued inflation, be it modest or great, but also because of weakening of support from the churches, which in turn is related to the continuing marginalization of the institutionalized churches in society as a whole, at least in our society, and because of continuing decline in resident theological school enrollments. To be sure, ATS figures seem to show a modest increase over the past decade, but this is entirely attributable to the increase in the number of female students, a development surely to be celebrated but one which, especially when combined with the growth of part-time and nonresident study, raises questions about the function, the resource base, and the direction of theological education.

Another kind of problem derives from the fact that theological faculty members are feeling themselves strained to the very limit of their resources by the multiplication of responsibilities that theological schools have assumed. This is often cited as a reason for the apparent decline in research and publication by theological faculty, a decline the ATS Council on Theological Scholarship and Research, chaired by Schubert Ogden, has documented. In our own situation in the GTU, the additional burden on faculty is often alleged to be due to involvement in the GTU's doctoral and master's programs, with the extra committee and advising tasks that ensue, and a consequent competition between "graduate" and "professional" educational tasks. Frankly, I don't accept that interpretation, at least as it refers to constriction of time for research and publication, for good graduate study supervision is a stimulus rather than a hindrance to research. Nor do I accept the hypothesis that the pressures result from the incorporation of new fields and foci of study into the theological curriculum.

Rather, apart from the quite wasteful duplication of effort among the

GTU schools, which may be a by-product of the relatively small size of those institutions, I see the growing pressures on our faculties as in large part a direct consequence of the increasing demands of continuing and extension education, and some of my faculty colleagues confirm this judgment. My impression is that nearly every faculty member in the GTU is spending a day or more a week, to say nothing of weekends, on off-campus activities in extension and continuing education programs, even in recruitment and fund-raising. This is not to deny the validity of those sorts of educational activities, for I agree that the responsibilities of theological schools must more and more include lay education and continuing education. My complaint is rather that these responsibilities are not creatively dealt with simply by laying them on the backs of faculty who are sent hither and yon to do the job.

Related to that problem is the fact that the entire function of the theological school is now under review. More and more in recent generations, it seems to me, the theological school has tended to be understood as a "trade school" for the training of religious professional functionaries rather than as a center of wisdom and inquiry for church and society.

Here it is worth recalling the kind of critique that Edward Farley has made in his recent book *Theologia*.[2] To be candid, the import of Farley's term "Theologia" does not always come through clearly to me. And his attribution of the problems to the particular developments of "theological encyclopedia" in the nineteenth century does not persuade me fully, though his account of those developments is illuminating history. Yet at least two elements of Farley's critique are important. One is the insistence that theology ought to be done as a whole, unified way of thinking, not as a concatenation of independent inquiries subject to unrelated disciplinary norms, even warring factions. The other element, more directly relevant to my present concern, is his showing, particularly well demonstrated for the Protestant world, of the extent to which theological education has come to be understood simply as clergy education, which tends to divert the theological school from being the center of learning for the whole church into being a mere training school for ecclesiastical, professional functionaries. That is surely inadequate to a proper theological vision. And in my experience, the "professional culture" of the typical theological student is very close to the antithesis of education.

Finally, and obviously germane to the role of the theological library, I note some changes in the patterns of instruction. It seems to me that faculty are relying less and less on "reserve lists" of books in the library and more and more on student purchase of paperbacks and on "handouts" of duplicated chapters and sections, etc. This means less reliance on the library for the bulk of theological instruction. The question can then be asked, "Is a theological library necessary for basic classroom-oriented theological study?" To put the matter in the quite personal terms of our GTU experience: given some of these changes in teaching patterns, particularly at the elementary level, member schools of the GTU might well ask, and have asked, "Why should we pay more than a thousand dollars a year per student and faculty member to support a library for our professional degree programs (assuming of course that the principal purpose of those programs is to train prospective clergy)?" And in all candor I would have to reply, "You shouldn't." Because the library's purpose is much broader; *it is not derivative from the classroom.* I shall return to that point. But let me suggest further a couple of the positive possibilities and opportunities that seem to me "givens" in the current scene.

Among the most promising possibilities is surely the technological advance of recent decades, ranging from computer storage, retrieval, and transmission to new bibliographical tools and controls, to automated circulation, to vast information networks which can provide previously unheard-of access to materials, and also to such things as decentralized instruction through videotape and satellites. Most important perhaps are the possibilities, through microcomputers, of a new "synergism between teaching faculty and library," as Steve Peterson has put it in his own recent reflections of Project 2000: "Because the same files, texts, and data are now as accessible to faculty members via micro-computers as they have been to librarians via terminal connections to mainframe installations, new patterns of cooperation are possible." So also, as Steve goes on to say, greatly intensified networks among libraries are feasible so that one can envisage "non-geographically determined consortia"—"electronic technologies now make it possible for institutions separated by substantial distances (there really are no effective limits) to establish viable and sophisticated cooperative library programs."

One must be careful here about prediction. I don't want to make the kind of mistake I made a dozen years ago when I was greatly enamored with microfiche reproduction and urged that never again should periodicals be bound, but should be preserved only in microform, and predicted that every working faculty member would find a microfiche reader as indispensable as a typewriter and might have most of his/her library in a file box on the desk. Obviously, that didn't catch on. We are going to have to deal with microform for preservation, but probably not for ordinary usage. Yet the computer has caught on dramatically, and I believe the future is quite different with respect to computer usage and even video transmission. (It bemuses me that there has been such widespread complaint about screen viewing for microfiche and microfilm, but something close to an addiction to the computer and word processor screen.)

A different kind of possibility stems from the call of the ATS for "globalization" in theological education.[3] Unhappily, much of that discussion has neglected the fact that Christianity, even in America, lives in a religiously pluralistic context and that internationally Christianity can exist only in engagement with non-Christian religions. And little attention has been paid to the role of libraries in documenting the literature of other religions. Nevertheless, I see the call for globalization, properly extended, as a great positive "given" in the current scene, and it appears to me that basic reconsideration of the relation of Christianity to other religious, i.e., of the nature of interreligious dialogue, is becoming more and more important in the theological enterprise. (And I may note here the forthcoming Third International Conference on Buddhist-Christian Relations, to be held at the GTU in August 1987.)

TOWARD A FUNDAMENTAL RECONCEPTION

According to the received tradition, the theological library is essentially only a support service; or, to use some of the more abominable language I have heard, a "service bureau." The faculty are the real educators, the teaching and research group. The library is an adjunct or a tool for the real business of the theological school, which is the training of religious professionals. The library is thus supposed to be curriculum- or course-driven, though it also serves the research interest of faculty. Collection policy is determined by those curricular and research parameters. The library's proper constituency is students, mainly in M.Div. programs, and faculty. The librarian is not looked upon as a proper faculty colleague (which is surely one reason why faculties have been so little interested in such things as the Peterson report), but as a servant employed to do the technical work involved in acquiring and circulating materials useful for the faculty in carrying out their real work of education. Thus library staffs can be very small, as in the case of the vast majority of ATS libraries. After all, one needs only a technician or two with library school training (or sometimes the job can even be left to part-time work of a faculty member with easily acquired technical skills, with perhaps some student assistance). The library degree is the primary qualification, theological literacy is secondary. For the essential task is to collect books, periodicals, and other materials (mostly written), to classify and store them, and to circulate them to faculty and students as required by the theological curriculum. And it is the faculty who define the range of requirements, not the librarians—though as I have suggested there are indications that for some faculty the library is quite dispensable for classroom instruction, and the growing reliance on part-time and adjunct faculty may well be intensifying such a tendency.

Now suppose, as our "project of thought," all this were to be reconceived, with the theological library as a real partner, a twin or a binary star, with the so-called teaching faculty—or perhaps as a major part of the teaching faculty. We could even reverse the relations and consider the teaching faculty and the classroom as adjunctive to the library as the resource and learning center. After all, one could conceive of a real educational and learning center without so-called teaching faculty, but hardly without a library. Think of such remarkable research and teaching centers as the Newberry Library, the Folger-Shakespeare Library, and the Huntington Library.

I suspect what I am proposing may be happily received by many librarians, but not so gladly accepted by my faculty and administrative colleagues. Actually, I find some such radical reconception to be at least implicit in Steve Peterson's report, when he notes with great understatement that "libraries are often found to hold literature of movements and topics before they make their presence felt in the curriculum or the faculty" and contents that focus on "the immediate documentation needs of the curriculum . . . is a less than sufficient understanding of curriculum support, an understanding which should not be encouraged as a primary or exclusive goal of library development."[4] The library should be involved in extending the curriculum, as in fact it is.

What would be entailed in the reconception I have in mind? A first requirement, perhaps even a presupposition, though one that I think libraries can help to effect, is doubtless a change in the self-understanding of the theological school as a whole. Instead of being a narrow training center for religious professionals, the theological school needs to see itself as a center of inquiry and learning for the whole church. I am not prepared to identify all the dimensions that such a shift in orientation would involve. But it is clear that the constituency of the theological school will not be just seminary students and faculty but *all* the clergy and laity of the religious community (and why limit this to the religious community?). Steps in responding to such a reality are of course already being taken in the movements into continuing and extension education, though as I have said I am uneasy about the way that direction has been pursued. The "market" for theological inquiry includes not just professionals and potential professionals but at least the whole people of the church. And unless the truth of such a statement is recognized, I don't really see any hope for the theological school (or even for the church). Simply to continue the past models will be profoundly uninteresting.

Why not therefore think of the library as the principal resource and learning center for lay and continuing education (even for all aspects of theological education), with a natural constituency no less broad than the entire spectrum of religious inquirers? Technology makes this quite feasible. And it seems to me that libraries are generally much better equipped to take advantage of the technological possibilities for communication through video- and audio-tape and through computers and the like. The library could well be directed by a Dean who would have the central responsibility for continuing and lay education, for bibliographical research, and for visiting scholars. Faculty who have special responsibility for lay and continuing education could be integral members of the library staff or could rotate into that staff for short or long periods.

Any such movement is obviously going to require much larger library staffs, and staff with different sorts of training and qualifications. And a great deal of retraining and continuing education for librarians will be needed. If librarians are not mere technicians to process faculty wishes, they will need to be prepared as scholar-teachers, as persons who are essentially interpreters and communicators, whose subject-matter competence is at least as important as technical skills in what is called librarianship. Special subject-matter competence may be less important for the general university or public library, but I believe it particularly valid for the relatively specialized center that is the theological library. Perhaps some faculty should be retrained as librarians. Or graduate programs in religion and theology should incorporate bibliography and librarianship as major fields of study. (Why should not this be promoted?)

Librarians will need to be *consciously* active in extending the horizons of theological inquiry. They can give leadership to faculty, for example, in enabling them to readjust their teaching and scholarship in the light of a changing and pluralistic world. In their acquisitions policies, they will themselves be shaping the future of theological and religious studies. In fact, those things are now happening. But we need to be self-conscious about it and recognize its implications.

As a consequence, librarians can and should be recognized not just as "professionals" qualified in library science who "serve" faculty and long for "faculty" status, but as integral members of the instructional community, just as much engaged in teaching (and research) as the professor of Old Testament, just as much involved in communication, interpretation, and inquiry as the theologian. Their bibliographical investigations, for example, can be properly recognized and rewarded as research activity. And they will function as teachers in enabling students of all sorts to encounter important materials creatively—which, after all, is exactly what I try to do in graduate seminars.

Now any administrator who happens to be present will say at once that such a transition has enormous financial implications. Of course, but not necessarily expansionist implications. As one who for a long time now has had to be concerned with library budgets, I find it a bit odd that nationally theological schools regularly seem to spend about nine or ten percent of their total Educational and General budgets on their libraries. But why only ten percent? That seems to reflect the old view of the library as a mere adjunct and material support to a curriculum-driven education. Why not thirty percent, if the library is to be understood as the kind of learning and

communication center I have suggested? And why not consider the library
as an integral part of the instructional budget, for the library is quite on a
par with the classroom as a place for teaching and learning. Maybe even shift
a third of the faculty and their salaries to the library account? However it be
done, I think I am suggesting the possibility of a wholesale transfer of
resources within the theological school, in order to carry out its teaching and
research function more effectively. Or perhaps the library can be supported
in important ways, not simply by allocations from current school budgets,
but by charges directly to the larger constituency that the theological school
should be serving, by user fees or something comparable. Surely that is an
area for exploration.

Can we think also of major budgetary reorganization *within* the library?
You will surely tell me if I am wrong, but I suspect that much of the detailed
and laborious work of accessioning and cataloging is no longer necessary for
individual libraries because of the technological revolution. Is there not less
need for technicians, if for example the current possibilities for centralized
cataloging are exploited? Granted that the Library of Congress may not adequately serve the cataloging needs of specialized theological collections, I
cannot see why more than one person (or one center) in the country should
have to engage in the cataloging of any single theological work. (On the
GTU library staff, we have a half-dozen people doing cataloging—which
seems to me insane unless everything they do is for the entire theological
library community.) And what are the implications of automated circulation? Would then a proper library budget therefore reflect a greatly increased
proportion for acquisitions and communication services as compared with
technical services?

Finally, we need to think of greatly intensified and expanded patterns of
library cooperation in a multi-institutional environment on both a regional
and a national basis. This is now both necessary and possible. It is necessary
if for no other than economic reasons. No single institution has the resources
to maintain and develop a truly adequate theological library in all areas any
more. But fortunately that is not necessary, given the current capabilities of
information exchange, and given the changing role of the librarian into that
of a genuine faculty researcher and communicator.

I suspect the current inventory project will show that we have in this country and Canada a large number of look-alike libraries. But if we recognize
that technology has led us to a world in which access is much more important than possession, then we should move away from the process of replicat-
ing collections just as fast as possible. I have suggested with reference to the
preservation project that the reasons our libraries (and others as well) should
support that project are not so that all of us can possess the microfiche—few
of us will need most of those works frequently—but so that all of us can
have ready access to those materials when we need it, however seldom that

may be. Similarly, with respect to the obligation to collect materials of the Third World, it is plain that not everyone can collect everything. And it is equally plain that not everyone should try. Rather, some of our libraries must be identified as the places where certain concentrations of materials will be developed as resources that are made accessible to all. One place ought to be collecting for sub-Saharan Africa, another for South India, another for Central America, and so on.

Even more broadly than this, it appears to me that *every* theological library will have to focus increasingly on collecting in limited areas. And if the inventory project can be refined to show us the locations and the contours of special collections, that will be a great gain—far more important than telling us, for example, that most theological library collections are twenty percent works on the Bible. But with the technology of communication, limited and focused collection on the part of all will be desirable, for everything will be available to everyone else. And librarianship will be more and more essentially the art of making materials available to a broader and broader constituency.

I see no good reason why we cannot begin to think (as many of you may well already be thinking) of a truly national theological library system, in which all the technical work of cataloging will be done by one for all and in which a master data base will be accessible to all. Such a cooperative system will inevitably incorporate a number of regional or even non-geographically defined consortia. The focus of those cooperative clusters can include the development of individual acquisitions policies and cooperative acquisitions. And they will involve innovations in service, in delivery systems, in access, and in transmission, i.e., precisely in those areas that reflect the real activities of faculties in research and teaching.

CONCLUSION

I realize that I may here be preaching to the already converted. It is probably not so much librarians as faculty and administrators who need to be persuaded of a need for radical changes. But I think there are many steps that librarians can take without waiting on the conversion of deans and presidents.

First, you can pursue the inventory project with all vigor, with a view not only to getting an overall profile of the holdings of theological libraries, but also to identifying and describing the contours of all the special collections and emphases, including archives, and ensuring that all this information is available in a central database. That would be a major step toward a national theological library system, in which each library unit is seen as part of a national (or North American) whole, a part that can be shared.

Second, you can press toward a single national center (or its equivalent) for the cataloging of all theological materials, at least for all libraries using the LC system.

Third, you can develop schemes for regional or non-geographical cooperative systems for collection development, with appropriate distinctive emphases for individual libraries. And you can plan for at least regional centers for acquiring and processing materials.

Fourth, you can broaden the marketing base for the preservation project, far beyond the limits of theological libraries per se, not with a view to possession but with the goal of access and use.

Fifth, you can begin to redefine the qualifications for theological librarianship and even devise graduate programs for the preparation of theological librarians who will see themselves first and foremost as educators, as teachers and researchers in the fullest sense of those words. As technicians, they will be primarily concerned with access, with transmission and delivery. Thus you will reconceptualize the theological librarian as a way of redefining the theological library.

There may well be many other concrete steps that can be taken now—but these I suggest as starters. And mostly what they require is more intense cooperative action.

NOTES

1. Stephen L. Peterson, "Theological Libraries for the Twenty-First Century: Project 2000 Final Report," *Theological Education* 20, Supplement (1984).

2. Edward Farley, *Theologia: The Fragmentation and Unity of Theological Education* (Philadelphia: Fortress Press, 1983).

3. See "Globalizing Theological Education in North America," *Theological Education* 22 (Spring 1986) and "Global Challenges and Perspectives in Theological Education," *Theological Education* 23 (Autumn 1986).

4. Peterson, "Theological Libraries for the Twenty-First Century," 26–27.

28

Religious Studies and Theology
41st Annual Conference, Berkeley, CA, 1987

John E. Wilson

Most simply, Religious Studies is one department in a college or university while Theology generally means the discipline of work at a seminary. So terms are defined first of all by the nature of the institution. Seminary Theology is traditionally defined as "faithful scholarship," therefore, as having a faith component in all its various disciplines. In a secular or state-supported college or university, in Religious Studies, the type of work done is explicitly or implicitly independent of faith; at least that is the conventional understanding. Scholars in Religious Studies may or may not be members of churches (Buddhist, Christian, etc.).

According to conventional understanding, in Religious Studies the scholarly method is "objective" insofar as it is independent of personal or subjective faith commitment. So the most comfortable "fit" for conventional Religious Studies are or should be those disciplines that make obvious claims to objectivity, especially sociology of religion, to a lesser degree history of religion and comparative religion. *But Religious Studies may include a wide spectrum of disciplines and points of view, including Theology.* When this happens in a secular or state-supported institution, the understanding is that no single religious tradition will rule the program, that there will be diversity and equality of points of view.

Up to this point I have said that the usual definition of Religious Studies is conventional, the convention being set by the type of institution. If we go back in history—back to the European universities from the High Middle Ages up to the Enlightenment—we of course find that the only religious studies taught were within the theological faculties. There was no difference between Religious Studies and Theology, and Theology as faithful scholarship in the university was taken for granted. Even today in many European universities, for example, in Germany and Switzerland, Theology is still a department within the university, and indeed so much so that, for example, sociology of religion is more likely found in the sociology department than in the department of Theology. In Germany and Switzerland the curriculum in the departments of Theology looks like that of a seminary in the U.S.A. That may change in the future, because in both countries, especially in Germany, there is pressure to separate church and state, to impose the "American solution," as it is sometimes called. But in fact, the debate on separation and its consequences for university Theology has been going on in Germany for two centuries.

In America, too, Theology was originally taught within the universities and colleges. Two factors, both dating primarily from the late 19th century, were of special importance in ending the traditional arrangement. The first was the popularity of the new state-supported colleges and universities. The second was the ideal of the university as a purely scientific institution. (The influence on schools with religious affiliations was profound, although it was not fully felt until the early 20th century.) Initially and for a long time such purely secular institutions had no interest in teaching religion. But religion proved to be too popular a subject to be excluded. When they did begin on a large scale to include religion in their curricula (in parallel, by the way, with the relative decline in American religious denominations in the 1960s) they gladly met the requirement of being independent of religious denominations. Religious Studies departments came into being generally under the rubric of an independent "scientific study of religion." But how was that different from a study of religion in the history department or in the philosophy or sociology departments of a university? The situation seems at first paradoxical. At least theoretically the scientific study of religion could be done entirely within departments already existing within the secular university. The real reason for a department of Religious Studies is simply interest in religion, which is considerable.

Consider the root of "interest": *inter-esse*, to be in, to be involved in. In our conventional understanding "interest in religion" in fact does mean to be involved in religion. Putting the emphasis on "involvement," which is personal, moves us in the direction of seminary Theology. So one might say that Religious Studies exists, thrives, because it is, as personal scholarly involvement in religion, a kind of Theology. There are many religious persons in the university who are not the kind of scholars likely to be found in a religion department, because they do not share that personal scholarly involvement in religion. For example, I know a very deeply believing Quaker who is a professor of psychology: for him, psychology and religion are of course not entirely separate, but his religious interests are not directly involved in his scholarship. There are very many similar examples.

What separates Religious Studies and Theology is more a difference in commitment than a difference in method. Theology is commitment to Christ and to a Christian church, Buddhism is commitment to Buddha and a Buddhist church or body of belief. In Religious Studies there is a far greater diversity and far greater freedom from commitment to specific traditions, which makes Religious Studies more attractive to many students and to many potential faculty members. Yet in Religious Studies there is also unity in the diversity.

Since the 19th century, secular studies in religion have been characterized by *Religionswissenschaft*, science of religion. The term expresses the 19th century ideal of objective knowledge. In the last century it was perhaps best stated by the Hegelians as "lifting" (*Aufheben*) the content of religious myth and symbol into objective philosophical or scientific knowledge that is generally valid above and apart from the religious or worship activity of religion itself. That idea is still with us, for example in a Freudian interpretation of religion. As scientific, the intention is usually, at least to some degree, to try to arrive at some universal aspects of religious truth. Very generally speaking the steps might be (1) converting the content of religious myth and symbol into concepts; (2) comparing religions for purposes of demonstrating how the same content might be expressed in different mythologies, rituals, or religious systems; (3) judging the validity of the concepts according to some measure of truth, e.g., ethical or moral truths, whereby the question arises about the origin of one's measure of truth. Whether one emphasizes the differences and diversity of the religions or their relative unity, the basic method remains essentially the same. It characterizes the work of such diverse scholars as Ernst Troeltsch, a watershed thinker in *Religionswissenschaft*, Mircea Eliade, and Joseph Campbell. And in an American college or university, especially one that is state-supported, this method suggests itself as the best for the purpose of understanding the unity of a department of Religious Studies, even when not all the scholars agree with it. For with it one can comprehend how the diversity is unified: by the ideal of universal religious knowledge ordered according to principles on which broad agreement can be reached.

One also has to recognize how close this same ideal is to that of a considerable body of Christian Theology. For Hegel, the most complete statement of religious truth was contained in the symbols of Christianity and not, for example, in those of Buddhism, and Hegel considered himself a philosophical Christian. Is he then a theologian? According to many contemporary seminary theologians, yes. In fact, much seminary Theology operates in a way similar to Hegel's philosophy, namely with the understanding that

Christian Theology should cover all fields of human endeavor, both social and scientific.

Other seminary theologians do not agree. They say that while Christians should certainly be involved in all legitimate areas of human endeavor, theologians should be responsible primarily for the faith traditions of their churches. Because of the dominance of this view, most seminary curricula still focus on the classical theological disciplines: Bible, Church History, and Systematic Theology, with the addition of Social Ethics and practical "how-to" courses. But around the periphery of this center there is much going on that reminds one of the curricula in Religious Studies.

Some theological schools (they are all nondenominational, e.g., the Divinity School at the University of Chicago) have broken with this model and have organized around concepts more like those in Religious Studies departments of the universities. They are very much influenced by the moral need to value no one tradition more highly than the other.

Is this trend "secular"? Compare colleges and universities that in the early 20th century were affiliated with religious denominations: By and large they have separated themselves from the particularity of denominations, but their Religious Studies departments seem to be alive and well. Moreover, there is much cooperation and exchange between Theology (at least in "liberal" schools) and Religious Studies. ("Liberal" is a conventional word distinguishing these seminaries from evangelical and fundamentalist seminaries, which focus more narrowly on their traditions.) The distinction between Religious Studies and Theology is in many ways fluid. In the Joint Ph.D. Program of the Religious Studies Department at the University of Pittsburgh and Pittsburgh Theological Seminary, the only significant differences involve expertise, not, for example, faith. Look once again to Theology in Germany: The most significant publication involving the whole field is the new, entirely revised edition of the *Theologische Realenzyklopädie* (Berlin and New York: Walter de Gruyter, 1977ff). It includes not only Theology, but also subjects conventionally understood to belong to Religious Studies.

In conclusion, I would like to turn to several specific questions given me by the steering committee.

Question: How should library collections in support of programs of Religious Studies differ from those in support of theological programs? How can librarians prepare themselves to be effective Religious Studies specialists?

It has been said that a literature is a symptom of its public. I assume that is also true of a collection of literature. Of course, a library should also be better than its public, but the first rule should be: know your Religious Studies program, especially since Religious Studies departments can have such different emphases and directions. Perhaps it would be a good idea to shape the collection around what are perceived to be the permanent needs of Religious Studies at one's particular institution. A practical step might be to have a good acquaintance especially with the senior professors and with the curriculum and policies of the Religious Studies department. Perhaps the professors could be asked to list books not only within, but also outside their fields that they think ought to be available. There is so much being published in religion today that policy decisions about collections have to be made in order to keep the collection from being haphazard or, worst of all, unused. It seems to me that this might well be made a subject for an ATLA training curriculum: how to go about making policy decisions for a library collection that serves a college or university Religious Studies department.

Question: Students in a secular institution come from an enormous variety of spiritual traditions or lack thereof. What are some sensitive ways to respond to queries in the area of religion and theology when there is uncertainty as to the patron's background or point of view?

My personal opinion is that it is best not to guess or ask about the motives of the person who makes such an inquiry, because I think privacy needs to be respected. I would recommend that one be attentive, be direct and clear with the information requested (perhaps also with reference to the library's collection policy), and offer to be of further assistance. If such persons want to make suggestions or further inquiries, they should of course be made to feel that their comments are welcome.

SOME SUGGESTED LITERATURE

Altizer, T. J. J., W. Beardslee, and J.H. Young, eds. *Truth, Myth and Symbol.* Englewood Cliffs, N.J.: Prentice-Hall, Inc., 1962.

Campbell, Joseph. *Hero with a Thousand Faces.* New York: Pantheon Books, 1949.

Eliade, Mircea, and Joseph M. Kitagawa, eds. *The History of Religions.* Chicago: The University of Chicago Press, 1955.

Farley, Edward. *The Fragility of Knowledge; Theological Education in the Church and the University.* Philadelphia: Fortress Press, 1988.

———. *Theologia; The Fragmentation and Unity of Theological Education.* Philadelphia: Fortress Press, 1983.

Troeltsch, Ernst. *Religion in History.* Philadelphia: Fortress Press, 1991.

29

Serving the Religion Information Needs of the Public

53rd Annual Conference, Chicago, IL, 1999

Mary A. Dempsey

Thank you for inviting me to speak to you today. For those of you who are not Chicagoans, let me welcome you to our city. It is rather fitting that your annual conference is being held here in Chicago, a city that, I can attest from personal experience, is definitely "library friendly." In fact, on Tuesday of this week, Mayor Richard Daley dedicated our new 15,500-square-foot Rogers Park Branch Library, less than one mile away from where we are meeting today. This was the 36th new library Mayor Daley and the Chicago Public Library have constructed and opened in his ten years as chief executive of our city. It is the fourth new library opened in Chicago this year—and construction has already begun on two more libraries that will open in the summer of 2000.

As you can imagine, I am very proud of the network of beautiful, new, well-equipped public libraries that we are building across the City of Chicago. These massive capital improvements, along with our updated book and serials collections and free public access to the Internet and to twenty-seven commercial online databases, are a direct result of our strategic planning process of five years ago. The library's strategic plan has truly been a blueprint for our success. Thanks to a steadily increasing budget for personnel, books and library materials, equipment, professional development and training, and capital improvements, the Chicago Public Library has regained its former status as one of the country's premier public libraries.

I hope that you will permit me such blatant immodesty; first, because everything I have just said is true; and second, because our improvements and growth are the result of the collegial efforts of many, many people starting with Mayor Daley and our Library Board right down to the members of our page pool, who handle even the most daunting shelving assignments with SWAT-Team-like efficiency and dispatch. This is a very good time to be a part of the Chicago Public Library.

In fact, this is a good time for public libraries generally. Although there are painful exceptions in some parts of the country, today's American public libraries generally enjoy a high public profile and an increasing level of fiscal health. Not only in Chicago but across the country, the public continues to patronize and to support increased funding for public libraries.

Today, there are over 9,000 public libraries in over 16,000 buildings in the United States. Cities like Chicago, Cleveland, San Antonio, San Francisco, and Phoenix have constructed new central libraries in the last ten years. Following Chicago's lead, Los Angeles and Broward County (Florida) have recently passed referenda to support the renovation and construction of several new neighborhood branch libraries. The rise of the mega bookstores, the phenomenal popularity of book discussion groups, and the introduction by libraries of the Internet and other forms of information technology have actually increased public library usage in the past decade. Some public libraries develop more library-based programming than others and some of us provide more access to technology than others. Nevertheless, our fundamental mission continues to be to provide access to the greatest range of information and other resources to the lay public, consistent with our collection development policies, patron needs, and financial constraints.

I am providing you with this general information about American public libraries in order to put my remarks in context for you. The conference planners who so kindly invited me to speak to you today have asked me to talk about how public libraries serve the religion information needs of the layman, and to examine whether there are collection development opportunities in which public libraries and libraries of theological seminaries and religious institutions can engage together. In order to bring this topic into sharper focus, I ask your indulgence as I digress into a brief discussion of the mission of the public library.

THE MISSION OF THE PUBLIC LIBRARY

About two years ago, I was asked to come to Australia to discuss the status and the future of American public libraries—a rather daunting prospect given the breadth of the subject and my personal belief that most audiences can endure a speech on most subjects—even libraries—for no more than thirty minutes. So you can appreciate my dilemma. In preparing my talk, one of the first things I did was to examine the mission statements of about fifty urban and rural American public libraries. Some went on for paragraphs while others were able to express succinctly the essence of what public libraries do, the patrons we serve, and how we attempt to accomplish our goals. Central to all of our mission statements, of course, are the concepts of public service, equitable access to information, and endorsement of lifelong learning.

I am happy to report that ours qualifies as one of the shorter mission statements: "We welcome and support all people in their enjoyment of reading and their pursuit of lifelong learning. Working together, we strive to provide equal access to information and knowledge through books, programs, and other resources. We believe in the freedom to read, to learn, to discover."

Regardless of what words are used, this is the essence of the mission of American public libraries. Our audiences range from newborns to senior citizens. Yes, we do believe that reading to children should start at birth and that reading is a health issue. There is no "typical" public library user and the reasons they come to the library vary widely. About two years ago, we asked approximately twenty-five randomly selected visitors to our central library the purpose of their visit. The answers included: check out a book; hear a lecture; borrow a foreign language tape; surf the web; play the piano; watch a dance recital; research a science project; borrow a video; and research investments. On any given day, an entirely different but similarly varied set of responses would be given.

Collection development decisions in public libraries are, as in all libraries, a function of our patrons' needs and our financial resources. There is no mystery there, but given the breadth of our patrons' needs and the reality of fiscal constraints, the process is often equal parts data analysis, meeting core collection needs, and instinct—better known as the little voice which tells you that this is the summer to invest in lots of books for adolescents about space exploration and science fiction. Because requests for information and resources about religions, philosophy, and theology are generally not as high as in other subject areas such as business, health, computers, literature, popular fiction, and children's materials, selection librarians tend to look for the broadest or the best religion resources since we do not enjoy the luxury of purchasing a variety of materials on what is, for us, a subject area that is not patronized as frequently as others.

This does not foreclose, however, an examination of the viability of engaging in collaborative education about collection development of materials concerning religion, philosophy, and spirituality with our colleagues in religious institutions. Indeed, the reality of limited financial resources balanced against the need to maintain sources that are useful to the lay public may be the most valid reason to pursue such opportunities to learn from those who have expertise in the field.

PUBLIC LIBRARY PURCHASES
AND ACQUISITIONS

Public libraries spend approximately $1.8 billion on books annually. That is roughly 10% of annual book sales in the nation. In a recent article, *Library Journal* reported that fiction continues to enjoy the highest circulation in public libraries, followed by art books, craft books, and health and medicine titles.

Within the category of fiction, mysteries enjoy the highest circulation among public library patrons, followed closely by romance. Interestingly, however, many librarians surveyed for the article also identified a growing demand for Christian fiction and religious nonfiction titles.[1]

Within that category, librarians and commercial bookstore markets are seeking a variety of nonfiction titles from publishers on a spectrum of religious topics including the Bible and Bible study guides; books on comparative religions, prayer, and spirituality; and applying theological matters to daily living. Publishers have recognized this increased demand and are developing sophisticated marketing campaigns for religious titles using some of the same methods they employ for books in other subject areas.[2]

The increased demand for religious titles is not entirely surprising, especially in light of the growing trend toward spirituality in the United States, as was recently reported by George Gallup, Jr. of the Gallup organization. Libraries, especially public libraries, are often an excellent barometer of the nation's mood and interests as evidenced by requests received from patrons for particular titles or for titles in specific subject areas.

Locally, when Loyola Press published *The Gift of Peace* by the late Joseph Cardinal Bernardin, it anticipated a run of no more than 50,000 copies, which it planned to market through Catholic bookstores. In short order, Target and other retailers began placing large orders for the book. To date, Loyola Press has sold more than 300,000 copies of the title, many through these non-bookstore outlets. At the Chicago Public Library, we ordered 100 copies of the book. Normally we place an order of that size for the "hot" new national fiction bestseller of the moment, not for a religious title.[3]

Notwithstanding our experience with *The Gift of Peace*, collections of nonfiction religious titles in public libraries are not particularly deep. Our responsibility is to collect resources that assist the public in the general subject areas of religion, philosophy, worship, and spirituality. We happily recognize that scholarly works of philosophy and religion belong more appropriately on the shelves of your institutions. Nevertheless, as the public's interest in spirituality and comparative religions grows, the lines of distinction are blurring.[4]

PUBLIC LIBRARY SURVEY

To prepare for today's talk, I developed and sent out my own survey to approximately thirty-three public libraries serving medium and large cities. The purpose of the survey was to ascertain the demand for religious titles from their library patrons and the potential, if any, for joint collection development opportunities with theological libraries. Twenty-four of the libraries to which surveys were sent responded.[5]

Questions included: What percentage of your budget for nonfiction titles is spent on religious materials (under 7%, but generally 1 to 3%)? What sources do you use to respond to reference questions about religions? Have you considered asking local churches, synagogues, theological libraries, or university religious studies departments for assistance in collection development of religious titles? Which religious subject areas of your collection need supplementing? And in the next five years, in what direction do you anticipate the demand for religious materials at your library to go? With regard to the last question, just over half anticipate an increase in demand while the remainder believe demand will remain the same. No one believes the demand will decrease.

Responses to the question about which sources are relied upon to answer religious reference inquiries offer few surprises: *Butler's Lives of the Saint, New Catholic Encyclopedia, Interpreter's Bible, Catholic Almanac,* and *Encyclopedia Judaica* are listed in several surveys. As I said there are few surprises—in fact, the lists are strongly reminiscent of the reference courses we took in library school—but there is one interesting omission. Not one of the respondents cited the Internet or any online database as a source for answering religious reference questions. That may be because the reference librarians who completed the surveys have greater facility with the traditional print resources or because access to the Internet by reference staff is not yet as widespread as is access to the print resources. I suspect that will change in the next five years, and that the trend will actually shift away from print and toward the use of more online resources by public library patrons conducting religious research.

Most of the libraries responding to the survey confirmed the *Library Journal* report by identifying a growing demand by the public for Christian fiction, which one librarian described as containing "no violence, no sex, no inappropriate language—always a 'happy ending.'" Since many of those titles are reviewed in *Library Journal* and *Publishers Weekly,* it is not surprising that the selection sources consulted by public librarians are the same as the sources consulted for purchases of "mainstream" fiction.

A smaller number of survey respondents indicated a need to purchase more nonfiction titles relating to the study and worship of Islam, other Eastern religions, and "New Age."

All of those responding to the survey indicated that they rely on traditional selection resources—published reviews and bibliographies—to select titles to fill in subject areas of the collection. Three-fourths of the respondents indicated that they would consider consulting theological seminary libraries, university religious studies departments, local churches, temples, or synagogues for some collection development assistance; however, only one had ever done so. Clearly, the libraries surveyed value traditional selection tools for selecting materials of a religious nature.

A few analogized the selection process for religious materials to be no different than the process for selecting books about law or medicine. Lawyers and doctors, they wrote, are generally not consulted about which materials to purchase in those subject areas and so neither has it occurred to those public librarians to consult their colleagues at theological institutions. As someone who is educated as both a librarian and a lawyer, the logic of that analogy escapes me. In fact, I see tremendous benefits in combining the knowledge gained from the librarian's collection of book reviews and selection tools with the practical experience gained by a practitioner who actively uses the resource professionally.

COLLABORATIVE COLLECTION
DEVELOPMENT AND TRAINING

What, if anything, do these unscientific survey results indicate about the possibility of collaborative professional interaction between public and religious libraries? There is no question that our audiences are quite different. The mission of your libraries and the focus of your collection development are narrower, by definition, than that of a public library which must be equipped to respond to thousands of inquiries daily, only a fraction of which refer to religion.

In light of the growing interest in religion and spirituality among readers that I mentioned earlier, however, it seems somewhat shortsighted if those of us in public libraries do not recognize that our knowledge base and sources in these areas will have to expand. Moreover, as new generations of religious scholars appear and present interpretations and theories which reflect the changing dynamic of the relationship between theology and popular culture, public libraries will be obligated to establish and maintain credible, current collections. That means adding titles beyond the tried and true reference sources which have been our mainstay for so many years, and it especially means developing a facility with resources available on the Web.

It would seem, therefore, to make sense for us to develop some joint collection development and reference workshops, especially in large cities like Chicago, New York, Boston, Los Angeles, and San Francisco where diverse populations and continuing immigrant waves ensure a consistent need for information about comparative religions and theology.

A few survey respondents indicated some concern that conferring with religious institutions might result in "uneven" collections, too heavily weighted toward one religion or philosophy. I must say that I find that reaction puzzling. The ultimate purchasing decision remains with the public librarian. If the collection becomes unbalanced, it is because the public librarian, not the religious institution, lost sight of the library's collection development needs. There may be something else at work here, too. Occasionally, I hear public librarians raise concerns about running afoul of the principle of the separation of church and state. That may be a convenient excuse, but it is not valid. The first amendment to the Constitution says simply that Congress shall make no law establishing a religion or prohibiting the free exercise of one. It does not say that there shall not be free and open discourse between a government-funded agency and a church-sponsored institution. If the opportunity exists to discuss collections or reference questions with you, our counterparts in religious institutions, I would urge my colleagues to take advantage immediately. Similarly, I believe that doctors and lawyers can assist librarians in evaluating the value of certain medical or legal titles, and they should be consulted in those subject areas as well. In all three situations, the librarian also has access to published reviews on which to rely and which should be consulted. For purposes of evaluating the actual utility of a book or database, however, the input of those who practice in the field is a benefit, not a detriment.

Personally, I would endorse our having selection librarians confer with library colleagues who have knowledge and experience with specialized subject area resources, including religious subject matter. Who better to advise us on the usefulness and reliability of a particular title than subject matter specialists who work with it daily?

Similarly, as we have learned here in Illinois through our multi-type library systems, there is enormous value in fostering professional development programs that involve librarians from public, special, and academic libraries in resource sharing programs and exchanges. I must admit to you, however, that until I was asked to explore this topic, I had not given much thought to how we public librarians in Chicago could or should be conferring with our colleagues at the many religious and theological libraries in the metropolitan area.

In our institution, which responds to over 5 million reference questions annually, we deem it important to provide ongoing training on current reference sources. While we concentrate on educating our librarians on the latest resources in business, health, municipal reference, science, and education, I must admit that we probably pay only cursory attention to refresher courses on religion information resources, either in print or online. Given the increasing demand by the general public for this information, it appears that we may be missing an important opportunity to better prepare our professional staff to serve the lay public.

It would appear then that some joint reference and collection development workshops involving public and religious institution libraries would not only be groundbreaking but enlightening. I believe this would be a worthwhile endeavor and I submit it to you for your consideration as a joint project for your institution and your local public library.

TECHNOLOGY AS A RELIGION RESOURCE

If you and your institutions elect to proceed with some collaborative continuing education programs with local public librarians, I urge you to include a discussion of the most useful online religious reference sources, including commercial databases and the Web. Unless a public library receives a higher-than-normal demand for reference information about religious studies and theology, it is not financially advantageous for our segment of the profession to invest in special religion-only databases.

It is more likely that we will continue to rely upon general commercial databases that index a variety of journals and publications including some religious titles. Nevertheless, a discussion and review of the most helpful databases could have obvious benefits for both types of libraries. Commercial databases are frequently a significant investment. As an administrator, each time we subscribe to a new database I worry that our staff and patrons are not fully cognizant of the existence of this resource in our libraries or on our Web site. A significant advantage of conducting collaborative workshops on using religious resources would be the ability to include sessions to explore the full potential of these databases to assist in responding to the religion information needs of the lay patron.

With regard to the Web, however, there are many more possibilities for joint analysis and review. As we are all aware, the factual reliability of sources on the Web is sometimes in question. In the area of religious information especially, public libraries would benefit greatly from your expertise in determining which sites are the most legitimate for use as reference sources. Although the professional literature often reviews sites in a variety of subject areas including religion, public librarians do not use religion sites with a great deal of regularity. Your input in evaluating the reliability and depth of these sites would be invaluable to your colleagues who are not as familiar with these sites.

CONCLUSION

Nothing that I am suggesting here is radical departure from what we all do on a regular basis within our respective institutions. Nothing that I am suggesting here advocates departing from consulting traditional book and database reviews from the literature; however, supplementing that information by developing a forum for communication about reading trends and research resources is a fundamentally sound principle. Developing that communication not only within but between institutions that coexist within the same municipal boundaries creates the possibility of producing cost-effective and positive results for our institutions and for our patrons.

Public librarians would gain practical in-depth knowledge about those religious resources—whether print, Web-based, or databases—deemed reliable by librarians who regularly consult those resources for research purposes. Religious institution librarians would be able to use the public library as a source of information about the religious information requests being made to public libraries from the general public. As I mentioned earlier, there is perhaps no institution better situated to observe cultural and societal shifts than the public library. As religions continue to examine their responsiveness to needs of the laity, the public library provides a perfect opportunity to observe the public's reading interests and trends relating to religion, philosophy, and spirituality. I invite ATLA librarians and public librarians to take the first steps toward developing these partnerships. I believe that the benefits will be great and the disadvantages nonexistent. Finally, I want to thank ATLA and especially the conference organizers for challenging me to examine this topic. It has given me much to think about regarding the continuing professional education of our librarians and for that I am grateful.

NOTES

1. Barbara Hoffert, "What Public Libraries Buy and How Much They Spend," *Library Journal* (February 15, 1998): 106–110.

2. Kimberly Winston, "Publishing Not Perishing," *Publishers Weekly* (November 16, 1998): 56–59.

3. Kimberly Winston, "Opening New Pathways to Consumers," *Publishers Weekly* (March 15, 1999): 56–58, s10–s11.

4. David Young, "Spiritual Awakening Ahead, Pollster Predicts," *Chicago Tribune* (April 23, 1999): Sec. 2, 7.

5. Religion Collection Development Surveys were completed and returned by the

following public libraries: Addison P.L. (IL); Barrington P.L. (IL); Bensenville P.L. (IL); Blue Island P.L. (IL); Chicago P.L.: central, Sulzer regional, Woodson regional (IL); Cleveland P.L. (OH); Evanston P.L. (IL); Flossmoor P.L. (IL); Fountaindale P.L. (IL); Gail Borden P.L. (IL); Indian Prairie P.L. (IL); Indian Trails P.L. (IL); Joliet P.L. (IL); Memphis/Shelby Country P.L. (TN); P.L. of Nashville (TN); Phoenix P.L. (AZ); Rockford P.L. (IL); San Francisco P.L. (CA); Schaumburg P.L. (IL); Seattle P.L. (IL); Skokie P.L. (IL); Wheaton P.L. (IL).

5

THE AMERICAN THEOLOGICAL LIBRARY ASSOCIATION: REFLECTIONS AND REMINISCENCES

30

Introduction

John A. Bollier

It has been said, "The road to tomorrow leads through yesterday." If that is the case, then revisiting the five papers in this part, which date from ATLA's first Annual Conference in 1947 to its 40th Annual Conference in 1987, is of contemporary as well as antiquarian interest.

IN THE BEGINNING

Lewis J. Sherrill's brief remarks, bringing greetings from AATS to the fledgling group of librarians who are soon to call themselves the American Theological Library Association, attempt to define the role of the theological librarian in the whole enterprise of theological education. Prior to the establishment of ATLA, theological librarians had no distinct professional home. They were not really members of the teaching faculty, nor of the administration of their institutions. They were not college, university or public librarians, although they shared certain common interests and expertise with all of these. Some attended the American Library Association conferences and participated in its Religious Book Roundtable. But before long the Roundtable focused its attention on the needs of public librarians, rather than theological librarians.

In the meantime, theological seminary administrators and faculty were becoming ever more aware of the growing importance of their libraries, in light of changing curriculums and student expectations. Thus, the time was ripe in 1947 for AATS to issue a call for the first national meeting of theological librarians.

Sherrill's remarks addressed one of the central issues facing theological librarians across the continent at that time. He states that a theological school is "a purposeful, working fellowship between five groups of people," whom he identifies as students, teachers, authors, donors, and administrators, then goes on to observe that the librarian "has the singular distinction of belonging, in some sense, to at least four of these five groups!" Today, in the aftermath of ATS and ATLA having jointly faced the challenges of six decades of rapid change in educational methods, in technology, and in the expectations of students, churches, and society, Sherrill's analysis may seem slightly facile. And yet his succinct remarks served to set the agenda for the future. As if to assure the fledgling ATLA librarians that his remarks were not just empty rhetoric, he concluded with the announcement that ATS "plans to devote the biennium of 1948–50 to theological libraries. Toward that end your best thought and planning are invited." Thus was initiated a whole new era for theological librarians.

The second paper included here fills in for us some more detail on the various organizations whose efforts led to the establishment of ATLA, a report on ATLA's organizing Conference, and its structure and achievements during its first six years, 1947–1953.

In discussing ATLA's founding Conference, Elliott is especially perceptive in identifying an important characteristic of the organization which was apparent from its very beginning, persists to this day, and undoubtedly accounts for much of its success through the years: collegiality. He writes concerning the two-day first ATLA Conference in Louisville in 1947:

> At the first session the atmosphere was rather reserved and cool. Some of the librarians knew a few of the others but for the most part those who assembled that first morning were a group of strangers. Between sessions introductions multiplied, backgrounds and contacts were discovered. Qualities of personalities were revealed in the discussions. Respect and appreciation for one another grew as evidence of ability and scholarship multiplied. At the close of the session a stranger would have thought a big family reunion was breaking up.

The spirit of that first conference has continued through the years. Certainly the warm interpersonal relationships and close friendships that ATLA has fostered through the years helps explain the members' loyalty to the organization, their willingness to serve in its wide-ranging programs, and their ability to attract a constant flow of new members.

YEARS OF GROWTH AND MATURING

Ernest White's paper recalls memories of 40 years earlier when he and his school, Louisville Presbyterian Seminary, hosted the first ATLA Annual

Conference. Writing four decades after the events (in 1987), he gently reminds ATLA not to forget its roots. "I believe that, in more recent years, we have been inclined to forget, or to overlook, the major role which AATS, now ATS, played in the start of our own organization, for this first meeting was called directly at the request of AATS." Fortunately, to the mutual benefit of both ATLA and ATS, ATLA has heeded White's gentle admonition. He also reminds us of the strong feeling of need for a theological library association that prevailed among those who attended this first Conference in Louisville. He cites Stillson Judah, for instance, who "had ridden all the way straight through on a railroad day coach from Oakland, California in order to attend this first meeting." White observes a phenomenon remarked by Elliott: the growing sense of friendship among those attending the first ATLA Conference:

> On the very first morning, several of the guests mentioned to me the fact that it would be most regrettable if they had to return home from Louisville and to admit that they had not seen Churchill Downs. So, at a point on the second afternoon, I rigged up an arrangement with our local bus company, and we had ourselves a bus tour! We made a quick stop at the Southern Baptist Seminary, to see Leo Crimson's excellent library . . . to keep the tour "legal!" . . . Interestingly enough, this was the single feature of the conference which made the greatest impression! At least, it was the thing mentioned to me more often in the years ahead, and it seemed to be remembered with the greatest pleasure.

GROWTH AND ITS CHALLENGES

Elmer J. O'Brien's presidential address was delivered on the occasion of ATLA's 33rd Annual Conference in 1980. By that time ATLA possessed a great many strengths, and had attained widespread recognition as the professional association for theological librarians in the United States and Canada. In addition to its Board of Directors, it had two semi-autonomous boards for its periodical indexing and micro-text (later called "preservation") programs. It also encouraged numerous interest groups, roundtable discussions, denominational meetings, and regional associations of theological librarians. It had also established the status of the theological librarian as a professional playing a key role in theological education.

The issue facing ATLA at this juncture in 1980 was whether to encourage continued growth through further decentralization or by centralization. In retrospect, it is apparent that ATLA did both. It continued to encourage the initiative of its members but in due course it reorganized its three boards into one Board of Directors; it established the position of Executive Director; moved into a central headquarters; and expanded its staff to meet its growing program needs. One major result of this reorganization was its enabling ATLA to apply for and receive substantial foundation and government grants directly, rather than through its parent organization, ATS.

DISCERNING THE FUTURE

G. Paul Hamm's paper was delivered in the same year as O'Brien's, just before the digital revolution burst upon the world. His insights can now be seen to have had a "prophetic" quality, challenging theological schools and their libraries to reconsider changing their centuries-old ways. He proclaims that holding onto the lecture as the only method of instruction and the incidental use of the library are no longer adequate pedagogy and, indeed, never were.

Yet he sees signs of hope, especially with the leadership of ATLA and ATS as they work both separately and in cooperative efforts. He cites, for example, the Library Development Program (1961–66), a joint effort of ATS and ATLA, funded by a major grant from the Sealantic Fund, Inc. It provided matching funds for libraries that would improve their services and increase their expenditures for books and periodicals up to a maximum of $3,000 per year. Thus, theological libraries spent $5,000,000 to increase their acquisitions, and most of them continued this new level of expenditure. Hamm concludes, saying, "Paradoxically, theological libraries have grown steadily in every respect . . . while the philosophy and method of theological education have remained basically the same . . . Theological libraries and their administrators are in a position unparalleled in history to exert a beneficial influence on the philosophy and methodology of theological education." With the library in the vanguard of the subsequent digital revolution which would soon engulf theological education, Hamm's insights helped encourage ATLA librarians to review their self-perception. Considering that the rate and extent of change has only accelerated in subsequent years, his insights have taken on a renewed timeliness.

31

Seminary Librarians (Greetings and Challenge from ATS)
1st Annual Conference, Louisville, KY, 1947

Lewis J. Sherrill

It falls to my pleasant lot to bring the greetings of the Executive Committee of the American Association of Theological Schools to the Theological Librarians. The call for this meeting, issued by that Committee, has been read, and need not be repeated here.

It seems to me that this gathering has much significance in the development of theological education in the United States and Canada. I should like to try to picture part of that significance as I see it in its larger setting.

Most of you serve as librarians in *theological schools*. A school of this and other kindred types is a purposeful, working fellowship between five groups of people. The first is a group of young men and women who wish to learn. They have devoted life to some form of Christian service. They have taken three, four, or even five years out of a short span of life, and have consecrated that period of time to God for specific preparation for some form of ministry. At their best they are eager for such learning of all kinds as will better equip them to serve their own generation, for they wish to take their part in building the City of God.

The second is a group of teachers, relatively more mature men and women, who have something to give spiritually and intellectually. At their best they too are eager to continue learning. They have long ago discovered that life is too short, and perhaps even eternity is not long enough, to permit them to accomplish all of their hearts' desires.

The third group is an invisible company of men and women who have lived richly, thought deeply, toiled diligently, and have given us some of the best of their life blood in the form of the writings which are in our libraries. They are of every time, present and past. They are of every stature, great, near great, and small. But once they have written a thing that is true and has value, their color, their ancestry, and their status in Church or State becomes of little account. Once they have done even one sentence well, they belong to the ages, and to us personally if we can possess it. The library, then, is a place where we may commune with this invisible company, and in so communing grow toward the ends we earlier chose for ourselves, all the while discovering still worthier ends toward which we shall forever after be inwardly driven to strive.

The fourth group consists of men and women who have given life blood in another form—the money which makes school possible. In part this is also an invisible company, for many of these people have long ago left the earthly scene. But night and day, year after year, generation after generation, the gifts which these people and their still living comrades have left, toil on, unseen in the background, working toward exactly the same ends as the students, the teachers, and the makers of books.

The fifth is a group of administrators and other co-workers who see to it that the enterprise of education goes on as smoothly as may be. Their job is to see to it that the numerous essentials of corporate life should always encourage, and if possible never hinder, the carrying forward of the central purposes of the community of persons.

This, then, is the goodly company in which your life is invested, a comradeship drawn from all sorts and conditions of men, in all times and from all places where men have dwelt. And the librarian, you are now to be reminded, has the singular distinction of belonging, in some sense, to at least four of the five groups! By virtue of his function he is at one and the same time student and teacher, for he must be constantly giving, out of what he learns, to the enrichment of both students and teachers, while he in turn learns yet more from them. And in virtue of his work he also is among those who administer the educational enterprise. Beyond this he is fairly to be counted also among the authors. For he and his colleagues construct the apparatus without which a library would be merely an unknowable pile of dead books. But *with* that apparatus a collection of books becomes instantly responsive to the wish of any person to commune with the silent spirits who inhabit the shelves, wanting nothing now so much as to be called down again into action.

Furthermore, many of you fulfill this function of librarian within the framework not only of your own school, but also within the still larger framework of the American Association of Theological Schools. Including as it does more than a hundred institutions in the United States and Canada, this comradeship is unique in Protestantism. In it schools of the most diverse persuasions work together in harmony, not by the sacrifice of any conviction, but because we have the common task, that of theological education. Fortunately that Association plans to devote the biennium of 1948–50 to theological libraries. Toward that end your best thought and planning are invited.

On behalf of the Executive Committee of that Association, I bid you welcome to this gathering, and God-speed in what you undertake.

32

Six Years of ATLA: A Historical Sketch
7th Annual Conference, Evanston, IL, 1953

L. R. Elliott

THE PREPARATORY INFLUENCES

In the unpublished Yonan MS of the old Syriac version of the New Testament, the opening phrase of John's Gospel may be translated, "In the beginning before the beginning." So it was with this organization. It began with the first conference in Louisville, Kentucky, June 23, 24, 1947; but there was a beginning before this beginning, or perhaps more accurately, several prior beginnings.

The earliest of these was the Religious Books Round Table of the American Library Association. At the ALA Conference, Asbury Park, 1916, there was established a Round Table of Theological Librarians. This name was enlarged the next year to read Round Table of the Libraries of Religion and Theology. By 1920 public libraries were included, and in 1925 the first of the now well-known annual lists of religious books was distributed. In the years following, the emphasis of the RBRT shifted to the needs of the religion sections of public libraries, with major attention to seminary libraries diminishing. However, some of the seminary librarians remembered the earlier character of RBRT and hoped for something that would better serve their particular needs.

Another beginning before the beginning occurred in 1918, at Harvard University, with the formation of the Conference of Theological Seminaries and Colleges of the United States and Canada. This Conference, which continued until 1936, apparently placed little emphasis on theological libraries.

In 1924, Robert L. Kelly's *Theological Education in America*[1] was published under the auspices of the Institute of Social and Religious Research. Out of more than 400 pages of text, this book devotes less than one page to libraries, and gives pictures of two libraries out of twenty-three campus and building scenes.

Under the same auspices came in 1934 the four-volume work *The Education of American Ministers* by Brown, May and Shuttleworth.[2] Volume Three contains a chapter of forty-three pages on theological libraries in addition to several other pages, all indexed. This chapter was prepared by our president, Raymond P. Morris, and at once took its place as a major document on the subject. The publication of this work exerted a large influence on contemporary thinking about theological education. One result was the reorganization of the Conference in 1938. Its name was changed to the American Association of Theological Schools. A commission on accreditation was established which published a statement of criteria for accreditation containing one on library standards and also four items on libraries in the list of notations. Eight years later the AATS took the initial action leading to ATLA.

A third contributory movement may be seen in the small informal meetings of theological librarians attending ALA conferences or at other convenient times. Such a gathering occurred after the scheduled meeting of RBRT in 1941. There were eleven persons present, nine of them from seminary libraries. Five of these nine (Raymond P. Morris, Winifred Eisenberg, John F. Lyons, Elizabeth Royer, and Lucy W. Markley) became charter members of ATLA, and two others (Helen B. Uhrich and Theodore L. Trost) joined later.

Other private meetings of theological librarians followed. These were regional and informal. They seemed to have been confined to the areas around Boston, New York, and Chicago. The last one was held in Chicago, December 28, 1946. Twelve persons attended, nine from the Chicago area. The other three were in Chicago in connection with the ALA Mid-winter meeting. Of these twelve, seven were present at the first conference of ATLA (Robert F. Beach, Ralph W. Busbee, Jr., E. F. George, Elinor C. Johnson, A. F. Kuhlman, John F. Lyons, and Evah Ostrander).

Another and indirect influence came from the colleges and universities which were placing increased emphasis on their libraries. The Association of American Colleges made a survey of their libraries in 1937. The results were reported by the director, Dr. Harvie Branscomb, in 1940, in his book, *Teaching with Books*.[3] This report stresses the educational function of the library, and Dr. Branscomb's book at once became an outstanding item in the expanding literature on this emphasis.

Under the impetus of this literature a southern seminary librarian discussed with two southern seminary deans, who were members of the executive committee of AATS, the implications of this emphasis for theological libraries. Their encouragement led to conversations with other members of the executive committee. From these conversations, which occurred during the latter part of 1945 and the early part of 1946, came the resolution voted by AATS at McCormick Presbyterian Seminary in June 1946, encouraging their executive committee to authorize the first national conference of theological librarians.

The invitation to the last Chicago area meeting in 1946 was dated December 14. In New York, on the day before, the executive committee of AATS appointed the committee to convene the first national conference. Some of the Chicago librarians had been thinking of calling for such a nationwide conference. Shortly prior to the date of their conference, December 28, they had learned of the action of the executive committee of AATS. With generosity and farsightedness they merged their efforts and ideas with the plans of the committee authorized in New York. Similar support was soon forthcoming from the librarians of the Boston and New York areas, as well as from individuals across the nation.

Thus from three widely separated sections, the East, the West, and the South, came the three main streams supporting the formation of ATLA. From this outline of the beginnings before the beginning, we turn to the beginning itself, and take a glimpse at the first conference and the committee activities which prepared for it.

THE FIRST CONFERENCE

The Work of the Convening Committee

The committee to prepare the program for the first Conference was composed of a dean of a school of theology within a university, a university librarian whose responsibilities included direction of a theological library, and the librarian of an independent seminary. Oddly enough, they were all from the South.

However, the three Southerners believed their duties were too important for a committee of three representing one region only. At their request, the committee was enlarged by four additions: two librarians from the North, one from the Midwest, and a seminary president from the Pacific Coast.

The committee recognized at least two handicaps: one, the inability to meet—all contacts must be by correspondence; second, the lack of personal knowledge of the librarians and their individual abilities to contribute to the program. The original committee of three received notice of their appointment December 21. On February 15 all librarians of schools which were members of AATS were notified to expect a call for the conference. Notices were sent April 5 to the various library journals giving the time and place of meeting. On April 12 the dean on the committee wrote all the presidents and deans, giving the time and place of the conference and suggesting each make it financially possible for his librarian to attend. The official notice of time, place, and purpose was mailed April 25 to all AATS librarians. The first draft of the program was ready by May 3. On May 24 the final program was finished. The conference met June 23–24.

The preparatory activity covered a period of six months. Many problems were encountered, much time was consumed, and more than 650 communications exchanged. At first the going was slow, uncertain, and difficult. The problems were varied, such as the cooperation of the librarians who were accustomed to area group meetings; the uncertainty of the financial support for the expenses of the librarians who should attend; the problem of time and place most favorable for the largest attendance; the competition of other national conferences of interest to some theological librarians; the frequency of meetings, whether annual, biennial, or triennial. On March 6, twenty-three librarians were committed to attend but a member of the committee thought this was not enough; where and how to house and feed the conferees; where to hold the sessions of the conference; how to organize a permanent body, especially the first officers and the constitution; and above all, the program—who should talk about what?

In the end the problems were all solved. A strong program was prepared and carried out. A permanent organization was set up. Not until the night before the first session had more than two members of the convening committee seen each other face to face. Success was due to a real and widespread desire for such an association and a splendid willingness on the part of all to do what was required.

The First Conference

Fifty librarians, one president, and one dean attended the first conference. All but three of these came from cities other than Louisville. Seven came from west of the Mississippi River: one each from California, Iowa, Minnesota, and Oregon, and three from Texas.

All sessions were held in the chapel of the Louisville Presbyterian Seminary, except one which was held at Southern Baptist Theological Seminary. President Caldwell, Dean Sherrill, and Librarian White of the former school and President Fuller and Librarian Crismon of the latter were cordial in their hospitality.

The main subjects on the program concerned (1) general background and relationship with AATS; (2) a survey of present operations and needs of theological libraries; (3) the contribution which the library should make to theological instruction; (4) what is adequacy for library accreditation; (5) the proposed study of member libraries by AATS during 1948–50; (6) additional indexing of religious periodicals; (7) cataloging and classification; (8) bibliographies; (9) the proposed AATS booklist; (10) reference work; (11) administration including in-service training; and (12) extension service. Nineteen names appear on the program—to read papers, to direct the sessions, and to contribute amenities and hospitality.

Parallel to the discussion program, committees were meeting and business sessions were held, so that on the afternoon of the second day a permanent organization was effected by adopting a name, a tentative constitution, and a slate of officers with an executive committee.

For the next annual program the conference set up a list of projects, each one aimed at the solution of a problem common to all or a majority of the librarians. A committee was appointed to study each problem and to bring a proposal for solution, or a program of action.

Each of the morning sessions was opened with a period of worship which in succeeding conferences has always included the reading of a portion of the Scriptures and prayer, and sometimes with the added feature of a brief devotional comment or the singing of a hymn.

Another characteristic of the first conference was the free and general participation in the discussion of each topic on the program. The convening committee encouraged the presentation of the total experience of the membership on each problem discussed.

Back of this emphasis was the principle of the democratic process, both with reference to the business sessions as well as to the program. The conference was convened to work out cooperatively the solutions of common problems, not to listen to authoritarian pronouncements on those problems.

At the first session the atmosphere was rather reserved and cool. Some of the librarians knew a few of the others but for the most part those who assembled that first morning were a group of strangers. Between sessions introductions multiplied, backgrounds and contacts were discovered. Qualities of personalities were revealed in the discussions. Respect and appreciation for one another grew as evidences of ability and scholarship multiplied. At the close of the last session a stranger would have thought a big family reunion was breaking up.

That the first session had proved to be all or more than was anticipated is revealed in the resolutions adopted at the last session,

> Be it resolved, That we here assembled express our profound appreciation of the insight of the American Association of Theological Schools which foresaw the need of such an assembly of librarians and of the efforts of the persons who dedicated themselves to the task of producing an interesting, instructive, and helpful meeting.
>
> *Second*, whereas, Much thought and time have been devoted to the preparation of these most helpful papers; therefore: Be it resolved, That we be recorded as expressing sincere thanks to all who have participated in the program.

Fourth, whereas, Great gains and much benefit have resulted from our association and from our sharing of insights in these two days; therefore: Be it resolved, That this fellowship which has been so auspiciously begun shall be periodically continued, and that the gains shall be conserved by all means which may be deemed feasible.

THE FIRST SIX YEARS, 1947–1953

Affiliations

Both before and during the first conference much thought was given to the matter of affiliation with similar national bodies—the American Library Association, through the division of College and Research Libraries; the Council of National Library Associations; the American Association of Theological Schools. It was soon recognized, if ever seriously doubted, that primary affiliation with AATS was the most important to the success of the new organization. The former was the parent body of the latter; the institutions we served were members of this parent body, and we were dependent on these respective institutions to make financially possible our common participation, without which no national association could be sustained. Relationship was established with ALA, through ACRL. An experimental affiliation with CNLA was soon discontinued.

The Constitution

The convening committee brought to the first conference a suggested constitution. It was adopted provisionally, with some minor changes. Final decision was made in 1948 at Dayton. Since then some amendments have been made for the purpose of more clearly defining a statement, or of making some operative provision more flexible or more effective.

The active membership consists of the professional members of the library staffs of the schools in AATS. Librarians in charge of denominational and other religious libraries are welcomed.

The executive committee is the responsible group for making arrangements for the conferences, preparing programs, and supervising the work of the project and other committees. The democratic process prevails in that the executive committee is elected by the membership and must work along the lines of policy adopted by them.

The Project Committees

The main work of the Association has been carried on by the project committees and their reports have been the chief features of the programs. By process of experience they may be said to have divided themselves into perennials, semi-perennials, and annuals. The perennials, those reporting all of the past six conferences are three in number:

- Periodical indexing
- Cataloging and classifying
- Survey, including standards and accreditation

The semi-perennials are those reporting on three or more of the six conference programs. They are:

- Building and Equipment, five times
- List of Master's Theses in Religion, four times
- Personnel, four times
- Periodical Exchange, four times
- Extension Loan Service, four times
- Audio-visual and Micro-Materials, four times
- The Educational Function of the Library, three times

Some of the annuals, especially those presented by speakers not professional theological librarians, were:

- Micro-Processes
- Microcards
- The Organization and Work of ALA
- Binding and Mending

Membership and Attendance Record

Table 1 reveals the consistency of the Association's statistics. They give an assurance of stability and value.

Results

Two projects of tangible form have been completed. One was the list of out-of-print books needing to be reprinted. This list was based on reports made by the members. As a result, a worthwhile list of important works was reprinted. The other is the list of master's theses in religion containing 2900 entries. It too was based on the cooperative responses of the membership. In both cases, however, the main burden was carried by the respective committees, especially the hard-working and devoted chairmen.

Another accomplishment was the devising of a system of duplicate periodical exchange. It operates on a minimum expense of time and money. Mem-

Table 1. Membership Statistics for the ATLA

	Attendance	Active Members	Associate Members	Institutional Members
1947	51			
1948	57			
1949	51	92	13	77
1950	59	95	11	75
1951	51	91	11	74
1952	63	81	11	77
1953	98	128	17	78

ber libraries are receiving needed periodicals at a cost of two postcards and transportation.

Help on building and equipment problems has been considerable. Beside information given on programs to the whole body, much individual assistance has been offered in private contacts between sessions.

The Association has been interested during the past year in the fifty-year catalog of the Doctor Williams Library, London, England. This outstanding non-Conformist library has not had a printed catalog since 1900. Our interest in this catalog and advance orders from our members seem to have encouraged the contribution from British sources of the amount needed for publication.

Spirit and Ideals

The most important part of any organization is its spirit and its ideals. During these six years and seven sessions the work and the personal associations have been characterized by friendliness and cooperation. The emphasis has been on teamwork. Members have shown a willingness to accept responsibilities and to discharge them energetically. Appreciation for services rendered has been sincere and generous without glorifying individuals. From the beginning the Association has emphasized the democratic process.

One of the chief ideals has been the professional quality of the work of the Association. This has been regarded not an end in itself but as the means to the constant improvement of service to theological education in the several libraries. Thorough scholarship is recognized as the liege man of both sound theological instruction and effective piety. The note is often struck on appreciation of and loyalty to permanent values, but without ignoring the usefulness of changed approaches and new methods.

The Association has passed through its experimental period. Its structure and program have been tested and approved by experience. Its worth and usefulness have been recognized by the American Association of Theological

Schools. Loyalty in the future to its purposes and ideals will assure its perpetuity.

NOTES

1. Robert L. Kelly, *Theological Education in America; A Study of One Hundred Sixty-one Theological Schools in the United States and Canada* (New York: George H. Doran, 1924).

2. *The Education of American Ministers* (New York: Institute of Social and Religious Research, 1934).

3. Harvie Branscomb, *Teaching with Books; A Study of College Libraries* (Chicago: Association of American Colleges, American Library Association, 1940).

33

Building on Our Strengths for the Future

33rd Annual Conference, New Brighton, MN, 1979

Elmer J. O'Brien

The presidential address is no longer a predictable ingredient of the annual conference program. In recent years some presidents have chosen to remain silent, probably because they were astute enough to know that by the end of their term of office they were lame ducks and lacked the necessary power to strongly influence the future. But in recent years there have been two presidential addresses that, upon reflection, performed a useful function. In 1972, President Genevieve Kelly spoke on the theme "The Eternal Quadrangle."[1] She spoke to the tensions between librarians, faculty, administrators, and students. In 1974, President John Batsel sketched "An Alternative Future for ATLA."[2] Both Kelly and Batsel attempted to express the situation in our Association at the time and offer some description of where they thought we might go in the future. I do think it is important that from time to time we express who we think we are and the possible directions in which we may move. My purpose in making a statement is to express some thoughts along these lines. Those of us who have been active in the Association for a number of years may take much of this for granted, but for those who are new in the Association I believe it is helpful to sketch what ATLA means and where it may move in the future.

Any of you who have used the curriculum materials produced by our friends in the field of religious education know that one of the persistent themes they emphasize is "Who am I?" A number of years ago I helped teach some pre-school children and the curriculum we used dealt with the question "Who am I?" *ad nauseam.* Having finished the stint of teaching pre-schoolers, I looked forward to joining an adult study group where we would deal with content. To my chagrin the first quarter of study was on "Who am I?" Not long after that, a change of employment followed and the present institution I serve was inaugurating a new curriculum. Almost before my feet were firmly planted on campus, the faculty decided to establish Core Groups. These are twice weekly meetings of students and faculty designed to integrate various aspects of the curriculum and to explore personal and professional concerns. The question "Who am I?" is always, eternally there.

Who are we? Obviously we are librarians. Most of us are theological librarians, working in institutions that prepare persons for some form of professional service in ministry. Most of us would tend to think of ourselves as professionals. I realize there is still considerable debate as to whether or not librarians are professionals. However, functionally we operate as professionals much of the time. Because educational institutions tend to be professional bureaucracies it is not surprising that we adapt ourselves to the prevailing pattern in our institutions. One analyst has said, "The Professional Bureaucracy relies for coordination on the standardization of skills and its associated design parameter, training and indoctrination. It hires duly trained and indoctrinated specialists—professionals—for the operating core, and then gives them considerable control over their own work."[3] This same analyst goes on to state, "Control over his own work means that the professional works relatively independently of his colleagues, but closely with the clients he serves."[4] Surely all of us recognize something of ourselves in these statements. Systems and standards loom large in our vocabulary today. Doralyn Hickey's column on standards in our *Newsletter* is indicative of an increasing professional concern in our Association, as is the Board of Directors' concern to broaden the scope of the former Committee on Cataloging and Classification to include bibliographic systems. We are striving more and more to develop and coordinate a standardization of skills and knowledge which mark us as a professional group. On the other hand, the work of the librarian is closely linked with the clients he or she serves. It is in this latter relationship that we operate independently and exercise discretionary powers. Personal contact with faculty, students, and other library clients is an arena where each of us exercises considerable freedom. Last year, Dr. Thomas Galvin made a strong case for formulating our collection policies so that they are more clearly client oriented. I sensed that most of us agreed with him. The ATLA Needs Survey, taken several years ago, verified that one of the major concerns of members in the Association is bibliographic instruction of clients. Again, these and similar concerns which you can cite indicate a growing professionalism among us.

An additional indicator of professionalism is that which relates to training and indoctrination. Initial training for most professions takes place in a university or special institution. In this setting the skills and knowledge of the profession are programmed into the would-be-professional. The degree one attains after satisfactorily completing the training amounts to a certification for the profession. As any library administrator can testify, there follows a period of on-the-job training. A library science degree does not a fully trained librarian make. The process of training never ceases. "As new knowledge is generated and new skills develop, the professional upgrades his expertise. He reads the journals, attends the conferences, and perhaps also returns periodically for formal retraining."[5]

One could go on to identify additional data in the literature of organization and leadership to strengthen the case that functionally most of us operate as professionals. The reason for sketching this identification is quite important, it seems to me, if we are to understand who we are. Knowing and recognizing who we are says a great deal about the possibilities that lie ahead of us as an organization. The professional is a particular breed of the species and will act and react in certain ways that are fairly well known. Let us now move more directly to the implications these observations have for ATLA and its future.

By and large it seems fair to say that ATLA is a voluntary association of professionals. I've never sensed that very many of us have been overtly pressured into either joining or participating in ATLA. For the most part we are drawn together by some common interests and goals. We are drawn together partly, one would guess, because we serve institutions that have a general educational goal of training persons for professional service in ministry. Presumably our institutions are similar enough that we consequently share similar interests and concerns. A few years ago a group of us were attending a meeting at one of our seminaries. Two of us were asked to step out of the room for a few minutes. We walked down the hall. There wasn't much to do so we began looking over the bulletin board at the end of the corridor. After reading some of the notices posted there, the other fellow turned to me and said, "You could take the bulletin board in any one of our schools, transport it to another campus and it would fit perfectly." There are differences among us, to be sure, but we come from institutions that are remarkably alike.

As theological librarians we share common interests. Our commitments and goals are reflected in our organizational structure. One senses there is a solid commitment to the Boards of Periodical Indexing and Microtext. For years we've had committees on library materials exchange, cataloging and classification, membership, annual conferences, and the like. In the past several years some new interests have emerged: collection evaluation and development, serials control, professional education and development, and the preservation of theological materials, to name the obvious examples. These newly emerging interests and our commitment to them remain to be completely tested. Their emergence, however, and the enthusiasm or lack of enthusiasm they generate tell us a great deal about the direction in which we are headed over the next several years. Clearly there are some new interests and some new leadership emerging.

How can ATLA capitalize on these new concerns, advance the state of theological librarianship, and accomplish some new objectives? Let me be bold enough to sketch what I believe is a possible paradigm for our future. My paradigm is certainly only one of several possibilities that could be suggested. I invite you to think of other possibilities besides the one I shall attempt to sketch.

First, ATLA will remain a voluntary association for the foreseeable future. As an association of professionals an even higher premium will be placed upon individual autonomy. Probably there will develop clusters of members interested in the achievement of certain goals. This autonomy and clustering is, it seems to me, a positive development and should be encouraged. In this way, there is an opportunity to develop expertise and leadership within our own ranks. As this trend is encouraged it will be important that communication between these clusters of interest be cultivated through the annual conference, the *Newsletter*, and in other ways.

Not only will we remain a voluntary association, but I suggest we build on that strength. Even with a new dues structure it is clear that we will still generate relatively modest amounts of revenue for our general fund. Even if we could somehow raise enough money to employ a full-time Executive Secretary with secretarial help, would that strengthen the Association? I'm not convinced it necessarily would. If we employed a staff it would be deceptively easy to assume that the staff will do the work. Staffing could destroy the commitment many members have to the organization. Bureaucratization and institutionalism could conceivably create a distancing between the members and the Association. Even with a staff there would not be any less need for voluntary membership time. With economic pressures being what they are, I believe our future remains one of drawing on the time, energies, and leadership of our own members to advance the goals of the Association.

There is a need to clearly identify our goals and to articulate them effectively. The annual conference serves as a forum where new ideas, proposed projects, and long-established interests in the Association can test new initiatives and receive feedback from the membership. The Board of Directors, working with the Committee on Annual Conferences, could more intentionally structure our June meetings to make sure this happens. The Board, over the past several years, has created internal committees to deal with this possibility in addition to other concerns. The annual conference, in this paradigm, would not only provide programs but would also help us define our goals more clearly.

After goals and/or projects have been clearly identified, an ad hoc or standing committee could be created or assigned the responsibility of developing an appropriate program. Here we could draw on the clusters of interest in the Association. If a project is involved the committee would define the program, identify its financial needs, and proceed to secure funding. If funding is required outside our regular budget, proposals could be developed and submitted to appropriate agencies and foundations. After funding is secured the committee would hire the necessary staff to execute the project. This discrete project approach has the advantage of avoiding many of the pitfalls inherent in permanent institutional staffing. In some cases it might eventually lead to permanent staffing, but that would emerge from rather than being a condition imposed on the project(s) from the beginning. This also leaves a large part of the management of projects in control of the membership where it is amenable to member concerns.

Let me offer an example of how this works. The Serials Control Project has been with us long enough that most of you are more or less familiar with it. Several members of the Association, a number of years ago, observed that regional groups of theological schools were compiling union lists of serials. If a particular regional group had several Baptist institutions within it, for example, that union list would reflect that strength, while a similar list generated by another regional group would reflect other strengths. Consequently, the suggestion was made that a comprehensive union list of theological serials was needed and desirable.

For several years the Committee on Publication worked with the comprehensive union list idea. In 1975 they identified one hundred twenty (120) theological libraries which were participating in regional listings of periodical holdings. The Ad Hoc Committee on Serials Control was formed the following year. During 1977–78 the Ad Hoc Committee worked on a Pilot Project, funded with a grant from the Association of Theological Schools, to test the feasibility of building a bibliographical data base via distributed cataloging using the Boston Theological Institute's CONSER capacity. Last June seventeen ATLA libraries were selected as initial centers of responsibility for phase one of the continuing project, and they met at our annual conference.

Currently the Ad Hoc Committee is drafting a proposal to submit to the National Endowment for the Humanities this December to fund a major phase of the project. If the funding is secured, a project director will be employed to supervise the work. There have been problems and delays along the way, but now the committee under Dorothy Parks' capable leadership is well on the way to generating the proposal.

There are several features of this project that offer a good model for other efforts of the Association. The idea of a union list has been well tested among us and there has been significant support developed for the project. A cluster of interested members has devoted untold hours developing the *modus operandi* and doing the investigation and fact-finding work preliminary to writing the proposal. The committee has engaged the services of Peter Oliver to write the grant proposal that will be submitted to NEH. Efforts are underway to secure CONSER status for the project so that it will complement the BTI's serial project.

Once we are successful in funding the project, a project director will be employed and a central office established. Denominational centers will contribute records to the database, thus reflecting regional participation. The project will last a stated period of time.

This model has a number of things to commend it. It has arisen out of expressed needs, it has been developed by the membership, it has received ATS support through the grant for a pilot project, and it is a discrete project with a definable goal. It will be managed by the same people as those who generated the proposal. The plan will work regionally so that the concerns of affiliation and representation are addressed. Yet there will be a central office to focus our efforts. The final result will benefit all of us.

I believe it is rather clear that ATLA's future is strongly linked to intentionality. As we are able to clearly state and identify our goals then we can marshal our resources to achieve our intentions. To do this I have suggested that we build on our strengths as a voluntary association of professionals. What has been sketched here by way of a paradigm is nothing new or novel. Many of you could sketch other paradigms, and I hope you will. In sketching this paradigm part of the purpose has been to state what I see emerging in the Association over the past six years. The question of "who are we?" can only be answered at a point in time. We are constantly in the process of becoming. I believe we are becoming a more professional organization, and I believe we shall become stronger and more effective as we structure intentionality into our organizational life.

NOTES

1. Genevieve Kelly, "The Eternal Quadrangle," *American Theological Library Association Summary of Proceedings* 26 (1972): 67–74.
2. John D. Batsel, "An Alternative Future for ATLA," *American Theological Library Association Summary of Proceedings* 28 (1974): 101–108.
3. Henry Mintzberg, *The Structuring of Organizations: A Synthesis of the Research* (Englewood Cliffs, N.J.: Prentice-Hall, 1979), 349.
4. Mintzberg, *The Structuring of Organizations*, 349.
5. Mintzberg, *The Structuring of Organizations*, 350–351.

34

A Look at the Past
33rd Annual Conference, New Brighton, MN, 1979

G. Paul Hamm

"Who am I?" "What is my role?" "What am I to do?" "What will I have done if I succeed in my new vocation?" were some of the questions I asked when I became a librarian in 1968. I had left the security of a pastorate to enter a new professional role. As a pastor, I knew my role. My function was clear to me. I had achieved a measure of success as a church leader. I assumed that my new role and function would be every bit as clear.

To my growing dismay and confusion, there were no satisfactory answers to who I was, what I was to do, or what constituted success as a librarian. My ignorance was not dispelled in the course of study for a Master of Library Science degree at the University of California. I was determined to discover my identity, however. When I later began research for a doctoral dissertation, I chose the general topic of the role of the library and librarian, knowing that the topic could be narrowed down when writing time came. For two years, I combed the libraries of the San Francisco Bay Area for information on the topic. When I arranged my resource material, I realized that the library/librarian role could not be discussed as an isolated entity but must be considered in relation to the philosophy and teaching method in theological education.

I will attempt to picture historically what the role of the library in theological education has been. I will discuss the major influences on the development of the theological library role. I will survey and summarize what theological educators have said about the philosophy and teaching method of theological education. I will delineate the historical development of theological libraries and then summarize this paper.

I realize that this topic is much too broad to be covered adequately. It is too general and limits specificity. My insights are dependent in large part on what theological educators have said about theological education. However, the fact that theological educators should be expected to be sympathetic with their profession makes their criticisms all the more devastating. I have hoped that this address, or my dissertation, or both, would incite or inspire others to use my work as an object of attack, point of departure, or springboard to do more specific study on the topics addressed.

MAJOR STUDIES OF AMERICAN
THEOLOGICAL EDUCATION

There have been four major studies of American theological education. Beginning in 1924, there was a major study every decade, the last one published in 1957.

The Kelly Report. As a result of widespread concern that Protestant ministerial education was inadequate, a comprehensive survey of 161 theological schools in the United States and Canada was published in 1924. Many were aware that there was a crisis because there were fewer and less capable ministerial candidates to lead the churches. All sorts of opinions and diagnoses of the problem and prescriptions for a cure had been made, but no careful study had been made of the seminaries. Robert Lincoln Kelly, Executive Secretary of the Church Boards of Education, New York, made a study to learn the facts and find a solution, and published a report of his findings.[1] The volume contained 400 pages, plus 56 pages of appendixes and index, but only one page was devoted to libraries.

The May Report. A massive, four-volume study was published in 1934 under the auspices of the Conference of Theological Seminaries in the United States and Canada and the Institute of Social and Religious Research. This was perhaps the most influential study of all because it resulted in the reorganization of the Conference of Theological Seminaries and Colleges, the establishment of a Commission on Accrediting, and the production of the first theological library standards. The report contained 14,000 pages, with 62 chapters in three volumes and one volume of statistics, questionnaires, etc. It contained one chapter of 43 pages which was a condensation of a master's thesis by Raymond P. Morris. A section entitled "Library Services" contained three paragraphs, one of which was less than three lines long, and a section entitled "The Seminary Library," which contained five paragraphs.[2]

The Hartshorne Report. A study of theological education in the Northern Baptist Convention was published in 1945. This one-volume report contained a great deal of information on philosophy and teaching method, but no comment on libraries.[3]

The Niebuhr Report. Perhaps the best known report was a volume jointly authored by H. Richard Niebuhr, Daniel Day Williams, and James M. Gustafson. The treatment of libraries in the study and report either reflect the general attitude toward libraries or illustrate factors that affected the role of libraries, or both.

The American Association of Theological Schools decided in 1948 to dedicate the next two years (1948–50) to "a survey of the libraries in relation to the curriculum and teaching methods" of the accredited schools of AATS.[4] At the same meeting, AATS decided to make another study of theological education. There was a question at first whether the library survey should be a separate one of major magnitude but it was decided to include it as a part of the survey of theological education. The report was published in 1956. Ironically, the authors declared in the report that it had not been practical to give sufficient time in the survey to a detailed study of the libraries and their problems.[5]

THE INFLUENCE OF RAYMOND P. MORRIS

The one individual who influenced the development of the role of theological libraries in America more than any other was Raymond P. Morris. His master's thesis, entitled *A Study of the Library Facilities of a Group of Representative Protestant Theological Seminaries in the United States and Canada,*[6] was somewhat of a bombshell in the theological world. Many of his findings were published in the May report. Morris's involvement in the Library Development Project in the early 1960s, the ATLA and its Board of Microtext, and other similar contributions makes his influence without parallel in American theological education.

THE INFLUENCE OF THE A(A)TS AND ATLA

The establishment in 1918 of the Conference of Theological Seminaries and Colleges in the United States and Canada (later AATS, then ATS) was probably the most influential single event in the history of theological education in America. ATS has been responsible for major surveys of theological education, accrediting standards, the securing of large foundation grants, and encouraging new approaches in educating ministers, as well as other important contributions to theological libraries.

The American Theological Library Association held its first meeting in

1947. It was the child of ATS, although forces were already at work that would have resulted in an association of theological librarians without ATS initiative. Since ATLA has worked very closely with ATS, it is difficult to assess its unique contribution. ATLA has provided a forum for librarians to voice the importance of the library in theological education. ATLA stimulated the revision of library standards, aroused concern for more adequate library resources and a more adequate library staff, organized and administered the Library Development Project, and has had an ongoing beneficial influence upon the role of theological libraries.

MAJOR EVENTS

Prior to the establishment of ATS in 1918, theological education in America had been sporadic and unorganized. The establishment of a headquarters office with an executive director and supporting staff, provision of committees, and standing commissions and accrediting functions provided for the upgrading of theological education in general and theological libraries in particular. The major studies and reports (1924, 1934, 1945, and 1957) provided concrete data for the examination of the theological enterprise, although libraries failed to receive adequate attention. The organization of ATLA in 1947 provided a unique vehicle for the improvement of libraries. The Library Development Project (1961–66) made the one most significant contribution to the growth and efficiency of theological libraries in America. It remains to be seen whether the ATS standards of 1971 will have a similar impact on theological libraries.

RELATION AMONG PHILOSOPHY, TEACHING METHOD, AND LIBRARIES

As has been indicated, the role of the library cannot be examined in isolation but must be seen in relation to the classroom. In addition, library holdings, lighting, salaries of personnel, and similar characteristics do not define the role of a library but they do tell us something of that role.

1636–1918. Theological education in America began with the founding of Harvard in 1636. The aim of theological education prior to the establishment of seminaries was to provide religious leadership in the new homeland. One objective was to safeguard against heresy and fanaticism. The method of training was tutorial, as a pastor would open his home and library to a ministerial candidate who would serve a kind of apprenticeship. As the number of candidates grew, pastors would train small groups, or "schools of the prophets." Of course, the libraries were small. Harvard began with 100 volumes, and one minister-tutor had one long shelf of books.

The early seminaries saw Christianity as a body of truth to be mastered, preserved, defended, and propagated. There were no electives and little opportunity for research. There was a decline in educational standards. The libraries of the schools were very small and their administration simple.

Following the Civil War, seminaries attempted to imitate the educational changes in the colleges and universities. They began to try to prepare students for specific ministerial tasks. They improved their teaching methods. These changes were minimal, however, and imposed little strain on the libraries, which were small, poorly administered, and inadequately supported.

Throughout this period, a knowledge-transmission, content-centered approach to ministerial training was practiced. There was little influence exerted between the philosophy and teaching method and the libraries.

1918–1946. The establishment of ATS provided the opportunity for study of and reflection on theological education from a national perspective. The studies by Kelly, May, and Hartshorne provided written data that could be carefully studied.

According to Kelly in 1924, the traditional isolation of the seminaries from their contemporary world was dramatically displayed in their approach to education. Many seminaries could not be correctly termed educational institutions because they used neither the language nor methods of modern education. The use of the lecture method and assignment of textbooks was employed in the classroom. This inhibited creativity and innovation.

Kelly cited the libraries as illustrations of the inadequacy of the current philosophy and methodology. The libraries were often locked and unheated and showed little indication of workshop conditions. The books were not accessible or convenient and lighting facilities were inadequate. Administration was poor, the collections were small, and expenditures inadequate.

The May report in 1934 showed little had changed in the decade since Kelly's report. The philosophy was content-centered and teaching methods consisted of lectures, discussions, recitations, and case, project, or similar methods. As one would expect, the May report (based on Morris's thesis) showed the libraries to be inferior, poorly housed, poorly equipped, understaffed, and their administration inadequate.

Hartshorne in 1945, in a study of American Baptist seminaries, stated that theological faculty members were brilliant in subject matter but ignorant of educational teaching theory. He failed to deal with library needs.

Theological libraries mirrored their environment. They were helpless pawns in their academic communities. They were poor but they were just what the schools deserved.

A curious development that has since been characteristic of the history of theological libraries was seen during this period. There were pressures to change the libraries, but they did not come from within the context of individual institutions. They came from farsighted individuals, reports from associations, and the first standard for theological libraries by ATS (1936).

1947–1960. The establishment of ATLA was the most important development of this period. This development demonstrated that seminary administrators were concerned about their libraries. ATLA provided a forum and vehicle for the articulation of the library's proper role.

Leading theological educators began to call for a more effective educational process that gave a more central role to the library. They called for a student- and learning-centered educational process.

The Niebuhr report in 1956 charged that theological education was concerned with the piecemeal transmission of knowledge and skills instead of companionship in learning. Teaching methodology was characterized by the "didactic stance," a disease characterized by lecturing to the exclusion of discussion, the urge to "get everything in," and the feeling that graduation was the end of a process rather than the commencement of life-long learning.

Although the Niebuhr report indicated there had been insufficient time to survey libraries and their problems adequately, there were encouraging words about the libraries. A central role for the librarian as an educator and counselor of students and teachers was called for. The depiction of the library was accurate and sympathetic. Acquisition expenditures had almost doubled since the time of Morris's report in 1932. There were a number of new or projected buildings. The salary, expertise, and status of librarians had improved. The libraries were still inadequate in terms of financial support, personnel, buildings, and collections but most of all in their utilization by the institutions they served.

Also in this period, a comprehensive report on library standards was approved (1952) by ATS, aimed at integrating the library into the educational process, and a scholarship fund was secured from Lilly Endowments, Inc. to enhance the qualifications of library personnel. The library standards were revised and upgraded in 1958.

1961–1972. This decade was characterized by the physical growth of theological libraries. The Library Development Project influenced the improvement of theological libraries more than any other single effort. A grant from Sealantic Fund, Inc.[7] provided matching funds for schools that would increase their expenditures for books and periodicals up to a maximum of $3,000 per year. But more than physical growth was involved. The program's four objectives were (1) to strengthen the book collections of the institutions by increased book expenditures; (2) to improve library operations and services; (3) to influence library expenditures as the academic community recognized the worthiness and importance of library needs; and (4) to attract stronger administrative personnel to take advantage of increased opportunity and incentive. A self-analysis was required and teams of librarians and faculty were available to implement the program and assist the institutions. An estimated $5,000,000 was added to the assets of about one hundred theological libraries in five years. The $5,000,000 did not include funds for building construction or improvement of physical facilities.

These improvements in libraries were not paralleled by improvements in teaching method or philosophy of education. Critiques by theological educators indicated that theological education had not escaped the ruts that had held it since its beginning. If these educators were correct, theological education still lacked a proper concept of its purpose, was isolated, parochial, and seemingly unaware of the chaotic change taking place all around. The teacher as knowledge-dispenser still stood at the center of the process, and the battle between continuing and terminal education continued. The same educators who lamented the sad state of theological education seemed unaware of the library's potential in alleviating that condition. Although the libraries and their administration were improving steadily, their importance was minimal to theological educators in general.

There was a polarization of some theological educators concerning the library. In their haste to promote a relevant theological education, some educators assigned the library a minimal role. Theological libraries should have minimal resources and nucleus libraries. Public libraries and the students' personal libraries were to be the resources of the students of the seventies. Others continued to insist on the library-as-heart-of-the-institution with the richest resources and utilization possible.

During this period, ATS took two actions that indicated the interest of theological educators in improving theological libraries. In 1972, a joint ATS-ATLA committee was created to study theological libraries in the light of current needs and trends. The title of the committee, "AATS-ATLA Task Force on a Strategy for Seminary Libraries and Learning Material Centers for the 1970s," was significant. The study and subsequent report of the committee had little or no impact.

The standards for accrediting were completely reworked and approved in 1972. Several changes were made that would enhance the role of theological libraries, but it remains to be seen how these will be interpreted and how seriously they will be enforced.

SUMMARY

Feilding stated that "The whole theological enterprise seems . . . to be off on a vast archaeological dig, preoccupied with long ago, and largely oblivious of the purpose of the expedition."[8] Feilding said again that "a cynic who observed that theology is learned to pass examinations would not be far wrong."⁹

Application of current educational theory has been lacking in theological education. This is due perhaps to the conviction on the part of many theological educators that Christianity consists of a body of truth to be preserved, defended, and propagated. According to the literature of theological education, these educators felt that the task of theological education was to convey this body of truth to the theological student and equip him to preserve, defend, and propagate it.

The teaching methods of theological education have mirrored the educational philosophy. Teachers have been chosen on the basis of their subject expertise, rather than educational ability. There is an amazing unanimity among theological educators that theological education has historically been lecture-dominated, content-centered, and textbook-oriented. The teacher has been the authoritarian figure in the process, dispensing knowledge and skill in a piecemeal fashion. Naturally, the role of the library has been a negligible one.

The role of the library has mirrored its educational context. The library has not been an active partner in the educational process. The library resources have tended to be little more than is needed to support the inadequate educational process and methodology. It has been necessary for the librarian to be an educator. One reason theological teachers have stayed in their rut is that they have had no choice. Few creative alternatives to the lecture method have been offered, so teachers continued to do the only thing they knew. The librarian has not been considered, even by himself/herself, a true colleague in the educational process.

It has been charged that theological education lags at least a century behind higher education in general. Creative, exciting alternatives to traditional methodology have been available for years. Through the proper adaptation and administration of learning resources (software and hardware), students should learn more in less time and with more enjoyment. The dull and repetitious can be eliminated; learning can be more colorful, exciting, and enduring.

Paradoxically, theological libraries have grown steadily in every respect (though they are still inferior) while the philosophy and method of theological education have remained basically the same. The improvement in the libraries has not been motivated from within individual institutions as much as through outside influences. The ATS, representing seminary administrators, and ATLA, representing librarians, have been the prime movers in the change.

Theological libraries have improved to a point almost beyond comparison to their earlier counterparts. The administration of these libraries is no longer charged to untrained persons such as a retired or part-time teacher.

Theological libraries are more and more being administered by professionally trained individuals who are the equal professionally of anyone else in the institution. Theological libraries and their administrators are in a position unparalleled in history to exert a beneficial influence on the philosophy and methodology of theological education.

NOTES

1. Robert L. Kelly, *Theological Education in America: A Study of One Hundred Sixty-One Theological Schools in the United States and Canada* (New York: Doran, 1924).

2. Mark A. May (ed.), *The Education of American Ministers* (New York: Institute of Social and Religious Research, 1934).

3. Hugh Hartshorne and Milton C. Froyd, *Theological Education in the Northern Baptist Convention* (Philadelphia: Judson Press, 1945).

4. Walter N. Roberts, "Steps Toward a Library Survey," *Summary of Proceedings. 3rd Annual Conference of the American Theological Library Association* (Chicago: ATLA, 1949): 2–3.

5. H. Richard Niebuhr, *The Purpose of the Church and Its Ministry; Reflections on the Aims of Theological Education* (New York: Harper, 1956).

6. Raymond P. Morris, *A Study of the Library Facilities of a Group of Representative Protestant Theological Seminaries in the United States and Canada.* Unpublished Master's thesis, School of Library Service, Columbia University, 1932.

7. Paul F. Stuehrenberg, "A Giant Step Forward: The Sealantic Fund and the American Theological Library Association Library Development Project," in *The American Theological Library Association; Essays in Celebration of the First Fifty Years*, ed. M. Patrick Graham, Valerie R. Hotchkiss, Kenneth E. Rowe (Evanston: The American Theological Library Association, 1996), 60–70.

8. Charles R. Feilding, *Education for Ministry* (Dayton: American Association of Theological Schools, 1966), 10.

9. Feilding, *Education for Ministry*, 30–31.

35

A Combined Greeting to ATLA 40 and Reflection on ATLA 1

40th Annual Conference, Kansas City, KS, 1986

Ernest G. White

Greetings to you who are attending this Fortieth Conference of ATLA and who are pausing for a few moments on this hot afternoon to reflect on ATLA's history and on your heritage as members of this organization.

I use the words "hot afternoon" advisedly, based on my own experiences of traveling through Missouri and Kansas at this time of year and on the conclusion that, if it's June, if it's an afternoon, and if it's in Kansas City, it's bound to be hot! I well remember the very first time ATLA met in Kansas City. St. Paul Methodist School was the host. It was an excellently constructed program, and the host was superb; but the meetings were held in what had once been a small hotel, somewhere to the south of downtown. There was not a shred of air conditioning available, and there was no relief to be found either inside or outside. So we had a very, very steamy time of it.

Two or three weeks ago your program chairman, Michael Boddy, telephoned me and invited me to come to Kansas City for this session. It was a flattering and enticing invitation, and I accepted it. Perhaps the chief value in my being here would have been for some of you to see what a living fossil looks like! Alas, however, we are still in a situation where the schedules of the next generation govern our own schedules. Our son, Peter, known to many of you, is to be married this very next Saturday, down near Chattanooga, Tennessee. I first thought that I would be able to manage both events, arriving home from Kansas City at 9:30 on Wednesday night and leaving for Tennessee early Thursday morning; but the closer the time came for it, the more I realized that I was not quite up to handling it. So I had to call John Trotti, the convenor of this particular session, and renege on my promise. John, in turn, asked me to prepare this tape for you; but, as I wrote to him yesterday, I think that it might have been easier to come to Kansas City than to prepare, or to dictate, this tape!

It is an historical fact that our institution was the first, in fact the sole or lone, host of the American Theological Library Association, and this is an historical statistic of which we are very proud. However, it must be said immediately that there is no particular credit due for this fact. No heroics were performed, and there was no effort made to be the first in line. It came about more or less as an accident, or as a natural development. I believe that, in more recent years, we have been inclined to forget, or to overlook, the major role which AATS, now ATS, played in the start of our own organization, for this first meeting was called directly at the request of AATS. My own Dean, Lewis J. Sherrill, was one of the founders of AATS and was a member of the Executive Committee of that group at that time, and he was appointed by AATS to serve as the convenor for our first meeting. Louisville is located in the center of the United States, and our school was very near the downtown area, so this location was a natural site for this gathering.

My earliest recollection of the event was early Sunday morning, very early Sunday morning, on June 22, 1947, when I was awakened by a loud pounding on one of the outside doors to the Seminary. When I got down there to the door, I found a very sleepy and disheveled-looking Stillson Judah, who had ridden all the way straight through on a railroad day coach from Oakland, California in order to attend this first meeting and who was looking for a bed. In that downtown location, we had much experience with street-walkers and bums of every description, so it was with great hesitancy that I finally decided to admit Stillson! But I have never regretted that I did!

That night, then, a group gathered in the lounge of the old Seminary to make final plans for the upcoming conference. I think that it is interesting to note that this was the very first time that the so-called committee had ever met face to face. All of the previous work in connection with the conference had been done by correspondence. Possibly there were others present, but I can recall Dean Sherrill; Ray Morris, of Yale Divinity School; Ken Gapp, of Princeton; Bob Beach, then of Garrett; Evah Ostrander, of Chicago Theological; and L. R. Elliott, of Southwestern Baptist.

It should be noted that this was a no-frills, no-nonsense conference. Future program committees might like to recognize the fact that it lasted for only two days. The sessions began at 10:00 a.m. on a Monday, and they were concluded with a closing gathering at 7:30 p.m. on the very next day, Tuesday. While a few of the conferees stayed at the Seminary, most of them stayed at the Brown Hotel, located just three blocks down Broadway from our school; and we all took our meals at the Brown or at other nearby places. I've often worried that hosts who have had to fret with such fancy additions as an opening reception and a closing banquet have blamed me for them, but such is not the case! They were all later additions to the program. We were responsible, however, for the conference tour which has come to be an annual event. On the very first morning, several of the guests mentioned to me the fact that it would be most regrettable if they had to return home from Louisville and to admit that they had not seen Churchill Downs. So, at a point on the second afternoon, I rigged up an arrangement with our local bus company, and we had ourselves a bus tour! We made a quick stop at the Southern Baptist Seminary, to see Leo Crismon's excellent library, then located on one floor of a wing of the administration building and, perhaps, to keep the tour "legal!" And then we headed for the Downs. At that time, the racing season lasted for only three weeks in the spring and three weeks in the fall, so the place was wide open for the guests to wander all around and to look at the various attractions. Interestingly enough, this was the single feature of the conference which made the greatest impression! At least, it was the thing mentioned to me more often in the years ahead, and it seemed to be remembered with the greatest pleasure.

Nevertheless, with all of its shortcomings, that first conference is not be sold short. Minute for minute, it probably had the greatest impact of any of the thirty-eight or so conferences which followed it. Superb papers were read, covering every aspect of library operation. The Periodical Exchange Program was virtually begun through the efforts of Evah Ostrander, and both a paper and comments from Jannette Newhall actually started the Periodical Index on its way. Lucy Markley, of Union, New York, read a paper on cataloging and classification. What she had to say is largely outdated by today's trends, but, in my opinion, at least, many of her comments are still valid. Other matters discussed had to do with library cooperation, with extension services, with bibliographic work, with accreditation and, especially, accreditation standards, apparently much more a matter of concern back then than they are now, for much of this was still in the formative stage, and, of course, with a constitution for ATLA. That is a story in itself, for it developed that it was a very long time in labor! But the basic constitution was presented at this very first session and was more or less in operation until it was finally adopted several conferences later. It was my dubious honor to be a member of that first Constitution Committee from start to finish, and I have painful memories of its being sent back to Committee time after time.

The success of ATLA was not immediate and was not automatic. Too much credit cannot be given to those Executive Committees of the early years who held the group together almost by sheer force. The first Executive Committee decided that it might be wise to meet in mid-year and at its own expense, and ALA made available to us a meeting room in the old Edgewater Beach Hotel in Chicago at the time of the ALA Midwinter. So we gathered there, reviewed what had taken place both in Louisville and during the time intervening since then, and made plans for the conference ahead.

The whole undertaking was very much a shoestring operation, and most of the basic expenses of those early years were covered either by the officers themselves or by the institutions which those officers represented. Special mention should be made of Bob Beach and the first *Proceedings*, which he published. He initiated these himself and was in sole charge of their preparation, and I believe that the pattern which he set for these continues to this very day. This was a great force in tying the group together and in making them feel much, much more unified. If you ever have the time and inclination, I would heartily recommend that you glance back over the minutes and papers of this first conference. I can guarantee that you will find some of them making for most interesting reading.

Too, memberships did not come easily. It's true that our original membership classifications were rather closely defined. This was done deliberately, because the leadership feared that this newly begun organization might meet with the same fate that had come to the old Religious Books Round Table of ALA. Our first membership dues were set at $2.00 for active members, $1.00 for associate members, and $5.00 for institutional members. During that first year, Bob Beach got out one mailing, and I myself got out two mailings, beating the bushes, so to speak, for membership subscriptions. At that time, and because of the limitations, it was possible for there to be only ninety-four institutional memberships, and it was with some pride that I was able to report at the second conference that seventy-two of the ninety-four eligible libraries had joined ATLA as institutional members. The active memberships at the end of the first year amounted only to eighty-six, and there was a total of five associate memberships. If you get the feeling that I am trying to make the point that those early years were fraught with difficulties, you are correct. But I believe that these difficulties have served to result in the splendid organization which you have before you today and are, indeed, its very solid foundation.

As was inferred at the beginning, you are to be commended for taking this time to pay a few respects to your past, but the real work for you remains in the future, and, as I have said on other occasions, the possibilities for further cooperation and development of every variety seem to me to be enormous. So it is best that you be getting on with this task, knowing that you have my own best wishes for every success in any undertaking which you may elect to tackle. You see, everything that you do by way of outstanding accomplishment serves to make us all the more proud to have been that number one host!

When I thought that I was going to be present in Kansas City, I planned to prepare and distribute a chart of where all you have met during these last thirty-nine or forty years. I think that ATLA has covered the United States most commendably, although a charted map of the meetings might produce some evident gaps. I do not have a list of the places before me, and my memory may be faulty, but, as I recall, we have met three times in the Chicago area, once at Chicago Theological, once at McCormick when it was on the north side, and once at Garrett, out in Evanston. We have also met three times in Louisville. The first one, as has been stated, was on our campus; the second one was on the campus of the Southern Baptist Seminary. This was a big one, for, in addition to our group, the Seminary also hosted AATS and the American Society of Church History at that same time. The third time around was again on the Southern Baptist Seminary campus. We served as co-hosts for that one, but they carried the major burden of the load, and a session over here met on only one afternoon. Consequently, you have probably met in Louisville more than in any other single city. It's really no longer within my province to say so, but this will serve to invite you to return again at any time! It seems most appropriate that you should come back to your birthplace every once in a while, and I am confident that both Ronald Deering, the librarian at Southern Baptist, and Joe Coalter, my own worthy and superb successor, will be most happy to welcome you! Also, when you come around to observing your fiftieth anniversary, in 1996, if someone will invite me and if someone will furnish a wheelchair, I'll promise to make every effort to be present in person!

Thank you very much for listening and for your patience as I have tried to wrestle with this recorder. Please forget as soon as possible the slips which I have made in handling the machine. Very, very best wishes to you for a most successful Fortieth Conference, in Kansas City, in June, in 1986.

6

CHANGES AND CHALLENGES

36

Introduction

Eileen K. Crawford

My first job in a theological library materialized almost by default. The position posting was for a Judaica librarian to fill an eighteen-month position, cataloging a special purchase of 6000 volumes. Not surprisingly, there was little interest from experienced Judaica librarians in a term position at the low end of the pay scale in a southern university. So I was hired, and confidently began to catalog the English-language material in the collection. I then moved on to the European languages, but eventually was still left with 1500 books in Hebrew. The jig was up; my cover was blown. There I was, a Presbyterian with one semester of biblical Hebrew, surrounded by the books of a Jewish scholar in a language with which I had only a passing acquaintance. I felt like the miller's daughter in a room full of straw, with directions to turn the straw into gold. But where was my "Rumpelstilzskin?" Who was going to save *me* from the fraud I had perpetrated by accepting the position?

To my surprise and profound relief, I discovered I could almost always transliterate a few words of Hebrew on each title page and then find copy cataloging for most of the books in OCLC. When subject headings or call numbers were missing, *Encyclopedia Judaica* provided information on authors and a brief summary of their books. It was analogous to spending each day working on the *New York Times* crossword puzzle: the more obscure the clues, the greater the challenge, and the more fun in solving the puzzle.

I mention this personal challenge to highlight the achievements of Julia Pettee, the creator of the Union Classification System. Several years ago, I discovered the address Julia Pettee delivered at the 1955 ATLA conference and was simultaneously amused, awed, and intimidated by the challenge she had assumed with what can only have been the audacity of a very strong and intelligent woman. A word like "intrepid" is required to do justice to the life and work of Julia Pettee.

As a young librarian in the beginning of the twentieth century, she was invited to reorganize the library at Union Theological Seminary in New York. Pettee accepted this challenge of incredible magnitude and complexity and devised a classification scheme that still remains a viable system today in a handful of theological libraries in the United States and Australia. Only belatedly did the Library of Congress develop its own classification for religion, but it had to compete for many years with a few Catholic and Judaica systems, and Pettee's Union Classification System. The forces of change prodded libraries toward greater standardization and eventually relegated Julia Pettee's system to an historic memory that has been all but forgotten: theological libraries, often unaware of the more elegantly tailored systems of the past, superimposed the Library of Congress and Dewey classifications onto their local collections and labored to accommodate those systems to the emerging theological movements and trends of the 20th century.

Gustave Weigel's address, delivered in the early sixties on the Catholic-Protestant *rapprochement* and the ecumenical movement that spawned this trend, offers a window into the intriguing and constantly-changing intellectual landscape in which theological librarians live. What appears to be no more than a trend in one context may turn out to be the foundation in subsequent decades for a revisionist theory, a new manifestation of an emerging thought, or a reactionary wave that reinvigorates traditional thinking.

This phenomenon of old topics and issues re-emerging in a new guise can also be observed at work within the professional literature of theological librarianship. Connolly Gamble's presidential address highlights some of the issues that challenged the profession in the year 1962: professional training and development, collaboration between faculty and librarians in the educational process, creating bibliographical tools, and recruitment into the profession. In all likelihood, he typed his speech on a typewriter and then sent copies to colleagues through the U.S. mail. Imagine Gamble's amazement if he were somehow able to walk into one of our contemporary libraries, where he would see OPACs that can be accessed remotely, interlibrary loan made easy through bibliographic utilities, difficult reference questions answered by colleagues within minutes of their posting on the ATLA listserv, and keyword searchable electronic bibliographic tools and reference works. As much as we take such innovations for granted, or at times complain about their glitches or slow performance, there is an enduring continuity between Gamble's issues and ours, as can be discerned readily from a look at the more recent ATLA conference programming. All our technological advances have only raised the bar of what is expected by patrons and required by our deans and directors.

ATLA has been an important vehicle in providing a collaborative structure which has enabled even relatively poor theological libraries to provide their patrons with bibliographic access to the literature in the field. Dickerson and Peltz's article on the history of the *Index to Religious Periodical Literature* chronicles the difficult decisions that, in retrospect, were made wisely and courageously. Without the leadership within the association to develop this early example of a bibliographic tool, none of the products and services currently offered through ATLA would be available. However, ATLA is much more than a source of products: the membership services that enrich our professional lives are possible only as a by-product of a healthy association.

ATLA's importance to theological librarianship is articulated in Decherd Turner's address on the Association's fortieth anniversary in 1986. Together as colleagues and friends, ATLA members have weathered the "revolutions, evolutions, and syndromes" that have aided or beset their work. Computers, copy machines, conservation, special collections, and what Turner refers to as the "Ransom Syndrome" are the dramatic changes he singles out for special attention. I expect none of us would select the same five today. Digitization, electronic holdings, access versus ownership, delivery systems, and shrinking budgets are only a few of the topics that characterize 21st century discussions.

Lest we theological librarians feel we are alone in dealing with perpetual change, publishing executive Clayton Carlson offers us a view into the world of academic religious publishers. Academic publishers, he claims, depend on a marketplace that will buy serious literature. From Carlson's perspective in the 1980s, popular culture was the threat, and his fear was that soon there would be no one left who was willing to publish a serious book. Publishers have even more to grapple with today. Free information on the Internet and copyright enforcement in an environment of easy duplication are only a couple of realities that complicate publishers' ability to profitably predict market share for their titles.

We know enough about our patrons to observe that the emergence of new and ambitious digital ventures is not likely to quell completely the demand for top-quality print resources. In the meantime, one ongoing dilemma for librarians is the allocation of limited funds to purchase the right balance of resources in traditional print formats and electronic formats (many of which have advantages over their print predecessors, while perhaps lacking their permanence).

Globalization is yet another of the exciting trends that remind us of our relative wealth in theological education. Robert Schreiter's article on this topic challenges libraries to assume their role in preparing their institutions for the commitment to globalization. Since Schreiter's article was written,

ATLA has created a committee on international collaboration and has made contact with many theological associations around the world. Many of them have websites where collaborative projects such as union lists, acquisitions resources, and member directories provide easy access to information that even a few years ago would have been unknown to libraries in the United States and Canada. There are regional theological library associations in Asia, Africa, Latin America, and Europe, and countless associations in individual countries.

Finally, Roy Stokes' address expresses the concern that, in a time of enormous change, librarians are "followers of trends rather than pioneers." One could argue this point on a number of levels. What remains unchanging is the commitment we as librarians have to long-held core values: excellence of service; commitment to learning; respect for individual beliefs; and preservation of the human record for future generations.

Although all I know of Julia Pettee are her words on a page, I think of her as my mentor. How would she have handled the changes and challenges we face in this new century? The answer comes to me without hesitation: undaunted, with an intrepid spirit, and a wry sense of humor.

37

On the Union Classification
9th Annual Conference, New York, NY, 1955

Julia Pettee

I really must thank Mr. Morris for giving you a rest before my speech. You perhaps can endure it better. When I spoke at Dr. Rockwell's dinner, Dr. Coffin introduced me as the author of the driest book he had ever set his eyes on. So it is really very gratifying to me to see so many of you here who are familiar with that dry book and have steeled yourselves voluntarily to listen to the author.

When I was invited to come and talk to you, I was delighted. When I tried to think what on earth to talk about, I got pretty cold feet. You see, it is fifteen years since I have used that classification that I made, and for the last four years I have been immured up on my hill farm, remote from both theological and library interests. So it seemed to me the only thing I could really talk about was to tell you younger people something of what theological librarians faced over half a century ago.

Now, in 1894, I was a student in the Pratt Institute Library School, a brand-new school just preceded by a few years by Albany. At that date, the library world was much smaller than it is now, and we underlings had a much better opportunity of being personally acquainted with the highlights in the profession. For several years I was on the Dewey Committee and so became personally acquainted with Mr. Dewey. Mr. Dewey was a large man

---

This discussion completes the series begun two years ago at Evanston when several seminary librarians discussed their experiences with the Dewey and Library of Congress Classifications. The following has been transcribed [by Ruth Eisenhart], with a minimum of editing, from a recording made at the Conference.

with black hair, piercing black eyes, and a very dominating personality. You gave Mr. Dewey the information that he asked for, and did not discuss things with him. He told you what was what, and that was the end of it. Now Mr. Cutter was a very different type of man. He had just then finished his dictionary catalog for the Athenaeum Library and had published his *Rules for a Dictionary Catalogue.* Mr. Dewey, at that date and in that century, was at the height of his fame as the author of a relative classification system.

I suppose classifications of knowledge are as old as civilization. But, when libraries came to use them, they applied the classification not to books but to the spaces in which books were contained. The old monastic libraries had cupboards along the walls with history and theology in them, and when the books were removed to rooms, the alcoves were allocated to certain topics. This custom of allocating spaces to books continued on down through the ages to the modern steel stack. The modern steel stack was given a Roman numeral, the section in the stack was given an Arabic numeral, and the shelves numbered from the bottom up.

Mr. Dewey was interested in making a classed subject catalog, and he devised his decimal classification for this purpose, for applying it to a classified catalog on cards. Then the brilliant idea occurred to him: if this system can be applied to cards, why can't it be applied directly to the books? This idea revolutionized the practice of a thousand years. In the last quarter of the last century, libraries were simply tumbling over each other to put in this new relative classification system.

But theological libraries lagged several decades behind. As far as I know, no theological library was classified by a relative system until the present century.

Fifty years ago I was a classifier in the Vassar College Library when the librarian of Rochester Theological Seminary wandered in and told me incidentally that the trustees had authorized the reorganization of that library the following summer. Naturally we began to talk about classification systems and methods of cataloging. The upshot of that was that I was invited to spend the next summer reorganizing the Rochester Theological Seminary Library, a library of some fifty thousand volumes.

That winter I visited every theological library within a convenient distance, but found very little, except that at Hartford they had an incipient classification scheme which we used in making an original scheme for Rochester. So, that summer vacation I went to Rochester to take charge of the reorganization of that library. We gathered a fine staff, and I turned over the non-theological books to an Albany graduate, giving her complete charge of putting them in the Dewey. I confined myself to the theological books. Well, the work out there just hummed, and the only fly in the ointment was labels.

Every library is accustomed to plastering on the backs of their books those great white labels to expedite their shelving. I laid in a bountiful supply, and when several hundred volumes were put through and duly decorated with these white labels, I gazed with pride upon theses symbols of a new dispensation. Then the president walked in. Now, if Dr. Strong had been half blind, he couldn't have failed to see those gleaming white labels . . . "Who," he said, "has been defacing our books? These labels must come off. This must be stopped!" Dr. Strong was willing for us to put on gold leaf, but that was too technical a process. We finally found a draughtsman among the students, and I went to the president and said that if he would allow this draughtsman to put on the white ink, he would do it so skillfully that he would really beautify the books instead of defacing them. The president was still a little skeptical, so to gain my point, I said, "Well, Dr. Strong, you know it would expedite the work, and I promise you that if you let this draughtsman put on the white ink, I won't varnish them, and when I'm gone, it can all be rubbed off and the books will look just as they did before." Dr. Strong consented to that, and before I left, the books were being permanently varnished, with Dr. Strong's full approval.

I completed that library in two summer vacations and a half-year leave of absence. When I got back to Vassar, I found an invitation to come down here to New York and take charge of the reorganization of this great library at Union Seminary. When I reached here, of course, I found the old fixed shelf notation, where Dr. Briggs, a former librarian, had gone through the stacks and very carefully assigned certain shelves to certain books, labeling the shelves and labeling the section which they were in. I suppose from some system he had in his head, because I never was able to get possession of it.

When I arrived, this was the practice at Union Seminary: The cataloger made one author card and placed it in the book. The books were assembled on a truck. The librarian, Dr. Rockwell, rolled the truck down to the stacks, and then, with the book in his hand, he would look around for the place where similar books were placed. When he found it, he would put the number of the stack and section in the book and on the card. Then he placed the book on the shelf and the card was returned to be filed in the catalog. Books were not *classed* in those days, books were *located*. We talked about "locating" books, and the catalogers had no responsibility either for classing books or for making the subject catalog. In the earlier period of library development, the chief librarian himself retained those functions.

Now, there is nothing static about a classification scheme. The way we sort our ideas is constantly changing, so it is not very strange that there should be found in the stacks of some fifty years ago an arrangement that would seem odd to us today. Union already at that date had quite a large collection on charities and social welfare, and these books were in the section that bore the label: "Home Missions." Then, there was quite a remarkable section in the stacks which we discovered. It bore the label: "Minor Morals."

Men have never known what to do with women. These theologians had an idea. They considered women a moral problem. And, as women were not a very great consequence anyway, they fitted very well under the caption "Minor Morals." And actually on the shelves here at Union under "Minor Morals" were these topics, in this order: first came Profanity; then came Drunkenness; Drunkenness was followed by Lotteries; Lotteries was followed by Women; and after Women came Dueling. The whole series of Minor Morals was climaxed by: War.

Classifying a great library like Union was quite a different matter from a smaller library such as Rochester. But at Rochester, thanks to Dr. Beveridge, I had learned a great deal. In the first place, I had a pretty comprehensive knowledge of the whole field of theology, and I had also handled a great many books in it. I was very much dissatisfied at Rochester with the dual system which we had introduced: one classification for non-theological literature and another classification entirely different for religious books.

When I was a student at Vassar, the president addressed the senior class, telling us that there were three distinct breaks in creation, with an impassible gulf between them. The first was between organic and inorganic matter. The second was between the animals and man endowed with the human soul. These were two absolutely distinct creations with no relationship whatever between them. The third absolute break was between the natural world and the spiritual world directly revealed by God in the Bible.

Now, even at that date, I could not accept this. It seemed to me that the universe was an integrated whole, composed of an infinite number of correlated parts. And I wanted one single classification that would represent this unity. Then, too, for practical reasons theological students are not encased in a glass cage separate from the world. Also, in their instruction both religious and secular books are brought together. So it seemed to me that a single unified classification based upon the uses and needs of the theologian would be the type of classification that would be most useful.

In my opinion a special library is better served by a special classification than by a general classification system. A general classification views the whole field of knowledge and each portion has equal value with every other portion. But a specialist views the field of knowledge from his own particular angle, and selects from this field of knowledge the portions that are useful to him and develops those portions. So I wanted a single, integrated classification scheme adapted to the purposes of theologians.

In order to make a classification it is absolutely necessary to have some framework upon which you can hang your topics. Where could we find such a framework? The Dewey didn't seem to answer our purpose, but one of our professors found a classification of knowledge that had just recently been put forth by a German, Dr. Munsterberg. Now I have no particular thesis for this Munsterberg classification of knowledge, but it did seem to serve our purpose by cutting down through the whole field of knowledge along lines that would bring the theological and non-theological material together in a useful juxtaposition with a minimum of overlapping topics. So we decided to adapt that classification in building our scheme for Union.

In making our classification scheme in those early days, we came upon some very controversial topics. In the first place, Mr. Dewey had been astute enough in the early days of biblical criticism to seize upon the then very new idea that the separate books of the Bible were literary documents composed at various different periods and finally brought together in one book. Upon that theory, Mr. Dewey set up the books of the Bible as separate entities, gathering under each book all the literature about that book. Now, curiously enough, Dr. Briggs, one of the Union professors and one of the founders of modern biblical criticism who fought valiantly for it, was very hostile to this idea. He much preferred the older system of approaching the Bible as a unit by different methods. The first method of approach was the study of the text, and textual criticism was one line of division in the classification. Then came the introductory approach, literary and historical criticism; then the study of the canon; and finally the exegesis and the commentary. In that older system, if you wanted to collect all the literature on the Psalms, you would have to collect it from these half-dozen different classification lines.

Another very popular method of approach in all the older classification systems is the historical approach. If you will study the older systems, you will see that the history of even minute topics is separated from the text of the topic. The history of the Bible was miles away from other literature on the Bible. It was considered as introductory to Church History, and the Bible stories of the Old Testament and the New Testament were followed by the history of the Christian church right on down to date. At Hartford, actually set upon the shelves was the series from the Creation of Adam right through Church History down to the Congregational Church in Connecticut, bearing the label: "History of the Kingdom."

I am greatly indebted in making this classification system to a subject catalog made by a former librarian, Dr. Gillett. He had worked out a really fine subject catalog on cards, classified, of course, according to the older theological encyclopedia. Although Union's system is not based upon the older theological encyclopedia, having these cards arranged by this older system gave me a very thorough comprehension of the older system, and when I broke away from it, I knew what I was doing. Then, too, since the cards were arranged by subjects, I could send the cards down to the stack and collect all the literature on a subject when I was reclassing. In making a classification system, especially, it is very useful to have a large body of literature on hand upon which to work. So the Union scheme is not only a theoretical scheme, but it is based on the actual handling of very many books.

Now, as I said, a classification is never static. Our ideas change constantly. As an illustration of this, one of the first classes that I reclassed at Union was the class of Irenics or Church Union. At that date, some forty or fifty years ago, all the books on Church Union dealt with doctrinal differences and attempts to reconcile these different doctrines; so, of course, it was set up in doctrinal theology. But before the classification was published, the churches were getting together on an entirely different basis, organizing to promote the practical interests of the church. The Federal Council of Churches and other organizations of that time were set up. Of course, these practical measures could by no means be classed in doctrinal theology; we had to set them up in the practical theology class. So, unfortunately, in the Union scheme, the whole movement of Church Union is divided into two very different sections.

I cannot conclude this very brief and inadequate sketch of a few of the problems we met in making the Union Classification scheme without expressing my indebtedness to the Union faculty. As each section was worked through, it was submitted to some member of the faculty who was interested in that section for his revision and suggestions, which were very freely given. And, also, I am most indebted to my former chief, Dr. Rockwell. Much of the work of the classification was due to him. He was practically responsible for the Church History and Church Law sections. And, too, in that earlier period, there was quite a good deal of criticism against the new scheme for breaking away from the older theological encyclopedia. I don't know how much Dr. Rockwell suffered, but he protected me, and I am very grateful to the administration for leaving me alone and allowing me unhampered to work out my own ideas.

I think the unique feature of the Union scheme is its Christian Literature class. When I was a student at Vassar, we studied literature by authors. The college library, disregarding the Dewey form divisions, collected all the works by or about an author in single author groups. When I came to Union, I found that some libraries were treating the Church Fathers in that way. I saw no reason why, as this was such an excellent way of treating literature, all the Christian writers from the Church Fathers right on down to date should not be treated in this way, and a great Christian Literature class set up to form a source class for both history and doctrine.

We set up the Church Fathers and followed them with the medieval writers. Saint Thomas Aquinas was followed by the Catholic writers right down to date. Then came the Reformation, and after it the Protestant divines by country and period divisions. This worked without a hitch through the Reformation, and I included the seventeenth and eighteenth centuries with the earlier periods. It is my ideal of a Christian Literature class that it be followed directly right down to date. But, when we come to the nineteenth and twentieth centuries, this Christian Literature class comes into a head-on collision with a basic rule of classifying by subject, which applies to theological as well as to secular writers. A British divine writes a book on Greek archaeology. Dr. Frame writes a book on China missions. The interest in the present period is in the subject matter of the book on archaeology or China missions, and not particularly in the author who writes the book.

You may ask why, if we class nineteenth- and twentieth-century books by subject, why do we fail to class them in the earlier periods? Well, there are several very good reasons for this. In the first place, a book written in the earlier period is not of particular practical value; its interest is historical. Then, too, we are talking about a special theological classification made for theologians. In the special literature class for theologians, the interest centers about the man in the earlier periods, and not in some one particular book that he has written. For example, Servetus wrote several books on the circulation of the blood. Theologians are not especially interested in the circulation of the blood, but they are tremendously interested in Servetus. For usefulness to theologians, these books on the circulation of the blood are more conveniently kept under Servetus than scattered off in Medicine.

Perhaps you will wonder, with this basic rule of classifying by subject, what Christian writers of the modern period stand any chance of getting into this Christian Literature class. Well, if any of you are Christian writers, and live long enough to have your collected works published, and you are not the founder of some sect, and you do not become internationally distinguished in some specialty, then you stand a pretty good chance of getting into the Christian Literature class. Then, too, if somebody writes your biography, and that biography isn't wanted anywhere else, you stand a slim chance of getting in.

This brings me to Biography. Now biography in a public library is a very popular class. I confess I love to browse among it and pick out one that intrigues me and take it home for recreational reading—just reading for pure pleasure. But I have my doubts that there is any justification for setting up in a theological classification a class for reading for pure pleasure. You see, we theological people are pretty serious minded. "When joy and duty clash, 'tis joy must go to smash." And, so, there is no place in the Union scheme for reading for pure pleasure unless it is the class: Sermons!

I have a firm conviction as to what to do with biography. It seems to me that the biography of a man is most usefully classed with the subject to which he contributed his major life work. A biography of a scientist with science; the biography of a theologian with theology. We class John Wesley with the Methodist Church in England. We class Joseph Smith with the Mormons. A minister who spends his whole life in some single parish contributes to the history of that parish. Where else would he be more usefully classed? The minister who serves several parishes under one denomination contributes to the history of that denomination. And I have been greatly impressed how much a biographical sketch of some obscure clergyman or circuit rider sometimes does contribute to the history of the denomination. If it were classed elsewhere the value to the denomination would be lost.

Well, in classing biography we come upon a very perplexing question: what to do with some of our leading Christian writers who transcend the bounds of denominational lines, and whose interests are too broad to be compressed into a single subject group? For example, take such an outstanding man as our Dr. Fosdick. He is a Baptist clergyman, a one-time preacher in a Presbyterian church, a long-time professor at Union, and the pastor of a great interdenominational church. Or, take another of our Union professors, Dr. Niebuhr. He is widely interested in social problems, and, as I understand, is a member of a minor denomination, but a man with an international reputation as a theologian. Now, if I were classing, which I'm not, I would unhesitatingly set up such outstanding men as these in the Christian Literature class when a biography or critical work came to hand, because they are interesting as personalities, and interesting for all that they stand for.

Then there is a group of profound thinkers, of theologians who have really evolved a special type of theological thinking which amounts to a school of thought. One of these moderns, Karl Barth, came along while I was still at Union, and I set him up in the Christian Literature class. I understand that Miss Markley and Miss Eisenhart have followed that example and have set other men of that character in that class. To my way of thinking, that is the best way of disposing of them.

In my theory, the Christian Literature class is open to any worthy Christian writer who is not more usefully classed somewhere else. And Christian Literature is not entirely composed of the great, but includes very many minor writers. There are many minor worthy Christian writers who have written several books of value, but who have gained no great distinction in any one field, who are not denominationally known, and it is sometimes a great puzzle what to do with them. I think the Christian Literature class is just the place for them. Though the books that they have written may be classed in other places, their biography goes here very well, because these men are known as writers and only as writers.

I understand that a perennial question arises as to the relationship of the Christian Literature class to the Dogmatics class. The Christian Literature class is a source class for doctrine. It is through the personalities and the writings of these great Christian leaders that we trace the sweep of Christian thinking down through the ages, as it is interpreted and accepted by our churches. The Dogmatics class takes up these doctrines, doctrine by doctrine, and discusses them separately.

Now, if a man is set up in the contemporary Christian Literature class, is it ever legitimate to class one of his books on some specific dogmatic topic— say Justification, or Sin—with the man in the Christian Literature class?

There is one valid objection: it does impoverish the Dogmatics class by removing from it a book by an outstanding author. But, that book can be found through the subject catalog. Then, too, in the stack, arranged under the period divisions of the Christian Literature class, is the total thinking of the period. This total thinking of the period is something which we cannot collect from the catalog and which can only be collected from bibliographies by consulting a number of different ones.

What each library chooses to do with the modern Christian Literature class, I think, rests with the particular library. That decision may be based upon a number of very different factors. It may be just space. It may be the type of library. It may depend on the special collections which it has. And, of course, it must be what the faculty and students wish. If the library prefers to develop and emphasize the Dogmatics class, it is perfectly possible for users of the Union Classification to transfer the total modern period of Christian Literature to the Dogmatics class. I think that the Union scheme is perfectly adapted to this, because there is space for it, and the notation scan be readily adjusted. I was very much pleased to see Dr. Ehlert's remaking of the class of Dogmatic Theology and I think he has done a very good job of it. I am very pleased to think that the Union Classification can be adapted to libraries of very different types with very different collections.

It goes without saying that a classifier can make a wise decision only if he has a very comprehensive and thorough knowledge of the field of literature with which he is dealing. He must know the classification system that he is using, and he must adapt the system to the library which he is serving. But this is not quite all, I think, that will give a classification a slight degree of permanence. I think that it is necessary to think back over the past ages and to note the changes in theological thinking: how it has developed from century to century, and then to try to evaluate the general trend of thinking in our present period, so that we can prognosticate just a little bit into the future to guess how the next generation will be wanting to use our library. And in my opinion, the young people of today are immensely interested in our current Christian leaders, in their personalities, and in their interpretation of our common Christian faith as a way of life. They have not so much the past century's interest in the intellectual and logical interpretation of the single dogmas.

38

When Catholic and Protestant Theologies Meet
15th Annual Conference, Washington, DC, 1961

Gustave Weigel

It is getting to be quite banal to refer to the current phenomenon called the Theological Revival. But the Revival is very real. Not the least significant aspect of its reality is the meeting of the theologies of the different churches. Only thirty years ago the members of the Woodstock College faculty, aside from those who were converts from Protestantism, felt no need to be acquainted with Protestant theological thought. In fact very few bothered with it at all. Today this is all so different. I personally know as many Protestant theologians as Catholic colleagues. My Protestant friends come to Woodstock and lecture to the community and I find myself more and more often speaking to Protestant theological audiences.

The causes and characteristics of the Theological Revival with its consequence of a Catholic–Protestant *rapprochement* can be solidly explained only after a rather long analysis of the historical changes we have experienced during the last thirty years. This task is too arduous for me and hardly accommodated to the purposes of a short consideration. However, we can quickly look at some of the more salient features of the phenomenon.

Ever since the Catholic and Protestant reformations of the 16th century, Catholic and Protestant theologies were necessarily linked to each other. Perhaps Protestant theology was more dependent on its Catholic counterpart than the other way around. Protestantism took a stand of opposition to many Catholic dogmas and perforce had to consider them in order to construct its own doctrine positively. The Catholic theologians living on a tradition and rationale which were derived from an epoch antedating the reformations could independently move on without necessarily heeding the observations made by the newer men. Yet, being human and being interested in the apologetic function of their discipline, they were influenced and excited by what was being done in Protestant circles. In the 16th and 17th centuries Catholic theologians were carefully reading works of Protestant thinkers. An outstanding example is Robert Bellarmine (1542–1621), whose knowledge of the writings of Luther, Calvin, and their associates was quite thorough. His presentation of their thought was objective, though not necessarily sympathetic. Unfortunately, the successors of Bellarmine just used the summaries of Bellarmine in their attempts to understand Reform thought with the consequence that a conventional abstraction called Protestantism took the place of the highly concrete vision which Protestant thinkers were developing. As time went on, the abstraction labeled Protestantism stood in the way of understanding the living thought of Protestant thinkers because this thought was always achieved after it had been unconsciously filtered through the screen of an abstract Protestantism which never had existed. I suggest that something very similar happened on the Protestant side when it tried to meet Catholic thought.

The fruit of this double wall-eyedness was, and to a degree still is, that neither Catholic nor Protestant theologian would see the other as they really were. Two sets of jargon had been set up which are unintelligible to the parties involved in the supposed conversation. We are finally breaking through the opaqueness of jargon, and today we find essays wherein it is clear that Protestants do understand what the Catholic is saying and vice versa. Among others, Jan Jaroslav Pelikan's writings about Catholic doctrine are quite acceptable to Catholics because he obviously does understand the Catholic position. Louis Bouyer's presentation of Protestant thought is generally admitted to be a valid description. What is more important, both men make their expositions with sympathy for what they are describing.

With these prefatory remarks let me, a Catholic theologian, indicate the trends in modern Protestant theology which attract the attention of a Catholic. They probably are not so significant for a Protestant who is quite accustomed to them.

The first thing which strikes the Catholic theologian as he encounters the living Protestant theologians of our time is their concern for speculation, or what is usually called by Protestants, systematics. Speaking in 1961 with a group of theological students at Wesley Seminary in Washington, I said that I thought it was a mistake for seminaries to dedicate so much time to the preparation for churchmanship: poimenics, homiletics, etc. To my pleasant surprise they vehemently agreed with me and somewhat embarrassed their professors of whom they asked for more formal theology and less courses in parish management or pulpit techniques. Paul Tillich for some time has been teaching an ontological theology and he is not too concerned with scientific biblical exegesis. I would venture to say that the present-day Protestant seminarian is not at all content with an exclusively philological analysis of the Scriptures or with a rapid survey of the history of dogma. He wants to investigate dogma itself and find a genuinely objective dogmatic system for his faith.

To the Catholic this trend is most congenial. He has long considered this to be the prime theological task. Systematic dogmatics must be the central concern of the theologian, be he a beginner or an adept. Theology should be what Anselm called faith in search for understanding. Piety should certainly be a by-product of the theological enterprise but it is not its professed goal. Theology wants to understand the Gospel to the degree permitted by the mystery of faith. Now understanding is one form of knowledge and what makes it formally itself is that concepts are used in the approach to the object under consideration. Most of us who are not at all versed in musicology can listen to music and derive great satisfaction from the experience, but we would not claim that we understand it. The musicologist comes to the piece of harmony with many concepts and through his concepts he understands.

It seems to me that in our time Protestant theology is taking kindly to conceptualization. Perhaps the finest monument to this kindness is Gerhard Kittel's *Theologisches Wörterbuch zum Neuen Testament.* This work is not a lexicon in the older style according to which we are given philological structures and their history. The writers for the Kittel lexicon consider their words as transmittors of ideas, and it is the concept which is the object of consideration rather than the historical wrapper around it. We have another instance of the same trend in modern Protestant ecclesiology which is certainly one of the liveliest branches of current Protestant theology. In the 19th century as well as in the first third of the present, church studies were always attempts to describe a concrete group called an *ekklesia.* Today this approach is less prominent. Protestant theologians have become fully aware that *ekklesia* is an idea in its own right before it is an historical fact. The historical *ekklesia* deserves this label only if it realizes the *ekklesia* idea.

In other words, Protestant theology is definitely receding from the exclusively empirical mode as the fruitful achievement of the Christian *kerygma.* The older theologians are not pleased with this new development. They are still looking for the historical Jesus. They do not realize what their younger colleagues see so clearly, namely that the Jesus who saves cannot be found by employing the inadequate apparatus of historical method.

This awareness has furnished the starting point of a second trend in current Protestant theology. This movement is not as widespread as the tendency toward conceptualization but it is certainly here and it produces some confusion in Protestant Christians in general. Before I name the trend, let me describe what has happened. As we have seen, the quest for the historical Jesus is over. Actually the hope which inspired it was laudable, salutary and valid. What failed this aspiration was the structure of the method which was employed. The historical method, in order to be safe for the generality of its questions, so restricted the laws of evidence that the religious in its proper being could not be treated according to such rules. This was evident in the days of historicism. The more you used the historical method on religious data the less religion you found. In the beginning this caused dismay because it was felt that religion was being exposed as a complete fraud with no possibility of saving itself. Then came thinkers who by reflection saw where the problem lay. It was not the unhistorical nature of the religious nor yet the invalidity of the historical method. It was the unconsciously but wisely planned uncongeniality of the historical method for the treatment of the numinous in history. A coin machine whose largest entry admits only a nickel can collect for you pennies, dimes and five-cent pieces. It cannot at the end of the process show you any quarters or half-dollars.

This recognition is a general achievement in our time but it can lead two different ways. The religious historian today is trying to set up a method to deal rationally with the religious object as it can be found in the sphere of the historical. He knows that he cannot simply borrow the apparatus of the secular historian. That much we have all learned. But we have not yet produced a generally recognized rationale for our work. In consequence there is some uneasiness in the undertaking. The method will certainly be an essay in subjectivity but it must at the same time eliminate subjectivism. But subjectivity and subjectivism lie very close together and it is no easy thing to draw a fast and sharp dividing line between them. Phenomenology will certainly dominate the newer method, but it is not at all desirable that its mode must be existentialism.

Because of the tricky nature of the project, some theologians, notably among Protestants, refuse to consider religious data as historical. They even tell us that if we look at them under the lens of historical method, we lose the religious. Divinity has nothing to tell us about secular events nor can it be derived from such an investigation. Religion as a merely empirical phenomenon is not different from other manifestations of human striving. True religion lies beyond the phenomenon. A neutral phenomenology is a good and necessary introduction to the investigation of the religious, but theology begins at the moment when phenomenology is finished.

The danger of this procedure is that we can land flat into the gnosticism of the past. Not only is there an utter despair of finding the historical Jesus but there is a persuasion that he is quite irrelevant to the theological task. I feel that there is a tendency toward gnosticism within the preserve of actual Protestant theology. Perhaps Rudolf Bultmann's star is declining, but it seems to me that he was moving far into the gnostic mist. What made the movement more disturbing was that it seemed to make existentialist interpretation of scriptural myth and symbol the only valid way to interpret biblical affirmations.

The result of this kind of effort is that the ordinary believing Christian is strongly tempted to drop Christianity. The Christ symbol is being explained not in the terms of the life and action of one who in history under Pontius Pilate was crucified, died, was buried, and then rose again. The Christ is divorced quite radically from Jesus of Nazareth. The Christ seems to be a floating vision somehow anchored to the historical Nazarene whose only function was to be a point in history serving as the occasional stance from which we can see beyond history. The Son of Man has been lost although the Logos has indeed been retained. We lose here the poignant cry of the English martyrs in the London Tower who scratched into their cell walls the words: "Sweet Jesu, be Jesus to me." They were committed to the man Jesus and that man, not some vision emanating from him, was the savior.

We have been frequently told in the last thirty years that Christianity, unlike some other religions, is historical and not a moralizing or esoteric allegory. This statement seems to be unimpeachable but we must be careful lest when we say historical, we somehow dehistoricize history to such a degree that it comes out as a most unhistorical thing.

So far I have pointed to two tendencies which I seem to detect in current Protestant theology. They are interrelated and mutually causative. There is a third tendency which springs from both of the preceding.

It is clear from the history of theology that conceptualization and allegorizing bring dangers with them. The conclusion from this truth is not that we should avoid concepts, symbols, and myths. This would be fatal because in these terms we find the *kerygma* and the dogma expressed. However, we must avoid an uncontrolled use of these elements whereby any kind of extravagance can be permitted to flourish in the name of the Gospel. It was perhaps this that the Reformers feared above all else. They wished to restrict valid statement of the Good News to scriptural affirmations. They felt that such expression would be safe.

It seems that today Protestant theologians are re-examining the methodological principle adopted by their 16th century predecessors. The reason is quite obvious. Biblical propositions are not at all free of ambiguity nor yet are they translucent to any reader whatsoever. Both Luther and Calvin were quite convinced that the Councils of Nicea and Chalcedon faithfully paraphrased the Gospel records. Yet during their own lifetimes this conviction was not universal. The Nicene Creed is undoubtedly Trinitarian in its confession just as Luther and Calvin were. But Michael Servetus and the two Sozzinis considered it quite unscriptural. They were unitarians and felt that the New Testament countenanced no doctrine about a triune God. Likewise

Luther could not accept the Calvinistic interpretation of the Eucharistic texts of the Bible. As time went on, it became clear in the many polemics within the Protestant camp that the Bible will not be understood in the same way by all readers. The old slogan which insisted that the Bible must be interpreted by the Bible alone does not solve all problems. The variations of interpretation gradually grew into alarming proportions. This was nowhere seen as clearly as in America which was the fertile field for so many kinds of interpretative schemes of Scripture.

Protestant theologians began to look for a norm of valid interpretation. In the 19th century they felt sure that sound scientific philology could be such a norm. With enthusiasm they applied the tool to the text but in the long run they found that the situation had not improved. Scientific philology could bring forth schemes as many and as varied as the older sectarianism. In consequence the theologians of our generation are looking elsewhere for a norm. They are cautiously returning to the idea of a normative tradition. Their basic recognition can be put into the few phrases I heard spoken by Jan Jaroslav Pelikan. Tradition is primitive; tradition is inevitable; tradition is exegetical. On the occasion Pelikan spoke these words, he also quoted the Orthodox theologian, Father George Florovsky, to the effect that the Christian does not have a choice between tradition or no tradition; he can only choose between good tradition and bad. What Ephesus taught and Nicea decreed are not mere sputterings of theological steam released in a squabble of ecclesiastical politics. They are the perennial Church communicating her understanding of the Gospel, just as she did when she bound together 27 brochures and called them solemnly the New Testament. When the word *homoousion* struggled to the death with *homoiousion*, it was not a fight for an iota subscript but rather for the saving faith in the God-Man Jesus the Christ. That is tradition and it keeps the centuries in line and true.

Protestants are only now beginning to see the dynamism in tradition. They have not yet moved far. Some still think that tradition is the history of the Church. This is not enough. The quest for the historical Christ failed and a quest for the historical Church will fail as well. Tradition is more than an attempt to recapture the past of the Church through the tools of historical science. Tradition is an ecclesiological dimension and can be utilized throughout the theological disciplines. This is beginning to be seen by not a few Protestant theologians and it is going to be most interesting to follow the future of this new theology of tradition. One grateful thing will inevitably result. The conflict between Scripture and Tradition will finally evanesce. It will not be one versus the other. They will both be simultaneously affirmed and in that affirmation Scripture will support the tradition and tradition will buttress the Scripture. They will be one after too long a separation.

If my gaze sees rightly, we can say that Protestant theology at this moment shows three characteristics. First, it is seriously engaged in the proper conceptualization needed to make the Gospel meaningful to our contemporaries. There is less preoccupation with the arid analysis of language and documents. Systematics are coming back into vogue in our theologates. Second, historicism is more than on its way out. It is gone. But by its departure a vacuum is being created. If historicism has left us, does it mean that history must be ignored and the whole Gospel understood as a symbolic presentation of the absurdities of existence in order to be overcome by hope in the great unknown? Can a new rationale be formed to furnish theology with tools to do the history of the Gospel with more adequate equipment than that supplied by secular historical method? These are questions which the near future will answer. Third, Protestant theology is coming to grips with the theological notion of tradition and we already see the beginnings of a clear awareness that tradition means much more than the history of the Church and is rather a theological recognition of an abiding dimension of the Church.

If it be so with Protestant theology, it would not be unreasonable that in the same time Catholic theology should move in similar directions. It seems to me that in fact it is. The work will be different because the starting point is different. Catholic theology has always used conceptualization in its enterprise. In fact it was far more interested in this phase of the theological work than any other. However, there is a new approach to concepts in our day. The whole procedure of Catholic conceptualization is now converging toward the mode employed by Protestants. The ideas used are no longer spun out of a foggy Aristotelian past but are searched for in the theological sources: Scripture and tradition. The return to the Bible has been fervent and enthusiastic. Now the key ideas of the sacred page are the ideas which are being hammered into useful links for the theological system. Here we have a convergence of Catholic thinking toward its Protestant counterpart. Both sides are moving away from their original stands to come closer to each other—but it must be confessed that the convergence has not yet situated the two brotherhoods on the same point, though they are certainly getting into the same area.

Catholic theology in the past was not highly skillful with the historical method. Today, however, it knows its value and structure. It has escaped the pitfalls of historicism but it has had to meet the challenge of history. Two concerns are evident in the confrontation. First, there is an awareness that we must set up some viable canon whereby we can validly do theological history rather than a mere history of dogma. In Catholic circles the big cry is salvational history, and there is a groping toward some scheme whereby it can be framed. Second, to avoid falling victims to the zombie Christianity of gnosticism, Catholic theologians are examining devices they have had for a long time. Those are the concept of analogy, which is a notion parallel to symbolism as understood by Protestants, and also the notion of the evolution of dogma. Both ideas are fruitful in a study of the nature of the *kerygma* which is something distinct from dogma, and both again distinct from theology. This is all thrilling work and it is going merrily along.

The third parallel movement in Catholic theology is the concern with the notion of tradition. Starting from the opposite side from the Protestant concept of tradition, the Catholics are bringing the Scripture into the tradition while the Protestants are bringing the tradition into the Scripture. The end result is that both sides are meeting in the Scripture-tradition complex.

These convergences are very real. As a result, for the first time in hundreds of years Catholic theology is relevant to the Protestant theologian and also the other way around. The scriptural scholars of both flags are already in close collaboration in their common work, and the theologians are now starting to feel a common concern and they are coming together, not as much as the biblical researchers but in a way that is palpable. More communications will still surely come in the days to come.

I have made no mention of the Ecumenical Movement. I tried to avoid the theme, but it cannot be done altogether. The Ecumenical Movement helped to bring the two theologies together, and the converging theologies strengthen the Ecumenical Movement. It is gratifying to see how Ecumenical conversations bring Catholic and Protestant theologians into friendly interchange of theological ideas. This is more visible in Europe than in America, but America is beginning to wake up, haltingly and nervously in these beginnings but gradually with greater confidence and surer foot.

The young theologians who are just beginning their professional careers are certainly entering into an age different from that which the men of my generation entered. At Woodstock College, Paul Tillich, Robert McAfee Brown, and Carl Henry lecture to the Catholic theological students. I, in turn, have lectured at Yale Divinity School and other Protestant theological centers. This is all new but it is glorious. Can we be blamed if we feel thrilled with the present buoyancy of theology which seems to promise an even more vibrant and vigorous action in the future just around the corner?

39

Contemporary Challenges to Theological Librarianship
16th Annual Conference, Hartford, CT, 1962

Connolly C. Gamble Jr.

Recently some American young people were asked, "Would you like to make the first trip to the moon?" One laconic youth replied: "I might as well. There aren't any more projects for pioneers on earth."

Few theological librarians, surveying backlogs of cataloging and book selection, eying desirable services not yet feasible because of inadequate facilities or insufficient staff or restricted budgets, would need to go elsewhere seeking excitement or purposeful labor. There is more than enough work to daunt the most industrious and dedicated in this profession.

A presidential address is sometimes expected to mount a figurative prophetic watchtower and view the distant horizons to bring a relevant word concerning the future for earthbound mortals. My objective is much less ambitious. Lacking a prophet's mantle or a seer's crystal ball, I seek rather to take a look at some of the elements that compose our normal responsibility as theological librarians. This critique of our profession may—hopefully—bring some new insight into our task and highlight some of the crucial issues that challenge our best thought and effort today and tomorrow.

My purpose is to stir the thought processes to identify and to begin to meet the dominant challenges. What problems need attention? What projects ought to have constructive thought and planning in the next few years?

Each of us will doubtless cite different needs. My aim is to stimulate your imaginative attack on the problems. Perhaps my reflections will be infectious.

I should add that I do not mean to imply that these matters have gone unnoticed by our predecessors. Competent leaders have pushed back the boundaries on some of these areas, and their contribution should be appreciated. Yet the frontiers remain: the territory still needs exploration and conquest.

Fresh urgency is given our inquiry by the ATLA Library Development Program. During the past twelve months attention has been focused upon the theological libraries of accredited members of AATS, alerting faculties and administrators to opportunities for library enlargement and increased proficiency. The number of AATS schools who have elected to take part in the program is most heartening. A full report on the program is scheduled later in the conference.

Our colleagues in the faculty and administration are involved with the objectives and program of library service more concretely and intensively than has been true in many seminaries heretofore. The spotlight is on the library more clearly than at any time in recent decades. Thus a magnificent opportunity is at hand: to use this program of library development as an occasion to educate the whole theological community to the central place of the library in theological education.

One challenge may be stated immediately: the need to be thoroughly competent librarians. A quick survey of *Library Literature* indicates the varieties of research and experimentation going on currently in the general library field: the applications of electronic devices to streamline circulation procedures; the use of photographic or electroprinting or punched-tape methods in catalog card reproduction; the possibilities of automation in storing or obtaining a given book. Astounding developments in almost every phase of library work give promise of revolutionary changes in the next years.

No theological librarian worthy of his profession will fail to attempt to keep abreast of the rapid developments in the library world, for he is a *librarian*. Nothing that works in the public or college or special library is meaningless to the seminary librarian. Yet there are also specialized concerns requiring particular attention because of the *theological* orientation of the divinity library. Without ignoring or depreciating the fundamental importance of the broader area, we must also focus upon the particular needs of theological librarianship.

Perhaps the greatest single need in theological library work is genuine reciprocity in the relations of faculty and library. Both faculty members and library staff must recognize this categorical imperative. Both have a stake in the teaching program of the school and should jointly consider the educational methods employed as these impinge upon classroom and library techniques. Both must appraise new methods, asking such questions as these: Is there still validity to Dr. Harvie Branscomb's thesis regarding *Teaching with Books?* Have mass media of communication made the printed book and periodical antique relics? To what extent are films and recordings supplanting books and journals in theological study?

Are classroom procedures pacing students toward ever greater self-reliance and self-dependent study? Are the most capable students led to educate themselves through books as their gateway and guide? By our pedagogy are we training a generation of voracious readers who are encouraged to range widely beyond collateral assignments to discover different viewpoints and engage in dialogue with many writers? Are creative teaching methods stimulating deepened subject study?

The library cannot develop wisely and well apart from consideration for and collaboration in the teacher's cause. In a certain school one professor spends about four hours a week on book selection for library acquisitions in his field. He fails to find a reciprocal interest in educational practice from the library staff. Unilateral concern is not enough: both faculty and library staff must work together in the one task of theological education.

This comes sharply into focus also in the matter of marginal acquisitions. Faculty guides must counsel in determining policy on the peripheral developments alongside subject fields, such as religion and psychiatry, religion and science, religion and history, religion and ethics. Without the sustained interest of the faculty, the librarian is greatly handicapped in foreseeing adjoining subject areas which should be built up to support the teaching program through the years.

Reciprocity between faculty and library should be expressed also in common understanding and interpretation of the library's place in the school's program. Faculty as well as library staff should feel responsibility for library orientation, giving the students more than the details of charge-out procedures. Both faculty and staff should interpret to the students the concept that the library is a central teaching agency of the seminary rather than a mere warehouse for book storage.

Faculty orientation to the library thus becomes indispensable. Counsel between librarian and professor in new course preparations should be an accepted practice. Thus the faculty may discover new or unremembered resources for their teaching, and the librarian may learn of important materials that should be acquired.

Reference service to students and counsel in their library use are likewise essential. The faculty may present to the student not the stereotype of the librarian as a technical specialist but the recognition of a worthy colleague in the academic community.

Another primary challenge is the need for an adequate propadeutic or theological encyclopedia. Each generation should establish its own rationale of theological orientation, surveying the entire theological bibliography, correlating the major fields and subject areas, and selecting the indispensable desiderata in the light of present-day and viable perspectives. *The Theological Encyclopedia* of Crooks and Hurst (1884), the *Theological Propaedeutic* of Philip Schaff (1893), the *Guide to the Study of the Christian Religion* edited by Gerald Birney Smith (1916), and Kenneth Kirk's *The Study of Theology* (1939) served earlier generations as guides to theological education from varying viewpoints.

Today's need is for a similar venture by which the basic bibliography in theological study may be identified, described, and evaluated in the context of contemporary theological developments. This project calls for the catholic breadth of capable bibliographers, meticulously detailed knowledge of learned scholars, and balanced appraisals by judicious theologians. Perhaps it may be initially the contribution of a group of theological librarians or a single seminary faculty. From this provisional start others may add representative and definitive works to bring further balance and proportion to the selections of the original compilers.

Building on this basic structure of theological bibliography, our profession may undertake cooperatively the compilation of a balanced and extensive list of definitive works of general interest to theological libraries. The groundwork for such a project seems already available in *A Theological Book List*, compiled by Raymond P. Morris at the request of the Theological Education Fund. More than ninety divinity professors and librarians gave critical appraisal and constructive advice in the compilation of the Morris list. The new project doubtless will take account of the emphasis upon Asia and Africa in that list, perhaps substituting more substantial scholarly studies for some of the more popular treatments named, and supplementing with later works. In view of the ATLA Library Development Program, it seems highly desirable to launch promptly this project, so that an extensive bibliography may be available as a guide to the constructive expansion of theological collections in the United States and Canada.

Another challenge confronting us is a revision of the standards by which theological libraries are evaluated for accreditation. This is not a new concern of ATLA and AATS. Not many years after ATLA was formed, a committee formulated the first statement of standards, adopted by AATS in 1952. Another committee five years later revised the statement of library standards in a report adopted by AATS in 1958.

Four years' experience with the revision suggests that still further changes may be wise, perhaps to tighten the tension between objective and achievement for those libraries that have reached a minimum but not much beyond. Too, the Standards of 1952 and 1958 have apparently had little effect upon the libraries that were already well beyond the minimum: no challenge for continuing growth and development appears in the Standards for such libraries. Is it unrealistic to hope that another essay will produce a statement that may call attention of administrators to unrealized potentials and desirable goals for even the finest libraries of theology on our continent? A comparison of library expenditures in leading schools of medicine, law, and theology indicates that theological librarians have decidedly the lowest budgets. More than standards is needed, but this may be a point of attack upon the problem.

Still another challenge is the complex of recruitment, training, and personnel placement in theological librarianship. Small comfort to us that this same subject seems to baffle competent legal and medical and public librarians! The triumvirate (recruitment, training, and placement) have to be considered together, though they may be separated for attention to each.

Able committeemen through the fifteen years of ATLA's history have sought workable plans for effective recruitment. Their reports indicate that personal enlistment is probably the only consistent answer to the problem of recruitment. Perhaps all that can be done is persistently to remind ourselves that each librarian must be (along with all the other roles!) a recruitment officer for our profession, taking the time and trouble to interpret to gifted young people the needs and opportunities in the divinity library. Here let me offer a personal testimony: I am in this work because my horizons as a student were enlarged by one who saw and imparted to me a vision of a boundless ministry in theological library service. I was drafted, and the enlistment became voluntary.

Recruitment is made easy or difficult according to whether the training and job opportunities are attractive or uninviting. Progress in special training for theological library work is substantial, thanks to cooperation between some library schools and some notable theological librarians. As courses in theological bibliography and librarianship and cataloging are widely offered, an increasing number of recruits may be expected to enter our field.

All of us were encouraged to learn that median salaries of librarians in AATS accredited schools were increased by 16% from 1958–59 to 1960–61—the highest percentage of increase of any professorial category. Yet a partial explanation is that the librarians' salaries were low to begin with, and the dollar increase for librarians was just slightly more than other professorial groups in this period. The median salary of $6,860 for librarians of accredited schools was more than $650 below the median salary of an assistant professor.

Dr. Jesse Ziegler, Associate Director of AATS, commented that librarian salaries "will need to continue to be increased in order to compete on any favorable basis with colleges and universities."[1] The median salary of college and university librarians was $1,300 above the median for AATS accredited schools' librarians.

Closely related to recruitment and training is an adequate placement service. Matching personnel and positions is exceedingly difficult in a field as highly individualistic as American theological education. Yet it seems clear that ATLA has an obligation to provide such a clearing house of available trained personnel, and that AATS schools would be wise to make use of this channel of information in obtaining the desired personnel for staff positions. Our imaginative attack upon this problem is urgently needed.

Our profession is challenged to assess the responsibility of the library in continuing theological education. Enlarged provisions for residential study on a number of campuses give promise that the tie will be maintained between seminaries and their alumni in the parish ministry. The involvement of the library in residential and non-resident programs of continuing education seems not yet universally recognized. Librarians facing increased service demands with inadequate staffs may regard their assumption of a leading role in continuing education as an impossible added load. Let me record my conviction that the seminary is the primary agency of the church in providing for the continuing education of the church's ministers. In my judgment this task is properly the work of the entire seminary, not merely a project of the library. Yet in many instances the library seems the most appropriate and competent agency to house and administer the seminary's continuing education program. May I also testify that new funds can be secured from constituents for this purpose, when the vitality and renewal of the church's ministers are shown to be a genuine prospect through such a program?

Without attempting to assign an order of priority, I have suggested that our profession faces challenges at these points: to be thoroughly competent librarians; to cultivate reciprocating interests between faculty and library in such areas as teaching method and library use; to prepare a basic theological propadeutic; to undertake revision of library standards; to become more effective in recruitment, training, and placement of library personnel; and to enlarge our understanding of the library's involvement in continuing theological education.

It is easier to identify problems than to solve them, but the first step is to pick out the critical issues. If this paper has served to focus attention upon this need, then perhaps we will be ready together to meet the crucial challenges.

NOTE

1. Monthly Report of the AATS Staff, April, 1962, p. 3.

40

The Index to Religious Periodical Literature: Past, Present, and Future
28th Annual Conference, Denver, CO, 1974

G. Fay Dickerson and John A. Peltz

Volume 1 of the *Index to Religious Periodical Literature* was published in 1953 and contains material beginning in 1949. This year is an appropriate time to pause and reflect on the progress of 25 years of indexing effort. Many of you recall the beginning. I would like to share some thoughts about the course of that progress, during the long and, at times, uncertain genesis of the *Index*, through the present and into the challenging future for which we are planning. I would also like to consider with you the place of the *Index* in the larger framework of national bibliography and abstracting and indexing services in particular.

In 1937 the Religious Books Round Table of ALA sent a questionnaire to 262 libraries to determine the need for better indexing of religious material. Although the response was incomplete, there was general agreement that more adequate coverage was needed, and 372 specific titles were suggested by 79 librarians. H.W. Wilson advised further explorations into the value of a religious periodicals index. In 1938 progress had been made toward launching such an index including Protestant, Catholic, and Jewish periodicals, but a full decade passed and this need was still unmet.

Imagine the effect on religious bibliography in the United States had the recommendations of 1937–1938 been followed. There is no adequate single index coverage for the period between the publishing of Ernest Cushing Richardson's *Periodical Articles on Religion*, 1890–1899 with the *Alphabeti-*

cal Subject Index published in 1907 and the *Author Index* in 1911, until the publishing of the ten volumes of the *Répertoire Général de Sciences Religieuses* and our own *Index* for the decade of the 1950s. If there had been a commercial American service for religious periodicals from 1900 to 1950 would the present be more or less adequately covered? Who is responsible for religious periodical indexing—the professional library society or an association of religion professors? American scholars responded to bibliographic needs by beginning *Religious and Theological Abstracts* and *New Testament Abstracts*, both in 1956. Fr. Brendan Connolly, in an address to ATLA in 1958, "Facets of New Testament Abstracts," justified the value of an English-language approach to many of the same titles covered in *Internationale Zeitschriftenschau für Bibelwissenschaft und Grenzgebiete*, noting that "with a more modest scope . . . the usefulness of presentation in English provided a further reason for believing that [they] were not merely duplicating efforts." Since then other groups have begun bibliographic publications.

Earlier, theological librarians had turned their attention to this problem. In 1947 the American Theological Library Association was founded. The need for indexing was surveyed through yet another questionnaire. Replies agreed with the earlier survey. Librarians wanted either a new religious periodicals index or more religious material incorporated into existing indexes. They compiled a basic list of 140 titles, of which 64 were suggested by ten or more libraries. Little reference is made during this period to European efforts at bibliographic control. On the other hand, care is taken not to duplicate titles already in such American indexes as those published by the Wilson Co. and *Catholic Periodical Index*. A need was expressed for specific subject heading indexing in the American tradition. Note that even in 1947 suggestions were made that a possible merger with *Catholic Periodical Index*, which had been established in 1930, be explored. A majority, though, favored a separate index and recommended a committee to work with H.W. Wilson Co.

ATLA had to get at this part of the American religious bibliography. There were more questionnaires. It was agreed that a new separate index was desirable. If this were impossible, multiple and incomplete sources would have to be relied on such as the *International Index* and *Essay and General Literature Index*, separate journal indexes, the use of European bibliographies, and specific subject bibliographies.

A periodical indexing committee was established by ATLA. Several years work and dialectic were consumed in deciding whether to produce a religious periodicals index, which titles to include, and how to produce it.

The early history of the *Index* is interesting. Read the *Proceedings* of the early years of ATLA. Through the initiatives of this professional society, a small milestone was reached. Initial response was not overwhelming, but it was encouraging. The primary concern was for current service, and, though in a limited way, a contribution was made to American national bibliography.

ATLA decided to prepare a cooperative index covering 30 titles not readily available in other American indexes. In 1953 Volume 1 (1949–1952) of the *Index* appeared with contributions from 20 libraries, edited by J. Stillson Judah. By the time Volume 2 (1953–1954), edited by Pamela W. Quiers, was published in 1956 the committee was sure that certain aspects of cooperative indexing should be abandoned and that the production should be under the direct supervision of a full-time indexing editor.

Mr. Robert Beach was appointed chairman of a committee to make ATLA requests to foundations. The proposal for an *Index* was written by Dr. Jannette E. Newhall and specified the work that was to be done. In 1957 a grant of $30,000 was received from the Sealantic Foundation. (In 1964 a second and terminal grant of $35,000 for development was made by Sealantic Foundation. Miss Helen B. Uhrich wrote this proposal.) The project Committee on Periodical Indexing resigned and a Board of Periodical Indexing was appointed. Dr. Lucy W. Markley accepted an invitation to become editor.

Most of you are familiar with the succeeding history. The *Index* was first housed at Seabury-Western Theological Seminary, and then moved to Princeton Theological Seminary for a number of years. By 1960 Volume 4 (1957–1959) had been published, and, after Dr. Markley's work was complete, a successor was needed. It does nothing for my ego to know I was hired to fill a position described as "a competent full time secretary [who] could carry on with cooperative indexing being channeled to her." I was designated "editorial assistant" most of the period from 1961 until 1965 when I was named editor. In October 1965 *Index* and Editor moved to McCormick Theological Seminary in Chicago where there has been cordial assistance in many ways. Much of the *Index* road over the years has been smoothed by the stewardship of Calvin H. Schmitt, Chairman of the Periodical Indexing Board and Head Librarian at McCormick.

The *Index* staff has increased steadily, and in 1970 John Peltz was appointed Assistant Editor and Sr. Nicole Goetz Book Review Editor in 1971. Volumes 7 through 11 will have been produced in Chicago with 180 journals currently being indexed.

As the *Index* has grown, its purpose has become more clear. The policy on titles included has always illustrated a plurality of interests. In 1948 the Committee on Indexing reported that a "popular vote [of librarians] was instructive but would not give a balanced list," inferring the bias of the sample from any particular group. Volumes 1 and 2, with 30 and 31 titles, respectively, though intended for an American audience, included a few German and French titles. Stated policy during the first several volumes of the *Index* was "to cover scholarly journals in the broad field of religion . . . foreign as well as American journals." The chief concern was "to serve the seminary community," but the *Index* was to be "popular enough to attract many subscribers in the university and public libraries." However, although the scope of the *Index* was broadened, *still*, titles covered by the Wilson indexes such as *Church History, Christian Century,* and *Religion in Life* were omitted. These have since been included.

Our current selection policy gives preference to basic North American scholarly journals and other journals publishing articles in English, with considerable inclusion of representative non-English titles. The alphabetical subject-author arrangement of the *Index*, following patterns developed in standard American indexes, has resulted in a service with international support.

One last comment needs to be made about the misconstrued nemesis, "duplicate indexing," and the dilution of resources due to multiple indexing services, which is suggested by that term. We cannot and do not build a corpus of titles indexed, around and between the lists of all other indexing services. Recent articles critical of some overlapping reach this conclusion by comparing lists of titles processed by abstracting and indexing services. These studies do not adequately consider the pluralistic nature of varied services and their clientele. Much duplication is more apparent than real. These publications differ in ways such as completeness of coverage, use of cross references, retrieval formats, etc. *Of course*, it behooves us all to foster serious cooperation of this type, and these efforts go on. Also, although many publications differ in services offered, some publications complement each other and should be used together. For example, *Catholic Periodical and Literature Index* covers 120 titles; the *Index to Religious Periodical Literature* 180 titles, with only five titles duplicated. Thus if these are used together, access is provided in very similar formats to almost 300 religion journals.

The projected addition of religion titles in the new *Humanities Index* will include 11 new titles that are not in the current *Social Sciences and Humanities Index* yet are indexed by the *IRPL* or *CPLI*. These additions were determined by one of the Wilson Co. user surveys. I believe they are acting responsibly. Public librarians have enough call for such titles for them to expect coverage of important current material in religion. This certainly does not mean that we should not index these same titles for our more specialized purposes.

I would like, at this point, to change the focus of our attention from the past to the present. As a vehicle for this transition, I would like to share with you some general comments and representative quotes from the questionnaire which we recently enclosed with the last semiannual mailed to subscribers this spring. Twenty-seven percent of the questionnaires have been returned thus far. The greatest response is from seminary libraries together with church-related college libraries. This fact must be kept in mind when making inferences from results so far. Non-church-related colleges and universities form a large subscriber group from which a smaller percentage responded.

A wide spectrum of concerns has been expressed; many support expanded coverage and yet a few warn against becoming too large; some are concerned that the subscription price stay low while others state a willingness to pay more for expanded service. About 12% mention a preference for more frequent publication. Many express appreciation for the *Index* as it is, for which we are grateful. Let me quote some responses. Some of you will recognize your own statements. "Satisfied in every respect! Even if you should adjust the subscription price to that of oil, we shall continue to support your excellent work." "We find the *IRPL* an increasingly important bibliographic tool in our library. Of all our indexes, it is the one used most heavily and most consistently. The expanding coverage has made it more valuable each year." Here are two statements which provide an interesting dialectic on the subject of "balance" being maintained within the profile of titles indexed. "The *Index* is being managed superbly and is of immeasurable service to us. Of course the indexing of 'more' periodicals is always welcome; but I would suggest that the *present balance* be maintained in any expanded list." Whereas another says: "I do not believe that the major concern of the *Index* is to have a *balanced selection* of materials. Rather, I think that the *Index* must press forward as rapidly as possible to cover all religious periodicals regardless of the specific area of interest. There should be two major criteria for inclusion. (1) Is the periodical primarily religious or is it essential to theological study? (2) Does it contain substantial and serious articles on the subject of religion?"

There were many suggestions for added titles—326 to date. Titles most often requested are all already indexed elsewhere, from which we infer that no significant title should be omitted as a matter of policy. Responding to another question, subscribers indicate interest in more indexing for areas reflecting contemporary religious and cultural phenomena. At the head of the list are "New and emerging religious movements" and "Culture and religion," followed by twelve other contemporary cultural and practical areas of interest. The more traditional disciplines of theology, biblical studies, church history, and missions are checked as less important for increased coverage. Such responses have to be balanced against the fact that most titles suggested for inclusion are in the traditional fields.

Regarding the language coverage in titles indexed, only a small percentage specify the need for more non-English material. Sixty-eight percent say the present balance of English, French, and German titles meets their needs. There are many requests to index journals of German Catholic theology and titles in Spanish although 30% say there is more non-English material than they need. One college librarian adds somewhat astringently: "The vast, vast majority of college students can't plow through a theological work in a foreign language. In seminary, too, very few students can read a foreign language well enough to read a theological work. . . . Most, but not all, of the teachers in theological schools can handle a foreign language. . . . Why then are one-fourth of the periodicals indexed in a foreign language?"

On another issue, we wanted to survey our users on the relative merits of abstracting as opposed to indexing. We asked the questions, "Do you have any comment on the value of an index without abstracts? Do you find current abstracting services in religion adequate for your needs?" These questions elicited interesting responses that represent the gamut of positions from those who are satisfied with indexing alone to those who would like our *Index* to begin including abstracts. However, a clear majority of responses took a middle position which may be characterized in this statement: "Add abstracts if you can, but we are equally concerned that you continue your *Index* as in the past. Consider indexing more titles and increasing your publication frequency. If adding abstracts means a major rise in price, a slowdown in publication or a change to inferior format, then we would discourage that step." There is an acknowledgement of the value of an index as a locating device for information while abstracts specify more clearly whether a particular article is worth searching out. "Your indexing is invaluable to us even *sans* abstracts. Abstracts, if well done, are primarily a timesaver to the researcher. We would greatly welcome more abstracting. Indexes without abstracts are helpful relative to their quality as indexes, and yours is good."

Again, there is strong support for the usefulness of the Book Review Section although two responses thanked us for pointing out to them that this section existed! They had never noticed it. Frequency is a crucial issue for book review information. Thus some indicate heavier use of *Book Reviews of the Month*. In general, many students use this section for reviews as do some librarians for book selection. One professor indicates heavier use of the Book Reviews than of the *Index*, since in his studies as a theologian he examines other persons' reactions to books he has read.

In addition to the above comments, users express a variety of concerns that they consider proper services of the *Index*. There are requests for retrospective indexing, biographical information on authors and their institutional affiliations, a request for a form entry for bibliographies (we squarebracket "bibliog." and "bibliog. essay" after titles), and numerous other interests.

In conclusion, I would like once more to refocus your perspective, this time on some critical issues for the *future*. There are many variables to consider: staff, relocation, inflation, changing habits of scholarly research, technology, the ever-growing number of indexing services in religion. . . . However, let me comment on three key immediate concerns: (1) the need for feedback from our student-professor clientele; (2) computer-assisted production; (3) our relocation, hopefully not just to a different place, but into an environment of wider information service. First user feedback. . . .

We want to continue our policy of gradual growth; producing a better product. Changes must be based on user needs. Our communication with the library world (though not perfect) is easier to tally than are the needs of students, professors, and the general public. For the *Index* to be valuable for research, we must be sensitive to changes in research interests and bibliographic search habits. Impressions gathered from limited conversations and surveys indicate that many religion scholars are skeptical about the usefulness of the *Index* yet may have rarely looked at it. Too many are even unaware of its existence. They depend on regular scanning of familiar journals and contacts with colleagues. If students and professors in seminaries and universities are to be educated to the importance of the service we are providing we must have more direct contact and encourage them to use it as a primary reference tool. Rising standards in graduate education in religion suggest increased dependence on indexing and abstracting services for the future.

Actually the field of the study of religion in this country is a relative newcomer among academic disciplines in the demand for information service in a contemporary sense. Too many use indexes inadequately. The typical professor is not going to admit that he doesn't understand how to use cross references to find his topic, and probably will not ask the librarian for help.

Another concern is for the implementation of a well-designed automated production system. For several years we have periodically looked into the feasibility of computer-assisted production. Such a step is complex and demands types of expertise not often available to a small operation. Our only approach might be in conjunction with some other agency which has worked through some of these steps. I quote from this year's report of the Board of Periodical Indexing: "We are pursuing the potential of cooperation with the Philosophy Documentation Center at Bowling Green University, publisher of the *Philosopher's Index*. Our conversations envision the possibility of agreements which provide for the modifying of certain computer programs currently in use by the *Philosopher's Index*, in such a manner so that they can be used jointly by both publications to their mutual economic advantage. If successful, the *Index to Religious Periodical Literature* might be in a position, in the near future, to provide for the expansion of the *Index*, the addition of abstracts, and the development of an information retrieval system at a capital cost we can afford and within the budget capabilities of subscribers. This information is intended as a progress report on study and planning for the future."

The third critical issue is a move from our present quarters. Plans have not been formulated but the potential for future growth and possible cooperation among religious abstracting and indexing services must be kept in mind.

The recent report of the Task Force on Scholarly Communication and Publication of the Council on the Study of Religion indicates comparable concerns. "[The Council should] collect and evaluate data on cooperation in bibliographic services, [work for] . . . the development of a common computerized system of providing annual and cumulative indexes for the various member-society journals. The CSR should . . . plan for more adequate . . . bibliographic services in the field of religion as a whole, . . . sponsor meetings of the editors of existing bibliographic services . . . cultivate association with various professional societies of librarians."

These statements, and similar ones made by the joint AATS-ATLA Library Task Force Report of 1973 and by the Association for the Development of Religious Information Systems, lead us to believe that what is needed in the field is a bibliographic and information center acting as a clearing house for such needs as expressed in the CSR report. Though the compilation of the *Index* would remain the main function of such a center, spin-off services might develop such as: reprint services, special bibliographies, a printed thesaurus, and microform publication. The scope of material included in the *Index* should be expanded to include any kind of document more properly handled by indexing than by subject cataloging such as Festschriften, annuals, and the proceedings of scholarly meetings.

A larger, more comprehensive identity suggests itself for the *Index* future, but it seems appropriate to end this talk about the *Index to Religious Periodical Literature* with a quotation, the third stanza of the hymn, "Strong Son of God, Immortal Love":

> Our little systems have their day
> They have their day and cease to be.
> They are but broken lights of Thee,
> And, Thou, O Lord, art more than they.

The *Index* is a "little system" that is being used to bring student, scholar, minister, or layman in touch with the articles he wants. The little system has developed into a somewhat larger "little system." It may be that in meeting current bibliographic demands the *IRPL* will become a part of an even bigger "little system." Our identity may change until it is completely different, but we are called to work and serve faithfully today—and, we jolly well better get on with the task.

41

Revolutions, Evolutions, and Syndromes: ATLA Anniversary Address
40th Annual Conference, Kansas City, KS, 1986

Decherd Turner

Either due to a lack of sufficient sentiment in my make-up (like the lack of calcium) or due to an over-presence of sentiment—I have never quite known which is the case—I have never been comfortable in extensive personal journeys back in time to events of former years. Having, however, been a portion of the academic community for four decades plus, I have been present at many retirement banquets or similar events, where the people being honored spent most of the time, in their responses to verbal-laurels already heaped upon their heads, doing a total vocal recall of events and persons involved in their past associations with the institution. And each time, I have always felt a strange embarrassment, almost as if they were revealing things which should be kept within one's mind and heart. I don't know why this is, but it is a character trait which I have, and thus will explain why I will not speak long concerning the early years of the ATLA.

I was indeed at the first meeting in Louisville, and in fact I was at the first thirteen annual meetings, attending in later years now and then so as to allow other members of my staff to be present. Travel funds were always a problem, and in many years I was so tied to the financial needs and excesses of my own children that I could not always afford to pay the fare out of my pocket, and there was none in the school-till to take care of it. Institutionally, I have always been so deeply in debt due to purchase of books for which there was no immediate budget to cover that every other fiscal facet of the operation suffered severely. But I'm glad that I did, for the libraries I have served are the stronger for such a stance. But of all organizations with which I have been associated, the American Theological Library Association will always hold first spot in my heart. It was, and remains, the instrumentality by which a very special group of people with a very special interest have been able to hone ideas and practices into a professional profile and ethic. The evidence is quite clear. All one has to do is to review the *Proceedings* of the ATLA. What is shown is an immense growth in bibliographic sophistication. This is as it should be. But such results are not automatic. It came about because many people worked hard to translate potential into reality.

I am a theological librarian who served Vanderbilt for four years (1946–1950) and Southern Methodist University for thirty years (1950–1980). I remain a theological librarian who has now served the State of Texas in the Humanities Research Center for six years (1980–1986). My theological background and continuing interest seem to be a source of immense curiosity among my current colleagues. Their curiosity, and my curiosity at their curiosity, creates something of a protective moat, as well at times a genuine verbal barrier. For instance, I remember remarking to a staff colleague that a particular book had profound Christological implications. His puzzled look alerted me to the fact that I had slipped into my old modes of conversation. Finally, he suggested, hesitatingly, that he had not seen anything about glass in the book.

Aside from a substantial change in verbal patterns, working in the director's office of the Humanities Research Center differs mainly in quantity of people and paperwork from working thirty-four years in a theological seminary. The reason for a basic similarity is subject matter. The nature of man and his relationships with his deity is the common concern of theology and the humanities. Certainly James Joyce and T. S. Eliot were among the greatest of 20th century theologians, with W. H. Auden following in a typology of apostolic succession. In the case of Joyce there is even an amazing parallel in the patterns of criticism. The Joyce industry, like biblical criticism, struggles with the problems of a basic text, and the various schools of Joyce critics have an amazing similarity to the schools of biblical critics.

Indeed, working in an institution where 90% of the holdings and research are based on a massive collection of manuscripts and printed books of 19th and 20th century American, British, and French literature has had a reverse educational result in instructing me in theological truths. For instance, I never fully believed in original sin until I started to work with State employees. In the many years when employed in theological institutions, I cherished and nourished an old-fashioned liberal bent toward the belief that in every man there was that spark of divinity which made a strong belief in original sin a type of poetic exaggeration. No longer do I hold such reservations. State employees can be persuasive teachers.

For the sake of a brief recalling of the first meeting of the ATLA in Louisville, Kentucky, let me center on one person—the wonderful man who chaired the first meeting and saw the organization through its early infancy—the late Dr. L. R. Elliott of Ft. Worth, Texas. At the time of the first meeting, I was a cataloger at the Joint University Libraries, Nashville, which served the bibliographic needs of the Vanderbilt School of Religion. When I moved to Southern Methodist University in 1950 to establish the Bridwell Library in Dallas, I, of course, became a neighbor of Dr. Elliott's.

I remember at that first meeting that Dr. Elliott insisted upon pronouncing Louisville as "Lewisville," and that he moved events onward with a firm hand. A man of great charm and great sweetness of spirit, he set in motion most of the projects which occupied the ATLA for years. It was at this meeting that many of the most meaningful friendships of my professional life were started. Unlike Sir Max Beerbohm who wrote that "having been at Oxford is much more comfortable than being there," I am profoundly grateful that I was privileged to be there at the beginning and also to be here forty years later.

The first four decades of the ATLA have been years of dramatic change in the library world. Without verbal inflation, we can call these changes "revolutions"—or at least "evolutions." Let's take five events or attitudes which have changed today's ATLA meeting from the first meeting 40 years ago. Two of the revolutions are mechanical: (1) the presence of the computer and (2) the presence of the copy machine; but let me remind you that culture has a very close relationship to machinery. The great impact of the Gutenberg Bible was not that it was a copy of the Vulgate text (the world didn't overwhelmingly need more copies of the Vulgate text at that time) but rather that the invention of printing was a technology which enforced the standardization of language. William Caxton, the first printer in English, in selecting words for his printed books, standardized English and set in motion the greatest flowering of English culture ever experienced, culminating in the publication of the first Shakespeare folio in 1623.

The third change is the frank facing of the most critical issue of our day—conservation. The fourth change is a change of attitude toward Special Collections, and the fifth change is the rise of the Ransom Syndrome. I will reflect briefly on each of these items.

1. The computer has brought the greatest imaginable change to our labors, and the surface has only been scratched. The computer is the instrument by which a vast cultural change will take place, as it too is standardizing a new language. One can anticipate that in four-five-six generations there will be a cultural explosion many, many times the size of the Elizabethan.

Only the most agile mind can project what our future with the computer will be.

2. The copy machine has been a source of infinite aid. It has also created major problems, problems enhanced by the fact that just as the copy machine was coming into full usage, the copyright laws of the land changed. We therefore live in a period of a tremendous ease in making copies at the same time that the laws concerning the right to make copies tightened tremendously. The issues are particularly difficult in the field of manuscript materials. The purpose of a research librarian's dollar is the gathering of unique materials into one place for the purposes of research. Before the rise of the copy machine, this was a relatively straightforward affair. Someone had a clutch of letters by an important person, the bookseller offered them for sale, and the librarian purchased them.

Perhaps no development has so identified the distinctions between the needs of the research librarian and those of the private collector. For the private collector, there is not the great difference in his love of his original letter by Charles Darwin even though a single copy or fifty Xerox copies exist. After all, the collector has the original. For the research librarian, an entirely different focus prevails. The existence of the copies, or even publication of the letter, has fulfilled the librarian's basic motivation—the letter has been saved. To spend institutional dollars on manuscript materials which have been copied and thus available somewhere is dubious wisdom.

This situation places serious responsibility upon the bookseller and the auction house. Certification that the item has not been copied, and that if copied, that the copies are being surrendered, is not easy. With all honesty, the present owner might affirm he has made no copies, but a former owner might have made a hundred copies. But without certification, the librarian is in serious jeopardy of spending resources for materials which are not unique, thus calling into question his judgment. At the present moment, no fool-proof answer is known, and thus the bookseller and the librarian struggle in a limbo of uncertainty.

3. Conservation is at this moment the single most important issue facing our institutions. We, and our progenitors, have merrily danced through the passing years, gathering swiftly all which we could reach, with small regard for the ultimate price we were to pay for keeping the materials now obtained. The basic truth is that we are going to lose a great many items over the next decades, for the time has simply run out on us. In my own institution my daily prayer is give me "one hundred men for a hundred years." What I do have is a staff of 23 conservators, armed with an amazing amount of equipment and skills. Sometimes, miracles of restoration are performed. But 10,000 miracles will not be enough. In spite of the fact that conservation is big business with us, we are still not going to get everything saved. What is required is an iron-clad priority system immune to special interests, but the fullest realization of such is much easier said than done. We have reached the last day of grace when self-destructing materials can be ignored. Every library administrator must now change styles, no matter how old or revered the style. Henceforth, judgment on his work will be structured on how much of his collection he managed to save, rather than how much new he added.

4. Another change, the growth of *special collections*, requires the full range of the decades to measure. Not as dramatic in its arrival on the scene as conservation but, nevertheless, a great change has taken place in the attitudes toward special collections—albeit strangely enough theological seminaries have never quite made up their minds concerning rare books.

When Melville Dewey established his library school in 1876, its whole approach was structured toward an authoritarian bibliographic democracy. Everything from the Gutenberg Bible to the latest Victorian novel was to be equally available to all people. Cards in pockets became the record of the movement of books to the reader and back to the shelves. There was regnant a genuine conviction that it was, at the minimum, poor administration to have any materials set aside separate from the central regular collection. The bibliographic egalitarianism made one basic assumption and that was that the rights of materials to proper conservation and care by limited access were secondary to the rights of people to use these materials. In other words, special collections were held to be subversive to sound library structure. And, with a few notable exceptions, it wasn't until the 1950s that this stance was challenged. The post-1950 world was to see one of the great sagas of bibliographic change, and that was the rise of interest in and support of special collections. Special collections, when properly conceived, become the bibliographic mirror to a subject, an idea, an event, which is judged important in cultural history. The central idea of special collections is that a special collection will more adequately capture and preserve that idea or subject when kept separate and discrete than would happen if all the materials were scattered in accordance with Deweyesque enforced democracy.

However, the revolutionary nature of special collections must not be overlooked, for such dramatically changes a fundamental concept of library structure. Special collections, because they do receive special care, transcend the old stance of the right of user over the right of materials, and works on the assumption that there is a larger heritage at stake at any single time than a single person or single generation. Indeed it demands that users certify their rights to usage by proper background, previous research, and genuinely articulated perimeters of research, for the materials themselves have preeminent rights to conservation and survival. Thus occurred in the post-1950 world a typology of division between the supportive materials of the academic enterprise—a division between those materials which could be deemed consumable as stack books and reference books and separating those materials whose claim to survival is deemed special.

Another contributing factor entered the picture with the rise of the massive reprint programs. The ultimate end product of wide reprinting is to make all libraries alike. But libraries, like people, will inevitably strive for some type of individuality and identity. And the chief road to this separate identity became the path of special collections.

This brought back into historic reality a facet of book life which had all but been lost during the pre-1950 world—the love of the book because it is a book rather than simply an instrument to an end. The unashamed rise of bibliographic iconography was nurtured through those special books of special collections whose presence proclaim the bibliographic faith—such as the Eric Gill *Four Gospels* which, because of its excellence of production and its position in bibliographic history, proclaims as does the Cross of Christ the genuine bibliographic faith. Not to be touched by ordinary hands or used by the unclean-of-heart, but rather by its presence to declare as surrogate for all lesser books that books are the most important structure for the continuation of Western culture.

Within the context of our mutual involvements in theological librarianship, let me turn to a facet of it which has puzzled my mind—never being able to arrive at an explanation. I am talking about the attitudes of theological libraries toward rare books. Now "rare books" mean many things, but I think you can sort out the specific contours about which I am speaking: the *incunable* period which saw the first printings of many of our most basic classical texts, the sixteenth-century printings of the foundations of Protestantism, landmark imprints of biblical text, etc. No intellectual discipline has such close relationship to these materials than theology—in content, in historic significance, etc. And, yet, generally speaking, it appears that theological libraries have not done the best possible job in this area. In fact, it is easy to slip into the conviction that theological libraries are anti-rare book, or hold so mild an interest that little is done to collect, hold, and use such materials. Again and again I see the foundational publications of our heritage removed from theological collections and sent via the auction room or other arrangements into the keeping of secular institutions. I guess my inability to understand the thinking which permits such must be added to my long list of personal perceptive flaws.

5. The last, but certainly not least, dramatic change I've seen since the first meeting of ATLA is the rise of the *Ransom Syndrome*. This will probably be something of a mystery to some of you, and maybe after I get through my explanation it will remain so. However, it has had such a profound influence upon literary criticism that I cannot think its patina has totally bypassed theological libraries.

The Ransom Syndrome is named for the late Harry Huntt Ransom who in the mid-fifties set out to modify bibliographic geography. And he did so. Mr. Ransom left no record of just when he decided upon the particular plan which had such profound results. I have hypothicated that in one of his 3:00 a.m. periods of sleeplessness he decided how he would break out of the box of fixed bibliographic geography and transform a good library collection into a great one. Think back to 1946. It certainly appeared that bibliographic geography was a fixed picture. The great libraries of the world were known. In the United States, the strong libraries of the East, along with a few institutions on the West coast, would inevitably get stronger. There were, and would continue to be built, good collections throughout the land, but, basically, the patterns of bibliographic dominance would remain as they were.

But substantial change came, and it was due to the Ransom Revolution. What was it? Reduced to its ultimate simplicity, the Ransom Revolution worked on one basic conclusion: that the first edition is not the beginning of the literary process, but rather its end. The first edition, the printed book, comes at the end of a long and at times torturous process consisting of (1) author's original notes; (2) manuscript; (3) corrected, rewritten manuscript— sometimes many times rewritten; (4) copy for printer; (5) galley proofs; (6) corrected galley proofs; (7) page proofs; (8) corrected page proofs; (9) and, ultimately, the printed book.

In other words, the true seat of analysis, criticism, and understanding the literary process is in the pre-published materials, and thus the need for complete archival collections. Later years, with sufficient distance from those often-misunderstood mid-fifties, reveal the dramatic changes brought about by the Ransom Revolution.

It is clear now that Mr. Ransom's central idea was an astonishing combination of foresight and necessity. Let's take the necessity first. The first edition came into its bibliographic kingship 100 years ago, in the 1880s. By the time of the Ransom Revolution, some of the profound tiredness of the dominance of the printed text of the first edition as a basis for literary criticism was all too painfully evident. Remember the shallow and thin and even grotesque schools of criticism which desperately tried to work exhausted soil in these years? But when Ransom turned the attention to the preliminary artifacts, it opened a fertile whole new world, and gave scholarship a massive area in which to work and come to a new understanding of the literary process. From the standpoint of literary criticism, this was the greatest event of our time for it released the scholar from the dominance of the first printed edition and provided entrance into the much wider range of archival collections. The Ransom Revolution made many other changes in the patterns and pricing of collections, the relationships between writers, booksellers, and collections. But the full coverage of those facets is best left to another occasion.

And so revolutions, evolutions, and syndromes will continue to develop the next forty years as they have in the past forty. Certainly it can be said that there have been no dull periods in the last forty years. I salute you for your work with deepest admiration and affection.

42

Can Serious Academic Religious Book Publishing Survive in an Age of Pop Culture?

41st Annual Conference, Berkeley, CA, 1987

Clayton E. Carlson

I have been asked to speak this afternoon on the state of religious book publishing, particularly as it relates to the serious, substantive book. I have chosen as my title for this paper the following: "Can Serious Academic Religious Book Publishing Survive in an Age of Pop Culture?" or to put it more popularly, "Will the Next Paul Tillich Survive in the World of Vanna White?"

It is no secret to any of us that religion is one of those areas in academic life in which it is tough to play a quiet, abstracted, and decorous elite scholarly game. While one can think of several academic disciplines in which peer group communication—scholar to scholar—goes on tranquilly, quite apart from the ongoing tides of the popular culture, religion-oriented studies exist as a thin strand of activity interwoven with the colorful and even boisterous ropes of popular expressions of related themes. The question is not the traditional one: what hath Athens to do with Jerusalem, but what hath Hermann Gunkel to do with Tammy Bakker?

I suppose one can point to other academic disciplines that also live interwoven with popular culture—psychology, which has to live with its Doctor Feelgoods, or aspects of science, which must contend with the creation scientists, or the literature people who have Danielle Steel—but I doubt that there is any other discipline in which the passions run higher or the discomfort deeper than in religion. The reason for this is, I think, that the traditional purpose for serious religious reflection is in the end still thought to be directly related somehow to the living of quite ordinary lives. Hence the quite ordinary has a way of intruding in the most disconcerting ways. No matter how "scientific" the religion scholars feel in the faculty lounge, people do wonder if they pray before going to sleep. Nobody wonders if Northrop Frye reads Barbara Cartland.

Let me see if I can put our question into some admittedly personal short-term historical perspective. I came to Harper's as an editor in 1967, in what was then called the religious books department. I had studied in philosophy at the University of Minnesota, where I was exposed to a weird mixture of logical positivism and Kierkegaardian theistic existentialism; then to Princeton, where reformed theology, analytical philosophy, and specifically philosophy of religion swirled in my mind; and then a year and a half at Cambridge in England, trying and failing to successfully do linguistic analysis of metaphysical language in the wake of Ludwig Wittgenstein's latter work. Moving from this ten-year stint in the hothouse atmosphere of academe into the swirl of New York commercial publishing, I, like all others who find themselves suddenly outside the walls of scholarship, was astounded by how unserious and how easily satisfied the public-at-large seemed to be. For some strange reason, it had never dawned upon me during those ten years that I had been leading a rather elite and specialized form of life. Surrounded as I had been by colleagues and mentors who shared my passions for serious thinking, I had been lulled into believing that except for the few people who tended shops, worked in factories, fixed broken pipes, worked in glass towers, drove cabs, rode subways, went to shopping malls, plowed fields, ran businesses, sold goods to retail outlets, and a few other admittedly necessary but quite mundane activities, all the rest were just like me. What I didn't count on was that all the rest turned out to be not very many. Incredibly, I was shocked to find out that there were only a few thousand who were just like me. And in the late sixties, we were demonstrably fewer.

Let me try to recapture what the world of religion was like in those days. God had died on the cover of *Time* magazine, and Anthony Towne had written his obituary for the *New York Times*. The assumption of the reigning New York–based High Culture was that Harvey Cox was right—the secular city was where the action was. Religion was going down the tubes, at least religion as we had known it. Religion's stock was so low that when Jürgen Moltmann published his *Theology of Hope*, it made front page in the *New York Times*. Any kind of religion-related hope was news. In book publishing, the secular houses that traditionally published serious religious and theological books—Scribner, Macmillan, Holt, Doubleday—were stumbling over themselves to get out of a dying business. Harper's had sold its Bible department in 1964 to Zondervan, only in the nick of time, they thought, because Grand Rapids hadn't yet heard the news. No one then dreamt that Evangelical Christian bookselling would become a bonanza business a few years hence. It was assumed that religion was on its way out and that psychology, psychiatry, Esalen growth therapies, and encounter groups would easily replace the obvious ongoing traditional religious-type needs and questions that the mainline churches traditionally dealt with. The paradigm had shifted and people were finally coming to their senses and abandoning mainline churches in droves. Harper's was able to keep its religious department alive only because its founding editor, Eugene Exman, had a taste for Eastern metaphysics and mystical religion. Those titles had quietly rested on the backlist until the kids in what was then called the counterculture picked them up. Until Charles Reich in his *Greening of America* gave it a name—Consciousness III—no one in New York knew what to make of all this long-haired "religion." It was all chalked up to the war and crazy California but in any case it had nothing to do with religious publishing as they knew it. What hath Baba Ram Dass to do with Reinhold Niebuhr?

Nashville, the mecca of Protestant denominational book publishing and catalog-selling to ministers, was hurting. The head of the Cokesbury bookstore chain was reorganizing all their stores by putting gift books and bestsellers in the window to keep business alive. Even the famed Cokesbury catalog was hardly distinguishable from Kroch's and Brentano's. The 55th Street Cokesbury store in New York was indistinguishable from the Doubleday store down the block except for the dusty black wall where yellowing religious books rested.

The publishing houses that built their religious publishing programs on Protestant European-style scholarly tomes of theology—the works of Tillich, Brunner, Barth, Niebuhr, Bonhoeffer—watched sales drop dead. Since my previous exposure to religious book publishing had been heavily influenced by the stock at Princeton Seminary's bookroom, this reality came as a great shock. What I didn't know at the time is that in the two little rooms in the basement of Stuart Hall was a high-volume account for the publishers of Protestant theology.

The question is, what happened? Where did all the serious people go? Why had they stopped reading? The scholars were still there. The clergy were still mostly there. The seminarians were still there. The lay people—well, they weren't all still there, but they never read those serious books anyway. What happened? It is clear that they did not stop reading, but they did stop buying the kind of book that had been thought of as the serious religious book. Maybe they came to your establishments to read them but they weren't buying them. My hunch is that they were buying other types of books—secular, even serious secular books. The times were such that student, scholar, and clergy alike all felt the call of the secular city and evidently felt they had a lot of catch-up reading to do in order to carry on.

Overnight, the comforting image of the scholar-preachers who spent twenty hours a week in their studies poring over texts, learning from the master religious thinkers, became a negative image. The new role of the clergy demanded that they not hide from the *Sturm und Drang* of real life by living quietly with theological books. Instead what was demanded was a life of relevance and action—a level of direct involvement in the real lives of real people. Theory was out. Practicum was in. Pastoral psychology—the role of the clergy as therapist—was very much in vogue. The assumption was that the people in the flock had real problems and therefore the reading habits of those whose job it was to tend the flock would be better focused on the key works in psychology and other behavioral sciences. New authorities were in the land. What was read and bought addressed the techniques necessary to survive the day-to-day life of the working minister. Since their training in seminaries had traditionally viewed this gutsy side of the role as more or less peripheral—to be accomplished in a few practicums in the late afternoon after the Greek, Hebrew, biblical theology, and systematics were done with—the typical working clergy felt that it was now up to them—on their own—and perhaps through a few extension courses with the more secularized parts of the faculty to catch up. And to the objective observer of publishing lists, the scholarly fare seemed to grow thinner and thinner until all professional publishing seemed to have some very practical handle.

While some saw their role as the caretakers of souls, the others who saw their real role in the midst of community and social concerns also moved their reading habits away from what had been thought to be "the basics." They spent whatever time could be salvaged between meetings and demonstrations reading books related to the world of politics, community organization, and general social concerns. Overall, there was enormous anxiety over whether or not the clergy, the church, and even preaching the gospel itself was relevant. By the thousands the front ranks of religious professionals seemed to abandon all scholarly concerns not directly related to their activist role. A pervading despair based on the sneaking suspicion that unless they were able to prove themselves as direct and concrete aid to the people and the community, the church, if not religion itself, would justifiably wither away. I remember manuscripts in those days from the working clergy flaying against their obscurantist training in the university and seminary world, declaring it all a complete waste, and that unless theologians and religious thinkers could adapt themselves to the reality of the world—their world as it existed—there was no hope.

And some theologians responded. Those were the days of the "Theologies Of": theology of play, of work, of leisure, of death, of sex, of relationships, of guilt, of—you name it. And the telling fact is that these theologies weren't practiced in the traditional manner in the context of church history, Christian ethics, biblical theology, and the Bible but rather in conversation with the scholarly world at large and in conversation with the traditional university disciplines rather than the seminary disciplines. New theology moved from the seminary to the university, and what resulted was a much hipper, more sophisticated form of religious reflection that presumed background and interest in secular disciplines rather than in holy disciplines. The ironic upshot of this is that ordinary preachers—even if they wanted to keep up—found themselves reading theoretical formulations that assumed knowledge often foreign to their own experience and background. Many tried to keep up but it was beyond them. They felt abandoned by the theoretical leadership who seemed to be playing to a grandstand of university peers and outsiders rather than directly to them, with their seminary backgrounds. In the end, they gave up. Seminary theology did, of course, continue to be produced, but given all the other demands of the working parish minister and the therapeutic and community roles I spoke of earlier, it seemed more and more arcane.

The target audience for this new form of university theology—the intelligent general reader (the famed secularized reader of the *New York Times*)— never really positively responded to this new wave of university-style religious reflection. For the most part, this audience, particularly the secularists, had put theology and religion into a conceptual box and in fact were quite offended by what was perceived as a tricky attempt to keep alive artificially what obviously ought to be left to die. To the genuinely secular person there is no more fraudulent character than a scholar or a clergyman who has lost the faith but does not have the courage to admit the fact and get out. Genuinely secular people often hate sophisticated, innovative religious reformulations and their half-breed rhetoric. Usually, with some condescension, they admit that religious belief is necessary for some people, usually confused and weak people. It's these clever, sophisticated foxes-in-the-chicken-coop-scholars and the preachers who know in their own hearts that there is nothing there in religion but nonetheless hold on—reinterpreting and stirring up the faithful only because they can't face the fact that there is nothing else that they can do in life—these are the worst of a rather tawdry breed. Most secular people see the civil merit of religion and its institutions and are therefore offended by those religionists who, from the secularist perspective, fraudulently play the game of slippery reinterpretation for the sole purpose of keeping their jobs and their place in respectable society. Secularists will usually respect out-and-out religious conviction—and even tolerate self-delusion on the part of religious types, but they will never stand for deliberate fraud. If you are smart enough to play these clever word-and-concept games, you are smart enough to know that there is no long-term health in conceptual manipulation. It would, they think, be better all around for the clever reinterpreters to go off and sell insurance and just face up to the fact that the understandable but regrettable decision to enter the field of religious studies during one's extended adolescence was just a bad mistake.

So, on the Protestant side of things, the serious theological book was in trouble. The traditional-plus markets—the markets that traditionally added on to the academic market per se—dried up. The working clergy were either off to learn other things, or didn't have the background to catch the drift of the new formulations. The intelligent general readers were not impressed with either the traditional or the new university theologies; the seminarians bought their textbooks but their related reading was an individualized and diffuse search for some grounding related to their private concerns. It was an era when many of the Protestant seminarians were there in the first place because they had come from explicitly Evangelical backgrounds—had "given their lives to the Lord"—only to find disturbingly that seminary seemed to have little to do with the fervor and motivation of that original decision. In fact, for most it seemed that one of the purposes of seminary life was to educate them out of that motive and calm them down into proper and dignified church leaders. Others found themselves in seminary because of the ugly reality of the military draft, part confused by the fervor of the born-againers next door, and part grappling with the demands of conscience in a very volatile political and social atmosphere. Others found themselves on a sane and sensible track toward graduate school and some form of doctorate to become themselves the theoreticians of the future. Somewhere along the line, they had decided that one or another of the specialized religion-related academic fields was a suitable way to live the life of a scholar. But as always, they were the remnant, sandwiched in between the activists and the pious, and importantly to our story, together with their purely university-trained colleagues, today form the core market for all serious religious and academic publishing. And therein lies, it seems to me, a critical issue in the fate of the serious, theoretical religious book. As near as I can tell, there are about twelve thousand such creatures in America today fragmented across at least forty compartmentalized academic religion specialties, six basic theological orientations, and in four quite distinct academic milieus. And what that means is that the market for any particular serious book can be sliced pretty thin, unless there are some bells and whistles that also draw a response from the remnant of scholar preachers or some ongoing text use in some level of graduate education. Or, hope beyond hope, some aspect in that book moves it into the current of general culture discussion through general trade book channels.

When one turns to the Roman Catholic side of the picture, the narrative of the story is distinct but the end result is much the same. In the late 1960s, Vatican II dealt almost a death blow to Catholic publishing. Overnight, the backlists of the traditionally strong houses went dramatically out of date.

The mainstay of pre-Vatican-II-style theology and devotional literature now seemed a relic of the past and quaintly old-fashioned. Since publishers live off their backlist—it's the books you published last year, two years ago, ten years ago and even thirty years ago that keep publishing alive as a business— there was trouble in the land here too.

Because Harper's was traditionally more of a Protestant house in the late sixties—reserving its Catholic publishing program to the more general market and heretical-type titles like the works of Teilhard de Chardin, Charles Davis, and the early Richard McBrien—my direct experience here was more as an observer than as a participant. It was Herder and Herder, Holt, and Doubleday that held the ground in this arena. New popular Catholic publishing in the late sixties was characterized by a flurry of short-lived "why I am getting out of the institution" books, and dramatic reformulations in which themes and trends were developing at almost a journalistic pace rather than at a pace appropriate to the production schedules of book publishers. New approaches quickly dated in the flux and flow of liberation from old rules and ways of thinking. Most interestingly and ironically, because of the open windows in the Catholic church, there was a lift in sales of the traditional, Protestant heavyweight titles, because a whole new Catholic readership wanted to catch up on recent Protestant thought long after the Protestants themselves had moved away from reading it. But it was the Catholic Europeans—the Küngs, the Rahners, the Schillebeeckxes—who ended up keeping the fires alive in serious publishing, along with a new breed of younger scholars such as Raymond Brown, David Tracy, and Charles Curran, who took John XXIII at his word and explored new ground. The vitality of this substantive publishing tradition long outlasted the Protestant equivalent and continues to this day with a much more respectable and vital track record.

Today, of course, it is still on the Catholic theological side where much of the vitality and the action can be seen. The new traditions growing out of post-Vatican II thought are now bumping up against the increased levels of wariness coming out of Rome, giving Catholic scholarship and thinking almost a melodramatic tinge. The assumptions, methods, presuppositions, and beliefs between the recent and the traditional are now making copy on the front page of the *New York Times*.

In sum: on both the Catholic and Protestant side of the spectrum, the last twenty years have not been very conducive to the quiet, tranquil, orderly development of the religion-related academic disciplines. The hurly-burly of the world, the explosion of knowledge at the university, the secular culture at large, and the repositioning of the churches have been the tail that has wagged the dog of scholarly concerns.

Serious religion has for my twenty years been caught in the vortex of general external concerns. Outside factors have effectively broken through into the self-contained, self-assured, constructive study of religion as a communal enterprise for the sake of something beyond just the enterprise itself. The result is stimulating chaos.

The ultimate effect of this phenomenon is an enormous confusion and fragmentation of the norms by which individual books can be judged objectively as valuable for the field as a whole. Valuable to whom is always the question. As the tides of academic fads and new languages and vocabularies rise and fall, the genuine question of what will be important a hundred years from now—a question that surely you must deal with daily—seems enormously complex. It is a world in which a dozen key scholars can make a new connection with a new theory or a way of thinking from completely distinct university disciplines and for a season be the rage, only to be swept away by yet another new set of concerns a few seasons later. Concurrent with this ebb and flow at the highly theoretical level, the ongoing constituency of the typical theological library—the theological student, the clergy from the neighborhood, the alumni on sabbatical, the earnest lay seeker—all need quite different types of books. People still have to preach at funerals, visit the sick, and get through their nervous breakdowns. I frankly don't envy your buying discretion in the midst of this milieu of fragmented norms, theoretical fads, conflicting needs, expensive books, and preordained budgets. It can't be easy.

It can truly be said that variations on this theme of external influence have almost always been with us in the history of scholarship. Therefore it should not surprise us all that much that it is with us today. But I do think that something genuinely new and different is happening now in the 1980s. It is one thing for the religion academe to stand in the winds of sophisticated general culture and quite another to stand in the winds of mass popular general culture. It is my thesis that there is a new worry in the land, that sophisticated general culture and especially the publishing future is on the brink of being overwhelmed and infiltrated by popular culture. Something quite distinct is happening this time around that may have dramatic implications for the future of publishing and the serious book. This new factor—one that any book publisher is keenly aware of—is that we now have *a literate pop culture. A pop culture that reads.*

Now there has always been popular culture. Obviously there is nothing new in that. There have always been people who live their lives quite apart from the High Culture of serious and systematic reflection on serious and specialized themes. In fact, such people have always formed the overwhelming majority of any population. The caste of highly educated specialists has always been a tiny minority.

What is new, and relatively recent on the historical scene, is that the book—the holy, totem object—the revered symbol of the elite caste—has become a familiar, comfortable, and common object for all sorts of people.

There is hardly a shopping mall in America where such objects are not found. There is hardly a subway car at rush hour where books are not seen. There is hardly a coffee table where some ornate variation of the book does not rest. There is hardly a vest pocket park in an urban area where books are absent. And this phenomenon, my friends, is something relatively new. And those of us who love the book, who associate the book with some form of student-based mentality where books are revered because they have been the holy instruments which have brought about in us fundamental changes in mindset and world-view, are quite frankly offended by this recent association of the book with all sorts of seemingly trivial pursuits. The book as a holy and revered object has been snatched from the hands of the elite and has been, many people think, soiled by its association with all sorts of unworthy people. Mass culture has snapped the chain that tied the book to the lectern in days of old and stolen the book away. The fundamental problem is that universal education has worked in this country, and it is frankly making many serious types feel damned uncomfortable and fearful that in the tide of print daily washing across the land, the book as we knew it, the book as we loved it, the kind of book that influenced us, is going to disappear.

Despite the statistics, despite the numbers of excellent serious books that roll from the presses of a wide variety of publishers each year, the undertow of anxiety among those in the High Culture is almost palpable. Yes, they say, we are holding on, but the future looks very bleak. Someday the powerful people, the people who make the decisions, the people in conglomerate publishing, the illiterate people who have for the basest of reasons inserted themselves into the publishing system that delivers the holy objects to us will wake up one morning and realize how small a minority we genuinely serious ones have become, and, for the basest of reasons, walk away from our concerns and go only for the subway car crowd. It is inevitable, they say. Why inevitable? Because even in the realms of genuine thinkers, quantification values—the values based on *how many*—has become the norm of judgment. And that's new.

It is as though the operative norm of value—the breath of impact—that one finds in mass culture standards has become the single most important norm of value for us all—potboiler author and scholar alike. It is as though the Nielsen rating standard—the bestseller list standard, the performance of the film in its first week grosses—has become *the* standard of value for mass and High Culture alike.

Look what has happened already, they say. *Vanna Speaks* sells hundreds of thousands in its first six weeks. My book sells hundreds. These business types in publishing may be crude and venial, but they are not dumb. If I can see it, surely they can see it too and someday soon, I am going to be sitting alone, me and my typewriter, with no one left to publish my serious book.

Maybe the solution is to do something that will get me on *The Today Show*. If I don't, all will be lost.

Now as a publisher I find that perception and the assumptions behind it absolutely fascinating. And if you think clearly about what is actually being said, absolutely damning in terms of the growing identification between the scholar and the culture at large, and damning on both sides in the perception of how publishing actually works. On the one hand it reveals a fear-driven admission that what one is doing, what one has devoted one's entire life to, has become obviously and genuinely marginal, and it is only a matter of time until the reality of that view is exposed to the world at large and acted on by the powers that be. On the other hand it assumes that shooting-star quantities alone influence judgment in publishing. And the fact of the matter is that this is just not true. One does not need to sell tens of thousands of units of a title to view the book as a success. You do need to sell that kind of number if you have an extravagant promotional budget, but certainly not if you have a targeted market.

What has happened in the world of academe and publishing to bring about this apocalyptic vision of the world to come? Where is the feeling of damn-it-all self-confidence and even old-fashioned arrogance that comes from a group of serious people who gather together for a common pursuit and purpose and see the value of their combined efforts wholly outside the norm of mass impact? Do we need to be on *Good Morning America* to feel the value of what we do? Was Andy Warhol right that the *summum bonum* of life is fifteen minutes of general celebrity? Surely not.

But it is the publishers, you say, who encourage this quantification. They are the ones who reject manuscripts because of "limited markets." They are the ones at the heart of the quality vs. quantity issue. They are the reason why quality norms are giving way to quantity-based norms. They are the reason why we are all being forced to sink to the lowest common denominator.

I suppose that there has never been a time when those living have not thought that the world is going to hell in a handbasket. That the old standards are declining. That quality is slipping away.

Around the turn of the century—in 1897 to be precise—G.P. Putnam's Sons released a curious book entitled *Authors and Publishers: A Manual of Suggestions*. Although written anonymously, it was obviously penned by a working publisher anxious to defend his profession against the charge of what one critic of the time had called "crass literary alchemy"—the unseemly conversion of an author's brains into a satisfactory cash equivalent. Listen to the charge: "Like the luxurious princes of old who fed upon small birds, so publishers fatten upon the brains of authors." If gross exploitation of authors was not bad enough, the charge gets worse. We are also the purveyors of cultural dross who seek to "build our palaces from the gold of a gullible public." This portrayal of publishers as cynical, ravenous despoilers was the view of our more vocal critics in 1897. And so, I fear it remains today. So much for the "good old days."

I know that there are those who think that we publishers today are naively obsessed with our economic bottom line and that therefore predictable mass sales potential has become our sole criterion and motivation. A publisher's bottom line is much more interesting and complex than just going hell-bent for the obvious commercial bestseller.

You see, book publishing today operates on two very distinct levels: first, the kind of publishing that is essentially an extension of the entertainment and therapy industries, that is, books that cater to and reinforce trendy values and obvious ongoing needs in the culture. And the second, books that are distinctive originals: fresh and genuine insights that genuinely contribute to the knowledge of the discipline and hence ultimately to individuals and in some cases even the welfare of society. Books whose value is added in the publishing of them. In the end it is this prophetic element in any publishing list that gives it its edge, its bite, its flavor, its quality.

I am old-fashioned enough to believe that books can still stir change. For me, at least, it is precisely this concept of originality and the capacity to open and even change minds in a wide variety of constituencies that speaks best to the question of quality in general and scholarly publishing.

The first level can be called *publishing as merchandise*: books that, although they may be judged as good of their "type," essentially capitalize on and exploit existing cultural facts and trends. The second level I call *wisdom publishing: distinctive, "original" insight works*: books that are potentially trendsetting. Though I have done my share of merchandising, it is the second type that gives me real pleasure and pride in my profession and will be the heritage—the backlist—I will leave to my successors.

Nonetheless, it is a true view that not only publishing, but the culture itself, is facing a crisis in the respective attention given to merchandise and originality. We must face the fact that ours is a culture more comfortable with glossy packaging than with genuine substance, with proven formulas than with the risks inherent in original thinking. For that reason, any publishing program must be run on two tracks: books published for their short-term return and those published for their long-term contribution. The first track is the exciting and dangerous game; the second is the essential one. The first requires an enormous amount of canniness and often an iron stomach. Bestsellers do not often come cheap, and since I have lived in a world in which they are part and parcel, the real question is how can we play that game without making it the definition of the total enterprise. My own perspective, both as one who cares about values in our book-related culture and as a businessman, is that to go after the brass ring of merchandise to the exclusion of distinctive "originals" would mean suicide—not just cultural suicide, but economic suicide.

Ours is a business that depends for its survival—its profitability—on what in publishing jargon is called "the backlist." The books that we published last year, two years ago, that continue to sell. Publishing economics are such that it is next to impossible to survive on the new books alone. At best, they are a break-even proposition. Money out—money in. It is our backlist that keeps us afloat, that produces profit dollars, that finances yet another new list. And to survive, some proportion of the new list must become the backlist of the future. Unless a healthy percentage of the books can stay alive— reprint and sell continuously not because of what they promise but because of what they deliver in terms of genuinely satisfying the expectation of the readers who bought them—a publisher will ultimately go under. Therein, by the way, lies the direct relationship between quality and commerce in all but the most hype-ridden, merchandise-oriented publishing operations.

Fortunately for those who care about serious publishing, there is the stark reality that there is nothing less salable than last year's merchandise. There is nothing deader or colder than last year's shooting star. The world of merchandise is like a fickle—and easily jaded—lover. Just when you think you have their undying devotion and attention, they leave you for yet another titillation, and there you are, stuck with a warehouse full of passé merchandise. It is the carefully chosen books of genuine substance and value—the not-so-glamorous, not-so-flashy titles—that keep us alive and sometimes even surprise us. Such books endure because of what they are. And for my money, they are the bottom line in publishing.

But my assumption in all this is that quality and substance endures. If I am wrong in that assumption, then there is little hope for the serious book. The rules under which a publisher must operate do assume that people want what we produce. If that in and of itself is not true, then we will obviously go under. It is possible to mix the quick and the long-term sellers but it is not possible to continue to produce that which no one wants.

Now there is nobody I know in publishing, religious or general, who is deliberately out to do that. I don't know anybody who intends to be giving money away. Even nonprofit houses like university presses, or denominational and religious order-sponsored houses, hope at least to break even. Thus for any publisher to say that they don't care ABOUT the financial bottom line is equivalent to saying: 1) It is my own money, and I am engaged in a personal form of philanthropy. 2) It is not my money, but the people whose money it is wish me to be philanthropic with it and are looking toward other purposes in my publishing activity than some financial return.

Here is where we may be facing an adjustment, or even a crisis, when it comes to the future of religious and theological publishing in particular. It seems to me that the day when we can expect ecclesiastical and religious denominations to underwrite the publication of unsalable religious scholarship is over. It is clear that, as sponsoring institutions, there seems to be an increasing unwillingness to underwrite religious publishing as a form of ministry either to their own constituency or to the religious community at large. As institutions, the times are economically tough and the traditional view that religious book publishing is worthy of subsidy seems to be waning. Instead of publishing arms being beneficiaries of capital and cash, in fact, many religious institutions seem to be looking to their publishing units as generators of income to be used for other institutional purpose and ministries.

You may be surprised to learn that frankly I regard this as clarifying good news for substantive serious publishing. I admit that it may be a mindset that arises from the reality that I, myself, have had to live within a publishing atmosphere where bottom lines are a day-to-day reality. But I have myself, through the years, superintended a couple of pro-bono programs, and—human nature being what it is—I have come to believe that something genuine is lost in the publishing process when the goal of having to play it smart is a clearly defined necessity. When there in no cushion to fall back on, there is, I believe, something real in the process to be gained.

And with that my basic point: the wisdom implicit in serious reflection growing out of disciplined scholarship is not, to my view, an optional activity for any society. Without it, the society dies. It is not a bauble in which we as a community indulge certain people because they like to do that sort of thing. It is the lifeblood of the future. It is not a marginal side game that runs parallel to real life and is therefore expendable in the crunch. It is not expendable in book publishing terms unless it has devolved into private games of one-upmanship among the participants.

The times for us as a culture are serious, and our needs both as individuals and as a collective are too serious for publishing to allow only the voices of the mass exploiter and the common minds to speak. But I have given up in asking those who have chosen a life of reflection and deliberate consideration to popularize either their language or their concerns so that scholarship can be read on that subway. That kind of lay interpretation is a special art and very special talent that, in my experience, falls outside the realm of possibility for most specialists. There will always be a level of talented people who can do that translation for us. Such popular writers are, by definition, derivative minds whose skill lies in translation, not in creation.

. But what I do ask is for a scholar-to-scholar rekindling of a united belief and confidence among themselves that the sum of the parts adds up to something that resonates with the life of the culture at large. I realize that most of the academic fields have become too complex and too fragmented to easily facilitate the appearance of those renaissance people of the past who, in their own minds, saw it all. I have, as a publisher, had to accept the fact that to find such may not be easy—but it is necessary.

Why is it, we must ask ourselves, that we have lost a sense of the whole? One possibility is the thing that struck me most dramatically in moving from the insider's world of the student to the outsider's observing role of the publisher, that strangely enough scholars give each other little support and grace. I am still amazed by that. I genuinely hope that I am wrong in this, but from where I sit, except for members of some clique who are in the midst of some battle with an opposing clique, there does not appear to be a lot of mutual support for each other's enterprises. And there is little sense of the growth and health of the discipline as a whole. Instead, one scholar's success or accomplishments seem to be perceived as an automatic diminution of the self by another. It is as though the real competition was between them and among them instead of beyond them to the world at large. As though the purpose of it all was the pursuit of some prestigious Distinguished Chair in the sky that could hold only one of them. I suppose the reasons for this most human of situations can be found in the nitty-gritty levels of competition throughout the path from graduate school to Distinguished Professor. But if that is true and cannot be overcome for the sake of the advancement and health of the disciplines, then I fear that there is no long-term health and future for serious publishing, to say nothing of the disciplines themselves. In such a milieu, scholarly publishing becomes only the most private of games. It becomes one scholar talking to another with a few knowledgeable interested parties listening to the conversation. Now, no one can deny the necessity of this kind of interaction. It is the first step—the working papers—for all advances in the discipline. Such are the first drafts of parts of genuinely serious books, serious in the sense of being capable of making some serious contribution to the world at large. What I am asking for from the academy is a serious discussion of what it is to be serious. And surely, the answer to that must be something more than just one scholar's temporal victory over another. Let the world of the journals record, disseminate, and document those conversations. The genuinely serious book is the next step in the conversation—when the single threads are gathered together, when one wise man or woman steps forward to speak to the discipline as a whole on what the pieces mean. And therein lies the difference between individualized gamesmanship and communal wisdom. And taking that step is as serious a matter as you can find.

Wisdom is admittedly a rare commodity and not to be found easily. But when we go looking for it, we think we know where it should be found. And that is in the academy. Will serious publishing survive Vanna White? Let me recast the question: Is there any wisdom in the land—or has it *all* become the wheel of fortune?

43

Globalization and Theological Libraries
44th Annual Conference, Evanston, IL, 1990

Robert J. Schreiter

In a reflective essay looking to future directions for theological libraries in the 1990s, Stephen Peterson identified three major factors that will shape decision-making in this final decade of the century: (1) the current configuration of resources, (2) trends in theological education, and (3) decisions made by institutions responding to those trends. While he does not identify any trends or the institutional decisions likely to follow upon them, he does provide a useful framework for exploring some important issues now before us.[1]

Using the suggestions he has made, I wish to examine with you here aspects of the second and third of those factors, namely, one trend that is likely to have a growing impact on theological education, and some thoughts on how institutions might respond to it. I am speaking here of the current interest in globalization, and how that will be influencing theological education, and especially theological libraries.

Globalization, as the very word suggests, is a broad and diffuse topic. Like any issue that presents itself as new to us, it is in danger of banalization and trivialization. But there are issues at stake here of great significance for theological education and the resources that we bring to bear upon it. Hence it is important to move with as much precision as possible in order to keep a clear picture before us of what actually will be involved in all of this.

In the hopes of achieving some clarity in the discussion, I would like to proceed in three steps. First of all, I will try to make clearer why the interest in globalization and why it is likely to be an enduring dimension in theological education, and not simply a fad. From this, we will move to a second stage, to identify some of the major issues that commitments to globalization entail, especially for theological libraries. And finally, in a third part, some reflections on implications and expectations for theological libraries. I enter this discussion knowing more about what is happening in the area of globalization than as any expert on libraries or information management. In fact, the reflections in the third part will be more a host of practical suggestions than a coherent plan for bringing librarianship to bear upon this new area. It seems to me that the more strategic planning in this regard is best done by those competent in the field—namely yourselves. But it would be my hope that what I suggest might stimulate your own thought to find ways to meet the challenges that lie ahead for all of us.

WHY GLOBALIZATION?

"Globalization" came into the vocabulary of theological education in the early 1980s. Throughout that decade, a series of committees (and later, task forces) were set up by the Association of Theological Schools in the U.S. and Canada (ATS) to explore the meaning and implications of globalization for the future of theological education. Surveys were conducted among the schools in 1983 and 1989 to gauge the levels of globalization that had been reached. Globalization was the major theme of the ATS biennial meeting in 1986; in 1988, the ATS set globalization as the overarching theme for theological education throughout the 1990s. To that end, an ATS Task Force on Globalization has been working on generating a literature to support this effort, as well as provide support for schools active in globalization through a summer institute for faculty and administrators, and grants for specific projects within the schools.[2] Thus, the theme of globalization seems already to be part and parcel of discussion in theological education today.

But just what is it? The fact that everyone is talking about it does not in itself make it an enduring quality to be reckoned with in theological education. To understand the interest in globalization, we need to trace its antecedents.

The term "globalization" was not originally theological in nature. In fact, it has come rather lately to our enterprise. As far as I can tell, the term first appeared in the early 1960s and first gained wide currency in the business world. It referred initially to the extension of one's manufacturing and marketing strategy across national boundaries to create a wider market, more efficient because of the larger scale. Globalization in business, then, meant an expansionist impulse of globe-embracing magnitude. By the mid-1970s, as multinational companies looked for new markets to penetrate, some of them started to realize that the attitudes and strategies that had led them to high market success and profitability in one country did not always transfer well to another context. Indeed in some instances, hitherto successful strategies were often resounding failures. Since that time, those companies that are truly "globalized" have allowed their strategies to become more modified by the cultural and social exigencies of each region, while not sacrificing the cost-lowering advantages of manufacturing and marketing on larger scale. Thus, this kind of globalization is expansionist but recognizes the importance and impact of difference as cultural boundaries are crossed.

A second place where globalization appeared was in political theory. It was called "globalism" in the 1960s, but that term gave way to "globalization" by the late 1970s. Globalization here meant the overcoming of national and ethnic differences for the sake of achieving and maintaining world peace. The threat of nuclear annihilation (and, more recently, of ecological catastrophe) has been a driving force in this interest in globalization. If globalization meant expansionism for business, in political theory it stresses interconnectedness and interdependence.

The third place where globalization began to be discussed was in education. Two sets of issues converged to make this an important area for reflection. On the one hand, in an increasingly interdependent world, and in a world where the oil-rich Muslim states and the "four dragons" of East Asia (Korea, Japan, Taiwan, Singapore) were reshaping the economic map of the world, Westerners had to begin to take more cognizance of the world outside their traditional North Atlantic ambit. Thus, for a person to interact in this changed world, nonwestern cultures and societies would have to be studied alongside the more familiar cultures and societies of the West. On the other hand, the migration of peoples was creating new configurations in societies in Europe and North America. There are now more Muslims than Episcopalians in the United States, and more Muslims than Protestants in France or Italy. The needs for bilingual and bicultural education in countries once considered more homogeneous have pressed this shift in perspective. If globalization meant expansion for business and interdependence for political theory, among educators it has come to stand for pluralism.

These three disciplinary areas—business, politics, and education—were largely shaping the globalization discussion when theological education came into the arena. Some of the issues for theology were being raised already in the mid-1970s (by such works as Walbert Buehlmann's *The Coming of the Third Church*),[3] but it was not until the end of that decade and the beginning of the 1980s that interest in globalization began to gain momentum. But what has been theology's interest in globalization? Has it been a kind of me-too attitude, secretly sharing the interests of business, politics, or education? Or has it had its own distinctive motivations?

This is an important question, since many critics from the southern hemisphere of theological education have eyed our globalization discussions with some suspicion. They wonder whether this sudden interest in globalization is not all that different from discussions of globalization in the corporate boardrooms and in the graduate business schools of America. They wonder whether it is not simply another way to regain the enthusiasm that world mission once provided for mainline seminaries, or whether it is a neocolonialist ploy to overwhelm and exploit our poorer neighbors once again. Globalization, from this perspective, is nothing more than a more acceptable face on aggressive evangelism, or an attempt to expropriate new forms of faith and community life to shore up dying theologies and churches in North America.

Now some of this may be true. It looks suspiciously so in some uncritical acceptances of liberation theology or base Christian communities here, taken out of the original contexts that gave them meaning. Each institution needs to test its understandings of globalization to discover what complexes of motives direct their efforts. But are there more honorable ones as well? I can identify two factors that make discussion of globalization imperative for theological education in any case.

First of all, the *environment* in which graduates of our institutions will teach and minister is becoming increasingly pluralistic. This is coming about not only due to the immigrant populations so noticeable on the West Coast and in the larger cities, but also because of economic interdependence. People in our congregations, even those connected to small companies, may fly regularly abroad as part of their business, thereby making the ministering context much broader than it once was. And the economic penetration, especially of Japan, is changing the face even of homogeneous rural America, as Honda and Toyota plants sprout in the cornfields and cotton fields of the Midwest and South. Furthermore, as the United States loses its relative share of economic power in the world, we will have to take on a greater awareness of other people and places, something we could afford not to do in times of greater wealth. Thus, the very context in which we work will demand a higher level of awareness of the planet.

Secondly, the *church* itself is changing. The statistics of those shifts are already well known to many of us. In 1900, eighty percent of all Christians were Caucasian, and lived in the northern hemisphere. Just thirty years from now—in 2020—the demographer David Barrett estimates that this datum will have been reversed: eighty percent of all Christians will be non-Caucasians and live in the southern hemisphere. Already some sixty percent of all Christians are to be found there. The fastest growing Christian continent is Africa; the fastest growing Christian country is South Korea.[4] For nearly fifteen years, one-third of all the novices of the Jesuits have been found in India. We are all dimly aware that the shape of the worldwide church is changing; those in denominations or communions that do not have their center of gravity in the United States are perhaps more keenly aware of this than others. But just look at our theological schools—how much more international in character their student bodies are than was the case two decades ago. Globalization is not something that we hope will occur; it is already, in some ways, a fact. To this extent, globalization is not going out and creating new territory, it is simply a matter of catching up. We must become more global in our awareness and attitudes if we are to be able to prepare men and women to minister in the church as it has become.

I believe that these two factors—the world in which we live and the church of which we are a part—are the principal reasons why theological education has come to consider globalization a priority. To be sure, the motivations of political science and education overlap with theological education here; here, too, are concerns about interdependence and living in a pluralist society. And we need to investigate our motivations regularly to see whether traces of the expansionist motivations of the business world have crept into our thinking and acting. We are becoming global because, if we are truly aware of what is happening around us, we have little other choice.

WHAT IS GLOBALIZATION?

Clarifying the motivation of globalization is one thing; giving the concept some definition is another. Some of the complexity involved in doing this already appeared in the previous section in looking at the motivation for globalization.

It should be noted from the outset that, within theological education, there is no univocal definition of motivation. What has emerged instead is a matrix of definitions within which theological schools try to locate themselves. Let me examine some aspects of that matrix as it is emerging.

The basis for the matrix is the four definitions of globalization proposed by Don S. Browning in 1986.[5] Browning noted that persons and schools tend to define globalization in any of four ways:

1. Globalization is the church's mission to evangelize the world; globalization is about missions and evangelism.
2. Globalization is the ecumenical cooperation among churches; globalization is about mutual respect and support and contextualization.
3. Globalization is dialogue between Christianity and other religions; globalization is about learning to respect other religious traditions.
4. Globalization is solidarity with the poor and oppressed and the struggle for justice; globalization is about liberation, justice, and peace.

In a recent and important contribution to this discussion, S. Mark Heim has suggested that we need to move further than simply identifying which of the four definitions most clearly typifies the approach to globalization in our institution; we must also be aware of which modes of analysis we use to exegete, as it were, the definition. Heim lists five such modes (symbolic, philosophical, functional, economic, and psychic) that in turn shape and direct our approach. These allow us to see with greater clarity not only which definition or definitions can best describe our approach, but also what kind of intentionalities shape our response.[6]

This mapping, or topological, approach seems to me to be the most fruitful for approaching globalization. No doubt all of us would give some credence to all four of the definitions, and probably most of us would find our institutions wanting to give some attention to all of them, though certainly not in equal measure. A recent survey among theological schools finds the first definition (evangelism) to have the highest priority most frequently (51 percent), and the third definition (interreligious dialogue) to have the lowest priority in most schools (7 percent).[7]

Another way of approaching the meaning of globalization is to realize that the word itself is a neologism, embracing adjectival ("global"), verbal ("globalize"), and nominal ("globalization") elements. Thus, globalization can be approached in descriptive terms, in processual terms, and in conceptual terms. All of these are necessary, it seems to me, to achieve the results hoped for in globalization. Let me expand just briefly on this.[8]

The nominal dimension deals with the understanding of what actually constitutes the framework for globalization. This dimension could be presented as Browning's four definitions: globalization as evangelism, ecumenism, interfaith dialogue, and justice, respectively.

Secondly, to be globalized is to enter into a process—a *mysterion* or rite of passage, if you will—that brings about change in an individual. Globalization, therefore, transforms, critiques, decenters, and includes in its process. This dimension of globalization emphasizes the dynamic process by which change from an ethnocentric or provincial approach to a more universal, multicultural approach can take place. Some globalization programs concentrate on one or other aspect of this transformative process. And finally, in what ways do we describe the end results of globalization? What qualities should characterize a globalized person or community? Adjectives that come to mind are comprehensive, equal, mutual, different, aware, and so on. These represent the qualities to be found in the globalized person or community.

However one wishes to go about a definition of globalization—using these or other suggestions[9]—what is incumbent on each of our institutions is a period of reflection whereby we come to understand where we see ourselves on the globalization map. No institution can pretend to cover the whole field in all the different ways that it can be approached. Coming to a clear sense, however, is important for planning and for the allocation of scarce resources. Given the continuing information explosion in the theological disciplines, no librarian needs to be reminded of this. Librarians, it seems to me, need to play an integral role in the theological school's defining its position in the globalization discussion.

ISSUES IN GLOBALIZATION FOR THEOLOGICAL LIBRARIES

This brings us to the second part of this paper; namely, what are some of the issues that face theological libraries in meeting the challenge of globalization?

The first and most important issue was already named at the conclusion of the last section. It is important for there to be some level of institutional clarity regarding which form of globalization is central to the school's mission and purpose, and in what manner it will be carried out. Without such a clarification, scarce resources will quickly be dissipated. Anything short of that kind of setting of priorities will amount to a bandwagon attitude of me-too.

But there are four other major issues that come to mind that I would like to identify at least for your further discussion:

Access to Materials. The electronic networks that we enjoy linking our libraries in North America and Europe largely do not exist outside that sphere. Not only can we not be assured that borrowing materials is possible, we often do not even know what is available. Because of the difficulty of access, the question of allocating funds to acquire these materials becomes an important addendum to an already overtaxed budget. A major issue, then, is knowing what is available and how to acquire it.

Criteria for Selection. Barrett estimated in 1982 that there were 8,647 periodicals published in Asia, Africa, Latin America, and Oceania. Many of these are church newspapers, and the like. He estimated at that time that the number of scholarly periodicals worldwide amounted to somewhat more than 3,000. He estimated for that same region of Asia, Africa, and Latin America a production of some 140,258 books, again without distinguishing scholarly from popular titles.[10]

If access is difficult, criteria for selection of serials and titles is even more so. Closely linked with selection is the matter of preservation. Many of the periodicals and books coming out of these regions of the world are printed on paper that is less likely to stand the corrosions of time. Preservation of these materials may fall more to European and North American libraries that have funds—however inadequate—to preserve at least those deemed most important.

The Nature of the Theological Library. The electronic age of communications has already done much to alter our understanding of what constitutes a library and what is its role within the institution that it serves. The Project 2000 study sponsored jointly by ATS and ATLA has already pointed to the new tensions that are present in the identity of the theological library today. On one hand, the impossibility of all but a few research libraries being able to collect everything with, on the other hand, the power of networking making materials accessible in a way never before realized. Likewise, the relative shrinking of the percentage of the budget allocated to the library comes at a time when libraries are called upon to offer more services than ever before. Because of familiarity with the electronic communication hardware and software to manage information today, the librarian is often in demand in areas of a theological school well beyond the confines of the library. So the very nature of the library itself is in flux.

The challenge of globalization raises the ante on this transition in yet another way. A question often raised about so-called Third World theological material is how much of it is worth collecting and preserving? Would comparable materials be sought in North America, or is it simply the fact that it is exotic that makes some feel they ought to be collected? Are the criteria of quality the same for these materials as for North American and European materials? If the criteria are different, how does this affect the rest of the library collection?

Not everything foreign is worth collecting, and the fact that so much of it may not be indexed makes it inaccessible even if it is proximate in space. Without wanting to sound paternalistic or colonialist, these questions need to be asked as they affect the nature and purpose of the library. There are, to be sure, materials in Asia, Africa, and Latin America worth collecting and saving. But like here, others are of an ephemeral nature. In many ways, this question has some little parallel with the question of collecting non-print materials. Judgments have to be made about their ability to support curriculum and faculty research.

Political Considerations. In some instances, political considerations may hinder the flow of information. Boycotts against the apartheid policies of South Africa, for example, may warrant not maintaining any communication with that country. These things have to be factored into any plans that might be developed. Likewise, complying with ALA policies in this regard would have to be respected. One would hope that in the general atmosphere of lessening of tensions in the world that this kind of consideration would be less important in the future than it is—unfortunately—still today.

IMPLICATIONS AND EXPECTATIONS FOR THEOLOGICAL LIBRARIES

This brings us to the third and final section of this presentation. Having tried to make a case for globalization, and having tried to locate some of the issues globalization will raise for theological libraries, it is now time to turn to some of the implications these issues raise and some of the expectations they are likely to create. I would like to organize them under three headings, followed by a list of suggestions for how to meet the implications and expectations. These lists are by no means exhaustive in enumerating what to expect, nor do they attempt to discuss any of the proposals in anything like complete detail. As was said in the beginning, the proposals are meant to stimulate discussion more than provide any answers.

Networking in North America

Networking is something that librarians have done extraordinarily well. They have been able to achieve levels of cooperation that are the envy of those of us in other sectors of theological education. There are two suggestions I would make as ways that librarians could bring to bear their uncommon abilities in this regard:

The first is, based on the understanding of globalization in each of our schools and our relative ability to collect materials, that we establish foci in our collections and decide upon who will maintain special collections. We all know that everyone cannot collect everything; the next step is to decide who will try to collect what. By setting up these kinds of special collections, we can serve one another through the already existing networks.

The second flows from the first. We need to develop catalogs or online access to these titles (many of which will not fall under Library of Congress or other classifications), including indexing and abstracting services. The Missio institute in Aachen already provides some of this for selected Third World periodicals, and has begun to provide bibliographies on certain topics.[11] IIMO, the Dutch inter-university institute, also does this on a limited basis.[12] We need to build upon these, as well as work together for building selection criteria. Again, this is a matter of using networks already in place to tackle the problems of access and selection that we face.

Networking Beyond North America

Networking beyond North America (and Europe) is still relatively new territory. It is more difficult not only because of the difference in technology available, but also because of a history of colonialism. Extra care has to be taken to maintain genuinely mutual relationships, relationships valuable for our partners as well as ourselves.

Let me begin with four suggestions for such networking along some already established institutional lines, and then turn to some suggestions about how to network in a non-colonialist way.

The first is that ATLA work with the nascent World Conference of Associations of Theological Schools. This group began with a meeting in Djakarta in 1989, and is looking forward to holding its first conference in 1993. Leon Pacala, the executive director of the ATS, is vice president of this organization. If ATLA could get itself involved at this level, it might have quicker access to a network of schools.

The second is networking denominationally. Many denominations already have elaborate networks in place that could be utilized more effectively by the theological schools. Patterns could be developed either along those lines of officialdom or through twinning with an individual or group of schools. This gets us into some of the discussion of non-colonial networking below.

The third is networking with major theological centers where there are also publishing houses, such as Nairobi, Manila, Singapore, Kyoto, Bangalore, and so on. This might be undertaken most profitably by consortia of schools (as in Berkeley, Chicago, Toronto, etc.) as a joint project.

The fourth is the judicious use of the services of our graduates to spot publications and to bring them to the librarians' attention. As will be discussed in the next point, ways need to be worked out to make the arrangement of mutual benefit.

This brings us to the fifth and most important point, of how to undertake such networking in a non-colonialist fashion. The most important aspect of this is honesty on our part and a willingness to listen. In approaching such a relationship we need to be clear and complete in presenting our needs. Instead of our guessing what their needs are or making some initial offer, we need to take the time to listen carefully to what needs they have and their proposals for our meeting them. Quite likely, we will not be able to meet all of them, but their presentation of their needs should be the starting point of the conversation—not what we have to offer. It should be remembered, too, that many of the librarians, especially in the smaller and poorer institutions, will have no training in library science. Thus, they may well feel intimidated by our professionalism—on top of the fact that we are already the rich and powerful figures that we are. Care and sensitivity are important in this. And it must always be remembered that any arrangement undertaken must demonstrably be worth their while.

When it comes to that point in the discussion, what do we have to offer them? Here are a few suggestions; I am sure that you could multiply them:

- Make an arrangement with your denominational publishing house to send them copies of new publications.
- Share with them syllabi and reserve lists. They have the same problem of access that we do: they often do not know what is available and what is of value.
- Offer to ship them last year's *Books in Print*. Again, this increases their knowledge of what is available.

- Send them the publishers' notices that you would throw away.
- When graduates want to will your school their library, suggest instead they will it to a specific school, *with* a provision of providing for the transport of it to its destination.

Again, a little brainstorming can go a long way to find creative ways to be of mutual help. Information and materials are the two most important items of exchange in establishing and maintaining such a relationship.

The Theological Librarian as a Leader in Globalization

Just as a commitment to globalization changes the nature and purpose of the theological library within an institution, so too a commitment to globalization changes the role of the librarian. Because information is an important part of bringing about the transformations that globalization programs seek, the theological librarian will be called upon to play a different role than the one heretofore assigned. Faculty will look to the librarian as a resource for course materials. Students will look for help in researching papers. And one of the most important things that the librarian can do for the institution is to model those relationships of respect and mutuality with other librarians that are so important for the success of globalization. The librarian has the best access to an important dimension of what is needed to make globalization happen: materials from nontraditional resources. To be most effective, the librarian must press the school to define its goals and purposes in globalization as clearly and as carefully as possible. Then, working through networks already in place or yet to be constructed, the flow of information can begin that will be needed to prepare students for a future in a globalized world. The networking tradition that librarians have already established will be essential for all of this. I hope these remarks have helped clarify some of the next steps to be taken.

NOTES

1. Stephen Peterson, "The More Things Change—The More Things Change: Theological Education in the 1990s," *Theological Education* 26 (Spring 1990): 137–51.

2. These developments may be found in "The Report of the Globalization Task Force," *Program and Reports of the 37th Biennial Meeting of the Association of Theological Schools in the United States and Canada* (Vandalia, Ohio: ATS, 1990), 71–80.

3. Walbert Buehlmann, *The Coming of the Third Church* (Maryknoll, NY: Orbis Books, 1977).

4. These statistics can be found in David B. Barrett, *World Christian Encyclopedia* (Nairobi: Oxford University Press, 1982). The major statistics are updated annually

338 *Robert J. Schreiter*

and published in the January issue of the International Bulletin of Missionary Research.

5. Don S. Browning, "Globalization and the Task of Theological Education in North America," *Theological Education* 23 (Autumn 1986): 23–59.

6. S. Mark Heim, "Mapping Globalization for Theological Education," *Theological Education* (Supplement I, Spring 1990): 7–34.

7. "Comparative Perspectives from the 1983 and 1989 Surveys on the Globalization of Theological education," in *Program and Reports*, 81–83.

8. I developed this in an unpublished paper for the Minnesota Consortium of Theological Schools, entitled "Globalization and Theological Education" (February 21, 1990).

9. See for example, Max L. Stackhouse, et al., *Apologia* (Grand Rapids: Eerdmans, 1988).

10. Barrett, *World Christian Encyclopedia*, 804-5; 951. Barrett also provides some useful directories for contacting publishers, 949–50, 971–74.

11. The Missionswissenschaftliches Institut "Missio" publishes *Theologie im Kontext* semiannually, an indexing and abstracting service. It has added bibliographies on church, ministries and Christology to its list. Address: Postfach 1110, D-5100 Aachen, Germany.

12. The Interuniversitair Instituut voor Missiologie en Oecumenica (IIMO) publishes *Exchange. Bulletin of Third World Christian Literature*. Address: Rapenburg 61, 3211 GJ Leiden, the Netherlands.

44

Shadow and Substance
47th Annual Conference, Vancouver, BC, 1993

Roy Stokes

I should like to begin this talk with a quotation. Unfortunately I am unable to verify the quotation, and to proceed in that manner before a professional audience would be a grave sin. The sin would be further compounded by the fact that what I am seeking is a Biblical quotation. The majority of us would, no doubt, agree that there does exist a reasonably large body of material which does not appear in the pages of most of our regular Bibles. Some of it has received scholarly attention and can be found in the several editions of Apocryphal literature. But there is also a kind of substratum of words, phrases, and events which bear no scholarly interpretation but which has passed into our folk memory. Perhaps my search should be directed to that ever-growing body of new versions of the Bible which descend upon us with the monotonous frequency of novels by Barbara Cartland. When I was in England last month I had the opportunity to check a new publication: the *Alternative Bible* by David Voas. I missed this chance but I did read a review of it by Kate Saunders in the *Sunday Times*.

Her review began as follows: "Ever since the sea of faith began its melancholy, long, withdrawing roar, the church has yearned towards the lazy, the young, the pig-ignorant—everyone who might be put off religion by long words. This century, there has been a hopeful belief among Christian teachers that translating the Bible into chummy contemporary slang will somehow distract from the strictness of the doctrines. [This version] looks like yet another attempt to turn dull old God into Terry Wogan [the English Johnny Carson]—something for intellectual purists to condemn unseen, as belonging with the *Good News Bible*, the *Alternative Service Book*, and dreadfully hip vicars with electric guitars." I should further whet your appetite by saying that the bulk has been reduced by 80% and the whole text is enlivened by a commentary by the Archangel Michael, who enhances our understanding with asides such as, "I remember those two in the Garden of Eden, and to be candid, they were poor company." Surely here I might have found my quotation, because it involves that unhip pair and the moment when Adam turned to Eve and said, "My dear, we are living in an Age of Transition."

If there is any reliability to be attributed to this quotation, and I am not prepared to deny or confirm it absolutely, then surely it must be the most frequently quoted of all Biblical texts. We use it, or equivalent words, on any occasion when we are mystified by the rate of change, or we are seeking to justify changes which appear to us to be both desirable and inevitable. We cannot, we are constantly being informed by innumerable vested interests, stand in the way of progress. We cannot continue to use last year's model when this year's is being lauded to the skies by those who invested millions of dollars in the improved model and will now spend millions more in persuading us to keep abreast of the times.

The corporate giants of industry and commerce are not alone in making us feel naked in the hurricane of new devices; something very similar is attacking us on intellectual and moral issues also. There is a widely held attitude current today which suggests that long-held beliefs and standards of behavior are no longer appropriate to this brave new world on the eve of the 21st century. The story was once current of the Allied soldier during World War II who was being shown around an Italian village church by the priest. "A candle has burned constantly on this spot for 500 years," said the priest. "That's far too long," said the soldier—and snuffed it out. Our age has become adept at snuffing the candles of history. All change is regarded as progress and the possibility of regression is not seriously entertained.

Our reading of history confirms that there have been previous periods of stagnation; Dark Ages are distributed like chaff over the histories of most continents and nations and no imagination is needed to acknowledge that, in many parts of the world, darkness is the only quality of the 1990s. My question today is a simple one. In a world which is always subject to change and which today is being pounded by forces advocating more and more change, even by the most violent means, how is our profession of librarianship, and the world of ideas of which it is a substantial part, adapting to the storm? To what extent are we riding the storm or to what extent are we helpless victims of something which is bigger and more powerful than we can imagine?

Back in the dim days of 1961 I wrote an editorial for a student journal, in which I posed a question which, at that time, I regularly asked in person during the progress of their studies. What do you think the world of librarianship will be like in the year 2001? What do you hope will be the process of change with which you will become involved before this date arrives—a date which I suggested at the time might well be the year of their retirement from the profession? I wrote, "If you pick up any work of science fiction today, and if that story starts off with a date in the time-honoured Harrison Ainsworth tradition so that you commence reading, 'It was a bright Spring morning in A.D. 2005 . . .' then anything which follows that introduction is regarded as reasonable. No one will laugh aloud if the hero and heroine set out for a honeymoon on Venus or visit relatives on Mars. No one will be surprised at whatever ingenious mechanical contrivances are introduced as part of that still-distant time. There is, therefore, no reason at all why we should not be equally open-minded as to what librarianship can do in those days of the future which belong to you." I also recall that, in many conversations, I expressed the opinion that if librarianship remained true to its past history, no enormous changes would be very likely.

I was of this opinion because, all too often, we seem to have been followers of trends rather than pioneers. At the beginning of this century we were writing and talking of library economy when, comparably, there was political economy and domestic economy. But these came to be regarded as inaccurate terms, so, in the wake of political science and domestic science, we moved along obediently with library science although it was a study which admitted of little or no scientific reasoning. But if I expected, as I did, that the year 2000 would find us largely unchanged from the situation in 1960, then I was monumentally wrong. I do maintain, nevertheless, that we have been subjected to changes due more to outside influences than to anything of our own making. We have inherited rather than created; but we can be congratulated in that we have accepted a measure of revolution with good grace and some inventiveness.

Our own internally inspired revolutions, as it were, although accomplished with some flair, have never been fully completed. On my first-ever visit to the public library in the town in which I was born, I was faced with an indicator. Only by gazing at this formidable barrier and checking whether the accession number of the book which I thought I required was featured in red or blue figures could I determine whether it was available for loan.

No browsing was permitted except through the pages of the printed catalogue. But an in-house revolution was on the way. By the time I joined the staff of that same library to launch myself upon my professional career, the words "open access" had been spoken and the barrier was removed. Or was it? Certainly the indicator had gone but the service area behind it, in which the staff had manipulated the all-revealing numbers, remained. I recall vividly my first sight of the women behind the barricade who had previously been simply disembodied hands. They were all women in those sexist days and eventually I entered, when I joined the staff, with fear and trepidation, accompanied by the snide remarks of my school friends, as the sole male among them. They were all clad in green coveralls which, because they were handed down with no reference to size or shape, succeeded in fitting nobody. It was decided at the highest level that, as an interloper of the opposite sex, I did not qualify for a coverall and so another revolution began.

It is, however, when we consider that completeness of the revolution of open access that we have cause to wonder at the long-term effectiveness of revolutionary methods. Some early writers saw the movement in terms of social justice. W. H. Brett, writing in *The Library Journal* in 1892, explained, "In some libraries it has been customary to admit certain classes of readers, notably professional and literary men and women, to especial privileges, but it has not been deemed feasible to admit a young man from the workshop who comes into the library with his dinner-pail on his arm, wanting a text-book of electricity or a volume of Herbert Spencer, to the same privileges as the professional man who may want possibly only the last good novel for his hours of relaxation." But today, one hundred years after Brett's pleas, the professional man or woman would have equal difficulty with the young workman with his dinner-pail in gaining unlimited access to all parts of all libraries. There is no library of any size which does not practice, and rightly so, the restraints of closed access, as witness most magnificently the glass-enclosed core of the Beinecke Library at Yale. So I suspect has ended every revolution since the world began. Violent enthusiasms begin the new world with eloquent claims by the instigators of change and then, as the years go by, some is absorbed, some rejected, and the remainder modified to meet the ever-changing situation. The Reformation was followed by the Counter Reformation, and the early libertarian and egalitarian ideals of the French Revolution developed their own tyranny.

Such, I believe, will be the final outcome of the revolution which has so drastically reshaped our profession during the last thirty or forty years. It would be foolish to attempt to deny the magnitude of the changes which mechanization, in all its forms, has wrought in the daily life of our profession, and it would be foolish in the extreme not to greet many of the changes with enthusiasm. I do not know when this particular revolution began. Most begin with a small barely discernible trickle which gives no warning of the later flood. I do recall, however, when my own consciousness was first raised. In 1950 the Windsor Lectures at the University of Illinois were delivered by Louis Ridenour, Ralph Shaw, and Albert Hill; they were published in the following year under the title *Bibliography in an Age of Science*. Shaw had developed not only his Photocharger which was already widely used in libraries but also his Rapid Selector which was greeted as a new "electronic brain" with important bibliographic potential. The world outside librarianship was equally cognizant that change was desirable and that it was within human grasp. In 1955 Dr. Vannevar Bush contributed an article to the *Atlantic Monthly* entitled "For Man to Know." He wrote of the enormous strides made in scientific research and the consequent astonishing increase in the quantity of published scientific data.

He wrote: "There is progress too in the storing of the record, with microfilm and new methods of printing. But our methods of consulting the record are archaic and essentially unchanged. The library, as we know it, cannot cope with the task before it." It is salutary to remember that this statement, with which nobody at that time could disagree, was written less than forty years ago. We have indeed made remarkable progress but it is no part of my intention to comment on those changes or to evaluate their effectiveness. I would rather look at some of the forecasts which are now being made regarding some of the developments which, we are reliably informed, lie just ahead of us. I have no deep concerns about the increase of functions within library administration which can now be passed over to mechanization. Many of them are tasks which never required human skills, and it is good that intelligent human beings who are warm to the touch have been relieved of them. But in one particular direction there is cause for anxiety. During the past forty years we have heard cries which proclaim that the book, like God, is dead. Both appear to be remarkably resilient corpses, but it is important that we should recognize trends. I am not greatly worried by the propaganda which assails us from the manufacturers and developers of such products. They have the optimism of salespeople everywhere.

But there are other indications which are more worrying. Earlier this year there appeared an article in the British periodical *The Spectator* written by a 16-year-old girl entitled "Reading Books is Not Worth the Effort." From this article I have culled a few sentences which, I assure you, do not go against the general tenor of the article.

"I can tell you only what I see every day at school. A teenager who reads is a rarity. . . . While the computer room is packed every lunch hour, the turn-out in the library is sparse at best. Occasionally people come to stick discarded bubblegum on the radiator. . . . With microwaves, satellite dishes and fax machines to back us up, we seem to have proof that gratification must always be provided instantly. Because I and all the other children of the 1980s never knew a time when things took effort, we have a different slant on reading. Times may be hard but living is still meant to be easy. It is screens and sounds that link us and give us our identity. . . . What use is Jack Kerouac's *On the Road* when we have no desire to venture beyond the boundaries of our bedrooms with their view of the world via satellite? Which of us can relate to the teenage trauma of *The Catcher in the Rye* when the cast of 'Beverly Hills 90210' tell us everything we need to know? I can sit all day watching MTV, eating Pop Tarts heated in the microwave, drinking lo-cal, nutrient-free Diet Pepsi, listening to electronic music created by people taking smart drugs. Sometimes it all makes me feel a bit queasy. It is then that I find myself reaching for a book to accompany my Pop Tarts. But much as I may enjoy a few stolen hours with black on white, I do not talk about my reading at school. It would be like saying I occasionally sleep with a fish under my pillow."

This is infinitely more scaring than waking up in the middle of the night to find Dracula standing by your bedside. It is also, as a later correspondent wrote, a great pity that she could not read because the packaging of Pop Tarts bears a notice that they should not be heated in a microwave. However much we may wish to dismiss such evidence as being juvenile, exaggerated, and designed to be nothing more than provocative, we also remain aware that similar predictions are constantly being made by older and wiser beings.

It is right that society in general should show some general concern regarding the growth of electronic media. Concern is expressed regarding the effects on the eyesight of coming generations. And the fears of many regarding the possible linkage of constant exposure to electro-magnetic fields with the rising incidence of cancer in children have certainly not been allayed. One of the strange fallacies of our time seems to be that whatever we believe to be good, and in the modern context that means profitable, will continue to increase in volume, and hence profitability, *ad infinitum.* Because there was a time when the number of people traveling by air seemed to be increasing year by year, it was presumed that it would be so forever and plans were developed accordingly. The result is that airline after airline goes into bankruptcy. Retail stores believed that the good years would last forever until the chill winds of reality forced the closure of thousands. Real estate thought that it had hit the gold-plated bonanza of all time, until even the Reisman empire collapsed, not to the disadvantage of the family itself but to the ruination of thousands of humbler mortals. So in the lush years of the development of electronic media we believed that there would be no other form of communication. The book was indeed dead; killed by the microchip.

Back in 1969 I remember reading Peter Dickinson's *Heartsease*, later to be one of his *The Changes Trilogy.* It postulated a Britain of the future when people had come to be frightened of, and to hate, all machines; cars, buses, trains, all disappeared because they were regarded as evil. I think that this modern Luddite spirit is not necessarily the greatest danger; much current opposition is based primarily on ignorance. But I think that there is a nightmare view of the future in which everything has come to a slithering halt because our sources of energy have dried up. We can envisage millions of pieces of equipment strewn around the world which have ceased to function because we have no electricity to power them. There is probably not one of us who has not gone into a bank to effect a transaction to be met with the statement that "the computer is down"—and not an abacus in sight! On that day when energy finally dries up and all the computers are down, shall we not be glad that *King Lear*, and *Bleak House*, and *Moby Dick*, and *The Country of the Pointed Firs*, the Bible, and *Peter Rabbit* have been committed to the old-fashioned security of print. Many of these worries are, of course, the problems of society in general, and some people regard any mention of them as ridiculously alarmist. But the time is not that far in our past when the killing of our rivers and lakes by acid rain, the depletion of the ozone layer, the sacrifice of our forests, the fouling of our oceans, the advocacy of a form of energy which can kill thousands if anything goes wrong; all these would have been regarded as alarmist when their virtues were first being extolled. Professionally, however, we have other worries.

Most of us are glad that the *Oxford English Dictionary* is available on CD-ROM and that the *C18 Short Title Catalogue* is available in machine readable form. The record is much more easily accessible. Those who cannot read music have for generations been glad that Handel's *Messiah* has been recorded, that we can listen to James Joyce reading his own work, that Matthew Brady left such an evocative record of the Civil War, that there is such a revealing motion picture record of the early days of the Russian Revolution. The blind and those who are visually impaired must be forever grateful that recorded books are available to relieve the problems of large type books or the frequent difficulties in old age of learning Braille. Nobody would wish to suggest that the printed word should be our only medium, but certainly for much which was designed to be published in that form there seems to be no adequate substitute. Matter does not transfer well or easily from one medium to another; the long and disastrous trail of film adaptations of books provides a grim reminder of the magnitude of the horrors which can be perpetrated.

My family has made many trips to the English Lake District; the majority of these has included a visit to Grasmere and frequently a pilgrimage to Dove Cottage. This is not only because of our affection for Wordsworth but also because of our interest in Thomas de Quincey who lived in the cottage for a longer period of time than did William. In 1848 de Quincey published his essay on "The Poetry of Pope" in which he produced his final elaboration of a topic which he had first raised in 1823 in his "Letters to a Young Man whose Education has been Neglected." This was his famous discussion on the division of the literature of knowledge and the literature of power. In this essay, which is worthy of so much more attention than we can devote at present, de Quincey wrote as follows: "In that great social organ, which, collectively, we call literature, there may be distinguished two separate offices that may blend and often *do* so, but capable, severally, of severe isolation, and naturally fitted for reciprocal repulsion. There is, first, the literature of *knowledge*; and, secondly, the literature of *power*. The function of the first is—to *teach*; the function of the second is—to *move*; the first is a rudder; the second, an oar or a sail. The first speaks to the *mere* discursive understanding; the second speaks ultimately, it may happen, to the higher understanding or reason, but always *through* affections of pleasure and sympathy."

The examples which de Quincey chose, those century and three quarters ago, still have validity today.

What do you learn from *Paradise Lost*? Nothing at all. What do you learn from a cookery book? Something new—something you did not know before, in every paragraph. But would you therefore put the wretched cookery-book on a higher level of estimation than the divine poem? What you owe to Milton is not any knowledge, of which a million separate items are still but a million of advancing steps on the same earthly level; what you owe, is *power*, that is, exercise and expansion to your own latent capacity of sympathy with the infinite, where every pulse and each separate influx is a step upwards—a step ascending as upon a Jacob's ladder from earth to mysterious altitudes above the earth. *All* the steps of knowledge, from first to last, carry you further on the same plane, but could never raise you one foot above your ancient level of earth; whereas, the very *first* step in power is a flight—is ascending movement into another element where earth is forgotten.

Today we might not express our classification in quite the same terms as de Quincey but I think that we can all appreciate the division which he recorded. We know that there is a difference between factual material and the inspirational, between informative material and the emotional. We know that not all material means exactly the same thing to all readers; that a treatise on fishing can become one of the favorite pieces of bedtime reading for those who will never handle rod and line; that the sermons delivered by an early seventeenth-century divine have inspired many who will never darken the doors of any place of worship.

Many will assert that de Quincey's literature of power is the more important of the two, for it is that which makes the imagination soar, which liberates the spirit and takes the mind far beyond its present confines. And if you think that de Quincey is a prejudiced literary witness—or Emerson, who said almost exactly the same thing—then remember that Albert Einstein wrote that "imagination is more important than knowledge." We are dealing with books which are capable of charting new worlds and challenging new heights. Do you remember Christopher Morley's *Haunted Bookshop*? "If your mind needs a whiff of strong air, blue and cleansing, from hilltops and primrose valleys, try *The Story of My Heart*, by Richard Jefferies. If your mind needs a tonic of iron and wine, and a thorough rough and tumbling, try Samuel Butler's *Notebooks*, or *The Man Who Was Thursday* by Chesterton."

We also know, with the certainty of our professional experience, that both of de Quincey's categories, with any others which we might invent, are essential to the overall intellectual health of any community. Long years have taught us that as new media arrive on the scene they do so with immense éclat, pass their peak of maximum effectiveness, and become absorbed into the whole apparatus of communications. The 1920s and the 1930s (when I began my career) saw the cinema as a monstrous threat to the reading habit. In our time we have seen cinemas turn into bingo halls, supermarkets, and even libraries, because fashions have changed. Medved's recent book has suggested an industry which has turned rotten at its core and all the evidence which we have, as consumers, confirm that he is, if anything, too gentle in his criticism. Radio was regarded as a threat but its best aspects have been channeled into programs which support the ideals of literacy rather than oppose them. Television was hailed as the biggest bogey of them all but we can already see the cancer in the rose. I recall, decades ago, seeing one of Mary Field's "Secrets of Nature" films, in which was promulgated the only sure-fire way of killing dandelions. The secret revealed was to overfertilize the root, which would then swell, burst, and die. The threat to provide us with over 300 television channels is as near an approach to overfertilization as we are likely to find. But in all these cases, society has absorbed the best feature and regurgitated the worst.

Modern libraries are faced with the problems and challenges of housing a vast amount of material in an ever-increasing variety of forms. In our constantly evolving societies we also have an ever-expanding clientele who seek our services. The combination of the growing complexity of collections allied to the increasing specificity of demand has led, and will lead further yet, to new technologies—technologies which we must be prepared to welcome and to subject to the most rigorous tests before we accept them into our professional heritage. I remain confident, however, that, although sections of our material will prove to be congenial to the changing new technologies, something very similar to the book as we now know it will survive and prosper. We should not expect it to be in precisely the same form. The printed codex with which we are familiar is a comparative newcomer on the scene. The clay tablet yielded to papyrus; papyrus to membranes; membranes to paper; manuscript to printing. We never stand still, and it would be disastrous if we did. But all the time we have had something which was portable, capable of being read in a wide variety of places and suited to whatever speed of assimilation we chose.

De Quincey wrote, "The directions in which the tragedy of this planet has trained our human feelings to play, and the combinations into which the poetry of this planet has thrown our human passions of love and hatred, of admiration and contempt, exercise a power bad or good over human life, that cannot be contemplated . . . without a sentiment allied to awe. And of this let everyone be assured—that he owes to the impassioned books which he has read, many a thousand more of emotions than he can consciously trace back to them." The sheer ease of readability has always had, and I believe will always have, a large role to play in our acceptance of these emotions. Our traditional book, with its physical attractiveness, even in some instances its sheer beauty, cannot be ignored when we try to assess the beneficial influences of great literature.

I think that the social role of our profession is an inherent belief that the myriad messages of great writing must be heard. In November 1918, Sir Arthur Quiller-Couch (one of my favorite critics) said, "I cannot, for my part, conceive a man who has once incorporated the *Phaedo* or the *Paradiso* or *Lear* into himself as lending himself for a moment to one or the other of the follies plastered in these late stern times upon the firm and most solid purpose of this nation." Or we may move to 1933 when A. E. Housman wrote, "All my life long the best of literature of several languages have been my favorite recreation; and good literature continuously read for pleasure must, let us hope, do some good to the reader: must quicken his perception though dull, and sharpen his discrimination though blunt, and mellow the rawness of his personal opinions."

Critics, and probably our own experience, tell us that the long-accepted great works of literature are the quarry of only a few in any generation. The *Phaedo*, the *Paradiso*, and *Lear* certainly do not rank in the best-selling lists with Stephen King, Jacqueline Susann, or Catherine Cookson. Nor is Boswell's *Johnson* as well thumbed as Kitty Kelley's latest exposé. But we must never despair. About a generation ago, American librarianship spoke and wrote frequently about the "the communications elite," a phrase which would probably be given short shrift these days. But it still contains an important truth. The literature of power is most effective when it is implanted in the minds and spirits of those who exercise power. And we humbler mortals live in the shadow of the world which they create. Do we not all hope that the reading of one Rhodes Scholar may turn out to be more influential for the benefit of mankind than participation in any number of B-rated movies? Crucial as such reading influence is at the highest levels of our secular lives, we also value it in our own most personal moments. In J. B. Priestley's play *Johnson over Jordan*, Johnson, Priestley's Everyman of modern times, came at last to the Inn at the End of the World. He found it peopled with the figures and the sounds of the literature which he had known while young and had forgotten in the years in between. At last, even if recalled with difficulty, there was the Lord's Prayer as he stepped out into the vastness of a starry space. At that moment, I can envisage no computer screen, no video game, no Hollywood movie, no TV special, which could supplant the consolation of words recalled from the deepest memory of our reading.

I am frequently disappointed that we do not pay sufficient attention to the history of our profession and the role which libraries have played in the development of our civilization. It is an honorable history and one in which we have cause to celebrate those who have played a part, however modest, in the long and continuing story. It is a saga of high hopes and myriad disappointments, of periods of neglect and periods of dire persecution. But it is also an account of unparalleled achievement. We have, as occasion demanded, been innovative, ruthless, imaginative, and faithful to our main purpose, which is to make freely available all that has been committed to a permanent form—and the forms have been many. But our purpose has held and so, I believe, it will continue to do.

May I offer you these words from Tennyson's *Ulysses*, with which I often committed our graduates to the rigors of the real world after their period of academic isolation:

Come, my friends,
'Tis not too late to seek a newer world.
Push off, and sitting well in order smite
The sounding furrows; for my purpose holds
To sail beyond the sunset, and the baths
Of all the western stars, until I die.
It may be that the gulfs will wash us down:
It may be we shall touch the Happy Isles,
And see the great Achilles, whom we knew.
Tho' much is taken, much abides; and tho'
We are not now that strength which in old days
Moved earth and heaven; that which we are, we are;
One equal temper of heroic hearts,
Made weak by time and fate, but strong in will
To strive, to seek, to find, and not to yield.

Afterword

Dennis A. Norlin

In the introduction to part 2, Theological Librarians at Work, Monica Corcoran writes "Unless a profession writes about its work it cannot measure its own progress; it cannot look to early members in the field for direction and comparison." The American Theological Library Association has written about its activities and members, goals and dreams for 60 years now. We are deeply grateful to David Stewart and Melody Layton McMahon for conceiving and editing this anniversary edition of selected writings from the 59 preceding volumes of the Association's Annual Proceedings.

Selecting significant contributions from among the hundreds available in that 60-year history and organizing them into coherent chapters was an important contribution not only to the Association and its members, but also to those who would learn about the profession of theological librarianship and seek to be better informed about the vocation of theological librarian.

And vocation it is. No ATLA member considers his/her professional involvement as merely a job. Anne Richardson Womack notes that the authors of the essays in part 1 ("The Distinctive Character of Theological Librarianship") view their profession as "a total lifetime commitment," one that is often misunderstood by institutional colleagues who are unaware "of the complexity of our work." Most theological librarians, Womack maintains, regard their work as a calling: "We respond to the gift of God's love for all humanity by devoting our energies to the respect and care of our staff and students, and we are energized by the reflective component of the theological enterprise."

The essays in part 2 help the reader to understand better the diversity of

351

tasks that theological librarians face, and, as Monica Corcoran points out, the articulation of those tasks falls to theological librarians themselves.

Roger Loyd sees continuity but also some major changes in the role of the theological librarian during the past 60 years. The essays in part 3, The Theological Librarian as Educator, begin with collaboration and extend to information literacy in the present day.

In part 4, Theological Libraries: Contexts and Constituencies, Michael Bramah finds that the context in which the theological librarian works still looks the same as it did decades ago, but notes dramatic change in the way users access the information available in theological libraries and the equally dramatic expansion that creates a global constituency for libraries that were primarily local institutions.

John Bollier helps the reader trace the association's roots in part 5, The American Theological Library Association: Reminiscences and Reflections, and provides a direct link to the vision and energy and determination of the Association's founders.

In the introduction to part 6, Changes and Challenges, Eileen Crawford not only identifies distinct challenges that continually face theological librarians but also testifies to the inspiration today's members can take from the example of the "intrepid" Julia Pettee who, when faced with reorganizing the important Union Theological Seminary library, devised her own classification system to do so.

On behalf of the current members of the Association, I want to express my profound thank you to the editors (David Stewart and Melody McMahon), to the original authors of the essays selected, to the current authors who so effectively and sympathetically introduced the selections, and, of course, to Father Simeon Daly for his graceful introduction, inviting the reader to enter his world of theological librarianship and to carry on the mission into the future.

About the Editors and Contributors

Robert F. Beach (chapter 25: Joint Panel Discussion) was Director of the Library at Garrett-Evangelical Theological Seminary (Evanston, IL) before becoming director of the Burke Library at Union Theological Seminary, New York.

John A. Bollier (chapter 30: Introduction to Part Five) was Assistant Divinity Librarian at Yale Divinity Library from 1971 to 1981.

Michael Bramah (chapter 24: Introduction to Part Four) is currently Head of Cataloguing at the John M. Kelly Library, University of St. Michael's College, Toronto, Ontario. He has also worked at Virginia Theological Seminary (Alexandria, VA) and at the Atlantic School of Theology (Halifax, Nova Scotia).

Lester J. Cappon (chapter 12: Archival Good Works for Theologians) served variously as Archivist at the University of Virginia, Director of the Institute of Early American History and Culture, and wrote extensively (and at times provocatively) on archival practice.

Clayton E. Carlson (chapter 42: Can Serious Academic Religious Book Publishing Survive in an Age of Pop Culture?) has been involved in the publishing industry for many years, most recently as a founder and Senior Vice-President of HarperSanFrancisco.

Milton J. (Joe) Coalter (chapter 7: On Spiritual Reading and Religious Reading in Peril) is currently Librarian at Union Theological Seminary and the Presbyterian School of Christian Education in Richmond, VA. He served previously as professor and Director of the Ernest G. White Library at Louisville Presbyterian Theological Seminary.

Monica Corcoran (chapter 9: Introduction to Part Two) is Library Director at Saint Meinrad School of Theology, Saint Meinrad, IN.

Eileen K. Crawford (chapter 36: Introduction to Part Six) is Assistant Director and Head of Technical Services at the Vanderbilt Divinity Library in Nashville, TN.

Paul A. Crow Jr. (chapter 20: Professors and Librarians: Partners in the *Oikumené*) served as Associate Professor of Church History and Registrar of the College of the Bible in Lexington, Kentucky, and as President of the Council on Christian Unity.

Merrimon Cuninggim ("The Seminary Library from the Faculty Point of View" in chapter 25: Joint Panel Discussion) was Dean of the Perkins School of Theology, Southern Methodist University, 1951–1960.

Fr. Simeon Daly, O.S.B. (Foreword and chapter 5: That They All May Be One) was for many years Library Director, Saint Meinrad School of Theology, Saint Meinrad, IN.

Mary A. Dempsey (chapter 29: Serving the Religious Information Needs of the Public) has been Commissioner of the Chicago Public Library since 1994.

G. Fay Dickerson (chapter 40: The Index to Religious Periodical Literature) was Chief Indexer for ATLA from 1960 to 1983.

James W. Dunkly (chapter 6: Some Values in Theological Librarianship and chapter 23: Theological Libraries and Theological Librarians in Theological Education) is currently School of Theology Librarian and Lecturer in New Testament at the University of the South School of Theology, Sewanee, TN.

Leslie Robertson Elliott (chapter 32: Six Years of ATLA) was a founding member of ATLA. He was Librarian at Southwestern Baptist Theological Seminary, Fort Worth, TX, 1922–1957, serving also as an instructor of Greek from 1925 to 1942 and as registrar from 1937 to 1943.

David William Faupel (chapter 4: Developing Professionally on the Job) is Director of the Library and Professor of Theological Research at Wesley

Seminary, Washington, D.C. He served previously as Director of the B.L. Fisher Library at Asbury Theological Seminary, Wilmore, KY.

Connolly C. Gamble Jr. (chapter 39: Contemporary Challenges to Theological Librarianship) was Associate Director of the Library (and Morgan Foundation Associate Professor of Bibliography) at Union Theological Seminary in Richmond, VA, from 1952 to 1976.

Thomas F. Gilbert (chapter 15: Circulation in Theological Libraries) was previously director of the Austen K. DeBlois Library at Eastern Baptist Theological Seminary, Wynnewood, PA, before working for Library Technologies, Inc.

G. Paul Hamm (chapter 34: A Look at the Past) was Library Director at Golden Gate Baptist Seminary from 1968 to 1979, and later served as Library Director at the International School of Theology, Arrowhead Springs, CA.

Arthur E. Jones Jr. (chapter 26: Some Thoughts on the Joint Theological School–Liberal Arts College Library) was Librarian at Drew University, Madison, NJ, from 1956 to 1986.

James J. Kortendick, S.S. (chapter 3: The Theological Librarian) was active for many years in library and information science education, serving on the faculty of the MLS program at Catholic University of America. He was also interim director of the library at Marquette University, Milwaukee, in the 1970s.

Roger L. Loyd (chapter 17: Introduction to Part Three) is Professor of the Practice of Theological Bibliography and Library Director at Duke Divinity School, Durham, NC. He was previously Associate Librarian at the Bridwell Library, Perkins School of Theology, Southern Methodist University.

Julia H. Macleod (chapter 11: Problems in Manuscript Cataloging) worked in the Bancroft Library at the University of California, Berkeley, from 1947 to 1963.

Melody Layton McMahon (co-editor) is Catalog Librarian and Liaison to Religious Studies at the Grasselli Library, John Carroll University, University Heights, OH.

Raymond Philip Morris (chapter 2: Theological Librarianship as a Ministry and "Orientation—An Indispensable Element in Making the Library Useful" in chapter 25: Joint Panel Discussion) was head librarian of the Yale Divinity Library from 1932 to 1972.

Jannette E. Newhall ("The Library Program Seen from the Point of View of the Library Staff" in chapter 25: Joint Panel Discussion) was Professor of Research Methods and Librarian at Boston University School of Theology from 1949 to 1964.

Dennis A. Norlin (Afterword) has served as Executive Director of the American Theological Library Association since 1996.

Elmer J. O'Brien (chapter 33: Building on Our Strengths for the Future) was for 35 years Director of Library and Information Services and Professor of Theological Bibliography and Research at United Theological Seminary, Dayton, OH. With his wife, Betty, he played an active role in compiling and indexing *Festschriften* and *Methodist Reviews*.

Leon Pacala (chapter 21: Theological Libraries Revisited) was Executive Director of the Association of Theological Schools in the United States and Canada from 1980 to 1990.

John A. Peltz (chapter 40: The Index to Religious Periodical Literature) was an Assistant Indexer at ATLA during the 1970s.

Julia Ensign Pettee (chapter 37: On the Union Classification) was Chief Cataloger, 1909–1939, at Union Theological Seminary in New York City. She is best remembered for devising a classification scheme for theological libraries.

Walter N. Roberts ("The Library from the Point of View of the Seminary Administration" in chapter 25: Joint Panel Discussion) was President of United Theological Seminary, Dayton, OH, from 1938 to 1965.

Robert J. Schreiter (chapter 43: Globalization and Theological Libraries) is Vatican Council II Professor of Theology at Catholic Theological Union, Chicago, and Professor of Theology and Culture, University of Nijmegen, the Netherlands.

Andrew D. Scrimgeour (chapter 22: The Structures of Religious Literature) is Director of the Library and Acting University Archivist at Drew University, Madison, NJ. He was previously Dean of Libraries at Regis University in Denver, CO.

John J. Shellem (chapter 13: Changing a Pile of Books into a Library) was Librarian of the Ryan Memorial Library at St. Charles Borromeo Seminary, Wynnewood, PA, from 1967 to 1978.

Lewis Joseph Sherrill (chapter 31: Seminary Librarians) was Dean of Louisville Presbyterian Theological Seminary from 1930 to 1950.

David R. Stewart (co-editor and chapter 16: Parchment, Paper, PDF) is Director of Library Services at Luther Seminary, St. Paul, MN. He was previously Associate Librarian at Princeton Theological Seminary.

Roy Stokes (chapter 44: Shadow and Substance) taught for many years at the School of Library, Archival, and Information Studies at the University of British Columbia, Vancouver, B.C.

Sharon J. Taylor (chapter 8: Power and Responsibility) is Director of the Franklin Trask Library at Andover-Newton Theological School, Newton Center, MA.

Decherd H. Turner Jr. (chapter 41: Revolutions, Evolutions, and Syndromes: ATLA Anniversary Address) was the founding director of the Bridwell Library at Southern Methodist University, serving in that capacity from 1950 to 1980. He then served as director of the Harry Ransom Humanities Research Center in Austin until 1988.

Helen Bordner Uhrich (chapter 10: The Cataloger and Instruction and chapter 19: The Community of Learning) served as Librarian of the Biblical Seminary (New York) and as Head Cataloger of the Hartford Seminary Foundation, and from 1937 until her retirement in 1974 was Cataloger and Assistant Librarian at the Yale Divinity Library.

Gustave Weigel, S.J. (chapter 38: When Catholic and Protestant Theologies Meet) taught theology in Chile, later at Woodstock College (Maryland), and lectured widely on Catholic–Protestant dialogue.

Claude Welch (chapter 27: The Theological Library) was President and Dean of the Graduate Theological Union (Berkeley, CA) from 1972 to 1982, and then Dean of the GTU from 1982 to 1987.

Caroline Whipple (chapter 14: Collection Development in a Theological Research Library) was Director of the Library at the Claremont School of Theology from 1980 to 1986.

Ernest G. White (chapter 35: A Combined Greeting to ATLA 40 and Reflection on ATLA 1) was Librarian at Louisville Presbyterian Theological Seminary from 1945 through 1985, thus serving as one of the host librarians for the meeting at which ATLA first gathered as an association in 1947.

John E. Wilson (chapter 28: Religious Studies and Theology) is Professor of Church History at Pittsburgh Theological Seminary, where he has taught since 1984.

Anne Richardson Womack (chapter 1: Introduction to Part One) is Associate Director of the Library at Vanderbilt Divinity School, Nashville, TN.